W9-CBC-652

congressional behavior

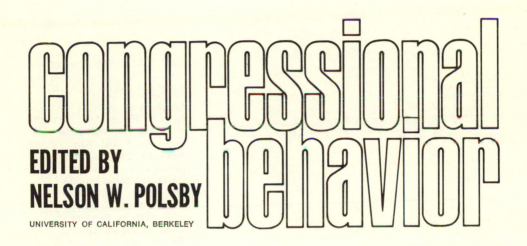

congressional behavior

EDITED BY
NELSON W. POLSBY

UNIVERSITY OF CALIFORNIA, BERKELEY

RANDOM HOUSE  NEW YORK

Copyright © 1971 by
Random House, Inc.
All rights reserved under
International and Pan-
American Copyright Con-
ventions. Published in
the United States by Ran-
dom House, Inc., New
York, and simultaneously
in Canada by Random
House of Canada Limited,
Toronto.
ISBN:0–394–31023–3
Library of Congress Cata-
log Card Number
70–122483
Manufactured in the
United States of America
by Kingsport Press, Inc.,
Kingsport, Tennessee
First Edition
987654321
Typography by Jack Ribik

This book is for Lisa Polsby and Emily Polsby,
masters of practical politics.

PREFACE

Poets believe that the pen is mightier than the sword; editors suspect that the scissors (especially when wielded in combination with a paste-pot) is mightier than the pen. As editor of this collection, I have contributed mostly scissors and paste. The authors have contributed the words and ideas, and it is to them above all that an editor and his readers should be grateful. Mark Ferber, H. Douglas Price, John Stewart, and the late Clem Miller, by contributing articles previously unpublished elsewhere, have been especially generous.

I want also to thank my speedy and efficient secretary, Kathleen Peters, and my research assistants, Bill Cavala and Byron Shafer, for their aid and good counsel as I muddled through this project in the midst of all the other things we have been doing. Lynne Farber of Random House has been most helpful.

For nearly a dozen years now, Linda O. Polsby has shared her living quarters with an ever-expanding pile of articles, papers, books, and essays on Congressional behavior, some of which have found their way into this book. By resisting her natural impulses to throw out, straighten up, or at least dust off, she has contributed more than she probably realizes to the availability of some of these pieces for publication here. My daughters Lisa Susan Polsby and Emily Ann Polsby enjoy seeing their names in the fronts of books. So do I.

N.W.P.

Berkeley, California
May 1970

CONTENTS

INTRODUCTION

The Congress of the United States is an institution ideally suited to the observation of the famous and anonymous spectator who professed not to know very much about modern art but knew what he did not like. Not many people actually like Congress. As the body that under the Constitution is charged with making the laws, it is Congress that must bear the dissatisfaction of persons—and they are legion—who think that the laws, or at least some laws, are unjust or inadequate.

There is very little doubt about the inadequacy and injustice of much that goes on under the color of law in this—or in any—society. But to pronounce oneself dissatisfied is scarcely to propound a remedy. Devising remedies is in turn less difficult than enacting them. And, in part, it is the fact that for nearly two centuries, national remedies have as often as not been the responsibility of Congress which has drawn the attention of people concerned with the problems of this society to Congress.

Frequently, Congress has not done very much about the problems of this society or this world, or very rapidly. It has, for many people, and on many issues, been something of a policy bottleneck, preventing or diluting attempts to deal effectively with serious social and political ailments. On other occasions, to be sure, Congress has moved swiftly and efficiently. On some matters, there has been protracted conflict; on others, unanimity.

On the whole, both committed liberals and committed conservatives believe, over the long haul, that they have been fighting a losing battle in and with Congress. Conservatives point to everything from social security through foreign aid to multibillion dollar federal budgets as indications of defeat. Liberals look around at the magnitude of the problems of modern life and despair at halting, parsimonious, and tardy governmental responses.

Who is right? It is impossible to say definitively. Probably both are, since they are taking their bearings from different landmarks. Congress, as a legislative body bound to do business by the rule of majorities, faces in both directions insofar as it is made up of people who do so. These people are in turn elected, so, in the end, and in some nontrivial sense, people get the Congress they want.

But it is also true that they may not know very much about what they want or what they are getting. This is a complicated matter to discuss. For each congressional district and each state, there may be dozens of different issues in the minds of voters—and nonvoters. Still other issues by some reasonable standards might well be on their minds—perhaps should be—but are not. Some of these issues may or may not be perceived by voters to be relevant to the choices they have before them in congressional and senatorial elections. Even if voters perceive and are ready to act on issues, the party processes that determine who the candidates are may or may not differentiate between candidates on the basis of these issues. Or all candidates may present a mixed bag with respect to all the issues that matter.

In the end, it is very difficult—perhaps impossible—to know whether people are getting the policy outputs they want from Congress by electing the congressmen they want. Presumably *in extremis* they can simply vote no until "the system" produces something better. But they have no reason to believe a "principled no" vote will not instead bring them something worse.

So they are caught (we all are) by the necessity to calculate marginal costs and benefits—to choose, as the saying goes, between the lesser of evils. On the whole, those people least willing to do this are those most optimistic about what would take place if the system were somehow different. Pessimists—people who believe that in all likelihood an American political system very much different from the one presently in use in America would probably be worse—are less uncomfortable about choosing lesser evils, in part because they can imagine greater evils more readily than greater goods.

Once these 435 congressional and 100 senatorial lesser evils (by some large number of majorities' decisions) are elected, they do not congregate at random or by alphabetical order. Rather, they enter into the life of an ongoing, powerful, social system, a community with a history, rules, a status ladder, roles, networks of friendships and enmities, rituals, staff, budgets, files, and work to do (collective and individual).

The puzzles of the election are nothing compared to the mysteries of the congressional community. Congressional behavior is determined more by the contours of this community, and by where congressmen and senators locate themselves and are located with respect to it, than by any other single thing. Who the congressman or senator is, where he comes from, what he stands for, his party, his prior life experiences, his ambitions and hopes, his alliances and enemies, all play a part in locating him, and of course his location determines what and how much he can do.

Many of the selections in this book look at congressional behavior from the standpoint of the congressman or senator. This should help readers to imagine themselves in the situation of members of Congress and suggest criteria to them by which they can judge what congressmen and senators do. Other selections look at Congress, or the House, or the Senate, as entities. Instead of taking up an observation post at the congressman's side, these selections adopt a perch somewhere up near the top of the ceiling in the chamber of the House, or Senate, or on a chandelier in a committee room. From there, the view takes on a more abstract design, and we can ask why the patterns of movement are as they are and what work is being accomplished by the collectivity as a whole. Both perspectives are helpful in understanding congressional behavior.

congressional behavior

part one

SOME COMMON CONCERNS AND CONTRASTS

The first four selections are about Congress; they discuss concerns common to both the House and the Senate or compare and contrast the two bodies.

1

STRENGTHENING CONGRESS IN NATIONAL POLICYMAKING

NELSON W. POLSBY

This essay talks about contemporary roles of the House and the Senate in the American political system and how Congress can be strengthened. It also takes up the problem of explaining and justifying a strong legislature as a part of democratic government.

The word is out that the Congress of the United States may have had something to do with the alteration over the past year and a half of American policy toward Southeast Asia. On the domestic scene, Congressmen can be observed taking the lead in tax reform and increasing federal appropriations for education. Consequently, it may briefly be fashionable to take Congress seriously, and perhaps those few of us who all along have been arguing this view *sotto voce* ought to say a word or two before Congress resumes its accustomed role of thwarting the domestic programs of liberal Presidents, and is once more relegated to the dustbin of historians if not of history.

– 1 –

To be sure it is easy enough to see why that popular guide to Washington politics, Casual Observer, finds Congress hard to understand. It is organized quite differently from the conventional bureaucracy, which Casual Observer

From *The Yale Review* (Summer, 1970), 481–497. Copyright © 1970 by Yale University.

professes to despise, but which he and his friends comprehend. Instead of having a single head, Congress looks like the hydra (or perhaps the Medusa) of Greek mythology. Instead of neatly delegating work downward and responsibility upward, Congress is a complex, redundant, not always predictable, and purposely unwieldy network of criss-crossing and overlapping lines of authority and information.

The mere contemplation of this organizational design customarily leads Casual Observer to assert overhastily that Congressional decision-making is inefficient, cumbersome, and in need of instant reform. Consider, for example, the frequently regretted fact that Cabinet officers are asked to justify certain aspects of their programs in much the same language before authorization and appropriation committees in both houses—adding up to four presentations in all. Clearly an inefficient use of a busy executive's time, according to the busy executive and his friends. Yet this same busy executive as a matter of course insists that programs coming up the line to his office be justified repeatedly to program review committees, bureau chiefs, department level staff, and departmental budget officers, and he would think nothing of justifying the program again to other interested executive branch departments, to the President and the Budget Bureau. Cabinet level officers quite commonly make presentations, formal and informal, justifying their programs to the general public, to interest groups, to newspapermen. Why, then, does the need for Congress to hear justifications as well constitute such an intolerable inconvenience? Why should this alleged inconvenience lead to recommendations that Congress revamp its structure? One observes that there is no comparable outcry to consolidate "Face the Nation," "Meet the Press," and "Issues and Answers."

Casual Observer also finds Congress hard to fathom because the political theories that are currently available do not help him resolve some basic choices that he generally has to make in order to defend his preferences with respect to the distribution of power within the national government. Does he want a strong Congress? A strong Congress means precisely one capable of asserting its will, even though Presidents, interest groups, courts, and ephemeral majorities of public opinion may find it inconvenient. A weak Congress means less effective oversight of executive policy-making and of the bureaucracies. It diminishes the capacity of Congressmen and Senators to play the roles of critic, goad, and ombudsman. Further, he must decide whether to vest power in Congress or in the majority party within Congress. If the former, he must be prepared to tolerate coalitions which occasionally—and perhaps persistently—thwart the will of the majority of the majority party. Of such majorities are the conservative coalition—and the progressive one that unhorsed Joseph Cannon

—made. If he opts for stricter party responsibility, he must accept the weakening of Congress vis-à-vis national parties, and whoever controls them—presumably quite often the President. For a long time, there were modish and unequivocal answers to these structural dilemmas—just as in the thirties Casual Observer's father knew what he thought of an innately reactionary institution like the Supreme Court. Now, however, while the idea of Congressional checks and balances and initiatives seems to make a little sense, it is possible to give these choices more evenhanded consideration.

The reasons why Congress and Presidents generally get along rather badly are too well known to require much reiteration. Differing constituencies arising, on the one hand, from the unit rule of the electoral college and, on the other, from the differential effects of party competition, the residuum of malapportionment, and the seniority system account for part of the conflict. So do purely institutional factors, the most important of which is the differing time scale of Presidential and Congressional careers.

President Kennedy understood this problem quite well, as the following quote from Theodore Sorensen's book suggests:

"Wilbur Mills," he said one day, "knows that he was chairman of Ways and Means before I got here and that he'll still be chairman after I've gone—and he knows I know it. I don't have any hold on him."

More generally, the argument is that the career expectations of political actors influence the rates at which they are willing to expend resources. By the standards of the operational leaders of Congress—Congressional party leaders, committee and subcommittee chairmen, their minority counterparts, and leading up-and-coming members in both parties—the career of any President is short: In the 91st Congress considerably more than a majority of both houses had already served with at least three Presidents of the United States. More to the point, the vast majority in both Houses could plausibly entertain the prospect of continuing to serve on into the indefinite future. Thus, while Presidents are under a constitutional injunction to seize the day, the men of Capitol Hill—even supposing they agree with the President and his programs—must calculate the consequences of their support against future demands upon their own resources. This leads to strategic dilemmas and to disagreements between Congress and the Presidency that are scarcely touched by proposals such as the 4-year Congressional term of office which seeks to coordinate the time of election but not the terminal points of Presidential and Congressional careers.

There is no definitive, universally acceptable answer to the question: How strong should Congress be? On the whole, gains in institutional strength are liable to be had at costs in institutional responsiveness. But there are many possible mixtures of these two qualities. A legislature that is merely an arena for the registering of the policy preferences of groups organized in the society at large is obviously not the only alternative to a legislature that is totally impervious to external sentiment. There is at present no very satisfactory description of Congress which assesses the developing balance between these somewhat incompatible goals. Thus Casual Observer is also handicapped in his attempts to understand Congress because Congress itself has been changing over the years, while our descriptions and justifications for it have not kept pace.

– 2 –

The accepted view of what a legislature contributes to government is that it represents the people, and it is as a representative body that Congress finds its ultimate justification in our political system. The difficulty that all modern legislatures face, of course, is the tremendous increase in the scale of modern government that makes it almost impossible for individual legislators genuinely to represent the people back home in any simple or straightforward fashion. And most legislatures collectively have pretty much stopped doing so. In most parliamentary systems, they are now mindless creatures of the political parties that run them.

But Congress is an exception. Principally because of historical accidents that destroyed the temporary unity of both the national parties earlier in this century, Congress built on some 19th century precedents in ways that have maintained and in some cases enhanced its independence in the political system. One major consequence of this process of institutionalization has been to shift the balance in the careers and life-styles of legislators from amateur to professional, from the status of temporary ambassador from home to that of member of the legislative group. Where Congress used to embody a popular will in some formal sense by its collective representativeness, it now does so de facto through the piecemeal pressures of oversight: case work for constituents, legislative committee hearings, and the appropriations process. Where representation—emphasizing the ambassadorial function—was once the characteristic, conscious activity of Congressmen and Senators, today it is deliberation—emphasizing the increasing centrality of Congressmen of their lives as members of a legislative work group and status system.

Thus in a sense Congress has been modernizing itself, through processes which have shifted the loyalties and the attention of Congressmen and Senators toward Washington and away from the grass roots, differentiated its internal functions, and professionalized the legislative service.

However, we have not yet developed a fully articulate rationale for a legislature that takes this developmental path; instead we are still relying both descriptively and evaluatively on notions of representation that made more sense when Congressmen spent most of their time at home and came from relatively knowable communities.

Thus a discussion of the strength of Congress in the political system might profitably consider the ways in which the House and the Senate organize to do business as a means of gaining insight into how a legislature can cope with the complex demands of a large heterogeneous society, including the rest of a big government. This may serve to throw some light on how or whether an effective legislature can contribute to democratic government.

– 3 –

As institutions, the House and the Senate differ markedly in their contemporary characters. The House is a highly specialized instrument for processing legislation. Its great strength is its firmly structured division of labor. This provides the House with a toehold in the policy-making process by virtue of its capacity to farm out and hence, in some collective sense, to provide for the mastery of technical details. House members are frequently better prepared than Senators in legislative conferences, and usually have the better grasp of the peculiarities of the executive agencies they supervise.

This is a consequence of the strong division of labor that the House maintains: members are generally assigned to one or two committees only. Floor debate is normally limited to participation by committee members. There is an expectation that members will concentrate their energies rather than range widely over the full spectrum of public policy.

Patterns of news coverage encourage specialization. General pronouncements by House members are normally not widely reported. Senators, because they are fewer, more socially prominent, and serve longer terms (hence are around long enough for newsmen to cultivate) and allegedly serve "larger" districts, can draw attention to themselves by well-timed press releases almost regardless of their content. One result of all this publicity (among other things) is that the Senate is increasingly the home of Presidential hopefuls, and this of course tends to generate still more Senate publicity. Some years ago I inquired of the chief of an important Washington news bureau if there was an imbalance between House and Senate news coverage. His response (bowdlerized) was: "The House! Look at them! There's no Presidential timber there at all."

The maintenance of a perennially timberless ecology like the House is difficult because it cannot entail excessive centralization of power. Decentralization of power is necessary for the House to sustain its capacity to cope with the outside world through its complex and specialized division of labor. The House's major career incentive is the opportunity accorded a tenth to a fifth of its members to possess the substance of power in the form of a committee or sub-committee chairmanship or membership on a key committee. At present seniority acts as a bulwark of this incentive system, by guaranteeing a form of job security at least within the division of labor of the organization. Without decentralization of power there would quite likely be no incentive for able men to stay in the House; without able men (there are few enough of these at any rate) there would be no expertise. Without subject-matter mastery, initiatives and modifications in public policy are capricious, responsive largely to prejudice, ineffective, and failing that, detrimental.

The essence of the Senate is that it is a great forum, an echo chamber, a publicity machine. Thus "passing bills," which is central to the life of the House, is peripheral to the Senate. In the Senate the three central activities are (1) cultivating national constituencies; (2) formulating questions for debate and discussion on a national scale (especially in opposition to the President); and (3) incubating new policy proposals that may at some future time find their way into legislation.

Where the House of Representatives is a large, impersonal and highly specialized machine for processing bills and overseeing the executive branch, the Senate is, in a way, a theatre where dramas—comedies and tragedies, soap operas and horse operas—are staged to enhance the careers of its members and to influence public policy by means of debate and public investigation.

In both the House and Senate the first commandment to newcomers is "specialize." But this means different things in each house. "Specialize" to a Representative means "tend to your knitting": work hard on the committee to which you are assigned, pursue the interests of your state and region. Consider, however, the consequences of these well-known features of Senate organization: Every Senator has several committee assignments. Boundaries between committees are not strictly observed. On the floor, quite unlike the House, virtually any Senator may speak for any length of time about anything. Thus the institution itself gives few cues and no compulsions to new Senators wondering what they should specialize in. For the Senate, specialization seems to mean finding a subject matter and a nationwide constituency interested in the subject that has not already been pre-empted by some more senior Senator.

It is a cliché of academic political science that in legislative matters, it is the President who initiates policy, and Congress which responds, amplifying and modifying and rearranging elements which are essentially originated in the executive branch. Not much work has been done, however, on following this river of bills-becoming-and-not-becoming-laws back to its sources. Where do innovations in policy come from *before* the President "initiates" them?

It appears that a great many newly enacted policies have "been around," "in the air" for quite a while. In the heat of a presidential campaign or later, when a President wants a "new" program, desk drawers fly open all over Washington. Pet schemes are constantly being fished out, dusted off, and tried out on political leaders. There is often a hiatus of years—sometimes decades—between the first proposal of a policy innovation and its appearance as a Presidential "initiative"—much less a law.

It is certainly not generally true that policy innovation begins with a Presidential message to Congress. For behind each Presidential message lurk months of man-hours of work and sometimes years of advocacy and controversy. The two great fountainheads of new policy seem to be: (1) Generally acknowledged "problems" producing the demands upon government that spur bureaucrats to ad-hoc problem solving. This often later has to be codified or rationalized as "policy." (2) A longer range build-up in the society of something that at first is not generally conceded to be a "problem." Those who see it that way may formulate demands upon the government in the guise of a "solution." This initiative may first be taken by a professor, or by technical support personnel attached to an interest group, or by a government "expert." On rare occasions, experts attached to a Congressional committee will initiate a policy. More often, I think, Congress is in on the beginning of a policy innovation because it provides the first sympathetic ear for an innovation concocted by outside experts.

Many of our most important policy innovations take years from initiation to enactment. Surely the idea of medicare, to take an obvious example, was not "initiated" by the Johnson administration in the 89th Congress. Proposals incorporating its main features had been part of the Washington landscape since the early Truman administration. Medicare, like other great policy innovations, required *incubation* —a process in which men of Congress often play very significant roles. Incubation entails keeping a proposal alive while it picks up support, or waits for a better climate, or while a consensus begins to form that the problem to which it is addressed exists. Senators and (to a lesser extent) Representatives contribute to incubation by proposing bills that they know will not pass, making speeches, making demands for data and for support from interest groups favoring the proposal.

Sometimes a sympathetic committee chairman can be persuaded to allow hearings on such a proposal. This focuses public attention, mobilizes interest groups for and against, and provides an occasion for the airing of a proposal's technical justifications. Policy incubation is, of course, not exclusively a Congressional activity; lobbyists may plant stories in the press, organizations may pass resolutions, professors may write books and articles. Most major policy innovations have been incubated by methods such as these.

The net effect of the Congressional process of gestation in any event is to develop a sense of community among far-flung interest groups that favor the innovation, by giving them occasional opportunities to come in and testify. It provides an incentive for persons favoring the innovation to maintain up-to-date information on its prospective benefits and technical feasibility. And it accustoms the uncommitted to a new idea.

Thus the Senate is in some respects at a crucial nerve-end of the polity. It articulates, formulates, shapes, and publicizes demands, and can serve as a hot-house for significant policy innovation. Proposals to increase the structuredness of the Senate, to force germaneness in debates, to tighten committee assignment procedures, and to reduce the number of assignments per Senator misunderstand the nature of the Senate and the contribution it uniquely makes to the political system. What is needed in the Senate is as little structure as possible; its organizational flexibility enables it to incubate policy innovations, to advocate, to respond, to launch its great debates, in short, to pursue the continuous renovation of American public policy through the hidden hand of the self-promotion of its members.

– 4 –

I do not mean by this to suggest that Congress is entirely self-sufficient in the policy-making process, or that all demands on Congress are equally well-treated. Far from it. In order finally to make new policy, Congress generally does need the power of the Presidency to set priorities and focus the energy sufficient to mobilize the successive majorities that law-making requires. A Presidential priority is a tremendous advantage in clearing away obstacles, but the President's support is usually purchased at a price: the proposal becomes his. This is not merely a matter of credit, although who gets credit is no trivial matter. It also affects the substance of policy. The executive branch begins the process of bargaining by including some features of a proposal and dropping others, adding bait here and padding there. In some cases (e.g., foreign aid, civil rights) executive branch control over bargaining is tight and continues right through the legislative mill. In others (e.g., surtax, medicare) influential members of Congress establish which provisions will survive and which will be sacrificed. Sometimes (e.g., the HUD [Department of Housing and Urban Development] bill in the Kennedy Administration) the most significant battle is precisely over who will control the bill.

But even with the President behind a bill, and despite years of Congressional incubation, the mortality rate for "new" proposals is high. Most Congressional policy-making takes place under adversary circumstances. Thus Congressional decision-makers ordinarily cannot enjoy the luxury of examining alternative means to stipulated ends. In an adversary process ends are not stipulated but contested. Agreement on means is often sought as a substitute for agreement on ends. Ends are often scaled down, pulled out of shape, or otherwise transformed. In short, from the standpoint of an outsider who cares about one or more pressing problems in society, the Congressional process of policy-making looks chaotic at best, perversely insensitive at worst.

If the perception of chaos is largely an optical illusion, the perception of insensitivity may not be. Insensitivity, slowness to register some kinds of new demands, exists in Congressional policy-making and is not altogether curable. It can come about because the strength of a demand in society as it is felt by an outsider has no counterpart equally strong within the Congressional process itself. Sometimes Congress does not reflect "needs" as defined in the society at large because Congress is malapportioned, or because the "wrong" sorts of people dominate the relevant committees. In this fashion a wave of short-run, intense demands might break futilely across the superstructure of any stable organization. Given the stately metabolism (fixed terms of office, staggered Senatorial elections) decreed for it by the founding fathers, Congress could hardly be expected to operate efficiently with respect to short-run demands in the best of circumstances.

A second source of Congressional insensitivity to innovation is of course the fact that many urgent demands are pressed upon Congress by groups with whom Congressmen—and quite often the bulk of their constituents—simply disagree. Not all righteous causes—not even all self-righteous causes—are popular. And, as a matter of fact, not all momentarily popular causes are necessarily righteous. Congressmen often have a keen appreciation of this.

It may be said that Congressmen are more concerned than they should be with popularity. But this constraint on their judgment is the result of the fact that they are popularly elected. They must ask who will get the credit —or the blame—for public policies. They must know who is for what and how strongly, because these matters affect not only their own future efficacy but also the present chances that a majority can be assembled.

Is there a practical alternative to a process of legislative policy-making in which alternative policies are put to stringent tests of internal political acceptability? If the internal politics of the institution did not matter, the legislature would be a mere arena, a place for forces as they exist in the outside society to contend. The group that captures such an organization may find it marginally useful in pressing claims upon leaders situated elsewhere, since victory in some arenas can give legitimacy to a cause. But as an organization develops independent power and internal structure as it begins to devote a portion of its resources to self-maintenance, it also develops a measure of insensitivity. To require total responsiveness of a legislature is to require it to be powerless.

– 5 –

Although Congress has developed institutional strength within its political system to a degree unrivaled by most contemporary legislatures, it does not follow that nothing can be done to increase its sensitivity to social problems or increase its effectiveness within the logic of its own developing character. To me the reason most reform proposals are uninteresting is not because reforms are necessarily less appealing than the status quo, but because they are usually addressed rather arbitrarily to "needs," and typically neither needs nor solutions are discussed within the context that includes the relevant features of the ongoing system.

A number of meritorious reforms

have been suggested that do not bear on the operations of the Congressional collectivity except insofar as the general reputations of all members are affected by the transgressions of a few. Reforms bearing on conflict of interest, disclosure of income, and other such matters do not materially affect the strength of the institution except as the institution's strength is mirrored in its general reputation.

Problems of Congressional morality cannot really be addressed responsibly without considering comparable problems in the private sector. Even under the new tax law American taxpayers will be giving rather substantial subsidies, far exceeding in their magnitude salaries and perquisities furnished Congress, to certain privileged persons and industries—most conspicuously oil companies and banks. How relevant is it to condemn Congressmen for allegedly taking "junkets" at taxpayer expense while in the private sector all manner of extravagance is routinely charged off to "business expenses" as a tax dodge? When Congress recently voted to raise Congressional salaries the news media were generally outraged. The fact is, considering the weight of their responsibilities, even at the new rates, Congressmen are far from over-compensated. It is necessary for them to maintain out of pocket two bases of operation and transportation between them. Their campaign expenses are not deductible as business expenses. Consider, also, the level of compensation of men carrying comparable responsibilities in the private sector as Congressmen and Senators do within government. It may be doubted that the top 535 men in the automotive industry, or on Wall Street, or in television make do with the equivalent of salaries of $42,500 plus small change in the way of stationery allowances, inexpensive haircuts, a few overseas junkets, and occasional trips home on military aircraft.

All this provides no excuse for Congressmen not to bring themselves within the conflict of interest laws as they presently apply to political executives. This may be more technically difficult than it sounds, since like the everyday activities of the Secretary of the Treasury, their votes touch everything, so no investment of capital is immune to a conflict of interest problem. There are, however, enough violations of propriety to make the problem worth thinking about.

Important as these matters are for public morality, they do not touch the institutional life of Congress. I propose now to list three suggestions that do go to the activities of the collectivity, that embody changes in present arrangements, but do not disturb most existing institutional values, except in ways I shall describe.

First, a scheme for mandatory retirement. Mortality is a melancholy fact, which comes upon us in different ways, and at different rates of speed. Most modern organizations protect themselves against its creeping effects by requiring the retirement of members after a certain age is reached. Congress now has a generous pension plan that works no economic hardship upon most members forced into retirement by electoral defeat. Instead of relying wholly upon local party systems to replace ailing, failing, and senile members, Congress should protect the efficiency and integrity of its functioning by providing for mandatory retirement at a stated age. If on college campuses these days 30 years of age seems about right for this purpose, perhaps for Congress the age 70 is suitable.

It will be argued in opposition to this proposal that (1) many valuable persons make Congress their second career, and Congress would be depriving itself of much-needed maturity and good judgment in legislative affairs; (2) no similar impositions are contemplated for other political offices, and thus the proposal is inequitable; and (3) the proposal places an unnecessary requirement upon electors in states and districts.

All three objections lack weight. The first ignores the extent to which Congress is presently a young man's game, though to be sure, a young man's waiting game. Men who arrive in Congress past the age of 55 rarely have a chance to accumulate sufficient seniority to acquire institutionally based influence. This proposal would over the short run in fact give some older new arrivals more, not less, of a chance to shine, since it would clear the most senior men out of the way at a predictable rate. But it would not materially affect the incentive system as it currently applies differentially to men of different ages.

The second objection has no merit with respect to the executive branch, since the President's term of office is strictly limited by other means, and other political officials serve at his pleasure. I have no desire to reopen the issue of court packing, but would have no objection in principle to the imposition of mandatory retirement upon federal judges.

Finally, there is the matter of the protection of the interests of voters. Presumably, if they want to send elderly Representatives and Senators to Congress, they should be allowed to do so. I merely assert a competing interest, one that has grown over the years, namely the interest that Congress has as an institution in maintaining a membership sufficiently vigorous to conduct its increasingly demanding business successfully. Surely each Congressional district and each state contains more than one potential Congressman or Senator, so the disability the requirement of mandatory retirement places on the voters of each district must be regarded as minimal. A more impressive objection is that the proposal is unconstitutional. This was not fully apparent until the Court decided *Powell v. McCormack* this year [1969]. But it now appears that it will take remarkable agility at textual construction, or a two-thirds' vote to expel in individual cases, or a Constitutional amendment, in order to give effect to a general retirement scheme.

A second proposal has to do with the improvement of technical knowledge available to Congress. Where does Congress get technical knowledge? Principally from committee staff personnel, who virtually monopolize the activity of explicit policy analysis in most subject matter areas. But while the executive branch has systematically been engaged in professionalizing its search for technical understanding over the past decade or more, Congress on the whole has not done so. It is romantic for Congressmen to think of themselves as not in need of expert and detailed explicit analysis because they are "generalists." Generalism is too often a genteel name for ignorance. Like all other modern institutions, Congress can only preserve its autonomy and effectiveness by reducing its ignorance.

Are there means by which Congress can do so? Two such come readily to mind. Both seek to apply to Congressional committee staffs lessons from the executive branch, where the professionalization of economic forecasting and defense procurement led to tremendous increases in the power of political decision-makers to identify options and choose among them. This is precisely the battle many Congressmen feel they are losing. Yet if they choose to do so, they can professionalize their own committee staffs, thereby increasing the efficiency of their explicit analytical activities and enhancing their own knowledge and power.

To "professionalize" implies continuous contact with a community outside the world of Capitol Hill. Professional economists, operations researchers, psychologists, and so on, maintain standards of performance by participating in their professional communities through meetings, scholarly journals, and similar specialized communications media. Typically, nowadays, the top economists of the executive branch—the men who formulate fiscal policy, anti-trust policy, international trade policy, and so forth—are first and foremost professional economists. The primacy of their loyalty to professional craft standards vastly increases the probability that the options presented to political executives will be feasible and technically sound.

Typically, Congressional committees are staffed by an older, less effective process of patronage. This produces loyal service, and by the standards of an earlier day, highly competent service. But unswerving loyalty to the chairman is seldom enough to produce technically advanced criticism of executive proposals, sophisticated insight into alternatives, or sensitive awareness of emerging problems in the world. Yet these are what Congress needs. Hence, two modest proposals. Committees should be encouraged to constitute outside advisory groups to advise the chairman on the technical competence of the work the committee is receiving from its staff. Secondly, more extensive exchanges for one- or two-year hitches of service should be instituted between Congressional committee staffs and staff persons in the executive branch, private business, labor unions, social service organizations, and universities.

The purpose of these proposals is to bring to bear upon explicit policy analysis on Capitol Hill the standards—and the considerations—that are commonly employed in policy analysis within the executive branch and elsewhere in society. It is not contemplated that steps such as these will necessarily bring Congress into harmony with the executive branch in areas where they now disagree, since there is no reason to suppose that a large number of disagreements over national policy are based on ignorance—though some may be. These disagreements should be resolved. Other disagreements may rear their heads if Congress chooses to equip itself with more professional analytic personnel, since not all executive branch proposals are free from controversy even when they are grounded in thorough professional knowledge. Thus more professionalism in explicit analysis can assist Congress in finding disagreements and weak spots in executive branch recommendations and can increase the probability that Congress itself can initiate policy. These proposals, therefore, genuinely attempt to strengthen Congress rather than the opposite, as is the case with so many proposals for Congressional reform.

My third suggestion is a simple endorsement of Representative Morris Udall's proposal to elect House committee chairmen at the start of each Congress. Udall's plan is not a return to king caucus. Rather, it provides for the selection of committee chairmen from a slate of the three most senior members of the majority party to be elected by secret ballot by all majority caucus members, with the ranking member on the minority side to be picked by a similar process in his caucus. This provides an institutional hedge against a too-arbitrary chairman, or one who is incapacitated or hopelessly out of step with his colleagues, without wholly vitiating the advantages of seniority or placing chairmanships in the hands of some centralized authority.

I have mentioned that the great advantage of the seniority system is that it decentralizes power in the House of Representatives by creating multiple centers of policy influence and increasing the number of good Congressional jobs. This adds to the incentives of the Congressional career. Proposals to centralize power must always be weighed against the damage they may do to this incentive system. The fragility and rarity of effective legislatures in world history is little appreciated. In most places, and at most times, they have been little more than arenas for the registering of organized group interests or electoral colleges for cabinets. The Udall plan has the advantage of even further decentralizing power—to Congressional party rank and file—rather than placing it in the hands of party leaders, and thus this plan increases the general level of incentives for House members to make careers in the House.

These proposals may seem hopelessly incremental. To a Congressman they may appear simply hopeless. At least they give recognition to the continuous needs for institutions to provide means by which they can respond to outside demands, yet at the same time retain the capacity to exercise independent choice. They recognize the peculiar contributions the House and the Senate make, individually and together, to American politics, and seek to enhance the participation of these institutions in the processes of policy-making by improving their capabilities rather than destroying their power.

2

THE CONGRESSIONAL CAREER
THEN AND NOW

H. DOUGLAS PRICE

This essay by H. Douglas Price, Professor of Government at Harvard, was originally drafted in 1964 and circulated privately to students of Congress, where it gave a tremendous impetus to the rediscovery of the historical dimension of inquiry into American political institutions. It is published here for the first time. It deals with changes in the character of the House from the end of the nineteenth century to today and how these have changed the careers of members; the relative stability of the Senate during this period makes a nice contrast. Since 1964 changes in the Senate's position in the political system have in turn changed the careers of senators, as I argue below in "Goodbye to the Inner Club," but these changes were not clearly visible when the following article was written.

A Tale of Two Texans

At one time or another tens of thousands of Americans must think, at least fleetingly, of what it would be like to be a United States senator or representative. To most the idea of a legislative career is not serious but passes as a sort of Walter Mitty daydream. To others, however, the ambition takes root, or perhaps the actual opportunity may loom on the not too distant horizon. To young Sam Rayburn the urge to become a congressman came at age thirteen after he listened to a spellbinding speech by Joseph Weldon Bailey, the Texas senator and one-time House minority leader. To Pierre Salinger the opportunity to become a senator from California inspired the ambition.

Joseph Weldon Bailey, Sam Rayburn,

Printed by permission of the author.

and Pierre Salinger represent not merely different types of political careers but also three quite different phases of American politics. The Congress of the 1960s is a vastly different institution from the days of the nineteenth century, as can readily be seen from the differences in the structure of a legislative career. The changes have been sharpest in regard to the House, as is evident from a quick comparison of the careers of Sam Rayburn and the hero of his youth, Congressman (later Senator) Bailey.

Joseph Weldon Bailey entered the House in 1893, one of 135 freshmen members (in the following Congress there were 165 freshmen). The Democrats were in the majority, as they had been in the previous Congress, but were engaged in a complex struggle over the speakership. When William Springer's Illinois delegation found themselves

14

unable to put Springer across, they swung their weight to Carlisle of Georgia, who was elected. Carlisle named Springer to be chairman of the Ways and Means Committee. Bailey, who had backed the wrong candidate, ended up on the Judiciary Committee, but young William Jennings Bryan, a Springer protégé, got a coveted seat on Ways and Means.

To make a long story short, in 1894 Bailey was reelected. Bryan, defeated in his bid for the Senate in 1894, captured the Democratic nomination for president in 1896, but lost under circumstances which further reduced the number of Democrats in Congress. The reduced Democratic contingent in the House turned to Bailey, then starting his *third term*, as their candidate for Speaker in 1897. Bailey was again his party's leader in the 1899–1900 sessions, after which he was elected to the Senate, where he served until 1913. Had he remained in the House and continued as Democratic leader, he would have been in line for the speakership in 1911.

Sam Rayburn's twenty-five continuous terms in the House represent the twentieth-century pattern of legislative leadership, just as Bailey's rapid rise, committee shifts, and switch to the Senate are typical of the nineteenth century. The general patterns of "Mr. Sam's" career are well known, but it is instructive to look at some of the less obvious turning points and some of the roads not taken. Rayburn ran for the Texas legislature in 1906 and was elected at the age of twenty-four. The great issue of the day was prohibition, and Rayburn characteristically moved to a compromise position in support of "local option." Rayburn, who had rapidly won a reputation for fairness and dependability, was elected to a third term in 1910 and was determined to go after the speakership. After a long and

complex struggle, Rayburn, who had the support of the then Senator Bailey, won the post—on the sixty-seventh ballot. (In Georgia young Carl Vinson— who later served for fifty years in Congress—was serving as speaker of the Georgia Assembly.) As speaker of the legislature, Rayburn was in an excellent position to bid for such statewide office as attorney general, a stepping stone to the governorship. But Texas was, in 1910, gaining two House seats, and the incumbent from what had been Rayburn's district was retiring to run against Bailey for the Senate.

Rayburn's bid for a seat in Congress was thus eased, both by reapportionment and by his predecessor's urge for "promotion" to the Senate. Still, there were eight candidates and Rayburn (who had bought a Model T Ford for campaigning) won with only 23.4 percent of the votes. He polled 4,983 votes, while his top two rivals received 4,493 and 4,365. When he arrived in Washington in 1913, John N. Garner, the Texas member of the Ways and Means Committee, helped to get him a reasonably good committee assignment, on the Commerce Committee. Garner, who had already served ten years, was eying the House speakership, an ambition it was to take him ten more years to reach.

Rayburn faced primary opposition in his first six reelection campaigns and was occasionally to face determined opponents even after becoming the Democratic leader of the House. But he maintained an effective campaign organization and kept in close touch with his district. Rayburn's progress toward the top in the House, however, was to depend in part on the career aspirations of his predecessors. Thus, on the Commerce Committee, Alben Barkley of Kentucky was immediately ahead of Rayburn—had Barkley remained in the House and on the committee, Rayburn would have remained the second-ranking Democrat during the 1930s, and for long thereafter (Barkley died in 1956). Fortunately for Rayburn, Barkley made the switch to the Senate in 1926. Still, the top ranks of the Democratic leadership consisted of his fellow Texan, John Garner, and such other figures as Rainey of Illinois, Bankhead of Alabama, O'Connor of New York, and Byrns of Tennessee. Garner, elected speaker in 1931, left the House for the vice-presidency in 1933, and was succeeded by Rainey, who had been his floor leader. But Rainey died shortly thereafter, and Rayburn made his move for the speakership. He was, however, defeated by Byrns, who had been majority floor leader under Rainey. In 1936, Byrns died. His floor leader was John Bankhead, who was in line for the speakership. Rayburn, sensitive to the apparent succession pattern, did not challenge Bankhead but sought the floor-leader post, which he won in January 1937. When Speaker Bankhead died in 1940, Rayburn moved up to the speakership, and John McCormack of Massachusetts, a key supporter of Rayburn's, became the new floor leader (and heir apparent).

Rayburn's accomplishments—and his longevity—were exceptional, but in many other respects his career illustrates the crucial turning points in any modern House career. He had the advantages of entering politics early, rising rapidly, and reaching the House by the age of thirty. He came from a one-party district, survived subsequent primary contests, and managed to avoid any damaging redistricting or at-large elections. He resisted temptations to seek state office or switch to the Senate. Early arrival plus sheer survival, physical and political, brought him to the chairmanship of his committee. Because he was acceptable to most of his colleagues and the administration, he was in a position to try for the leadership. That he reached the top was due in large part to his skill, persistence, and stamina. But it also was due to the fact that Barkley and Garner were elected to other offices, and that Rainey, Byrns, and Bankhead did not long survive their elevation to the speakership. In the two decades between Bailey's first election to the House (1892) and Rayburn's (1912) the whole pattern of a House career had drastically changed.

The structure of the legislative career and the relationship between the two houses on Capitol Hill are largely the result of changes which occurred in the late nineteenth and early twentieth centuries. Throughout most of the nineteenth century service in the House was likely to be a matter of one or, at most, a few terms. Turnover of House membership ranged from 30 to over 60 percent at *every* election, and the average number of terms of prior service represented by a new House generally ranged from one term (or even less) to one and a half terms. The Congress elected in 1900 was the *first* in American history in which new members constituted less than 30 percent of the membership, and it was also the first in which the average of prior service was more than two terms. This, of course, is vastly different from the twentieth-century pattern.

Up until the 1890s only a handful of men had pursued substantial lifetime careers within the House, and they were often the occasion for puzzled comment. Committee chairmen, minority leaders, and even speakers of the House would leap at the chance to leave that body and become freshmen senators (or sometimes governors). Power within the late nineteenth-century House was highly fluid. Not only was there high turnover of members, there was also frequent alternation of

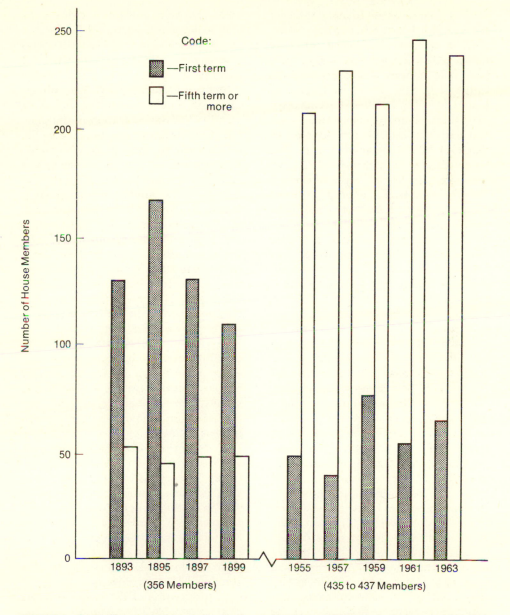

FIGURE 1   Seniority and turnover in the House: comparison of number of members serving first term with number serving fifth or higher terms, 1893–1899 and 1953–1963

party control. Since relatively few members had substantial seniority, there was no real seniority influence to buck. All committee appointments, both for majority and minority mem-

bers, as well as the designation of chairmen, were up to the winning candidate for speaker.

All in all the nineteenth-century House was vastly different from its modern counterpart. In many respects the pre-1900 House was similar to the average current state assembly: It was a part-time body (in session perhaps nine months out of twenty-four, rather than nine out of twelve), with a high degree of membership turnover, with sharp fights for party leadership, and with the leaders in a position to make all committee appointments and name committee chairmen. The nineteenth-century House was even physically different from that of more recent decades: Members sat at individual desks (rather than on the modern benches), which were often bedecked with flowers, traditionally wore their hats in the chamber (until the 1830s), and were permitted to smoke (until the 1870s).

Lengthy and powerful speeches were still common in the House into the 1890s when Reed's speech on the Wilson tariff bill ran to 15,000 words and required two hours. William Wilson's reply for the Democrats so elated them that they hoisted him onto their shoulders and carried him triumphantly from the chamber. Members often used bitter and outrageous language, scathing ridicule, and sarcasm. Outbreaks of physical violence were not infrequent, and guns and knives were on occasion carried into the chamber.

Constituents were a problem, then as now, but in different ways. There was little mail, and very little departmental "case" work. But members were plagued with continuous demands for government appointments (of which there were many, even after the beginning of civil service in 1883), for local postmasterships (of which there were a vast number, many part time), and for special pension bills (which became something of a national scandal). If modern legislators fret over the heavy mail and case work—most of

which can be handled by the member's staff—they can be thankful for the lessened concern with pensions, rural postmasters, and the whole array of government jobs.

Anyone accustomed to the importance of seniority and the extent of stability and specialization in the modern House is apt to find the nineteenth-century House difficult to understand. And yet the key to the development and maintenance of the modern pattern is to be found in the changes which destroyed the old system and laid the groundwork for the modern, professionalized legislative career. By and large these changes have been sharper for the House than for the Senate, but it is important to keep in mind the relations between the two bodies and between the two careers of representative and senator.

Service in the Senate was highly prized, and after the 1820s it was generally regarded as preferable to *any* position in the House, including the speakership. Henry Clay was only the first speaker to move to the Senate; he was followed by James G. Blaine, John G. Carlisle, Charles F. Crisp, and Frederick H. Gillett. And several minority leaders who did not serve as speakers also shifted to the Senate: Joseph W. Bailey, John Sharp Williams, and Oscar W. Underwood. Chairmen of House committees—even of Appropriations or Ways and Means—would similarly leave the House to run for the Senate, or for governor.

In the context of the past twenty or thirty years such behavior is unthinkable. Since the 1920s no speaker, majority leader, or minority leader has left the House to seek any other elective office. And the departure of major committee chairmen is almost as rare. Since the LaFollette-Monroney Act of 1946 the only chairman, or ranking minority member, of a major House committee to run for the Senate was Kenneth Keating—in New York in 1958—and he did so only under intense pressure and heavy prodding from such Republican figures as President Dwight D. Eisenhower, Vice-President Richard Nixon, and Attorney General Brownell. Even from the lesser committees of the House, the only two men making the switch to the Senate were Everett M. Dirksen, top Republican on the unimportant House D. C. Committee, and Clair Engle, who had been chairman of the House Interior Committee prior to his election to the Senate from California.

Even before the Civil War a major lifetime political career could be carved in the Senate. Thomas Hart Benton's twenty-nine and one-half years (1821–1851, defeated in his bid for a sixth term) is only one extreme example. Despite shifting party lines, the six-year term and the possibilities for maneuver within the legislative election at the state level made a long-term career possible. Since the Senate had only one-third of its membership up for election every two years, it operated as a continuing body. Committee selections generally were made as vacancies occurred, and once made they were usually held for as long as a senator served. The deposings of Stephen A. Douglas by the Democrats in the 1850s and of Charles Sumner by the Republicans in the 1860s were highly exceptional. Like the four-minute mile, serving thirty years in the Senate seemed an impossible goal. But once the barrier was broken by John Sherman of Ohio in 1895 and then by Justin Morrill of Vermont in 1897, careers of that length became commonplace. Since 1900 at least twenty additional senators have reached or passed the thirty-year mark, with the all-time

record (so far) going to Arizona's Carl Hayden.

The situation in the nineteenth-century House could hardly have been more different. Every two years a member's committee assignment and even his continued service were at the mercy not only of the voters but also of the majority party and the speaker. A member of the minority might be, and often was, removed from House membership by resort to the notorious "contested-election" process. So-called contests could be claimed in almost any district, whether Maine or Georgia, and the candidate of the majority party in the House declared the winner. Until 1907 only 3 of 382 "contests" were resolved in favor of the candidate of the minority party! Improvements in election administration and heightened public sensitivity to fraud have almost completely eliminated this threat to a member's career. And nineteenth-century party nominations, made in the confusion of the delegate convention, were subject to little regulation.

If a member was fortunate enough to be renamed by his party, reelected by the voters, and escape a partisan challenge to his right to his seat, he would return to a House where committee assignments and chairmanships were openly bartered for in the process of determining the party leadership (especially in the majority party, which elected the speaker). The support of freshmen members was courted as avidly, or more, than that of the relatively few veteran members. Thus after the Democrats captured the House in 1890, there was a sharp four-way fight for the speakership among Roger Mills of Texas, who had been Ways and Means chairman in the 1887–1888 Congress, Charles Crisp of Georgia, William Springer of Illinois, and Benton McMillin of Tennessee. A long-time Washington reporter summarizes the contest as follows:

On the first ballot in the caucus only a few votes separated Mills and Crisp, the leaders, and it was regarded as certain that one of them would be named. Then the dickering began among the managers of the candidates for high committee places, and the Crisp men outgeneraled the Mills' forces in that line of work. Judge Springer withdrew his name and voted for Crisp, and that settled it. Mr. Crisp was nominated, and Judge Springer secured the chairmanship of the Ways and Means Committee, and, as the floor leadership went with it as usual, he was satisfied with the outcome. The other Crisp managers got important committee assignments.

The fluidity of the process is indicated by the events of the next Congress, also Democratic-controlled. Crisp, who had been speaker, was reelected but faced a contest for the leadership with his former supporter, William Springer. When the jockeying was over, William Holman of Indiana, the famed "watchdog of the Treasury" and Chairman of the Appropriations Committee in the preceding Congress, was moved to the chairmanship of Indian Affairs; and Springer, Chairman of Ways and Means in the preceding Congress, was demoted to Chairman of Banking and Currency—the new chairman of Ways and Means was William Wilson of West Virginia. To round out the story, in 1894 Speaker Crisp managed to get himself elected to the Senate (thus following former Speaker Carlisle), while Wilson, Springer, and Holman (the key committee chairmen) were all defeated. And the new chairman of Appropriations, Joseph Sayers, left the House in 1899 to serve as governor of Texas.

Translated into the House of the early 1960s, this would mean a sequence of events something like this: Speaker Rayburn would give up the speakership to become a freshman senator and would be succeeded by John McCormack. After the next election McCormack would be challenged for the leadership by Wilbur Mills, who would then be dumped from Ways and Means and made chairman of Banking and Currency. Clarence Cannon, the latter-day watchdog of the Treasury, would be switched to the chairmanship of Interior. If this sounds a bit unlikely, consider further that McCormack would then leave the House to become a freshman senator, and that Mills, Cannon, and the new Ways and Means chairman might all be defeated at the next election. Cannon's successor on Appropriations, George Mahon, would serve a couple more terms and then run for governor of Texas. That is what the script would call for if current House politics were conducted nineteenth-century style!

Such a system provides flexibility, of one sort or another, but virtually rules out making a systematic career of serving in the House. The contrast can be seen by a quick comparison of the careers of the Democratic House chairmen of the ten leading substantive committees (Appropriations, Ways and Means, Judiciary, Military, Naval, Commerce, Foreign Affairs, and Agriculture, Rivers and Harbors, and Banking and Currency) when Grover Cleveland took office in 1893 with the chairmen of the same committees when Franklin D. Roosevelt took office in 1933. Of the chairmen in 1933 seven were eventually carried out of the House office building feet first, and three retired (after serving an average of thirty-three and one-third years in the House). None of the ten ever ran for any other office, and none of the ten was ever upset in his home district. By contrast, of the ten Cleveland chairmen four were defeated in 1894 and one in 1896. Two were elected to the Senate and subsequently served as governors, while a third went directly from the House to the governor's mansion. The ten Cleveland chairmen served an average of 7.4 terms (in several cases with interruptions in service) and only *one* served *more* than ten terms (he served eleven). The 1933 chairmen served an average of 16.2 terms (better than thirty-two years) apiece, and only *two* served *less* than ten terms, while three served more than twenty terms (prior to 1900 *no* member of the House had *ever* served that long). Of the 1933 chairmen four outlasted FDR and served with President Truman, three with President Eisenhower, two with President Kennedy, and one (Carl Vinson of Georgia) served with President Johnson (who in 1937 had been a freshman member of the committee of which Vinson was then chairman).

Lest it be thought that the House in the 1890s was atypical, it should be emphasized that a similar pattern prevailed from the end of the Reconstruction. Thus, of the seven regularly elected speakers serving from 1870 to 1894, one was elected in his third term of service, two in their fourth term, two in their fifth (one of these having just returned to the House after being out a term!), one in his sixth (Reed, who had sought the speakership unsuccessfully in his third term), and one in his seventh term. Of these seven, one (Kerr) died within a year of his selection as speaker. Of the remaining six exactly half (Blaine, Carlisle, and Crisp) left the House to go to the Senate. Keifer, who had defeated Reed for the Republican choice in 1881, was denied renomination to the House in 1884. Randall, who had the longest service of the seven, was upset in the Democratic caucus of 1883, and he served the next three Congresses as Chairman of the Appropriations Committee. Reed, embittered that McKinley rather than he had been nominated by the GOP for president in 1896 and out of sympathy with the Spanish-American War, resigned from the House and joined a Wall Street law firm.

Since the speakership was obtained by the appropriate parceling out of committee chairmanships and memberships, these also were subject to substantial shifts as well as to the high turnover. Thus, Henry L. Dawes was Chairman of Appropriations (1869–1870), then Chairman of Ways and Means (1871–1874), and then went to the Senate. William Morrison was Chairman of Ways and Means in 1875–1876, but lost the position to Fernando Wood in 1877–1880, only to return for 1883–1886. James A. Garfield went from Chairman of Banking and Currency in 1869–1870 to Chairman of Appropriations in 1871–1874. Frank Hiscock, congressman from Syracuse, New York, became Chairman of Appropriations in his third term (1881–1882), subsequently served as a minority member on Ways and Means, and then was elected to the Senate. William Holman, one of the few really long-term nineteenth-century members, specialized in appropriations during Randall's chairmanship. But instead of succeeding Randall on the committee, Holman was switched to Public Lands in the Fiftieth and Fifty-first Congresses, and in the latter, the Republicans named Sayers of Texas as top minority man on Appropriations. In the Fifty-second Congress Holman returned to Appropriations as Chairman, but in the succeeding Congress he again lost the post (to Sayers) and had to be satisfied with Indian Affairs.

Although *total* experience in the House was of some importance, *continuous* service meant virtually nothing prior to the twentieth century. The misuse of "election contests" meant that removal did not necessarily constitute rebuke, and the lack of reliance on seniority meant that many members dropped out for a term or so, held other offices and then returned, or came back to pick up their House service virtually unimpaired afterward. The lack of importance of continuous service was most obvious in the pre–Civil War era. Thus, Henry Clay served two short tours in the Senate *before* he ran for the House in 1810. Speaker Clay then resigned from the House in 1814 but came back again for the next three Congresses (in which he was again speaker). He then skipped a whole Congress but returned for the next two (in which he was again speaker). He returned to the increasingly important Senate in 1831, resigned in 1842, but returned once more in 1849. To the extent that *continuous* service constitutes a congressional career, Clay had no less than *seven* separate and distinct congressional careers, which is only to say that continuous service had nothing to do with his two real careers in the House and Senate. Indeed, Clay (as chairman of a select committee) fashioned the epic Compromise of 1850 at a time when his continuous service in the Senate dated from March 4, 1849!

In the nineteenth-century House, continuous service was even less important and defeat for a term (or being ousted in a "contest") had little or no effect. Michael Kerr was defeated in 1872 (after serving four terms) but came back in 1874 to be elected speaker (when he had *zero* continuous prior service)! Joe Cannon was defeated in the Democratic sweep of 1890, but returned to Congress in 1892, and after the 1894 Republican victory, became Chairman of the Appropria-

tions Committee (he then had ten terms of service but only *one* term of continuous prior service). Continuous prior service, then, was of no consequence for either standing on committee or election to party leadership. To understand how and why this was changed is to understand the twentieth-century Congress.

The extreme fluidity or even near chaos of the House in the twenty-year span from 1875 to 1894 came to a sudden stop and was succeeded by a sixteen-year period (1895–1910) in which change in the House was virtually imperceptible. There was no change of party control in the latter period, and the "team" of leaders which Tom Reed brought to the top in 1893 continued to dominate the picture, with only a few replacements, up to 1910. Reed, who had done so much to mold the rules of the modern House, was also the master architect of the only real centralized "machine" to ever dominate that body over a substantial period of time. And it was the reaction in 1910 and 1911 against this centralized control which brought into being the "modern" House and further shaped the pattern of the House career.

Thus, there have been three main patterns of House politics, each with its particular type of career. Just as nature abhors a vacuum, so most politicians abhor excessive conflict and uncertainty. But conflict and uncertainty prevailed in the House up to 1895, and the stable oligarchy of 1895–1910 was destroyed by the events of 1910–1911. The great transformations in the structure of the House, and thus of House careers, were not the conscious result of any one man's will or of any one event. Rather they were the net result —often unintended—of a number of trends and decisions. As Marx once noted:

Men make their own history but they do not make it just as they please; they do not make it under circumstances as chosen by themselves but under circumstances directly found, given and transmitted from the past.

In retrospect it is not difficult to specify the crucial preconditions which served to maintain the fluidity of the nineteenth-century House. As these factors were changed, the career possibilities and motivations of the members were changed, and *this* amounted to a change in the political structure of the House. Table 1 lists the more important preconditions for fluidity and the factors which changed. The

TABLE 1   Factors Sustaining Fluidity and the Origins of Seniority in the House

NINETEENTH-CENTURY CONDITIONS	CHANGES IN CONDITIONS
1. Prior to Civil War a member might be left off the roster by the clerk of the House in a move to effect majority control.	1. A member's right to a seat was not threatened in this way after the Civil War.
2. A member of the minority was always in danger of being unseated by a questionable "election contest," decided on strict partisan vote.	2. Improved election administration, and publicly supplied ballots made this unlikely after 1900.
3. Voluntary turnover was very high; norm in some districts required rotation or a two-term limit (even Lincoln had been limited to a single term).	3. Efforts at reelection increased around turn of the century; norms against reelection declined.
4. Until the 1890s competition was on a much more even basis throughout the country than after 1900.	4. The 1896 campaign polarized the country, and local one-party dominance was reinforced by: a. Rise of white supremacy and decline of GOP in South b. Urban–rural split c. Catholic–Protestant split d. Immigrant–native split.
5. Party control of the House alternated frequently.	5. There was no alternation in party control of House from 1895 to 1911, and there has been only infrequent alternation since.
6. All committee assignments, majority and minority, and all chairmanships were designated by the speaker for each new Congress.	6. After 1902 speaker dealt with only his party's assignments, leaving minority assignments to minority leader.
7. There was frequent competition for party leadership, and rapid turnover of leaders (who frequently ran for the Senate).	7. Leaders became more likely to remain in the House, less likely to run for the Senate, and more difficult to challenge because of: a. Infrequency of alternation in power b. Fact that the minority leader after 1902 was buttressed by power to make minority-committee assignments.
8. Few members had much seniority so there was no effective guide to apportioning positions.	8. After 1895 seniority, and continuous service, became more common and harder to ignore.
9. House was not a continuing body, in law, in practice, or in most of its membership.	9. Although still not a continuing body in a legal sense, the House *has* become one in much of its practice and in the great majority of its membership.

cumulated effect of these changes was to make possible a new-style organization of the House under Speaker Cannon, but it proved intolerable. When Cannon was cut down to size, and the Democrats captured the speakership, the "modern" House was the result. To go back to the centralized control of a Cannon, or the fluidity of the pre-1895 era would require changes in the crucial factors which underlie the origins of the modern House career pattern. Empty talk about changing the rules or practice of the House ignores this simple reality.

In summary, the nineteenth-century pattern of flexibility reflected both the lack of continuity in membership (resulting from high turnover plus contested elections) and the lack of continuity of structure within the House (resulting from frequent alternation of party and movement of party leaders to the Senate). A change in the latter factor permitted a unique centralization of power under Reed and Cannon, but the situation was not as stable as it looked. The Democrats had never accepted the idea of a presiding "czar" (indeed, they had even opposed the Reed rules). And the spectacular drop in turnover produced inevitable pressures, even under Cannon, for adherence to seniority.

If not the best of all possible rules, seniority at least has the advantages of being an operational criterion and an automatic one, which "merit" or "ability" are not to an equal degree. It thus tended to avoid controversy and was soon wrapped in a glow of legitimacy. Length of continuous service on a committee soon became a legislative fetish, complete with special procedures for breaking ties. But it should be emphasized that *new* appointments to a committee continue to constitute a vital exception to the general reliance on seniority, especially in the House.

No amount of seniority will guarantee a member admission to the elite committees, such as Rules, Ways and Means, or Appropriations. In the Senate, however, seniority is much more important as a criterion for making committee shifts; for the Republicans it is usually decisive.

Seniority is not a "rule" to be adopted or repealed, but a habit, a way of life, and a means of resolving conflict. It is used by the Supreme Court to determine its seating (and the assignment of opinions if the chief justice is not with the majority), by the District of Columbia's government in assigning license plates to diplomats, by unions to determine job rights, and by people throughout the world who line up in queues (whether at the A & P or Lenin's tomb). It rests on no very rational basis, but neither does monarchy or counting ballots. Since the basic reliance on seniority in Congress is unlikely to be reversed, it is all the more important that its sway be limited. This can be done by providing more democratic procedures within committees, by maintaining flexibility in the Committee on Committees where the Democratic reliance on Ways and Means to make committee appointment has the advantage of adding five new committee members when the party shifts from minority to majority position (thus bringing new blood into that crucial body), and by awareness that congressional careers can be—and in the past have been—organized on other bases.

The Senatorial Career

The Senate career seems not to have changed much over the past hundred years, although the formal process of election and the types of individuals elected have been sharply altered. In contrast to the House, however, service in the Senate has from early in the nineteenth century constituted a potential lifetime career, in which seniority plays an important role. Recent descriptions of the Senate have made much of the true Senate type, the "inner club," the emphasis upon protecting each senator's rights, the lack of importance of speechmaking per se, and the importance of specialization. Walter Wellman, a perceptive Washington correspondent, hit on all these themes in a piece published in 1906, in which he described the great influence of Wisconsin Senator John C. Spooner:

The Country's estimate of a public man does not always agree with the Washington estimate. When they conflict, Washington is usually much nearer the mark. . . . It is coldly critical; it studies at close range; it is behind the scenes. . . .

The man who rises to the first rank in a body like the Senate is a man of power. Only ten or a dozen of fourscore and a half form that select company. . . . Accident or wealth may get a man into the Senate, but it will not get him into the inner circle. . . . The Senate is largely controlled by this inner circle of a dozen men. Actual personal leadership it will not have. According to the ethics and tradition of that body, no man may aspire to such commanding influence in it as Speakers have wielded or chairmen of Ways and Means Committees have enjoyed in the House. . . . It is a stickler for a theory of equality. . . . But in practice there is the dominating inner circle; and when one thinks of that circle, the first man who comes to mind is Spooner of Wisconsin.

Influence in the Senate is acquired in many ways. The popular impression appears to be that it is best won by making speeches. . . . Some of the most influential men in the Senate do not speak at all, or but rarely. Some of the best and most prolific talkers have little influence. . . . A large measure of his [Spooner's] success is due to the fact that he rarely uses his energy or capitalizes his influence in the pursuit of trifles.

In Congress, as everywhere, the tendency is toward specialization. Senators take up one line or another, become as proficient as possible in that, and give very little attention to other subjects. . . . He is so willing to work, so eager to investigate, so tireless and so alert, and his sincerity and judgment are so highly valued, that all the specialists consult him. . . . As a lawyer and maker of laws, as a watchdog against the furtive slipping in of blunders, as a suggester of stronger and better methods, as a deviser of practical schemes which will meet existing conditions in the Senate and the country, he is without a peer in public life. The natural result—despite himself, and not at all through his seeking—is that his finger is felt in nearly every big legislative pie. His impress is more or less upon every policy, every great act.

It follows, as a matter of course, that such a man is much sought; that other senators are constantly running to him with their knotty problems; that to him come many opportunities to give his country the benefit of his talents.

The above analysis has hardly been improved upon by more recent students of the Senate. Still, change has taken place. The mind boggles at a Pierre Salinger moving to Rhode Island to challenge Nelson Aldrich in the 1900s. And there is no denying that business domination, by fair means and foul, of many nineteenth-century state legislatures, did lead to a period when many Senate seats (especially in the Northeast) came perilously close to being for sale. Shortly after the turn of the century one observer (not a muckraker) summarized the situation as follows:

If you will take Montana's Clark, Senator Gorman, and Tom Patterson from the Democratic side of the Chamber, nearly all the wealth of the Senate will be on the Republican or rich East Side. There are ten Republican senators that represent one hundred million dollars, and ten others who are millionaires. There are only four or five millionaires on the Democratic side; as we rate wealth these days, twenty-five out of the thirty-one Democratic senators are comparatively poor men. . . . It is refreshing in these days of graft, however, to mention that it is an exceedingly rare case, where a senator from a Southern state is accused of fraud and bribery in gaining his seat in the Senate. . . .

Take, for instance, John T. Morgan of Alabama, who is serving his fifth term in the Senate. He is a poor man, and yet consider what a great railroad president he would have made, and the vast fortune he would have acquired, had he entered the business world, instead of the political field. His long head is filled to the brim with brains. . . .

The extent to which the Senate had become a rich man's club by the turn of the century might have led to a constitutional crisis such as involved the British House of Lords in 1911 or the U.S. Supreme Court in 1937. As it happened, however, the trend toward corporate domination which developed in the Gilded Age was halted and then reversed by the informal undermining of the process of having senators chosen by state legislatures. As William Riker has shown, the practice of sending written legislative "instructions" on specific bills, or of forcing resignation of a state's senator had virtually disappeared by 1850. Throughout the latter half of the nineteenth century new and more democratic devices were developed to provide a clear, and sometimes legally binding, mandate for a candidate whom the legislature would elect pro forma.

Thus, everyone has heard of the debates between Lincoln and Senator Stephen A. Douglas, but few realize just why the two candidates were campaigning all over Illinois when the actual election would take place in the legislature. The answer is that direct popular campaigning by such celebrities was used to elect slates to the legislature, less as local representatives than as virtual members of an electoral college. Later, actual popularity poll elections were authorized, and Oregon made the results of its senatorial poll binding on the legislature. Thus the legislative arena, in which business control bulked so large, was outflanked, and long before the adoption of the Seventeenth Amendment. When direct election of senators finally became part of the Constitution (1913), it was *already* the existing practice in twenty-nine or thirty of the states.

The direct election of senators and the spread of the direct primary for making nominations both tended to reduce the political life chances of the wealthy businessman or the skilled legislative bargainer. The gainers were those candidates skilled at making an impact on the public, whether on reform issues (as with LaFollette, Borah, Norris) or—in the South—the race issue (Vardeman, Tom Watson, and Bilbo). A well-known political name, such as Taft in Ohio, Talmadge in Georgia, Long in Louisiana, or Kennedy in Massachusetts, is a major political asset. And the real public figure—or celebrity—who has won fame in another field may well be able to cash it in for votes in a campaign for the senatorship: Consider only the enthusiasm generated for Astronaut John Glenn in Ohio, for football coach Bud Wilkinson in Oklahoma, or for Robert Kennedy in New York State, or the California Senate contest between White House press secretary Salinger and Hollywood's George Murphy. Once in office, the celebrity stands or falls on his political performance, but being a public "name" can be a great help in winning a nomination or election—especially in situations where party leaders evaluate the prospects as discouraging, or at best touch and go (the pro's willingness to fight for a nomination rests on a close estimate of the likelihood of winning). It is then that a party is most likely to look outside its own ranks for a candidate.

The steadily growing size of constituencies, both state and district (the average population of the latter has doubled since 1900), also makes the possession of at least some wealth a very substantial advantage. Tom Watson and Bob LaFollette could, in part, finance their political operations from the incomes received on the lecture circuit or from their own political magazines. Latter-day candidates find that they often must dip into their own income to acquire public exposure.

In modern times it is highly exceptional for a senator to leave that body for any other office. In earlier decades the Cabinet might have been tempting, but that is no longer the case. Of the state governorships only those in New York and California are likely to tempt a man away from the Senate, and then only if he has presidential ambitions. The presidency remains the great goal of American politics, a goal which has tempted even Speaker Rayburn and Senate leaders like Kerr, Russell, and Johnson. Just as leadership in the House is likely to take one out of the running for the Senate, so leadership in the Senate generally takes one out of the running for the presidency. Senate floor leaders, however, are frequently called upon as vice-presidential nominees—since World War I Republican floor leaders Curtis and McNary and Democrats Truman, Barkley, Johnson, and Humphrey were nominated as vice-presidents.

By contrast the House serves as a stepping stone for a wide range of offices. The decision to leave the House and try for the Senate is an especially tough one, since it involves giving up that post in order to seek a Senate nomination (except in the case of off-year elections to fill a Senate vacancy). But the members of almost any annual class of the House will be found to provide a number of future senators and governors. Thus the House class of 1946 included a larger-than-average group of ninety new members—by 1960 nine of the group had been elected to the Senate, and four others had left the House to wage unsuccessful campaigns. Among the better known House alumni of the class of 1946 were John F. Kennedy, Richard Nixon, George Smathers, Kenneth Keating, Jacob Javits, and Thruston Morton. The class of 1946 also has provided three governors, a federal district judge, and a number of administrators.

3

WHAT DO CONGRESSMEN HEAR?[1]

LEWIS ANTHONY DEXTER

Although Lewis A. Dexter is quick to point out that most of the field work upon which the following selection is based had to do with a particular policy area—the tariff and reciprocal trade—there is no reason to believe that for most issues this is a distortion of what congressmen hear and how they hear it. To the contrary, the experience of many congressional researchers has time and again confirmed that congressmen and senators have a great deal to do with structuring the communications they receive—and heed. Lewis A. Dexter has taught at many colleges and universities, most recently at Dalhousie. He is also a private consultant, based in Belmont, Massachusetts. Rand McNally will publish, in 1970, his new book, *The Sociology and Politics of Congress.*

I. The Mail's the Thing (Superficially, at Least)

Every congressman and senatorial assistant, when asked, "What do you hear . . . ?," or words to that effect, starts telling you about the mail. Most of the businessmen with whom we talked when asked, "What have you done about such-and-such an issue?" tell you (if he has done *anything*) that he's *written* to his congressman or senator (or possibly telegraphed).

In the importance attached to it both by congressmen and by business constituents, mail outweighs every other form of communication. Strangely, many congressmen do not raise any explicit question as to whether the mail *represents* the views of the district. Some congressmen do, of course, question this. A senator, for instance, who received 100 letters from a particular city urging that he support legislation for a higher minimum wage, checked

Copyright © 1955 by Lewis A. Dexter.

on the senders and found out that at least 75 of them were eligible to vote but only 33 of these actually were registered.

Senator Service's assistant says, "If you put faith in that sort of thing [stimulated mail] you're lost. We can tell the day and hour when somebody or other starts those calls or doorbells ringing [to get people to write]; so what?" Another senatorial assistant says it is easy to identify stimulated letters by the fact that someone nearly always encloses a copy of the letter to the letter-writer asking him to write his congressman. This assistant estimates that in any batch of 1,000 letters, at least fifty will enclose the original request.

But these are the exceptions so far as formal statement goes. It is true that many congressmen and senators run counter to the mail in obedience to the dictates of conscience, party, or committee. But they frequently appear to think they are controverting something very significant. This may be merely a habitual genuflection toward the right of petition and the sovereignty of the citizen; in some cases it probably is. For whatever reason, older congressmen were much less inclined to quote the volume of mail as an authority than younger ones. This may simply mean that older ones had become sufficiently familiar with the point of view expressed by the mail (since it is similar on this issue over the years) that they do not pay as much attention to the current inflow on this subject. It may also be due in part to the fact that older congressmen are busier. It is also possible that older congressmen, by the very fact of being older, come from districts which seem safer and may therefore be less anxious to ascertain the views of the electorate. But even they on the whole appear to think that the mail is important and civically significant. There are several reasons that lead them to this attitude.

In the first place, members or their staffs spend an enormous amount of time on mail. And having invested that time on it, they like to feel that it means something.

Second, a great deal of the time congressmen operate in a pretty complete vacuum so far as the voters of their district go. Most people seem to prefer to know what they are supposed to do (if even in some cases merely so that they can protest or revolt). The mail gives a sense that one is doing something that excites large numbers of people.

Third, as Paul Appleby and others have pointed out, many congressmen are irritated and annoyed because they come to Washington expecting to do and be something important; and because of the complexity of government and the seniority system they find they are hampered and shut off from effective action at every turn. Granted this rather general exasperation, handling mail is almost the only thing on which a congressman finds himself quite free; he can write any sort of letters he likes without let or hindrance from anybody. Thus letter writing becomes a disproportionately significant aspect of his job, for it represents the freedom and importance that he thought he would find when he got to Washington (but rarely does).

Fourth, most congressmen genuinely treasure the right of petition and the opportunity of the individual citizen to complain about mistreatment. This right has great importance on many issues where bureaucrats mistreat or overlook individual rights.

Fifth, whether realistically or not, some congressmen actually believe and many others like to feel that on any issue of national significance, rational communication between them and any constituent is possible. For this reason they spend a quite irrational amount of time on correspondence that is essentially academic in the sense that it is fairly clear that no political or legislative purpose is really served by the time they give it.

For these, and perhaps other, reasons congressmen come to believe that the mailbag is the secret of success. Senator Kefauver (D., Tenn.) reports that when first elected to Congress he asked Speaker Bankhead (D., Ala.) how to get re-elected, and that Mr. Bankhead replied:

Members get re-elected term after term without substantial opposition (because they) give close and prompt attention to mail. Votes and speeches may make you well known and give you a reputation, but it's the way you handle your mail that determines your reelection.[2]

Nearly all the businessmen we talked with also regarded *writing* congressmen as the basic political-legislative act. In view of the supposed popularity of public relations in a wider sense, this was a little surprising. But nearly all of them said, "I wrote," "I telegraphed," or "No, I haven't written," when asked if they had done something about the issue.

In this article we shall review some of the characteristics of the mail that seem extraordinary in so highly valued a source of information.

Little or no mail on many vital issues

A substantial number of congressmen and probably all senators received a noticeable amount of mail about reciprocal trade legislation. This in itself differentiates reciprocal trade from many crucial issues. For example, a senator from a major industrial state heard *nothing* in the 1955 session of Congress on any of the following issues, all of which were considered by the Senate during that session, and several of which were decided so closely that he could have exercised a crucial vote: the Capehart Amendment on Policy Responsibility of dollar-a-year men (WOC's), the Hickenlooper Amendment on permitting construction of an atomic-powered merchant ship, Home Rule for the District of Columbia, the Statute of Forces Agreement (Jenner Amendment), Marine Corps increase, Mutual Aid Programs for Europe and Asia, the stockpiling of minerals, confirmation of SEC and ICC Commissioners (both controversial in the extreme), a Serviceman's Voting Proposal, the Congressional Amendment (actually passed by the Senate) permitting governors to appoint congressmen in event of emergency, the sale of rubber plants, the Housing Act of 1955, and the restriction of wheat and cotton acreage. Several of these are very important *in fact* to his state;

some of them are considered by his committees. His experience is typical.

Most of the mail comes from few sources

In 1955, probably a majority of congressmen received a good deal of mail on the tariff. However, many rated it as tenth or fifteenth, relatively low in volume compared to mail received in connection with other issues. A few in 1954 heard nothing. Such figures mean relatively little, however, because a very large proportion of the mail on the tariff issue was organized and sent by a few sources. Westinghouse, Dow, Monsanto, and Pittsburgh Plate Glass may by themselves easily have stimulated 40 per cent or more of all mail received by all congressmen in 1954 on reciprocal trade. In addition to them, on the protectionist side, there were the coal, independent oil, and textile interests. One congressman is reported to have received well over 5,000 letters on the topic from textile workers in early 1955.

On the reciprocal trade side, there is only one big producer of mail—the League of Women Voters. Very probably three-fourths of the mail received by all congressmen in favor of reciprocal trade was directly or indirectly stimulated by the League. Even in tobacco or automobile districts, League members produced a majority of the pro-reciprocal trade mail; and in districts where there was no strong protectionist group, the congressmen may have heard mostly from League members. In general, protectionist mail outweighed pro-reciprocal trade mail at least 10 to 1.

Inspired mail tends to seem unduly uniform

Congressman Simpson (R., Penna.) received a number of letters and postcards in 1953 urging him to vote against the Simpson Bill for the imposition of a fuel oil quota. To one of his colleagues this simply represented the ineptness and political uninformedness of the much-abused "women's groups."

By and large, most protectionist mail quantitatively speaking takes the line, "Save my job." Printed cards are distributed and often collected and mailed by firms in the woolen textile industry. A manufacturer in one big port city explained why his organization had gone to the trouble of collecting and mailing the cards.

Oh, we found most of these people just didn't know who their congressman was, or they sent it to their state senator or something, so we asked them just to fill in their address and we did everything else.

One congressman from that city consequently got about 6 per cent of the cards with an address but no name signed. A senatorial assistant comments, "That's doing better than par for the course."

Mail from almost any given industry tends to have its own special characteristics. The cherry industry, for example, seems to promote letters which are particularly "reasonable" sounding: "We know foreign trade is necessary but ours is a special case." It is almost impossible to organize a letter writing campaign so skillfully that an experienced mail clerk does not spot it at once as stimulated and even identify its source.

The mail is direct

We found that most of the mail to congressmen is quite direct; Mr. X writes to his congressman, and that's that. In the letter, Mr. X may identify himself but more often is simply satisfied to say he is a constituent. Mr. X does not go through channels to write his congressman. For example, I never

saw a single letter from a county chairman or other *party* official on trade and tariff matters with one exception— an official Republican group in Midland, Michigan, had petitioned their senators against reciprocal trade. This is interesting because it differs from the prevailing political pattern on patronage where endorsements are often sought unless one is personally known to the congressman (and frequently when one is). It is unrealistic because in fact the attention a congressman pays to mail is *in part* a matter of how important the writer is; frequently the content or title make this obvious, but frequently they do not.

With letters to senators in the larger states, such endorsement or identification would seem still more appropriate since mail clerks for senators often know little about the state. I know one fairly skilled lobbyist who thinks that when he really wants something from a senator's office it is a good idea to write the senator a letter beginning "Dear so-and-so (first name)." Then the mail clerk, not to take a chance, will give the letter to one of the assistants instead of handling it himself. Ordinarily the assistant handles the subject, and the senator will never see the letter—so it will create no embarrassment.

Since we found that many senators and congressmen simply disregard out-of-state mail altogether, it is particularly odd that people who write them from out of state do not take some steps to identify themselves. Altogether, many thousands of dollars of postage must be spent in out-of-state mail which is unread except for the address or first sentence.[3]

Chaff in the mail

I have hardly ever seen a letter which indicated any technical mastery of reciprocal-trade legislation. I have never noted a letter which contained a new or unfamiliar thought about the issue; nor have I happened ever to read one (out of several thousands I have looked at) where one could say clearly as one sometimes can with letters. "Here is someone who writes with real conviction." (Letters I have seen on McCarthyism or on defense issues such as civil defense and stockpiling occasionally create such an impression.) Put another way, a detailed study of the phrases and sentences in letters on reciprocal trade and the tariff would almost certainly show an enormously high proportion of clichés and stereotyped phrases. I do not recall seeing a coherent presentation of protectionist *theory;* the Careys and the other mercantile political economists and nationalist theorists might as well never have lived as far as the mail goes.

Handling and effect of senate versus house mail

In several cases, I read mail to a senator and also mail to one or more congressmen from the same state. I noted little difference as far as the congressmen's district was concerned.

A good many and perhaps most representatives read all their own mail, except that which is clearly routine. If they do not dictate answers themselves, they indicate who should be queried about the letter, etc. How they handle it—whether they pay attention to out-of-district mail, how much use they make of reference facilities in the Library of Congress or the Executive Departments, how far they try to use the letter as a basis for thinking of something *else* that will interest the constituent—depends enormously upon the representative, the subject, and how busy he or his staff [is] are at a given time.

In the Senate, the situation is quite different. Senators from the larger states with whom we talked have mail clerks who handle the mail, attend to much of it themselves, and if in doubt consult one of the senator's assistants. But most senators rarely see their mail; some of them try to keep control by signing answers.

The inability to see mail results in odd situations. Senator Philip's legislative assistant assured me that no one in the state was concerned about reciprocal trade—the Senator got practically no mail on it, for instance. However, the chief mail clerk told me that it was either first or second among the issues that the Senator got mail about. One of the mail clerk's favorite ways of treating such mail was to reply, "I am turning your letter over to the Chairman of the Senate Finance Committee which is now considering H.R.1. and I am sure he will be interested in your comments." I looked at him quizzically. "No, I don't do it," he said, "but I don't think I'm being dishonest in saying that. I would if it said anything new." And this was probably true; every once in a while a letter that poses what is (at least to the senatorial or congressional office) a new question is sent to the staff of Ways and Means or Finance for comment or with the request that an answer be written for the appropriate signature.

No great difference in mail to committee members

Mail to members of House Ways and Means or Senate Finance, the committees that consider reciprocal trade, did not seem to differ much in volume from mail to congressmen and senators not on these committees. This is surprising, since sometimes lobbying organizations list the members of the pertinent committees.

The Senate version of the Reciprocal Trade Extension Act of 1955 was quite different from the House version; so necessarily a conference committee (of 5 Representatives and 5 Senators) was appointed to decide on the final version. The measure was in conference for a number of weeks.

The conferees could have decided for a more "liberal" or a more "restrictive" measure. One would have thought, that they would have been bombarded with communications and attempts to influence them. There was a real question how far Messrs. Cooper and Mills, two Democratic conferees from the House, would go in opposing the Senate version; conceivably Senator George (D., Ga.), who had traditionally been a strong advocate of the old Hull position, and Senator Kerr (D., Okla.), who was then a potential Democratic candidate for President, might be open to some compromise on the numerous restrictive amendments written in by the Senate. Most observers felt Senator George sympathized with the House rather than the Senate version. So from the reciprocal-trade standpoint, one might have expected a campaign directed at these four men at least. None took place.

On the other side, Senator Morse (D., Ore.), one of the most vociferous advocates of local interests in the Senate on economic matters, had succeeded in getting into the Senate Bill an amendment that was desired by Northwest fruit and nut producers and that would presumably have especially benefited them. The cherry producers in February and March had put on a fairly intensive campaign of letter writing; but as far as I heard, neither they nor the other Northwest, Michigan, and Georgia fruit-nut producers put on a campaign in May anywhere near resembling the March campaign. Yet, the fact was that in May they were in a special position where a campaign would have been more helpful. In any event the only loss "the" protectionists suffered in conference was the deletion of the Morse Amendment.

Generally constituents with ideas suggest something that is procedurally impossible

For our present purposes, it is sufficient to point out that because of the elaborate and technical nature of congressional procedure most letters to congressmen suggesting that they should do something, recommend things that they cannot, practically speaking, do. Procedural decisions or legislative custom may have allocated the responsibility to somebody else or have set the question up in such a way that what the constituent wants cannot be achieved. For instance, a large number of letters were sent to Senator Hennings (D., Mo.) asking that he support the Curtis Amendment.[4] But the Curtis Amendment never came to the floor of the Senate; it was not to the best of my knowledge seriously considered by the Senate Finance Committee; Senator Hennings belongs to more than a dozen subcommittees of his two major committees (Judiciary and Civil Service) and in addition serves on Rules;[5] and this is quite enough to keep the Senator and his staff busy; it would be difficult for them to take on new responsibilities of the magnitude involved in an effort for the Curtis Amendment even if he should be convinced by the letters that this was important.

Of course, occasionally some senator or congressman is looking around for an issue or is impressed by particular ideas; so there is always an outside chance that letters of this sort may have direct influence. They may certainly have a long-run "educational" effect, so that if the matter does some day come to the floor it may be received with more friendliness.

"You don't know what they mean"

Several congressmen pointed out—and a number of others implied—that much of the time "When they write you, you don't know what they mean." For instance, a very large portion of the mail calls for protection for some one particular industry. Sometimes it says, "but we realize the necessity of foreign trade in general." What can the average House member do with this mail? For example, under the closed rule procedure under which tariff bills are usually considered, the House as a whole is very unlikely to have an opportunity to vote to protect the domestic cherry processors and producers. The members will have to vote for or against the Reciprocal Trade Extension Act as reported out of committee. They can of course urge the members of the Ways and Means Committee to do something to help the cherry growers and producers, but precisely what? Either there has to be somebody on Ways and Means who works out the method—or somebody in the cherry growers' association—or somebody in the cherry processors' association—or the congressman himself must do it.

On the cherry industry, three legislators at least have tried to make an effort to work out a tailor-made solution—Senator Morse (D., Ore.), Senator McNamara (D., Mich.) and Congressman Holmes (R., Wash.). But most of the time on most of the mail they get, most congressmen and senators make no such effort. They simply receive the mail, and read and file it.

Or suppose a congressman gets—as some have—letters saying, "Vote for free trade." There was no free trade measure on the calendar; there is not likely to be one. Probably in January this means support the Reciprocal Trade Extension Act, as reported from committee. The measure was so riddled by amendments in the Senate that some people felt it was no longer a free trade measure; a New Deal congressman who voted for the Cooper Bill voted against acceptance of the Conference Report for the reason that the revised bill was so restrictive and protectionist.

In January, 1955, a letter from a [member of the] League of Women Voters or a Chamber of Commerce in favor of "more liberal" trade presumably meant "Support the Cooper Bill"; a petition from a cotton textile local to "protect our jobs" in January meant "Oppose H.R.l"; but after the Senate had adopted the committee amendments, what then? How many of those who wrote letters on either side had any idea of the significance of the changes made by the Senate? Actually, the newspapers and newsmagazines and newsletters had given only a very general and frequently a misleading picture of the drift of these amendments.

"You always hear from business too late"

Congressman Amiable says, commenting on his wide experience in a state legislature and in Congress, "You always hear from business too late." And this is true *in general* because businessmen and their representatives respond to the news; they write in to protest a bill that has been reported out of committee, for instance, because that is when they hear about it or when it really comes to seem a threat. But by the time it is reported out of committee, it is difficult to amend it; legislators have to say either

"Yes" or "No." And by the time it is reported out of committee, the battle lines have formed, commitments and promises have been made, and it is harder for congressmen to change. For example, take Mr. L., a member of Ways and Means; he joins the committee in reporting out such-and-such a piece of tariff legislation. Then he hears that the manufacturers of some product in his district would very much like a particular change in the bill; however, several members of the committee majority are opposed to this change. If Mr. L. had advocated it before the measure was reported out, he might be free to continue his advocacy or look for supporters of the position. But he is under the obligation that most decent men feel—not to throw over an implied agreement without very strong reasons.

And this obligation is backed by a very real sanction or threat. If Mr. L. wants to keep on friendly terms with his colleagues, to preserve their respect, he cannot break many such agreements; if he does he will lose his influence with them. And if he wants to serve his district *not only at the moment but over the years, he must preserve his colleagues' respect.*

II. Sources Other than the Mail

It is apparent that the mail is but one of a number of important sources of information for congressmen. Hattery and Hofheimer, in a study of legislators' sources of expert information, listed ten.[6] These were ranked by the congressmen as follows: (1) committee hearings, (2) personal reading and consultation, (3) office staff, (4) committee staffs, (5) arguments on the floor, (6) Legislative Reference Service, (7) executive departments, (8) interest groups, (9) political party, (10) Legislative Counsel.

No congressman mentioned to me his office staff, committee staff, the Legislative Reference Service, or Legislative Counsel as sources of communications which had shaped his thinking about the tariff issue. All four of the sources, of course, are not supposed to try to influence members but merely to aid them as requested, so the omission is perfectly natural. It will be helpful to comment more specifically on the role of a number of the others with respect to the tariff issue itself and to mention still other sources of influence that are absent from this list.

1. *Committee Hearings.* I asked a distinguished member of the Ways and Means Committee early in 1954 whether there would be hearings on the Reciprocal Trade Extension Act in that year. "O my God," he said, "I hope not. I get so bored with those repetitious hearings. We've been listening to the same witnesses saying the same things the same way for ten years."

Statements by witnesses from different industries are extremely repetitious not only from year to year but from witness to witness. Almost all of the statements were criminally dull. I spent portions of several days listening to the Senate hearings, and I wish I may never go through the same boredom again. Even some major government witnesses, such as Assistant Secretary Butz (Agriculture), who led off for H.R.1 before the Senate Committee, sounded as though they were reading statements which they only half understood and found thoroughly boring themselves.

After the first few days of House and Senate hearings, a good many of the members found it necessary to be absent. Since they walk in and out a good deal, no figures are available on how many hearings the "average member" attended.

Some of the questioning, particularly by Mills (D., Ark.) and Eberharter (D., Penna.) in the House, and by Millikin (R., Colo.) in the Senate, was adroitly contrived to embarrass witnesses opposed to the questioner's position. Very few witnesses seemed prepared for fairly obvious questions; yet a reading of hearings several years back or consultation with informed sources would have shown that Millikin, for example, has certain "traps" he has successfully baited his opponents with. Secretary Butz, the government lead-off witness, fell into several of these— apparently he had not been briefed on what to expect.

There was practically no evidence of any effort *systematically* to check facts or to follow through a line of argument except by Senator Malone (R., Nev.), an extreme protectionist who asked probably more than half the questions in Senate Finance. His questions were designed to get all witnesses to admit the unconstitutionality of the reciprocal trade program.

The reciprocal trade issue is, of course, an old one—and many of the members have heard it all before. But the factual basis of the subject has to some extent altered since the matter was last considered by Congress, and many of the members had probably had no occasion to consider the economics of the matter or the political theory, systematically, for years.

No member outside the committee in talking with me referred to the hearings in any way.[7] Probably with them, as with the public, it is the indirect effect of the hearings that counts rather than the direct ones. Newspapermen take the press releases of witnesses and write stories on them, and these stories are often published. So members of Congress read the stories. Since newspapermen are far more apt to get the releases than they are to sit through a session and listen to the questions, even quite inane testimony has a better chance of receiving publicity than quite pertinent questions have. Limitations of time affect the press as well as members of Congress.

2. *The Floor Debates and the Record.* Some debate takes place in the House and often a good deal in the Senate on issues such as reciprocal trade. Some Senate speeches cover a subject widely —for example Senator Gore's four-hour speech on reciprocal trade in 1954, and speeches by Senators Douglas, Langer, and Malone in 1955 on that topic.

It is unusual for many Senators or House members actually to listen to a speech; during most of Senator Gore's speech six other members on the average were in attendance, and those who paid closest attention were close sympathizers and supporters on the reciprocal trade issue.

On this basis, it might seem that the fairly common impression that the floor debate makes no difference and is chiefly for the benefit of the galleries is correct. However, there seems to be general agreement among those in a position to know that Senator Gore's speech in favor of the Randall program in 1954 was four hours long for this reason: The Senator and his associates, in offering the amendment which would have provided for a three-year extension (instead of the one-year extension voted by the House), feared that he would not be taken seriously; they felt the general attitude of his colleagues would be (1) "Gore's trying to put the Republicans in a spot," or (2) "Gore's just trying to show that he fills Hull's shoes."

But his associates felt that if the Senator made a four-hour speech developing the issue in terms of the relationship of reciprocal trade to the discouragement of East–West trade then it would make clear the fact that he really was serious in pushing his amendment.

Hattery and Hofheimer, commenting on the importance of floor debate, assert:

[Our] findings present a challenge to some assumptions which may have been too readily accepted. . . . One of these relates to floor debate. . . . Although it is true that members of the committee which studies the bill obtain little additional information through floor debate, the majority of legislators have not had the benefit of the committee deliberations. . . . Floor debate in cases of controversy often represents the results of careful research and marshalling of facts and consideration.

Several congressmen cited floor debate as the best source of information on minor matters . . . [and] on amendments (to the bill) it may be the only source of information available to the member before a vote is called for.

Unfortunately, neither their report nor this study enables us to distinguish between the importance of floor debate *as such* and floor debate and speeches as preserved in the *Record,* which members may study at leisure. I suspect it is the latter which is important.

However, no member referred directly to the debate as influencing him; although several members stated that when they went on to the floor February 17, 1955, before the key votes on the closed rule, they did not yet know how they were going to vote.

3. *How Much do Congressmen Hear From Congressmen?* It is likely that congressmen hear more from other congressmen about most legislation than from anybody else. Our study unfortunately was not conducted in such a way as to make it possible to be as certain on this point as we might wish.

Relatively few congressmen in answering our questions referred to other congressmen as sources of information or ideas.

Evidently, the communication of ideas and information between congressmen take place in such a matter-of-fact way that the congressmen who had heard something from a colleague did not often think of it as "hearing" something from an external source, but as an exchange of views within a work or friendship situation. Nevertheless, party leaders in the Congress, as well as individual congressmen with a specific interest in given issues, are clearly in a strategic position to influence congressional thought, and we have some evidence that they do so.

4. *"Pressure" From Other Congressmen: The Leadership.* A number of references were made to the "pressure" exerted by the Democratic leadership on the 1955 vote. This pressure is indicated by Speaker Rayburn's often-quoted remark at the breakfast of the freshman congressmen just before the vote: "If you want to get along, go along." Those who had read or heard the 1954 debate might also remember that the Speaker (then Minority Leader) had made an impressive speech stating his view that the Reciprocal Trade Act ought to be extended for 25 years. Similarly, one of the Boston newspapers reported that Majority Leader McCormack (D., Mass.) made a remark to Representative Macdonald (D., Mass.) which indirectly and euphemistically, but quite clearly, implied that Macdonald, by voting against the leadership, had let his district down—in front of a newspaper reporter! Since Macdonald was serving his first term, and since Medford, the key city in the district, was the scene of unusually public factional struggles, and since the district is traditionally very close, McCormack's remark, under the circumstances, was, in design or not, a threat.

Far more important than such hints are direct efforts to get members to change. On some measures, this is effective. One bill which was extremely vital to the leadership in 1955 actually appeared to squeeze through by five votes or so, but the leadership had in its pocket about twenty-five sure changes if the bill were in danger.

"Changes" take place in this fashion. A member answers to his name and votes "Yea" or "Nay" as the case may be, but while the vote is being checked changes it. A member may also announce an intention to vote "Yea" or "Nay" but fail to answer at the appropriate point in the roll-call and switch if the vote is close. On the closed rule votes on February 17, the leadership in fact won by one vote according to the *Record*. But at one time, members report, it had lost by seven votes.

5. *"Pressure" From Other Congressmen: Cleveland Bailey.* The only other member reported as exercising "pressure" was Representative Cleveland Bailey (D., W. Va.). Representative Bailey is unusual among members—probably unique—in that protection is the most important issue to him and that he creates the sense of having a deep-felt conviction on the subject. In 1953–54 he went around and pleaded individually with a number of members to vote against reciprocal trade and for the West Virginia miners. As one member put it, "He was rough, real rough. . . . I had to be rough with him." Another said, "In the 1954 vote, Cleve Bailey was worth fifteen votes to his side easily." In 1955, Mr. Bailey was generally admitted to be the leader of the protectionist fight.

Members who propose something *new* are likely to send statements about it to their colleagues. For example, Congressman Thomas Curtis (R., Mo.), who introduced the Curtis

Amendment which would materially change the basis on which reciprocal trade is administered, made an effort to publicize it and even testified before the Senate Finance Committee on its behalf. Similarly, Congressman Bolling (D., Mo.) circulated amongst his colleagues explanations of his measure for facilitating industrial dispersion.

6. *Informal Contacts with Other Congressmen.* As has been noted, the influence of other congressmen is very important, but frequently this is exerted in a casual, unplanned way, so it is not recognized or remembered except in the clear-cut cases. The study of legislative bodies as work groups is one of the crying needs of political science at present.

A couple of cases where friendship seems to have been the dominant factor in the vote in 1955 may be cited. A newspaper correspondent told me:

Oh, yes, you know those two boys [congressmen]. . . . Well you know why Jack voted against the leadership? Just to oblige Joe to whom he's very close. Joe was afraid he'd be the only fellow from the state to vote against the leadership and he'd get into trouble with the leadership and party organization so Jack went along with him to prevent his sticking his neck out all alone. Then of course on the final vote Jack switched back, so he's OK if anybody in his district asks him.

Similarly, the whip for the area told me:

Oh, Don went along against the leadership on this, but I don't think he cares at all or heard much about it from his district. It was just that Dave to whom he's very close is pretty strong against foreign imports and Don was more concerned to help him out than to help the leadership. And Tom rather wanted to go along with the leadership, but he found Dave and Don and four other guys from surrounding districts were against the leadership, and he decided he better go along with them, because after all he's hearing a lot from his district against it, and how could he explain his being for it and Dave and Don and the rest being against it?

7. *Personal Contacts.* No congressman in any way indicated that his wife or secretaries influenced his views, but I suspect that this was the fault of our method of interviewing plus the fact that in many cases congressmen are quite unaware of views picked up through daily contacts.

8. *Visitors.* Visitors do come in and see congressmen. Congressmen also talk with people back home about issues. On some matters, congressmen get as much and hear as much from visitors as they do from the mail, but it seems to be quite generally agreed that the tariff and reciprocal trade are mail issues, not visitor issues. To my knowledge, no congressman except a representative from Detroit received a visitor *from his district* simply to talk in favor of reciprocal trade. Most of the protectionist people from a district come in to talk about the sad state of their sales. Now, in regard to any given commodity, there are a number of ways government can help, of which tariff legislation is only one.

Mr. Serious Consideration, for example, and Mr. Fourth, who were certainly open to persuasion, had according to their statements, no visitors come to see them particularly in behalf of protection.

The few cases I know of where someone came to see a congressman *specifically* against reciprocal trade extension and nothing else fall into two types:

(1) People who, it sounded, were glad of a trip to Washington; and if the congressman helped them on gallery tickets, hotel accommodations,

etc., that more than offset any disappointment on his views as to trade.

(2) People who buttonholed congressmen in the lobbies the day of the vote, February 17–18; I'm not sure how many (if any) of these were actually from congressmen's districts, but some of them may have been. However, the opportunity for influencing congressmen by a hurried word just before they went on the floor was not great.

One reason why delegations and informal conversations back home count for little in what a congressman does on reciprocal trade is that many congressmen are much more expert in diverting visitors than visitors are in influencing congressmen.

9. *Reading.* Few of the congressmen interviewed quoted specific published sources as the basis of their opinions. With one probable exception (Mills, D., Ark.), there was little indication of familiarity with the economic literature on international trade, convertibility, and so forth. This may depress economists, but it should be remembered that many congressmen feel that economists are generally biased in favor of free trade. This history of economic thought tends to support this feeling. Thus, those congressmen who are much worried about unemployment or threatened unemployment among their constituents will find little credible in the published material on international trade. Journalists and newspapermen, on the other hand, may be encouraged by the fact that several congressmen evidently had obtained ideas from columns. Perhaps a dozen referred to some item in the press (e.g., an article by George Sokolsky, the most active protectionist columnist). The local and business press was not referred to by any of the interviewees.

In addition, few congressmen referred to the various reports recently issued by government agencies or distributed by interest groups; in most cases they had probably skimmed rather than read them.

On these points, congressmen appear to differ in degree at least from the executive department officials with whom I talked. Very likely, however, some executive department officials make a greater effort to impress a scholar than congressmen do. On the other hand it must be remembered that there was little or nothing available in 1956 which was of any real use to congressmen on the topic of foreign economic policy. For essentially what they need is material which *reconciles* the claims and desires of their individual constituents with the over-all general economic problems. What they find for the most part is (a) theoretical (e.g., abstract, high-level) discussion of the virtues of international trade, and (b) occasionally a theoretical response to that argument.

Congressmen—and everybody else in this area—also badly need *simple* or at least *simpler* explanations of what the whole apparatus of quotas and tariffs achieves and how they hang together legislatively. But there was nothing clear, usable and readable on the topic, thus blocking this significant material as a source of information for legislators.

NOTES

1. This article derives from Lewis Anthony Dexter, *Congressmen and the People They Listen To* (Cambridge: Center for International Studies, Massachusetts Institute of Technology, Dittoed, 1956). The copyright of this article belongs to M.I.T., and permission for reproduction should be obtained through the author (536 Pleasant St., Belmont 78, Massachusetts).

   Copies of the duplicated report, now out of print, are available in part at the Library of Congress and some university libraries; and it may also be obtained through University Microfilms, Ann Arbor, Michigan (Ph.D. Dissertation in Sociology, Columbia, 1960).

   The report was done at the Center for International Studies, M.I.T., in connection with a transactional study of business communication about foreign economic policy. The reception on Capitol Hill of the communications from business was studied partly by interviews (more than 50 with congressmen and a similar number with congressional staff members, and about 500 with businessmen, lobbyists, and leading constituents) and partly by reading the incoming mail of a few members of each house. Except where otherwise indicated, the names of all congressmen in this report have been disguised; the words and illustrations are, however, reported exactly, except that where some interviewee used a phrase which would serve to identify him, this has been changed also.

2. Estes Kefauver and Jack Levin, *A Twentieth Century Congress* (New York: Duell, Sloan, and Pearce, 1947), p. 171. It may be an interesting comment on public preconceptions and expectations that a columnist in a popular magazine, who frequently summarizes academic articles, summarized the present piece from the *Public Opinion Quarterly* by giving the Bankhead quote *as though it were the point of my article* and stated, when I protested, that that was what I had in fact said.

3. In other words, where the mail seems routine, repetitious, or uninspired, or

where the mail clerk of the congressional office is busy, much such out-of-state mail gets little attention. But a serious, original letter from a person who obviously knows what he is talking about or has some known claim to attention may and often does receive careful consideration.

4. No doubt this occurred because both he and Mr. Curtis are from St. Louis and Mr. Curtis had stimulated local attention on the matter.

5. A minor committee in the Senate, although a very major one in the House.

6. Lowell H. Hattery and Susan Hofheimer, "The Legislators' Source of Expert Information," *Public Opinion Quarterly,* 18 (Fall, 1954), 300–303.

7. There can be little doubt that committee executive meetings, where the text of the bills is discussed and amendments considered, often involve a lot of give-and-take and also result in members on both sides changing their minds.

4

CONGRESSIONAL STAFF AND PUBLIC POLICYMAKING: THE JOINT COMMITTEE ON INTERNAL REVENUE TAXATION*

JOHN F. MANLEY

There are upward of 10,000 congressional staff members presently at work on Capitol Hill, working in congressmen's and senators' offices, for committees and for the Congress itself (as doorkeepers, employees of the sizable Capitol branch post office, and so on). The following article discusses the activities of a group of highly professional and relatively autonomous staff workers employed by a joint committee of Congress. John F. Manley is Associate Professor of Political Science at the University of Wisconsin.

Many students of Congress have observed that, due to the increased scope and complexity of governmental activity, congressmen need expert staff assistance if they are to legislate in an informed way and retain some inde-

Reprinted from *The Journal of Politics*, **30** (November 1968), 1046–1067, by permission of the author and publisher.
* This study is based on interviews with 23 members of the House Committee on Ways and Means, eight members of the Senate Finance Committee, five members of the congressional staff, and three high-ranking Treasury Department officials. Support was provided by the Congressional Fellowship program of the American Political Science Association (1963–1964), the APSA's Study of Congress under the direction of Ralph K. Huitt (research assistant to Richard F. Fenno, Jr., 1964–1965), and the Brookings Institution Research Fellowship Program (1965–66), all of whom are absolved of any responsibility for the content of the study. I would like to thank Professor Fenno for commenting on a draft of this paper.

pendence of the executive branch and its expertise.[1] Confronted with multifarious demands on their time, the argument goes, legislators have a difficult time mastering the intricacies of substantive policy proposals; partly as a result, many policy-making functions theoretically reserved for the legislative branch have been transferred, in fact if not always in form, to the executive. Carried out to its logical conclusion this development would appear to culminate in the suggestion made by Samuel P. Huntington that Congress give up whatever lawmaking power it still has: "Explicit acceptance of the idea that legislation was not its primary function would, in large part, simply be recognition of the direction which change has already been taking. It would legitimize and expand the functions of constituent service and administrative oversight which, in practice, already constitute the principal work of most congressmen." [2]

Should Congress arm itself with a professional staff which may equip it to compete with the sources of information available to the executive and help it stem the tendency toward de facto executive lawmaking? Or should Congress recognize its inability to legislate and maximize the functions for which it is best suited: constituent service and administrative oversight? Or should Congress adopt, as a sort of via media, Representative Henry Reuss's (D.-Wis.) proposal for an American version of the Scandinavian ombudsman who would relieve congressmen of some of the details of constituent service and give them, it is hoped, more time for lawmaking activities? [3]

Like other questions of congressional reform the question of staff has been raised before political scientists have produced descriptive and analytical accounts of the activities of the staff which Congress already employs. Shooting from the hip does not necessarily mean that one will miss the target but Ralph Huitt makes a persuasive argument that the low level of knowledge about how Congress works impedes the effectiveness of suggestions for change: "The difficulty is that too little is known about how Congress actually operates now and what the effects of various procedural and structural arrangements really are. *What we lack is a solid base of research which would make possible educated guesses as to who would be served by what kinds of changes and what the costs would be.*" [4] The most recent full-length study of the congressional staff provides, as one reviewer noted, "some useful background and some data, but the analysis remains to be done." [5]

The purpose of the present study is to analyze the role of one staff in the policy-making process. Because little is known about the staff of the Joint Committee on Internal Revenue Taxation, Part I sketches its origins and current status in terms of size and expenditures. Part II discusses the staff as a link between the two tax-writing committees of Congress, the House Committee on Ways and Means and Senate Finance to the executive branch and to non-governmental groups. Attention is paid to the norms which are supposed to govern the staff's role vis-à-vis the committee members, the degree of conformity to these norms by the staff under two different leaders, and to the importance of how the Chief of Staff sees his job in relation to the competing blocs that are involved in making tax policy. Part III investigates the role of the staff in linking one of the committees, Ways and Means, to the executive branch and to non-governmental groups and individuals who are concerned with taxes. A final section discusses some variables which affect the staff's role and which may serve as starting-points for future research.

– 1 –

The Joint Committee on Internal Revenue Taxation (JCIRT), established forty-two years ago, is the oldest joint committee of Congress. As originally planned by the House in the Revenue Act of 1926 the "Joint Commission on Taxation," as it was called, was to be composed of five Senators, five House members, and five members appointed by the President to represent the general public. The job of the Commission was to investigate the operation, effects, and administration of the internal revenue laws with the purpose of simplifying the statute and improving its administration. Better phraseology and administration of tax law, not policy innovation, were the objectives of the Commission as envisaged by the House.[6] The Commission, expected to last less than two years, received an authorization to spend $25,000 on clerical and traveling expenses; quarters were to be provided by the Secretary of the Treasury.[7]

The Senate drastically altered the House plan. Making liberal use of its authority to amend revenue bills passed by the House, the Senate called for a Joint Committee on Internal Revenue Taxation made up solely of congressmen: five Senators and five Representatives. The primary stimulus for this action was the sensational revelations of tax evasion aided by misconduct on the part of Internal Revenue Bureau employees, revelations which stemmed from the work of a select committee headed by Michigan Senator James Couzens. The new Joint Committee, *through its staff*, was designed to: (1) obtain information from taxpayers to assist in the framing of future revenue legislation; (2) gain a "closer insight" into the problem of the administration of the tax laws (a euphemism for preventing corruption in the Internal Revenue Bureau); and (3) gather data bearing upon revenue legislation.[8] The House receded on the Senate amendments and the Joint Committee, a combination watchdog and law-simplifying organization, was set up—with a staff.

Shortly after its inception the Joint Committee was given the job of reviewing large tax refunds planned by the Bureau of Internal Revenue. Today, the Joint Committee relies upon its staff (three of whom actually work in the Internal Revenue Service) to review the refunds. The Joint Committee, which has only an informal veto over refunds, acts mainly as an appellate court for IRS when the congressional staff and IRS cannot resolve a case. Under the current Chief of Staff, Dr. Laurence N. Woodworth, the Joint Committee has not yet reversed its staff; it did rule in favor of the Bureau under Woodworth's predecessor, Colin F. Stam, in rare instances.

In addition to checking on refunds the Joint Committee has met in recent years to discuss tax regulations and to be briefed on the computerization of tax returns, but it has not evolved into a policy-making body for revenue legislation. With no role in the general policy process the importance of the Joint Committee is that it serves as the institutional excuse for maintaining the joint staff, a body of experts which early in its history was praised for its work on the technical aspects of tax law.[9]

From modest beginnings, and with an uncertain future, the joint staff grew until for the period July 1, 1966 to July 1, 1967 it employed three dozen people at a cost of almost $440,000. Twenty of the 36 were professional staff, including three economists.[10] Most of these people spend their time helping the Ways and Means Committee and the Senate Finance Committee write tax laws; the staff needs of the Joint Committee as such are minimal.

– 2 –

It may be true that in some fields Congress needs more staff assistance but in the area of revenue legislation the Joint Committee staff provides the legislature with a professional, independent, highly reliable source of information. The few studies which mention the staff invariably cite its competence, expertise, and influence with congressmen. Two articles, one in *Business Week* and the other in the *Wall Street Journal*, stress the quality of the staff,[11] and in a well-known book Roy M. Blough observes that the members of the tax committees place "heavy reliance" on the Chief of staff and that the staff plays a "highly important" role in tax legislation.[12] A member of the Ways and Means Committee goes so far as to contend that, "Between the Joint Committee staff and the House Legislative Counsel, Congress has developed a more competent staff for drafting tax legislation than has the Treasury." [13]

Congressional experience with the Joint Committee staff is so favorable that this device has been taken as the model for changes in the legislative process. In the recent hearings before the Joint Committee on the Organization of Congress, for example, Senator John L. McClellan (D.-Ark.) used the JCIRT to support his proposal to establish a Joint Committee on the Budget. This arrangement, he felt, would give Congress the same type of technical assistance in the appropriations field as it enjoys in the revenue field, and as the Budget Bureau provides the executive branch.[14] The National Taxpayers Conference and the Tax Foundation stated that the JCIRT could be a precedent for a similar organization to deal with expenditures, and Senator Boggs used it as the prototype for a fully staffed Joint Committee on National Strategy.[15] These proposals may never materialize but the fact that the JCIRT is taken as the model for further institutional innovations is evidence that in many quarters the view of the joint tax staff is a positive one.

What does the Joint Committee staff do for the tax committees which leads people to think that a similar device would be useful in different contexts? Are members of House Ways and Means and Senate Finance happy with the work of their staff; if not, why? What is the staff supposed to do for

these committees and does it live up to congressional expectations?

The most obvious, and in some ways the most important, function of the Joint Committee staff is one of linkage: what continuity the tax legislative process has, apart from informal contacts between leading members of the committees, arises from the central role of the staff in both the House and Senate deliberations on tax bills. In the executive sessions of the Ways and Means Committee the staff is not merely on tap for the members but it is actively engaged in the examination of policy proposals made by the members, the Administration, interest groups, and lobbyists. After explicating for Ways and Means how individuals and groups will be affected by changes in the Internal Revenue Code the staff, and most prominently the Chief of Staff, crosses the rotunda and explains the bill to the Finance Committee, going through the same basic routine except that now there exists a detailed bill instead of the tax message with which Ways and Means normally begins. For many years, and until Russell Long (D.-La.) became chairman of Finance in 1965, about the only professional staff available to the Finance Committee was the joint staff.[16]

In performing its tasks for the Ways and Means Committee and the Senate Finance Committee the staff is expected to follow certain norms. Three such norms are: objectivity, bipartisanship, and neutrality. As a body of professional tax experts the Joint Committee staff is supposed to be objective in its handling of data, bipartisan in its handling of member requests, and neutral on public policy questions. "Our job," says the present Chief of Staff, Laurence N. Woodworth, "is to see that members of Congress get the facts on both sides so they can make their own decisions." [17] "If I can come away from those meetings," he has said, "knowing that the committee has made its own decisions in the light of this knowledge, then I'm satisfied." [18] The staff's job, according to Ways and Means Chairman Wilbur Mills (D.-Ark.), is "to bring facts together for our use, to do the spadework for us." [19] A former Republican staff assistant noted the bipartisan nature of the staff: "When I tell Woodworth or those guys something I expect confidence and I get it." Recruited without regard to party affiliation ("I'm very proud of the fact that Mr. Stam [former Chief of Staff] never asked me my party politics and as far as I know never asked any other member of the staff.") the staff, as one aide put it, acts "as a coordinator for the Ways and Means Committee. We serve Curtis and Byrnes [Republicans], Boggs and Mills [Democrats], in addition to Senator Byrd." Woodworth has on occasion, helped write the majority report on a bill and then turned around and helped the minority write its dissenting views.

Given the controversial nature of tax policy, given the well-known complexity of the Internal Revenue Code which puts a high premium on technical advice, given the difficulty of facing choices without forming opinions, and given the strategic role of the quartermaster corps in the conduct of any war it is not surprising that the staff, which obviously affects the decisions made by the policy-makers, has been criticized for failing to live up to the above norms. One norm in particular, that of neutrality on public policy, has, some policymakers feel, been broken by the staff, especially while Colin F. Stam was Chief of Staff.

"It has been estimated," Stephen Bailey and Howard Samuel note, "that Stam exercised more influence on the preparation of tax legislation than any other single person in the federal government." [20] Little known outside of Washington, Stam accumulated so much influence with the Ways and Means Committee and the Senate Finance Committee that only one (Harry Byrd) of 20 people interviewed by E. W. Kenworthy for his perceptive study of Stam was willing to have his views of the corpulent technician attributed to him.[21] Stam did not control tax policy, in Byrd's opinion, but he "has made very many vital decisions. He has made recommendations that have carried great weight with both committees." [22] For another piece of evidence in support of Stam's key role in the tax legislative process consider the tribute to Stam contained in the following remarks made by a Republican member of Ways and Means in 1953 in defense of the policies of the then chairman, Dan Reed (R.-N.Y.):

He [Reed] had the assistance of the best tax expert anywhere in the United States, and I refer to Mr. Colin Stam, who is the chief of staff of the Joint Committee on Taxation. . . . *These two gentlemen, Mr. Reed and Mr. Stam, have as much capacity to decide what is best in the tax field as anyone in this country.*
Mr. Reed and Mr. Stam agreed on a program, not that they were trying to force it upon anybody, but they advanced it as a suggestion.[23]

And, to cite but one more piece of evidence, a Republican Senator commented on Stam,

He'd been here so long that he wasn't like other staff men. He was the only staff man I knew who could tell a senator to go to hell without getting his face slapped. Not that he did it, understand, but there wasn't any of this subjugation or kowtowing which you sometimes see in the staff, no "sir" business. He was here when I first came in . . . and he cut quite a figure then.[24]

Inevitably associated with influence in Washington is controversy, and Stam had influence in the tax field despite his stated view of himself as a technician who merely supplied analyses and counsel to the decision-makers.[25] Not everyone would agree with the citation on his Rockefeller Public Service Award given "in recognition of distinguished service to the government of the United States and to the American people." Specifically, Stam's activity as Chief of Staff has been severely criticized by liberal Senators concerned with making changes or, as they see it, "reforms" in the internal revenue laws.

For these Senators not only was Stam of little help but his expertise was sullied because it buttressed, in the main, the views of their antagonists, men who were in effective control of both committees. Though Stam was certainly not the linch-pin in the conservative coalition which Senate liberals feel has controlled tax policy for many years, he was a conservative, he identified with the conservative leaders of Finance and Ways and Means, and his key position and acknowledged mastery of the Code were used to frustrate liberal attempts to "purify" the tax laws—so, at any rate, say the liberals.

"This fellow Stam was an autocrat, he played everything close to his vest, and I always felt that he was an ally of big business. Never trusted him." A Senate staff aide agreed with this view of Stam and complained about the assistance available to liberal senators: "First, they never offered help. They'd never come in and say, 'Here's an important bill, let's go over it.' Two, they were nominal in their assistance. And you couldn't trust it so we just went out and got our own." One disenchanted Senate liberal, who once asked Stam to leave the committee room, declared that he never had trouble getting help from Stam,

I just never got anything out of him at all. He wouldn't do any work for me. He was here 25 or 30 years and he never deviated from the line of Millikin, George, Harry Byrd. You could ask Stam if something was black and he'd say, "Well, there are several shades of blackness. . . ." On a tax bill he'd say, "This came up in the committee in 1862 and they thought . . . or in 1904 the committee did this," and when he was all done he hadn't said a goddamn thing except, "Therefore, we ought to take the bill as it's written."

He concluded, "I never did think Stam was reliable."[26]

It appears, then, that the impact of the staff's work leaned toward the conservative side under Stam's leadership—norms of neutrality and objectivity to the contrary notwithstanding. What the staff does to some extent affects what the committees decide, and even the conservative members of Finance admit that in Stam they had an important friend. "Colin Stam's personal philosophy," said a Senator in praise of the staff chief, "was that the tax law should be used for raising revenue and not for social reform. If that makes him a conservative then I suppose he's a conservative. I think this is Larry Woodworth's philosophy too, and it's certainly mine." Commenting on the demands for more minority staff, a Republican Senator confirmed the liberals' charges when he observed that on Finance the minority, plus the Byrd Democrats, had all of the staff they needed because Stam was a conservative. "Gore and Douglas and a few others were the ones who didn't have any staff," he chortled; "our coalition had the staff." In defense of Stam he ticked off a number of famous conservative Senators saying, "Stam's career was woven into theirs. He did nothing more than discharge the responsibilities given him by his employers." In further support of the breakdown of staff neutrality under Stam a member of the Joint Committee staff admitted that his former boss broke the rules: "Quite frankly, on occasion, I think Mr. Stam, who used to identify himself pretty much with what the majority leadership of the committee felt, would really go too far in supporting their position. He'd become too committed."

Politics and policy preferences have, as reformer dissension shows, affected the role of the staff, its standing with its principals, and its relationship to the formulation of public policy. An institutional device such as the Joint Committee staff may not be an unmixed blessing to all of the participants in the policy-making process; it may, depending upon such variables as the policy orientation of a Colin F. Stam, support one viewpoint over another. For one group of Senators the staff under Stam was merely doing its job for the majority; for the minority of tax reformers he was a *bête noire.* Their complaints about him testify to the high quality of the job he did for those with whom he identified; his expertise could—and apparently did— mean advantage for some and disadvantage for others.

Given the difficulty of remaining neutral in the policy-making process it would be tempting to look upon the above policy consequences of the staff attitudes as all but inevitable. Men in Washington form preferences, the political system is designed for the airing and resolution of preferences, and it may be unrealistic to ask any man to be a policy eunuch, especially one who must operate amid the competing demands which surround the tax legislative process. But the history of the joint tax staff since Stam's retirement

and the ascendancy of Woodworth to the top position necessitate caution in accepting this conclusion. Perfect conformity to the norms of neutrality and objectivity is probably impossible but the degree of attainment and deviation varies with different individuals. And, experience shows, there is no reason to conclude that the staff *cannot* both serve and please diverse masters.

When Woodworth took over as Chief of Staff in 1964 he was aware of the liberal criticism of Stam and he took steps to restore the staff to its position as a useful aide to *all* members of the Senate Finance and Ways and Means committees. He assured Senate Liberals that he and his assistants stood ready to assist all members, regardless of policy considerations, and that, in effect, the staff would not play politics on revenue bills. Woodworth's campaign worked: the critics of Stam laud his successor. "I'd say the staff is 500 percent improved over what it used to be," said one liberal Senator. Hired by Stam in 1944, Woodworth is more skillful than his mentor in retaining the confidence of the factions that make tax policy. Whether or not he can always avoid all commitments to individual policy positions, or operate in such a way that although the staff research does in fact enhance one position at the expense of others he does not alienate any members, remains to be seen, but at present he is doing precisely that. "I honestly have no idea whether he's a Democrat or a Republican," says one long-time associate of Woodworth's. "He's about as straight down-the-middle as you can get." [27] If Woodworth can function in accordance with this inclination he may be able to play his role as he— and the congressmen—think it should be played.

It should be noted, in passing, that criticism of the joint staff has been found on only one side of the Capitol: the Senate. The Ways and Means Committee is populated with Democrats whose voting behavior is as liberal as the Finance Committee reformers, but there are crucial differences in style between the two groups. There are really no reform-minded liberals like Paul Douglas (D.-Ill.) (before his defeat) or Albert Gore (D.-Tenn.) on the House Committee, although some House members would no doubt vote for the same reforms—if pressed. The one Ways and Means member who in personal philosophy and public statements most closely resembles the Senate tax reformers is Chairman Mills, but in practice if not preachment he has been a disappointment: "Wilbur Mills has always been for reform right up to the opening day of Congress. . . . He pulled this three or four times until he found out he couldn't fool anyone anymore." [28] This statement, whether an accurate assessment of Mills or not, indicates that to date not much steam for tax reform has come from the House. Consequently, not much criticism of the staff for blocking reforms has come from the House either. The general attitude was probably well illustrated by a liberal Ways and Means Democrat who, in reply to a question about the criticism of Stam, dismissed it with the observation: "I think that's just a characteristic of some liberal Senators. They have to have something to complain about and if it's not the staff it's something else. I think complaining is their common denominator."

As a link between the two tax committees of Congress, in summary, the Joint Committee staff, as seen by the policy-makers, has had mixed results. Possessed of so much expertise that one House member was led to observe that "they are the legislators, we are the politicians," the staff has played

its role appropriately under one head and inappropriately, in light of the norms which the members and staff espouse, under another. Having gone through the process on the House side the staff is equipped to inform the Senate Finance Committee on the technical —and political—problems involved in various sections of the bill. But it is a job which affects the kind of decisions made in the legislative process; as such, it is endowed with influence and, potentially, controversy. The existence of the former and avoidance of the latter [are] delicate business. Under Stam the expertise of the staff resulted in some disaffection; under Woodworth the expertise of the staff, in no way diminished, has been used in a more neutral—or less offensive—way. Time will determine whether or not this is a permanent revolution.

– 3 –

In addition to linking the Ways and Means and Senate Finance committees directly in the legislative process, the Joint Committee staff acts as an important point of contact between the committee and two key participants in the tax-making process: the Treasury Department and interest groups. In this section we will analyze the staff's relation with these actors, putting special emphasis on the initial stage of the process which revolves around the Ways and Means Committee.

Ways and means—treasury department relations

It is a maxim, by now, that although the Constitution separates authority among the three branches of government there is a good deal of overlap among the institutions and that, in fact, they share power and responsibility for legislation. To date, however,

there are relatively few empirical studies of how the branches have bridged
the formal separation and organized
their interaction; there are even fewer
studies of arrangements between individual congressional committees and
related executive department agencies.[29] Congressional oversight of administration has received a fair
amount of attention, but much work
remains to be done on the interaction
between the branches in formulating
policy, marking up bills, and striking
a balance between the competing demands which are involved in the
policy-making process.

One bridge between the branches is
through the professional staff of Congress and its counterpart in the executive departments. For many years
Joint Committee staff experts, under
Stam and continuing under Woodworth, have worked with Treasury Department experts on technical tax problems in what are called staff "subcommittees."[30] A member of the Joint
Committee staff summed up the purpose of these subcommittees:

We work very closely with Treasury people. Before a message is sent by the
President we have these staff subcommittees composed of Joint Committee on
Internal Revenue Taxation staff, Treasury
people, and IRS [Internal Revenue Serv-
ice] people. We discuss proposals drawn
up by the Treasury's economists. These
economists compose big ideas and general
notions as to what Treasury ought to do
on taxes—this is where it all starts. Then
we get together in our subcommittee and
discuss these ideas as to feasibility and
technical possibility. Many times they
aren't practical. We represent the Ways
and Means Committee and let them know
what the Committee may or may not accept. What we do in these meetings is
kick ideas around, we brainstorm ideas.

The primary task of the subcommittee
is to discuss, in a professional way,
various tax proposals, the technical
problems involved in drafting the language necessary to put them into effect,
and the likelihood of congressional
policy-makers responding positively or
negatively to them.

Through the staff mechanism, then,
the Ways and Means Committee members may learn what the Treasury Department is contemplating or not contemplating and Treasury receives technical assistance and valuable information about what the Committee is likely
to accept or reject. Neither staff contingent has the authority to bind the
policy-makers, of course, and the Joint
Committee staff is careful about appearing to speak for its superiors. But
policy questions are discussed, technical barriers to changing the Internal
Revenue Code are resolved, and the
subcommittees do serve as a way of
combining the expertise of both staffs
in the initial stage of the policy-making
process. The prognostications of the
congressional staff may or may not be
heeded by Treasury. For example, in
1963 the joint staff warned the Department that Ways and Means would not
approve the controversial proposal to
limit itemized deductions to five percent of the taxpayer's adjusted gross
income, but Treasury, committed to
the five percent floor, proposed it anyway. The issue was not even put to a
vote in Ways and Means. In other
cases, however, the views of the congressional staff are taken into account
when Treasury is deciding what to include in a tax message, and in this way
the probable response of the Ways and
Means Committee has a bearing on the
initiation of tax legislation.

After the preliminaries are over and
the Ways and Means Committee is in
executive session, the Joint Committee
staff, having spent hours in consultation with Treasury Department experts,
is prepared to explain arcane tax pro-

posals to the members. Since Ways and Means allows Treasury officials to attend and participate in its executive deliberations, both staffs are involved in explaining the Treasury Department's proposals to the Committee. If the Secretary of the Treasury is especially well versed in tax matters, as was Douglas Dillon on the proposal which became the Revenue Act of 1964, he will carry a large part of the burden of presenting the Department's case, and the Treasury staff will serve as a backstop to him. (One Committee member said Dillon spent so much time with the Committee in 1963 he began to wonder if the Secretary was using Ways and Means as a "hideout.") But the Joint Committee staff, playing the role of *Congress's* staff, ensures that the Committee hears all sides of the issues and, by so doing, the staff affects the decisions that are made. One staff man told how he helped a Committee member against Treasury:

Really, as far as I was concerned it was six of one and half a dozen of the other. Treasury was opposed to it but I pointed out that on the other hand these considerations could be taken into account and the Committee said since this is the case let's pass it. Later, after the Committee had done this, O'Brien [Thomas O'Brien, D.-Ill.] met me in the hall and he really went out of his way to thank me. He was very grateful and really all I had done was stated as near an objective opinion as possible.

As the above quote shows, when there is disagreement among the experts the Committee members are inclined to rely on their staff, not Treasury's. The general feeling is that the Joint Committee staff, which generates its own studies and data independent of the Treasury Department, has demonstrated that in a dispute with Treasury its studies are more reliable than the executive's. Two examples, one pertaining to the reduction of excise taxes, the other to raising the national debt limit, illustrate the Committee's faith in its staff and the ways in which the work of the staff affects policy outcomes.

In 1965, as part of a long-awaited excise tax reduction bill, the Administration proposed that the excise tax on automobiles be reduced in steps from ten percent to seven percent, and then to five percent by 1967 at which time the five percent levy would be permanent. Detroit's spokesman on the Ways and Means Committee, Martha Griffiths (D-Mich.), proposed that the tax be removed altogether and at once, a proposal that would have cost the federal government over $1 billion in revenue. The Treasury Department, not wanting to increase the budget deficit by this much, opposed the Griffiths motion, and so did Chairman Mills. In the course of building his argument against the motion Mills argued that the Committee could not lift the automobile excise and stagger the tax on telephone service, so he asked Treasury how much reducing the telephone tax all at once would add to the deficit. Assistant Secretary Stanley Surrey replied that it would cost a half billion dollars. At this point Eugene Keogh (D-N.Y.) asked how much a compromise proposal on the auto excise would cost and Mills then recognized Woodworth, the Chief of Staff. Woodworth informed the Committee that the joint staff figures showed that the federal budget deficit would be higher than that estimated by the Treasury, an observation which further argued against the Griffiths proposal. Representative Keogh asked a rhetorical question about whose estimates have usually been nearer the mark, Treasury's or the Joint Committee's staff, and Mills answered for Woodworth: the congressional staff. With the case made against the car makers' amendment Ways and Means voted. Griffiths, beaten on a voice vote, did not bother to press for a roll call. Mills, the Joint Committee staff, and Treasury, in concert, defeated the Griffiths amendment.

In the case of excise taxes the expertise of the Joint Committee staff buttressed the Treasury Department, but the congressional staff's work also helps the Committee take and support positions contrary to that of the Executive Branch. One such incident was the Committee's handling of the 1966 debt bill. On the basis of calculations about federal finances made by its staff, Ways and Means rejected the Administration's request for a $332 billion temporary limit on the national debt and recommended instead a $330 billion ceiling. The $2 billion cut was predicated on the joint staff's studies which showed that federal receipts would probably exceed the amount estimated by Treasury, the deficit would consequently be less than expected, and, therefore, a lower ceiling could be justified. The Committee's faith in its staff was not misplaced: a week after the House passed the bill Treasury Secretary Fowler acknowledged before the Senate Finance Committee that the Department, though squeezed, could live with the House figure.[31]

Thus Congress, through the staff of the Joint Committee on Internal Revenue Taxation, has a body of professionals which links its principal revenue-raising organs bicamerally, which serves as a communications link between the Ways and Means Committee and the Treasury Department, and which is so expert that the legislature has an in-house check on the expertise of the Executive Branch—so much so that the congressmen feel they can rely on their staff even in the face of con-

flicting information from the executive. Important as these functions are they do not exhaust the functions of the staff. One more aspect of the staff, its relations with interest groups, needs to be explored before one can appreciate the extent of the staff's services for the Ways and Means Committee.

Ways and means—interest demands

Access to the Committee on Ways and Means is obtained in many ways. Members of the Committee act as the spokesmen for particular interests (e.g., the oil industry), the practice of holding public hearings on major bills is firmly rooted, and group spokesmen have on occasion been invited into the Committee's executive session to assist it in writing legislation (e.g., representatives of Blue Cross–Blue Shield were summoned to a closed meeting on Medicare in 1965). Another line of access is through the Joint Committee staff. The staff is a common target for informed Washington lobbyists and the first stop for many constituent demands.

There is abundant evidence in the anecdotes which travel the Washington grapevine, the public record, and the perceptions of those involved in the policy-making process to support the observation that contacts between the staff and interested parties are frequent, legitimate, and important.

On the anecdotal level the story is told of Colin Stam that he carried so much weight with the formal policy-makers that a lobbyist who had difficulty getting to see him bought a dog and walked the canine around Chevy Chase Circle in hopes of encountering the tax expert on his nightly dog-walking strolls. Apocryphal, perhaps, but the circulation of the story testifies to the importance of the staff to interest groups. "Nobody's been up to my neighborhood to see me yet," Woodworth has been quoted as saying,[32] but this may be because no one has yet had difficulty seeing him at the office.

Normally, access to the staff is not difficult. Stam, for example, used to hold quasi-hearings at which lobbyists would present their views on tax matters (a measure of his influence in the process), and Woodworth does the same. Many lobbyists have heard a member of Ways and Means or Senate Finance say, "See Stam" (and now, "See Larry"). Kenworthy quotes a tax attorney on how congressmen use the staff to winnow tax proposals and how the staff, contacted first, can reverse the procedure and assist a lobbyist:

The congressman says to the lawyer, "Go see Stam and then let me get a report from Stam." If Stam thinks there is no merit in the idea, the congressman will usually drop it. If Stam thinks there is merit, the congressman is likely to sponsor it.
An attorney will call on Stam to tell him what he would like to do and see whether it is in the cards. Stam may say, "Don't waste your time," or "You might be able to interest so-and-so in that." If Stam himself is interested, he will explain the proposal to the congressman in friendly terms, without necessarily urging it, and so help put it across.[33]

"Stam's staff," as one Ways and Means member put it succinctly, "is very influential and that's why they are lobbied so much."

By receiving and analyzing tax proposals the staff increases the Committee's contacts with interested parties, which is an important part of the Ways and Means Committee's job, and at the same time it helps the members cope with the tremendous number of demands for changes in the Code. Many times, in fact, these demands are stimulated by the Committee itself as part

of its legislative procedure. Prior to the passage of the 1954 Revenue Act, for example, the staff mailed a tax questionnaire to thousands of individuals and groups. Over 15,000 replies were received and over two dozen national associations did studies of various tax proposals before passage of the Act, the first major revision of the Code since 1939. So much [of] the work was done by the staff that one member, Jere Cooper (D-Tenn.), argued that the Committee, with six weeks' labor, still did not understand the bill reported to the House:

The staffs of the Joint Committee on Internal Revenue Taxation and the Treasury Department together have spent over two years preparing recommendations for the bill. Extensive hearings were held, and some 15,000 replies to questionnaires were reviewed preparatory to making recommendations to be included. In contrast to this, the committee deliberated on the bill for only six weeks. In my opinion, such a complete overhauling as this bill proposes to make involving the most complicated laws which Congress has ever written, would require at least one year to fully understand. . . .[34]

Another revealing example of the contacts between interest groups and the staff occurred in 1956 when the House considered a bill dealing with the renegotiation of government contracts. In this case the Committee did not make policy as much as it legitimatized the recommendations of the staff and business organizations. Thomas Jenkins (R-Ohio) said of the bill:

Mr. Speaker, this bill is the result of an exhaustive study by the staff of the Joint Committee on Internal Revenue Taxation. This study was conducted pursuant to statutory directive and lasted for many months. *Industry had a complete opportunity to present its problems to the staff.*[35]

Jenkins acknowledged that it may have been unfortunate that Ways and Means did not hold hearings but: "On the other hand, I believe that Mr. Stam and the Joint Committee staff did a magnificent job in developing these needed improvements in the act." [36] Small wonder that interest groups and individuals pay attention to the staff.

The testimony to the important role of the staff which is found in the public record is, of course, the reflection of the staff's activities in countless private meetings with lobbyists and in the executive sessions of the Ways and Means Committee. When the members of Ways and Means descend from their dais and begin marking up a tax bill the staff becomes an integral part of the process. According to Thomas B. Curtis (R-Mo.), when the doors are closed the staff represents the views of the people with whom it has been in contact:

The role of the Joint Committee staff is even more important during executive sessions when administration officials are the only outsiders present. Then the staff must represent the views of all other "interests" whose positions are often discounted by the sometimes parochial outlook of Treasury and Internal Revenue Service officials and experts. [37]

The staff, in other words, brings to the discussion the results of its meetings and communications with people on the outside, thereby keeping the Committee informed on the views and arguments of those who will be affected by the Committee's decisions.

One example of this part of the staff's role will be cited. In 1965, when the Committee was considering President Johnson's proposed cut in excise taxes, the question arose as to whether or not the announcement of excise tax reductions would induce consumers to postpone buying certain items until the tax

was removed, thus, in effect, creating a buyer's strike. Woodworth reported to the meeting that the Joint Committee staff had contacted different industries to see if they thought a refund of any tax paid on such goods was needed to ward off a drop in sales. It first appeared, he stated, that the electrical appliance industry favored the refund idea, but consultation with the national organization of electrical manufacturers revealed that the only appliance to which the refund should definitely apply, due to the closeness of the summer selling season, was air conditioners. He also informed the meeting that many manufacturers were not too anxious to pass the tax cut on to consumers by way of lowered prices, and providing for a tax refund would increase the pressure on them to do so. This, together with the administrative burdens of handling the refund, argued against applying refunds to articles other than air conditioners. Ways and Means, guided by the information gathered by the staff from interested parties, decided to make the refund applicable to air conditioners.

Interest group representatives in Washington go where power is, or where they think power is, and the Joint Committee staff is not shortchanged when it comes to contacts with lobbyists. A favorable response from the staff does not *assure* the same reaction from the tax committees, but with the complexity of tax legislation and the concomitant need of congressmen for expert guidance the likelihood of the decision-makers following the advice of the fact-finders is high. This does not mean that congressmen are captives of their staffs. By and large the staff probably reflects the views of the members more than it determines those views. But the above evidence shows that the staff can and does play an active role in the process. The input of the staff, one more variable for students of policy-making to consider, has received scant attention to date but it may warrant greater attention in the future.

Conclusion

From a case study of one staff it is impossible, of course, to answer the question of whether or not Congress needs more staff in order to compete effectively with the executive branch. All we can say is that in one significant area of public policy, revenue legislation, Congress is equipped to do much more than service constituents and oversee the bureaucracy. The House Ways and Means Committee is so well equipped in this area that the Treasury Department usually presents its requests in the form of a tax message as opposed to a draft bill. The bill is the *product* of the Committee's work, not the start of it.

Having shown how the Joint Committee staff may affect the decisions of policy-makers, and discussed the linkage functions of the staff, we may speculate on some of the variables which are pertinent to the role of the staff. First in probable importance is, obviously, the nature of the subject matter handled by the committee. As the complexity of the decisions facing legislators increases so too does the likelihood that the staff will exert influence on the outcomes. Tax policy, infinitely complex, maximizes the importance of expertise. The importance of the staff is likely to vary on other committees with different tasks (e.g., the House Rules Committee, Government Operations).

Another factor that affects the influence of the staff is the scope of the decision. It is no accident that much of the criticism of Stam centered around his role in drafting and defend-

ing narrow tax provisions which helped particular industries, companies, or, in the case of Louis B. Mayer, one individual.[38] The more salient the issue is to a large number of participants the less likely the judgment of the staff will direct the decision. On purely economic grounds, for example, the Chief of Staff believed in the fall of 1967 that a tax increase was advisable but Chairman Mills led 19 other Ways and Means members in tabling the President's request until Congress and the President resolved the question of limiting federal expenditures. Staff studies, though not without some importance, bowed to the political barriers to passing a tax increase in the House.

Highly personal factors such as the relationship between the staff and leading members of the committees also deserve attention. There is in Congress a cadre of professional staff assistants who, like Stam, develop firm ties with influential congressmen, thus partaking of their sponsors' influence while they simultaneously contribute to it. Thomas J. Scott and Senator Carl Hayden, Oliver Meadows and Representative Olin Teague, Colin Stam and Representative Robert L. ("Muley") Doughton, John Barriere and Representative Albert Rains—these present and past relationships are important in the legislative process, too important to escape the attention of political scientists.

Other interesting questions about the role of the staff in the legislative process are not hard to imagine. On a committee such as House Post Office and Civil Service, for example, what are the consequences of having an unstable committee membership but a long-term professional staff director? How does the staff of a highly centralized committee (e.g., Ways and Means which does not work through subcommittees) differ from the Appropriations

Committee which does almost all its work in subcommittees? Why is it that not one member of the current Democratic party leadership in the House has a staff confidant other than House Parliamentarian Lewis Deschler? How do congressmen rely on the staff without becoming captives of the staff? Why are some highly capable men willing to refuse lucrative jobs outside of Congress in order to toil anonymously and at relatively low pay for congressmen? These questions, and others, will not be easy to answer but they appear to be sufficiently important to require some investigation.

It should be noted, in conclusion, that it is very difficult if not impossible to determine how much "power" the staff has in the policy-making process.

On certain kinds of issues under certain conditions a staff man such as Colin Stam did indeed have power. But it was a curious kind of power. It depended upon the congruence between his judgment on policy and the judgment of the majority whom he served. In their frustration over the failure to change the internal revenue code one would expect the liberal critics of Stam to exaggerate his importance as a pillar of the status quo. Future research will demonstrate, I think, that Stam and other leading staff experts perform important functions in the legislative process but, in the final analysis, they take more cues from the formal policy-makers than they give.

NOTES

1. George B. Galloway, *The Legislative Process in Congress* (New York: Thomas Y. Crowell, 1953), pp. 605–12. Stephen K. Bailey, *Congress Makes a Law* (New York: Columbia University Press, 1950), pp. 61–64. Ernest S. Griffith, *Congress: Its Contemporary Role,* 3rd ed. (New York: University Press, 1961), pp. 86–89. Alfred de Grazia (ed.), *Congress: The First Branch of Government* (Washington, D.C.: American Enterprise Institute, 1966).

2. Samuel P. Huntington, "Congressional Responses to the Twentieth Century," *The Congress and America's Future,* in David B. Truman (ed.) (Englewood Cliffs, N.J.: Prentice-Hall, 1965), p. 30.

3. See Reuss's statement before the Joint Committee on the Organization of Congress, 89th Cong., 1965–66, *Hearings,* pp. 80–100.

4. Ralph K. Huitt, "Congressional Reorganization: The Next Chapter," unpublished paper read at the annual meeting of the American Political Science Association, Chicago, September 8–12, 1964, p. 8. Emphasis added.

5. Hugh Douglas Price, Review of Kenneth Kofmehl's *Professional Staffs of Congress,* in *American Sociological Review,* 28 (October, 1963), 859. Other studies of the staff which contain some helpful information are: Gladys Kammerer, *The Staffing of the Committees of Congress* (Lexington, Ky.: University of Kentucky Press, 1949); James D. Cochrane, "Partisan Aspects of Congressional Committee Staffing," *Western Political Quarterly,* 17 (June, 1964), 338–48; Warren H. Butler, "Administering Congress: The Role of the Staff," *Public Administration Review,* 26 (March, 1966), 3–13; Norman Meller, "Legislative Staff Services: Toxin, Specific, or

Placebo for the Legislature's Ills," *Western Political Quarterly,* 20 (June, 1967), 381–89.

6. U.S. Congress, House, Committee on Ways and Means, 69th Cong., 1st Sess., 1926, H. Rept. No. 1 to accompany H.R. 1, *The Revenue Bill of 1926,* p. 23.

7. *Congressional Record,* 69th Cong., 1st Sess., 1925, Vol. 67, Pt. 1, pp. 696–97.

8. *Ibid.,* Part 3, p. 2870.

9. See the remarks of Representative Collier, *Congressional Record,* 70th Cong., 2nd Sess., 1929, Vol. 70, Pt. 2, p. 1198.

10. *Congressional Record,* August 2, 1967 (daily edition), p. H9876.

11. "Where Tax Bills Run the Gauntlet," *Business Week,* June 11, 1966, p. 106; Arlen J. Large, "Help on the Hill," *Wall Street Journal,* June 25, 1965.

12. Roy M. Blough, *The Federal Taxing Process* (New York: Prentice-Hall, 1952), p. 64.

13. Thomas B. Curtis, "The House Committee on Ways and Means: Congress Seen Through a Key Committee," *Wisconsin Law Review* (Winter, 1966), p. 8.

14. *Op. cit.,* p. 477. McClellan's proposal has passed the Senate many times but to date leaders of the House Appropriations Committee have responded negatively.

15. *Ibid.,* pp. 1983, 1985, 800–01.

16. In justifying his successful request for more staff Long contended: "Under our Government the legislative branch is not supposed to be a lackey or the tool of the executive and is not to take the word of the executive on matters but should be able to acquire information itself." *Congressional Record,* April 20, 1966 (daily edition), p. 8239. He admitted that the Joint Committee staff does a good job but when they are working for Ways and Means the Finance Committee has only a secondary claim on their services. Long also argued that Finance has much nontax work to do and needs help which the joint staff cannot provide.

17. Quoted in *Business Week, op. cit.,* p. 106.

18. Quoted in Large, *op. cit.*

19. *Ibid.*

20. Stephen K. Bailey and Howard D. Samuel, *Congress at Work* (New York: Henry Holt & Co., 1953), p. 342.

21. E. W. Kenworthy, "Colin F. Stam," in *Adventures in Public Service,* Delia and Ferdinand Kuhn (eds.) (New York: Vanguard Press, 1963), p. 109.

22. *Ibid.,* p. 115.

23. *Congressional Record,* 83rd Cong., 1st Sess., 1953, Vol. 99, Pt. 6, p. 8493. Italics added.

24. After an apprenticeship with the Internal Revenue Bureau Stam joined the Joint Committee staff in 1927, became Chief of Staff in 1938, and ran it for a quarter of a century until his retirement in 1964. He suffered a stroke and died in January, 1966.

25. Kenworthy, *op. cit.,* p. 115.

26. Huitt reports similar complaints about Stam. See Ralph K. Huitt, "Congressional Organization and Operations in the Field of Money and Credit," in *Fiscal and Debt Management Policies,* William Fellner *et al.* (Englewood Cliffs, N.J.: Prentice-Hall, 1963), pp. 452–53.

27. Quoted in *Business Week, op. cit.,* p. 111.

28. See Mills's plea for tax reform, "Are you a Pet or a Patsy," *Life,* November 23, 1959, p. 51 ff.

29. Notable exceptions include: J. Lieper Freeman, *The Political Process: Executive Bureau–Legislative Committee Relations,* rev. ed. (New York: Random House, 1965); Richard F. Fenno, Jr., *The Power of the Purse* (Boston: Little, Brown, 1966), chapters 6, 7; James A. Robinson, *Congress and Foreign Policy-Making* (Homewood, Ill.: Dorsey Press, 1962), chapters 5, 6.

30. For brief descriptions of these subcommittees, see Blough, *op. cit.,* pp. 107–09, and Kofmehl, *op. cit.,* pp. 158–59.

31. Hobart Rowen, "Fowler Accepts House Dept Action," *Washington Post,* June 14, 1966. Before the Rules Committee, with Woodworth sitting behind him, Mills backed the Committee's action in these words: "I'm prone to believe that the staff itself may be more accurate than the Treasury."

32. Large, *op. cit.*

33. Kenworthy, *op. cit.,* p. 119.

34. *Congressional Record,* 83rd Cong., 2nd Sess., 1954, 100, Pt. 3, p. 3,420.

35. *Congressional Record,* 84th Cong., 2nd Sess., 1956, 102, Pt. 9, p. 12,726. Emphasis added.

36. *Ibid.,* p. 12,726.

37. Curtis, *op. cit.,* p. 7.

38. For a study of special tax provisions see Stanley S. Surrey, "The Congress and the Tax Lobbyist—How Special Tax Provisions Get Enacted," *Harvard Law Review,* 70 (May, 1957), pp. 1145–82. Surrey estimates that the Mayer amendment saved the tycoon about $2,000,000 in taxes. See also Philip M. Stern, *The Great Treasury Raid* (New York: Random House, 1963).

 **part two**

THE SENATE

Because the Senate is a relatively small group whose membership is stable and persists over long periods of time, to understand the Senate at any given time one must understand senators. Thus much of the commentary that follows concerns itself with how senators respond to one another, how they confer and use leadership, how their ambitions have changed over time, and how variations in their ambitions produce variations in their behavior.

5

TWO STRATEGIES OF LEADERSHIP: JOHNSON AND MANSFIELD

JOHN G. STEWART

John G. Stewart, a political scientist, was special assistant to Hubert Humphrey while Humphrey was Senate Democratic Whip and Vice-President. Thus Stewart's discussion of the leadership styles of Senators Lyndon Johnson and Mike Mansfield is based in part on long and close personal observation. This selection is taken from a chapter in Stewart's doctoral dissertation. Stewart received his Ph.D. from the University of Chicago in 1968 and is now executive director of the Democratic Policy Council of the Democratic National Committee.

The consecutive incumbencies of Lyndon B. Johnson and Mike Mansfield as leaders of the Democratic majority in the Senate illustrate two strikingly different approaches to the same job.[1] A product partially of their individual notions as to the proper role of the party leadership, as well as their respective techniques for executing that role, these differences also reflected the pressures of the political environment on Johnson and Mansfield in their development of a strategy of party leadership. This analysis will attempt to describe the opportunities for control of the senatorial party which are available to the majority leader, as well as the limited effectiveness of this position.

The Leadership of Lyndon B. Johnson

Expressed in baldest terms, Lyndon Johnson's tenure as majority leader of the Senate (1955–1960) is likely to stand for some time as the classic example of

Printed by permission of the author.

an elected party leader who with unusual zeal, dedication, and skill sought to control the realistic choices open to senators in such a way that a sufficient majority saw their immediate political interests better served by supporting the senatorial party program than by opposing it.[2] Johnson will be remembered not only for his efforts to wring the last ounce of effectiveness from his meager store of institutionalized power but also as a leader who set about diligently augmenting these fragments of power in a number of informal and highly personal ways. He set for himself no less an objective than *running* the Senate, in fact as well as in theory, by wielding decisive influence in generating majority support for the issues he permitted to come before the Senate for decision.

His election as leader of the senatorial Democrats coincided with the party's loss of the presidency to the Republicans. But the presence of Dwight D. Eisenhower in the White House provided Johnson with a crucial measure of independence and flexibility usually denied a majority leader of the president's party. Operating without the constant pressure and the inevitable restraints imposed by the obligation to push forward the legislative program of his party's president, Johnson was in a position to exercise greater personal discretion in picking his battles, choosing his tactics, and defining for the Democrats what would comprise an acceptable outcome. And he made full use of this relative independence and flexibility. Although Johnson was also denied the political leverage which a Democratic president might have provided from time to time in support of presidential legislative initiatives, the assets of flexibility and independence more than compensated for this deficiency (whereas Mansfield would have probably discovered the absence of presidential leverage to have been a serious handicap).

As Democratic leader, Johnson's most pressing challenge was to identify areas of agreement between the northern and southern factions of the party. He recognized that unless a minimum of approximately forty Democratic votes, necessarily drawn from the ranks of both North and South, could be delivered on most roll calls, his ability to control the outcome of issues would be seriously impaired. Grounds for common action had to be established. Johnson attacked this problem with the conviction that the interests of reasonable men, even northern and southern Democrats, could be served simultaneously if an affirmative effort was made to structure each legislative encounter in a way which recognized in some manner the legitimate interests of those senators most interested in the pending issue and which offered those senators a basis for justifying and defending their vote.

"Party loyalty" in itself was seldom sufficient, especially for southern Democrats who often acted as though their political survival depended upon a posture of opposition to the national party.[3] There was, moreover, no Democratic president to dramatize more forcefully the need for party unity and support. Johnson knew he would have to produce additional reasons in order to convince a senator to follow his party's leadership, reasons which spoke primarily to a senator's political interests and standing in his state or his position within the Senate. He therefore sought to develop for any given legislative issue: (1) the methods to identify the vital interests of a majority of the senators, (2) sufficient political leverage to take account of these interests through bargaining and accommodation among the contending parties, and (3) the ability to control the parliamentary situation, especially on the Senate floor, so that these accommodations would not be undone by pressures from other sources. The effect of this strategy of leadership went beyond closing the traditional breach between North and South within the Democratic party; its use in lining up any senator's vote was equally feasible.

In accumulating the resources to render this strategy operational, Johnson drew from two basic sources: (1) the institutionalized powers at his disposal as majority leader and (2) the influence developed through his personal involvement in almost every aspect of senatorial life. Looking first at Johnson's institutional powers, his election as Democratic floor leader also brought with it the chairmanship of the Democratic Conference, the Policy Committee, and the Steering Committee. From each of these formal assignments he sought to extract a maximum contribution to the total bundle of resources he needed to sustain his three-pronged strategy of leadership.

Floor leader

Although Johnson's techniques for controlling events on the Senate floor will be discussed below in greater detail, it should be noted at this point that his only recognized prerogative as floor leader was the traditional right of recognition by the chair over the competing claims of other senators.[4] This permitted Johnson to seize the parliamentary initiative whenever he desired, but it did nothing to ensure the outcome of the issue at hand.

Party conference

The Democratic Party Conference is composed of every Democrat senator.[5] Party leaders are chosen by decision of the conference and, in theory, it provides a forum for the discussion of issues facing the senatorial party. Due to its unwieldy size and the practice of not binding senators by decisions of the Party Conference (a practice superseded briefly by building votes upon the urging of President Wilson during John Worth Kern's tenure as majority leader), Johnson viewed the conference as a place ill suited to execute his highly personalized strategy of leadership. During Johnson's years as leader the conference met primarily to ratify his selections for party officers, party committees, and standing committees and to provide an appropriate platform for dissemination of his "state-of-the-union" message presented at the opening of a congressional session.[6] Given his strong distaste for any device which could exacerbate and highlight differences within the Democratic senatorial party, these meetings were infrequent: From 1953 through 1958 a total of only five Party Conferences were held. During the Eighty-sixth Congress (1959–1960), largely in response to pressure from a band of liberal Democrats,

Johnson called six conferences, one more than the total for the preceding three Congresses.[7] Nevertheless, he never considered the conference, and it never became a place for hammering out the delicately balanced compromises which served as Johnson's principal device for lining up the majorities he needed to function successfully.

Policy committee

Traditionally charged with drawing up the schedule of legislation on the Senate floor rather than formulating specifics of party policy, the Policy Committee during Johnson's regime served several additional functions.[8] Its regular membership of seven Democrats appointed by the majority leader included a hard core of independently powerful senators whose cooperation, or at least whose acquiescence, was required for the successful execution of the majority leader's major stratagems and tactics. The members generally carried over from one Congress to the next. In this sense the Policy Committee served as a council of major power holders of the Democratic senatorial party, i.e., such men as Richard Russell (Ga.), Robert Kerr (Okla.), and Lister Hill (Ala.), along with other less influential but highly respected men, such as James Murray (Mont.) and Theodore Francis Green (R.I.).[9]

Johnson also saw the Policy Committee as capable of providing the party's major geographical and ideological factions with a recognized position in his leadership system. Although distribution on the Policy Committee did not necessarily correspond with a faction's numerical strength in the party, the imbalance on the committee against the more liberally disposed Democrats in comparison to their numbers in the party became severe after the Democratic landslide in the 1958 elections. Johnson responded by inviting the three freshmen members of the Legislative Review Committee to sit ex officio with the Policy Committee in its deliberations (the whip and the secretary of the Party Conference already met with the committee as ex officio members). This adjustment brought three additional liberals (Hart of Michigan, Engle of California, and Bartlett of Alaska) into the higher councils of the party without any formal change in the committee's structure or composition. Such a formal alteration would likely have been opposed by the southern Democrats, thereby producing among the Democrats the kind of North–South battle which Johnson sought to avoid.

In practice the Policy Committee did little more than formally ratify scheduling decisions which in most cases Johnson had already made on the basis of more informal consultations with the minority leader, chairmen of standing committees, and other senators involved with the legislation under discussion. But the comments of Policy Committee members on the bills Johnson proposed to call from the calendar helped him refine his tactics and avoid pitfalls during the floor debate. The major factions within the party represented on the committee were also afforded a final opportunity to voice their feelings in a confidential setting. In the event of unforeseen difficulties, the majority leader could use this safety-valve procedure to delay legislation until the problems had been worked out to Johnson's satisfaction.

In summary, the operations of the Policy Committee, together with the work of its staff, contributed primarily to two components of Johnson's three-pronged leadership strategy—the identification of the interests of major senatorial factions and the control of the parliamentary situation on the Senate floor.

Steering committee

Composed of fifteen members selected by the majority leader, the Democratic Steering Committee met principally during the opening days of a new Congress to assign Democratic senators to the various Senate committees. Although the Steering Committee made the formal assignments, the committee members seldom ignored Johnson's recommendations.

The standing committees provide more than an arrangement to handle the Senate's work load. Given their recognized authority in determining substantive policy, they also represent important allocations of power within the senatorial party and the Senate. The process of assigning senators to the committees distributes this power in a way which can affect how the party leadership is able to function. For example, a Committee on Appropriations controlled by Johnson's allies was a distinct asset; one controlled by his critics would have been a major handicap. It was, therefore, not surprising that Johnson sought to exercise tight control over the assignment process.

Johnson also viewed each committee assignment as an opportunity for augmenting his personal resources for bargaining and negotiation on other issues. A desirable assignment could reward a senator for past support and assistance, or, more likely, establish a fund of credit to be drawn upon in the future. In addition, the distribution of cooperative senators among the committees expanded Johnson's communication and intelligence system: A strategically placed ally could help guide a bill still in committee or suggest the elements of subsequent negotiation which would ensure its passage on the Senate floor. Finally, assignments to the major standing committees provided one important measure of the party leadership's responsiveness to the interests and concerns of individual senators. Johnson's decision in 1953 to guarantee every senator, regardless of seniority, at least one major committee assignment reflected, among other things, a conviction that the choice spots should be available to all members of the party and not remain solely the province of the senior senators. This decision also served to advance Johnson's standing among the more recent members of the Senate.

Operating with the close assistance of Robert Baker, Secretary to the Democratic Majority, Johnson weighed and balanced these considerations carefully in evaluating the competing claims of various senators for the existing vacancies. The criterion of seniority in the Senate was a relevant factor in these decisions, but under Johnson it no longer served as the controlling consideration in each case. Seniority would be evaluated in relation to other objectives of the majority leader, e.g., the assignment of a particularly cooperative senator to Appropriations or Foreign Relations. Moreover, since the factor of seniority was totally predictable, a practice of reaching all decisions on that basis would have eliminated the sense of personal obligation to Johnson which a senator might otherwise hold for a favorable assignment.

In summary, the activities of the Steering Committee, although limited to the early days of any Congress, supported all aspects of the Johnson strategy of leadership. The work of the committee was especially valuable in helping Johnson accumulate political resources and other leverage to expend in bargaining and negotiation and

in controlling the parliamentary environment by placing reliable senators on the crucial committees.

Finally, Johnson appointed the chairman and members of the Democratic Senatorial Campaign Committee. Charged principally with raising and disbursing funds to assist in the reelection of incumbent Democrats, the committee's duties were less related to the activities of the senatorial party and the party leadership than either the Policy Committee or the Steering Committee.[10] But by his appointments Johnson made sure the Campaign Committee was run by senators who were responsive to his judgments on channeling funds to senatorial races where the contributions would be appreciated by the recipients and would expand the majority leader's fund of personal credit.[11] In short, the committee provided an informal source of influence which, in a given situation, could help Johnson achieve a particular tactical objective.

Johnson relied little on his whip, or, as he is also called, the asssistant majority leader. Earle C. Clements (Ky.), who served from 1953 to 1956, was a strong personal friend, adviser, and intelligence agent in both the conservative and liberal camps. But he assumed no regularized function of leadership, such as preparing estimates of voting strength; Johnson had no intention of handing these duties to anyone, not even a good friend like Clements. Upon his defeat in 1956, Clements was succeeded by Mike Mansfield (Mont.), a well-liked and noncontroversial senator whose choice avoided a scrap between the northern and southern Democrats. But given the differences in personality and interests between Johnson and Mansfield, the new whip played much less of a role in Johnson's operations than even Clements had done. He would occasionally monitor the Senate floor when Johnson was absent but only to see that routine business was transacted according to the majority leader's schedule.

The extension of influence

Despite Johnson's vigorous exercise of these formal prerogatives of leadership, he recognized clearly that such fragments of power could never provide the information, leverage, or access he needed to meet his expectations of control. He therefore developed a variety of more informal and personal techniques to build the influence that could compensate for the institutional deficiencies of the majority leadership.

Johnson believed that simply knowing more than anyone else about all facets of a legislative situation would generally prove to be decisive, first, in identifying the various interests of those senators who held the balance of power on a given bill, and, second, in designing the precise set of tactics which could capitalize on these interests. As noted above, the deliberations of the Policy Committee and the distribution of allies among the standing committees helped Johnson achieve his objective of knowing more than anyone else about the activities of the Senate. But his intelligence and communications system reached far beyond these bounds. Johnson himself ceaselessly roamed the Senate floor and the cloakrooms talking to senators and staff, listening, questioning, probing, and persuading. His principal assistants, particularly Majority Secretary Baker, scoured the terrain for useful reports, tidbits of information, or speculation. Various members of the Washington political community—executive branch officials, lawyers, newsmen, party officials—kept him abreast of developments beyond the immediate confines

of the institution. Little escaped his notice.

Any fact that related to a pending issue, such as the political standing of a senator in his state, his principal financial backers, a senator's pet legislative project, his private priority bills, or the identity of a senator's friends and enemies in and outside the Senate was meticulously assimilated by the majority leader for immediate or future use in helping structure parliamentary situations to produce the desired legislative outcome.

Other miscellaneous activities became part of Johnson's efforts to compensate for the lack of institutionalized power in the majority leadership. He apportioned office space in the Senate office building with an eye toward the level of cooperation a senator had displayed in the past or might be encouraged to display in the future. He willingly helped cooperative colleagues secure banquet speakers, locate additional staff assistance, or attend overseas conferences. Scarcely any aspect of senatorial life, however routine and seemingly removed from the formulation of national policy, escaped Johnson's watchful eye or his uncanny talent for translating these activities into resources which could be used in running the Senate according to the Johnson formula.

Floor business

Johnson's maximum use of the prerogatives of the majority leadership and his diligent efforts to develop additional sources of persuasion and influence ultimately had a single objective—to control the senatorial party program when it reached the Senate floor. His extensive preparation and diligent attention to the minutiae of Senate life had little rationale unless Johnson could produce a sufficient majority when the crucial roll call votes were taken.

Johnson viewed each difficult legislative encounter as a puzzle: Once one had identified all the pieces and knew their precise location, the rest was easy. By the time a bill reached the floor under Johnson's strategy of leadership, the solution to the puzzle should have been in hand. He did not view the Senate floor as a place for identifying or locating the various pieces; rather, the floor debate was the point in the legislative process for unveiling the previously determined solution and passing the legislation. It was, in short, on the Senate floor where the full impact of Johnson's strategy of leadership could be experienced and appreciated.

Working from estimates of voting strength provided by Majority Secretary Baker and consulting with committee chairmen and other key senators, Johnson would strive to identify as early as possible those senators who held the balance of power on the given legislation. His subsequent efforts could be focused on devising and executing the tactics which would capture these crucial votes. This would sometimes require substantive change to the bill itself and the adjustment of certain features of the legislation which the senators wanted passed. Some situations might call for commitments from the majority leader for his assistance on other legislation in which the crucial senators were interested. The prearranged absence of a senator or two or a well-timed parliamentary maneuver might be sufficient to secure the margin of victory.

In collecting the margin of votes necessary for victory, Johnson might concentrate his prefloor efforts in winning the support of an influential senator considered to be a likely opponent of the bill in question. Support from this unexpected source could then be used to encourage and justify similar backing from less prominent senators: "If Bob Kerr is voting with Johnson, I guess I can." In these negotiations and consultations prior to the crucial roll calls, Johnson would not hesitate to approach Republicans for the winning votes if that was necessary. But while he consulted regularly with the minority leadership, he never relinquished his initiative or control of the legislative situation simply to encourage a more cordial bipartisan climate (a charge later directed against Mansfield). And once a sufficient majority had been counted, Johnson would seldom attempt to enlarge it: Why expend limited bargaining resources which might be needed to win future battles?

In each specific legislative situation Johnson followed the same guiding principle: Control the choices of senators in such a way that a sufficient majority would conceive their interests better served by supporting the majority leader than by opposing him. Seldom did a senator achieve all he wanted, but seldom did he go home empty handed.

Due to his control of the legislative schedule through the Policy Committee and his ability to influence the shape of legislation through his allies on the various standing committees, Johnson could usually delay those bills deemed likely to run into serious difficulties on the floor until the necessary adjustments were made and a sufficient majority of the votes clearly identified. Johnson also regulated carefully the timing and pace of the floor debate, stalling for time when additional votes were needed and driving the issue to a conclusion when victory was assured. He became especially proficient in reducing the Senate's natural proclivity for lengthy discussion by limiting debate under the terms of a unanimous consent agreement specifying the precise time that a vote would occur. Since a single objection would prevent such an agreement to limit the debate, Johnson engaged in lengthy consultations with all major parties to the pending issue to discover the combination of provisions that would protect the basic interests of all concerned. Once the unanimous consent agreement had been propounded and accepted, Johnson could concentrate on making sure his majority would be on the floor when the roll was called. He also arranged the Senate's schedule so that periods of intensive activity, often running into the late evening hours for days at a time, would be interspersed with periods of relative inactivity when Johnson could prepare the next bundle of legislation for floor action and the senators could catch their collective breath.

Ultimately this strategy of leadership depended on Johnson's ability to persuade other senators that their interests were irretrievably bound up in his objectives. This, in turn, called for a prodigious expenditure of energy in identifying relevant interests, in accumulating the currency of bargaining and compromise, and in man-to-man negotiation. But since he worked longer and harder than anyone else at the business of running the Senate, he became a legend in his time, a man who allegedly never made a move until he had the votes, a man who clearly established himself as the most crucial single factor in deciding what the Senate accomplished.

But the Johnson strategy was not without its deficiencies, and these became more evident during the Eighty-sixth Congress, the last two years of his incumbency as majority leader. His willingness to accommodate a broad spectrum of interests in round-ing up votes for a particular bill tended to blur the differences between the positions of the Democratic majority in the Senate and the positions advocated by the Eisenhower administration. Following the congressional elections of 1958 which increased Johnson's majority from two to thirty Democratic seats, the larger contingent of activist northern and western Democrats grew increasingly dissatisfied with his reliance on tightly structured accommodations and his preference for avoiding sharply partisan attacks on the Republican administration.[12] Moreover, in these latter years Eisenhower became more emboldened to veto even the more moderate Johnson bills, leaving the Democrats with neither programs-in-being nor sharply defined issues to take to the electorate in the presidential election of 1960.

The majority leader operated very much in the senatorial arena—charting his course on the basis of the solutions which were acceptable to the existing Senate membership—and gave no special primacy to the guidelines and proposals staked out by the national Democratic Advisory Council established in 1956. As the presidential elections of 1960 approached, this aspect of the Johnson strategy became ever more distressing to the more nationally attuned Democratic senators.

The deep involvement of the majority leader in a broad spectrum of senatorial activities and his efforts to establish centralized control of the senatorial party program also tended to restrict the opportunities of other senators for personal participation or responsibility in legislative decision making. They came to see themselves increasingly as minor functionaries on the execution of the majority leader's elaborate strategems and maneuvers. Moreover, Johnson's constant attention to detail and the effectiveness of his intelligence and communications system often left them with a feeling that someone was constantly peering over their shoulders. Gradually the Johnson strategy exacted a toll in terms of their patience, good humor, and willingness to submit indefinitely to this style of hard-driving and intense leadership. Although few persons have ever questioned Johnson's strong personal attachment and loyalty to the Senate as an institution, it is ironic that his ability to structure the total legislative situation and generally dominate the actions of the senatorial party tended to detract from the Senate's traditional aura as a place which highly regarded and protected the prerogatives of individual senators to order and control their activities and decisions. This became a matter of increasing irritation to many senators in the final two years of Johnson's incumbency.

Finally, it is worth noting again the importance of the Eisenhower presidency in creating a political environment hospitable to Johnson's style of leadership. It seems clear that this added measure of personal discretion and independence which Johnson acquired by not having to bear responsibility for a presidential legislative program was an essential condition for his method of operations. His efforts could be less consciously directed toward rationalizing the separated powers of the executive and legislative branches and the disparities of interests between the national and senatorial parties and more toward producing legislative decisions which were viable in the senatorial arena alone. It is, however, also true that his efforts to produce *some* action by the Senate in a period of divided government helped avoid total stagnation and deadlock between a Republican administration and a Democratic Congress. In working to achieve this more limited objective, Johnson demonstrated that party leaders could exercise significant control over the activities and decisions of the Senate; in the process, he developed an impressive collection of techniques and procedures for maximum utilization of the leadership's formal powers and for augmenting these powers through personal and informal actions. Operating in a political environment with the potential for Democratic party leaders to exercise unusual initiative in managing the Senate, Johnson used his great talents and energy precisely to this end.

The Leadership of Mike Mansfield

In nominating his senior colleague from Montana for his fourth term as majority leader, Lee Metcalf said of Mike Mansfield: "we have a majority leader who regards every senator as an equal in a peerage he respects. He enjoys the profound respect and deep affection of all who have served—not under him, the majority leader—but with him as a coequal." [13] This word, "coequal," sums up Mike Mansfield's view of his role as leader of the majority Democrats in the Senate: His principal duty was to maintain a system which permitted individual, coequal senators the opportunity to conduct their affairs in whatever ways they deemed appropriate. A more distinct departure from the approach of his immediate predecessor, Lyndon Johnson, would be difficult to conceive.

Having served as Democratic whip during the first four years of Johnson's tenure, a position of little responsibility in that highly centralized system of leadership, Mansfield nevertheless was the logical and undisputed choice to assume the party leadership in 1961. Reserved, almost austere in bearing, unobtrusive, considered a liberal but respected by the conservatives, and possessing immense pride and affection for the Senate as an institution, Mansfield's selection as party leader satisfied all major elements of the Democratic senatorial party. Moreover, after eight years of Johnson's hard-driving, take-charge leadership, many Democrats seemed eager for the reins to be loosened and for the leadership to encourage broader and less structured participation in the affairs of the senatorial party. "After eight years of Lyndon Johnson," one observer noted, "a lot of senators were just worn out."

During the Eisenhower years Johnson had provided the senatorial Democrats with a rallying point and an identifiable spokesman; his strategy of leadership met the clear need of reducing the Democrats' penchant for factionalism and intraparty strife as they assumed responsibility for organizing the Congress in six of Eisenhower's eight years as president. But the election of John F. Kennedy as president and the continuation of the Democrats' thirty-seat majority in the Senate (sixty-five to thirty-five in the Eighty-seventh Congress) placed upon the majority leader, regardless of his identity, the primary task of moving the president's program and sharply reduced the need, and the latitude, for him to function as an independent and identifiable personality.

In addition, there existed a substantial backlog of Democratic legislative proposals which had never passed or which had been vetoed during the Eisenhower presidency. These proposals, principally in the areas of housing, education, minimum wage, depressed areas, and social security, seemed destined to occupy the Senate for most of the Eighty-seventh Congress. Given the top-heavy Democratic majority and the presence of a Democratic president, approval of these measures in the Senate appeared to be only a matter of time.[14] In other words, the senatorial party program for the Democrats was largely defined even before President Kennedy's inauguration and the votes to enact it seemed to be in hand. In these circumstances the majority leader likely would be concerned with routine direction and maintenance of the decision making machinery so that the potential for Democratic success would be realized. Mansfield seemed ideally suited to perform this task effectively.

An enthusiastic admirer of John F. Kennedy, both the man and the president, Mansfield conscientiously sought to bring his legislative program before the Senate for prompt and favorable action. For example, although he had been identified in earlier years as one of the senators attempting to reform the Senate's procedures for limiting debate, Mansfield opposed the reformers' efforts to renew this biennial struggle in 1961 because he feared it would hinder consideration of the president's priority bills. In fulfilling what he considered to be both a personal desire and party obligation to move Kennedy's program, Mansfield did not attempt to retain Johnson's centralized system of party leadership or to employ his techniques for controlling the choices facing the senatorial party.

Indeed, in striking contrast to his predecessor's constant efforts to expand the power and influence of the majority leadership, Mansfield, free of the burden of implementing Johnson's high-powered strategy, refrained from using even the fragments of institutionalized power at his disposal, much less did he attempt the more difficult task of augmenting these limited resources. One could even say Mansfield deliberately abandoned recognized powers of the majority leadership. He encouraged a decentralization of leadership responsibilities and a reassertion of the Senate as an independent institution of government which, at least in the short run, appeared to run certain risks as far as the president's legislative program was concerned.

Operationally the Mansfield strategy produced almost a mirror image of Johnson's methods. Where Johnson saw the process of controlling the choices of senators as necessarily involving a rather direct appeal to their individual political or legislative interests, Mansfield believed he could achieve sufficient leadership control by relying on each senator's ability to act responsibly in most legislative situations and to participate more actively in the life of the institution, in addition to each senator balancing his obligations to party and constituency with a proper respect for the Senate's reputation and integrity. Temperamentally unsuited to operate in the style of Lyndon Johnson, Mansfield based his leadership strategy on an appeal to the senatorial interests of institutional pride and personal participation, interests seemingly far removed from Johnson's harsh world of political reality. As one observer remarked, "Mansfield seemed to believe that belovedness would become the guiding force in the Senate."

Despite the striking differences in conception and execution from Johnson's strategy, Mansfield believed that his approach, if applied consistently across the range of his responsibilities, would deliver adequate levels of support for the senatorial party program in the political environment created by the Kennedy administration. Moreover, his strategy would help achieve another objective which Mansfield valued highly—the strengthening of the Senate as an effective and independent institution of government. In the process of working for passage of the presi-dent's legislative program, Mansfield had no desire for the Senate or its members simply to become functionaries of the New Frontier. He considered it feasible to operate in a manner which testified to his loyalty both to the president and to the Senate.

How, then, did he execute this strategy? How did his methods differ from the ones employed by Johnson?

Party conference

Under Mansfield's chairmanship, the Party Conference became a more genuine forum for reaching decisions affecting the senatorial party and the legislative program. Johnson had zealously used the recognized prerogative of the majority leader to choose the senators he personally wanted to fill other positions of party leadership and the party committees. Approval by the conference of Johnson's choices was strictly *pro forma*. But after Mansfield's formal election as leader, the conference, on January 4, 1961, adopted a resolution sponsored by Senator Proxmire directing that membership on all party committees should reflect more accurately geographical and philosophical distribution within the senatorial party and that the majority leader should consult with the president pro tempore and the other party officers before recommending the members of party committees to the conference. It is likely that this resolution, motivated at least in part by the liberal Democrats' growing disaffection for Johnson's methods, set forth a general procedure which Mansfield would have followed even if the resolution had not been passed. At the Party Conference convened the day before, a number of senators also expressed great dissatisfaction with Mansfield's proposal that Johnson, as vice-president, should continue to serve in the capacity of conference chairman. This dissatisfaction stemmed not only from the reluctance of many senators to run the risk of continuing the rigors of the Johnsonian system of leadership but also from their conception of the vice-president as an officer of the executive branch who had no business meddling in legislative affairs. Although the conference approved Mansfield's resolution authorizing the majority leader to invite the vice-president to attend and preside over the conference, Johnson took the hint and seldom appeared in this role.[15]

Mansfield remained totally uncommitted in two subsequent contests for party office, one in 1965 to fill the post of whip vacated by Hubert H. Humphrey upon his election as vice-president, and the other in 1967 to elect a conference secretary to succeed George Smathers who had resigned. In both races the slightest indication from Mansfield of his preference would have settled the issue without further argument or bitterness; in fact, many senators urged Mansfield to disclose his favorite and thereby spare them the problem of having to choose from among several of their colleagues. But his choices were never revealed, and genuine contests developed in both instances. The elections were conducted by secret ballot, a procedure which further masked the majority leader's preferences and protected each senator against any manner of retribution for his vote. It has been suggested that the results of these two contests, the election of Russell Long (La.) as whip and Robert C. Byrd (W. Va.) as conference secretary, elevated to the party hierarchy men opposed to crucial aspects of the president's legislative program, particularly in the area of civil rights, and men who were little help to Mansfield personally in the exercise of his leadership duties.[16] As in the other

areas of leadership activity where Mansfield actually abandoned power, it was a question whether the majority leader could afford this commitment to neutrality and noninvolvement, given the expectations of accomplishment which normally attend his position.

Although Mansfield recommended senators to fill vacancies on the other party committees, he did so after explicit consultation with the president pro tempore and other party leaders, as spelled out in the Proxmire resolution adopted by the conference in January 1961. The conference was then asked to concur in these recommendations after an opportunity for additional nominations from the floor. Johnson simply announced his selections after informal checking among the influential Democratic senators.

The Party Conference was convened more frequently during Mansfield's tenure as chairman. He considered it to be an appropriate forum for deciding routine housekeeping matters facing the Senate or, less frequently, for proposing procedures to follow in more difficult and controversial matters. He encouraged full discussion and debate of these questions within the conference. The interchange among individuals and factions was useful to Mansfield in evaluating the tenor of opinion within the senatorial party and in determining the course of action to follow. Everyone had the chance to go on record in the presence of his party colleagues. Johnson had gathered this information through more informal and private consultations and from his intelligence and communications system. But though the conference became more active under Mansfield and even served as an instrumentality for choosing party officers in contested elections, it remained a body of secondary importance in senatorial party affairs, still eclipsed by other party committees and the far more significant standing committees of the Senate.

Policy committee

Although members of the Democratic Policy Committee are normally carried over from one Congress to the next, the composition of the committee under Mansfield became somewhat more representative of the total party membership than was the case during Johnson's chairmanship. The Legislative Review Committee members continued to attend as ex officio members and provided additional representation for the more liberal Democratic forces.

The Policy Committee met more frequently during Mansfield's tenure. The deliberations within the committee were less concerned with ratifying the majority leader's predetermined objectives, the approach followed under Johnson, and more concerned with discovering the course generally acceptable to committee members. Mansfield usually listened to the members discuss the prospects of bills and resolutions currently on the Senate calendar; he would formulate a schedule of bills ready for floor debate on the basis of these opinions. For the legislation that needed additional consultation or attention, Mansfield would usually delegate to the principal proponents and opponents the task of working out as many of the snags and disagreements as possible before it was cleared for action by the full Senate.

Occasionally the Policy Committee has refused to clear a given bill deemed by the committee members to be objectionable. However, this power is used with great discretion and restraint, since its abuse would undoubtedly produce some countermove by the Senate to curb the prerogatives of the Policy Committee in this respect.

Moreover, the committee never holds up priority legislation recommended by the president. In this sense, the Policy Committee in no way exercises the impressive discretionary authority of the Committee on Rules of the House of Representatives.

Johnson usually conducted prefloor negotiations personally, and they were an important aspect of his interlocking system of bargaining and control which generated a high level of influence by the majority leader over the Senate's operations. Mansfield also kept in close touch with Everett Dirksen, the minority leader, and afforded the Republican viewpoint full consideration in determining the Senate's work schedule.

From time to time during a congressional session, the Policy Committee staff would request from each committee chairman a general estimate of the legislation likely to be approved in the coming weeks, but rarely would the majority leader or his staff attempt to interfere with or disrupt the chairman's plan for processing the business before his committee. Mansfield believed that the party leadership's responsibility for any bill must await its final approval by the standing committee when the bill would then go to the Senate calendar and be considered by the Policy Committee.

Steering committee

In a manner fully consistent with his general strategy of nondirective and decentralized leadership, Mansfield radically changed the procedures for appointing Democrats to standing committees. Johnson had exercised close personal scrutiny and control over all committee assignments, and he considered this function to be a crucial aspect of his leadership system. On the other hand, Mansfield relinquished almost all personal control and influence over the Steering Committee's decisions. It was estimated that under Mansfield about 90 percent of the decisions were based on careful, preliminary decisions reached by the majority leader's staff, i.e., matching up requests with vacancies, applying the Johnson rule of one major committee assignment for every Democrat, and using the factor of seniority to help resolve competing claims for a committee seat. Of the remaining 10 percent of the cases where the staff failed to provide a recommendation which the Steering Committee considered acceptable, about half were settled by the Steering Committee through further discussion until a consensus was reached and about half were decided by secret ballot. Once again, this procedure deliberately curtailed Mansfield's opportunities for personally guiding the Steering Committee to a particular outcome; he concentrated instead on facilitating the discussion and stating the consensus of the committee members when it developed. This also provided an opportunity for factions within the Steering Committee to reach certain decisions which some segments of the party found to be inimical to the legislative agenda proposed by the president.[17]

Mansfield continued to follow the recognized procedure of the majority leader selecting the chairman and members of the Democratic Senatorial Campaign Committee, although he did not participate or attempt to control the committee's decisions on allocating funds among senators up for reelection. The majority leader simply gave the chairman a free hand in running and staffing the committee in whatever fashion he deemed appropriate.

Regardless of the forum, Mansfield displayed a remarkably consistent approach to his formal duties as Democratic leader: (1) He sought to decentralize and broaden the base of participation in the decision-making process; (2) he encouraged full and unstructured discussion of the matter in question; and (3) he limited his own participation primarily to that of neutral chairman and executor of the decisions finally reached. This strategy of leadership rested fundamentally on Mansfield's view of the coequal status of the majority leader with all members of the senatorial party and his rejection of the notion that the party leadership assumed special responsibility for leading the senatorial party in certain directions or affecting decisively the outcome of legislative decisions.

Floor business

Just as the conduct of business on the Senate floor reflected Johnson's strategy of leadership in various ways, Mansfield's style had its impact on the procedures and techniques used to handle bills during floor debate. As discussed above, the pace established by the individual committee chairmen determined in large measure the flow of bills to the calendar. The movement of bills from the calendar to the Senate floor was largely determined, in turn, by consultations between the majority and minority leaders and unstructured deliberations within the Policy Committee. Mansfield maintained this pattern of minimum control and intervention by the party leadership once legislation reached the Senate floor.

He instituted the practice of clearing the Senate calendar regularly of all noncontroversial items. The large majority of bills passed by the Senate, not requiring extensive floor debate, were approved immediately with the consent of both parties upon being called from the calendar. It was, however, within the province of the majority leader to hold certain of these bills on the calendar for extended periods of time, a practice which had been known to strengthen his bargaining position with senators whose help was being sought on other issues; i.e., cooperation with the majority leader's request increased the probability of the senator's legislation moving off the calendar. But in line with his established hands-off policy, Mansfield seldom used his position to delay action on these more minor bills otherwise ready for final passage. Mansfield would generally clear the Senate calendar of all noncontroversial "consent" items at least once every week of the session.

Once the floor debate on a bill was under way, the floor manager, usually the chairman of the committee or subcommittee reporting the legislation, assumed major responsibility for bringing it through in acceptable shape. Mansfield remained in the background, following the debate and standing ready to offer his assistance to the floor manager should it be requested. (Compare data on Johnson's activity in managing the floor debate with Mansfield's performance in this regard.) This aid was limited generally to the logistical tasks of locating absent senators, maintaining a quorum, working out with Dirksen agreements on the time to vote, arranging pairs for absent senators, and moving the Senate along to the next item of floor business. Only on rare occasions did Mansfield assume command of the specific tactics for passing a particular bill or attempt to use his influence as majority leader to round up crucial votes.

The application of Mansfield's strategy of decentralized and nondirective leadership fostered conditions on the Senate floor where unforeseen crises occasionally erupted in the midst of debate, and it placed a premium upon a senator's capacity for fast footwork and parliamentary improvisation.[18] Compared to the precise estimates of voting strength on every bill prepared under Johnson, the nose counts conducted by Mansfield and his staff were less frequent and sometimes inaccurate. In the later years of Mansfield's incumbency, the problem of accurate nose counts became less severe, primarily because the majority leader's staff had become better able to estimate quickly the doubtful senators on any bill. But Mansfield still remained opposed to the open nose counting that went on continually by Johnson and Baker.

Since Johnson's intelligence and communications system no longer functioned, it was more difficult to receive advance warnings of potential trouble, and less information existed about ways to resolve these difficulties once they were known. In these circumstances the business of floor leadership became more of a collective enterprise and drew upon the talents of lesser party officers, committee chairmen, legislative specialists from the White House, and other executive agencies as a means of executing certain essential leadership activities.

During his tenure as whip (1961–1964), Humphrey performed a number of tasks which Johnson had reserved to himself. He would, for example, often draw up nose counts on legislation in consultation with the Policy Committee and White House staff, the bill's floor manager, as well as lobbyists and other groups backing the legislation. Humphrey's departure in 1965, and the failure of his successor, Russel Long, to assume these duties, tended to bring executive branch officials and members of the standing committees more directly into the process of estimating voting strength and working out parliamentary obstacles prior to floor debate. Mansfield, moreover, appointed four assistant whips in 1966 to perform various routine functions on the floor and to increase the leadership's resources for controlling the debate more effectively. (Mansfield again turned to the members of the Legislative Review Committee, Hart, Inouye, Muskie and Brewster, in his decision to appoint assistant whips. This lessened whatever feelings might have existed that Mansfield had acted with uncharacteristic arbitrariness. As it developed, the assistant whips did little except relieve Mansfield of certain routine tasks, such as closing the Senate in the evening hours.) In short, these minimum tasks of floor leadership were not so much abandoned under Mansfield as they were taken over by persons other than the majority leader himself. But this necessarily resulted in a much less centralized system of floor management than existed under Johnson, one less able to predict and control the Senate's response to the president's legislative agenda.

On the other hand, Mansfield's great restraint in using the prerogatives of the majority leadership also produced certain advantages that contributed to the impressive record of achievement compiled during his tenure. Senators of both parties, for example, genuinely respected Mansfield's willingness to let the legislative process proceed with minimum interference from the party leadership. There developed among many senators a sense of obligation to live up to Mansfield's assumption that a senator would conduct himself responsibly and honorably; those Senators who abused the majority leader's permissiveness for personal advantage found themselves the object of their colleagues' opprobrium.

The Mansfield strategy encouraged greater individualism in the Senate and a broader participation of senators in important aspects of senatorial party life. Although he shunned the center stage himself, Mansfield could help others function in a more visible and self-satisfying way than was generally possible under Johnson. Since most senators valued this sense of greater importance and the attendant opportunities for personal recognition, they generally responded favorably to these policies despite their disappointment or frustration over a particular parliamentary crisis which might have been avoided through more forceful leadership.

This posture of encouraging greater individual participation by the majority leader dovetailed effectively with Mansfield's sense of the Senate's crucial role in the operations of the American democratic system and his willingness to encourage the Senate to function as an independent and self-respecting body, obligations of party notwithstanding. His occasional, outspoken statements on foreign policy reinforced this impression of the high value placed on personal and institutional independence and integrity. These attitudes also shielded Mansfield from any intimation that he was functioning solely as the spokesman for Presidents Kennedy and Johnson and ignoring the legitimate interests of the senatorial party.

In his relations with the Republicans, Mansfield established an unusual degree of trust and mutual respect. In recognition of his efforts to take their views into account and of his unfailing habit of consulting frequently with Minority Leader Dirksen, the Republicans seldom took any action which might have embarrassed Mansfield personally in the course of achieving some short-term partisan advantage. Moreover, blind obstructionism and partisan sniping were largely forsaken in the expression of the normal differences and disagreements between the parties over the major portions of the president's legislative program. One Republican senator, for example, described how he would often go to the floor in the late afternoon and deliberately snipe at Johnson, "just because Lyndon would always get mad and irritated." But this senator said he would never treat Mansfield in such fashion.

Some of the more active northern Democrats, however, expressed the view that Mansfield's strategy of leadership permitted, in effect, the organized factions within the Senate, principally the southern Democrats and conservative Republicans, to exercise more than their share of influence and control over the activities of the body.[10] They alleged that a lack of coordinated, positive initiative by the leadership allowed the Senate to entangle itself unnecessarily in parliamentary snarls and needlessly sacrificed elements of the presidential and senatorial party programs. Although the performance of the senatorial party under both Johnson and Mansfield will be evaluated later in this chapter, it is worth noting that many of the same senators who criticized Mansfield for lack of leadership also spoke out sharply against Johnson's brand of assertive and centralized direction of the senatorial party.

In evaluating the effectiveness of Mansfield's strategy, one must always remember that he served during the administrations of two active Democratic presidents. Following passage of the initial legislative program of President Kennedy, essentially holdovers from the Eisenhower years, the pace of legislative achievement slackened in both House and Senate. By the fall of 1963, party leaders were faced with a growing logjam of priority measures. Whether this logjam would have been broken in 1964 under Kennedy's leadership can never be known. But it is a fact that the shock over Kennedy's assassination and President Johnson's vigorous assumption of the Kennedy legislative program propelled the Congress into a period of great legislative accomplishment, one which was extended through the Eighty-ninth Congress by Johnson's landslide victory over Senator Goldwater and the election of large Democratic majorities in both houses of Congress. In sum, with the exception of the first nine months in 1963, Mansfield served during periods when a two to one Democratic margin in the Senate, combined with substantial momentum for action flowing from the White House, provided an environment ripe for legislative achievement. In these circumstances Mansfield did not face for any sustained period the burden of rationalizing substantial disparities of interest between a Democratic president and a Democratic senatorial party.

His posture of restraint also contributed to an environment within the Senate conducive to building a viable relationship between the legislative and executive branches, a relationship which made it possible for the Democratic senatorial majority to act without the likelihood of revolts caused by an overzealous application of leadership pressure in support of objectives established by the president in his capacity as chief of the executive branch. But despite Mansfield's ability to reduce the bickering and dissension caused by a feeling of executive coercion on major policy issues, the Senate's performance record might have been less impressive if other persons, such as Humphrey and the White House legislative operatives, had not moved in to assume certain more routine tasks of party leadership which the majority leader tended to avoid, e.g., nose counts and other prefloor planning and preparation.

Whether Mansfield's strategy of leadership would prove adequate in periods of greater partisanship, or if the size of the Democratic majority in the Senate was significantly reduced, is another question. Given the normal disparities between the interests of the president and the senatorial party, compounded by the impact of the separation of powers, the need for more forceful and self-conscious leadership would likely become evident. This situation would increase the desirability of the majority leader's greater use of the institutionalized powers at his disposal and of his attempts to augment these resources. But this judgment, even if true, cannot detract from the considerable record of accomplishment compiled by the senatorial party under Mansfield or dispel the affection and support which he received from other senatorial party members during his tenure as majority leader.[20]

Impact of the Johnson and Mansfield Leadership Strategies

This section will attempt to analyze the effect which a particular leadership strategy has on operations of the senatorial party as a whole. Similarly, this section will examine how changes in the senatorial party affected the strategy of the party leaders. The analysis will compare (1) the composition of party leadership, (2) the participation of senators in party activities, and (3) the performance of the senatorial parties during the Eighty-fifth and Eighty-sixth Congresses (1957–1960) with Johnson as majority leader and the Eighty-seventh and Eighty-eighth Congresses (1961–1964) under Mansfield.

Composition of party leadership

The Democratic Policy Committee is composed of all principal elected party leaders, although some serve ex officio, and other generally influential senators. This committee, especially for the majority Democrats, is more actively engaged in the on-going tasks of leadership, e.g., clearing legislation for the Senate floor, than any other established party instrumentality. For these reasons, the membership of the Democratic Policy Committee will be used as a means of analyzing the composition of the senatorial party leaders, e.g., geographical distribution, ideology, seniority, from the Eighty-fifth through the Eighty-eighth Congresses.

This analysis will attempt to delineate more precisely the effect of a given leadership strategy on the instrumentalities of senatorial party leadership, as well as the impact of the political environment, especially the composition of the senatorial party, on the nature of the strategy itself. This complex, often reciprocal, relationship is largely interstitial in nature and difficult to quantify. Yet the highly unstructured nature of the majority leadership suggests that the incumbent must take account of various internal party pressures, but that a measure of latitude also exists for his initiating changes in the party apparatus to correspond to his concept of party leadership.

Although one cannot hope to "prove" which force was dominant in a given set of circumstances, it may be possible to document and illustrate trends which support the foregoing descriptions of the leadership strategies of Johnson and Mansfield. These trends will provide additional insight and understanding as to the capacity of the senatorial party leaders for controlling the performance of the Senate itself and their limitations in this regard.

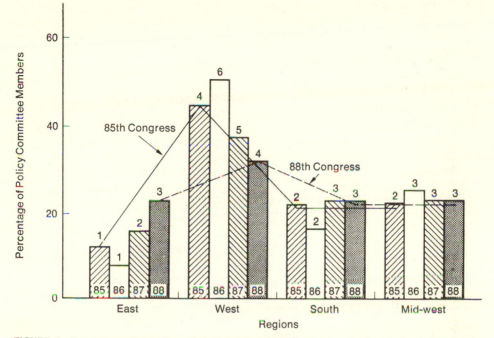

FIGURE 1 Percentage distribution of Democratic Policy Committee members, by region, Eighty-fifth and Eighty-sixth Congresses. In the Eighty-fifth Congress, the Policy Committee was composed of seven regular members and two ex officio members. In the Eighty-sixth Congress three ex officio members were added with the inclusion of the Legislative Review Committee. In the Eighty-seventh and Eighty-eighth Congresses a fourth member of the Legislative Review Committee was added to the Policy Committee.

Both Johnson and Mansfield conceived of the Policy Committee, among its other functions, as a forum for the representation of major geographical and ideological factions within the senatorial party, although neither leader attempted to achieve an exact correlation between a group's strength in the party and its numerical representation on the Policy Committee. However, Mansfield's greater restraint in directing the decisions of the committee and his greater reliance on these decisions in determining the Senate's schedule of floor business would suggest the wisdom of his guaranteeing all principal elements of the party ready access to the committee's deliberations through reasonably equitable representation on the committee. To the extent that the committee became a place where genuine decisions were made affecting the outcome of legislation, senators would likely be more concerned that their views receive adequate recognition and attention on it. They would want to be assured of dependable allies among the committee members.[21]

Figure 1 compares the percentage distribution by region of Democratic Policy Committee members during the Eighty-fifth through Eighty-eighth Congresses. The more nearly horizontal path of the broken line, signifying the distribution by region in the Eighty-eighth Congress, contrasts clearly with the more irregular path of the solid line, denoting the distribution in the Eighty-fifth Congress under Johnson, one highlighted by a marked concen-

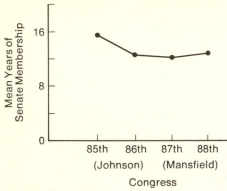

FIGURE 2 Mean years of Senate member-ship of Democratic Policy Committee mem-bers, Eighty-fifth through Eighty-eighth Con-gresses.

tration of western senators. When one takes into account the Democratic practice of retaining incumbent Policy Committee members from one Con-gress to the next, Mansfield nonethe-less reduced the percentage differential among regions from a low of 12 per-cent for the East and a high of 44 per-cent for the West found in 1957 to a low of 23 percent for the East, South, and Midwest and a high of 31 percent for the West in 1964. In essence, Mansfield achieved this greater balance within the committee, albeit one which still did not correspond to the regional distribution within the senatorial party as a whole, by increasing eastern repre-sentation at the expense of the western states. The de facto expansion of the Policy Committee from nine to twelve members which took place under John-son in 1959 with the addition of the three freshmen members of the Legis-lative Review Committee provided Mansfield with two (Muskie of Maine and Brewster of Maryland) of these three eastern seats. (John Pastore of Rhode Island, appointed by Mansfield to the Policy Committee in 1961, pro-vided the third eastern member.) The greater equality among regions was

also in line with the resolution adopted in 1961 by the Party Conference direct-ing a more equitable distribution in the membership of party committees.

This broadening of the access of the Democratic senatorial party to the Policy Committee is indicated by other criteria. Figure 2 illustrates the reduc-tion that occurred between the Eighty-fifth and Eighty-eighth Congresses in mean years of Senate membership of Policy Committee members. The pri-mary drop—from 15.8 years in the Sen-ate during the Eighty-fifth Congress to 13.3 years in the Ninety-sixth Congress —correspond with Johnson's decision to include freshmen senators of the Legislative Review Committee as ex officio members, a decision which rep-resented *his* response to the altered na-ture of his senatorial constituency.

Figure 3 uses the annual ranking of senators released by the Americans for Democratic Action (ADA) to gain some rough approximation of the relative liberal–conservative distribution on the Policy Committee.[22] Figure 3 illus-trates the same trend noted above, that Johnson's decision in the Eighty-sixth Congress to include the Legislative Re-view Committee members produced a

FIGURE 3 Median ADA score for Democratic Policy Committee members, Eighty-fifth through Eighty-eighth Congresses.

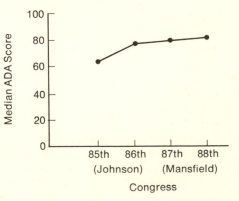

noticeable change from the preceding Congress and, in this case, a rise from sixty-four to seventy-eight in the median ADA score of Policy Committee members. This upward trend toward a more "liberal" Policy Committee continued under Mansfield and corresponded to the influx of generally liberal Democratic senators in the 1960 and 1962 elections.

Finally, Figure 4, which illustrates the percentage of Policy Committee members who also served as committee chairmen, suggests that Johnson's conception of the Policy Committee serving as a forum of major power holders in the senatorial party was clearly modified in the Eighty-sixth Congress as the percentage of committee chairmen dropped from 67 percent to 50 percent, a change again illustrating the effect of the 1958 election on Johnson's leadership strategy. One must, however, acknowledge an obvious fact: A reduction in the percentage caused primarily by expanding the size of the committee with freshmen senators was not likely to affect in any significant fashion the influence of the chairmen who served on the committee prior to the expansion. Access to the councils of the Policy Committee did not guarantee influence, especially for freshmen senators during Johnson's tenure as majority leader. But it is noteworthy that of the seven Democrats added to the Policy Committee by Mansfield, only one (Magnuson) also served as a committee chairman. By the Eighty-eighth Congress, as noted in Figure 4, less than half (46 percent) of the Policy Committee members held committee chairmanships.

In summary, these data support two principal conclusions: First, although the Johnson and Mansfield strategies differed greatly both in conception and execution, both leaders responded to the political environment which pre-

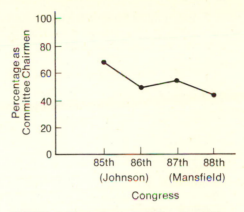

FIGURE 4 Percentage of Policy Committee members also serving as committee chairmen, Eighty-fifth through Eighty-eighth Congresses.

vailed during their respective tenures through adjustments in the composition of the Democratic Policy Committee, the principal party instrumentality related to the on-going duties of the leadership. The leadership structure began to change with Johnson's response to the 1958 congressional election by his adding the Legislative Review Committee members to the committee. These trends continued under Mansfield, trends away from a Policy Committee dominated by the more conservative southern and western senators, with relatively high seniority, and with a high complement of committee chairmen, to a Policy Committee more evenly balanced geographically, with greater liberal representation, less seniority, and fewer committee chairmen.

Second, these data are also consistent with the notion shared by both Johnson and Mansfield that the major factions of the senatorial party should have some measure of representation in the deliberations of the Policy Committee, as well as the additional proposition that Mansfield's strategy of leadership would call for greater access to the Policy Committee by the major groups within the senatorial party. By the Eighty-eighth Congress the committee's composition had shifted considerably to accommodate the enlarged ranks of the northern Democrats in comparison to the more senior and conservative membership of the committee in the Eighty-fifth Congress.

Participation of senators in senatorial party activity

Much has been made of Johnson's decision in 1953 to guarantee one major committee assignment to every senatorial party member regardless of seniority. But since Johnson retained control of the assignment process, this action was not inconsistent with his attempts to maintain tight control of the opportunities for participation by individual senators in most legislative activities. These opportunities were generally dispensed with an eye toward enhancing the majority leader's personal influence in directing the operations of the senatorial party: Some process of rationing was necessary to preserve the value of this currency for

subsequent bargaining and negotiation. Given Mansfield's disposition to see these opportunities expanded as part of his general decentralization of leadership responsibilities and lacking any workable procedures for rationing or control by the majority leader, one would expect to find greater participation by individual senators across a broad spectrum of senatorial party activities.

For example, in describing Johnson's and Mansfield's conduct as party leaders earlier in this chapter, it was noted that a greater number of Party Conferences and Policy Committee meetings were called by Mansfield than by Johnson. Figure 5 portrays the extent of this increase—from only two Party Conferences convened by Johnson in the Eighty-fifth Congress to twelve conferences called by Mansfield in the Eighty-eighth, as illustrated by the solid line, and from eight Policy Committee meetings in the Eighty-fifth to a peak of nineteen in the Eighty-seventh (which subsequently declined again to fifteen in the Eighty-eighth), as noted by the broken line. As in other areas of senatorial party behavior, the effect of the 1958 elections is reflected in the differences between the Eighty-fifth and Eighty-sixth Congresses: The liberal Democrats called for more involvement in party affairs and Johnson responded.[23] But Mansfield exceeded these higher levels of activity in both the Eighty-seventh and Eighty-eighth Congresses. Moreover, under Mansfield the number of Party Conferences approximately doubled from Johnson's high of six in the Eighty-sixth Congress, whereas the increase of Policy Committee meetings under Mansfield proved to be much smaller; e.g., in the Eighty-eighth Congress, Mansfield held fifteen meetings, only one more than Johnson called in the Eighty-sixth Congress. This would appear consistent with

FIGURE 5   Number of party conferences and policy committee meetings convened by Johnson and Mansfield, Eighty-fifth through Eighty-eighth Congresses.

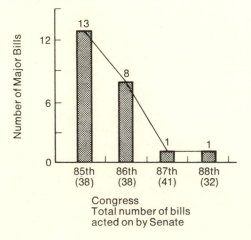

Congress
Total number of bills acted on by Senate

Mansfield's inclination toward encouraging a broader base of participating in party activities: The Party Conference involves *every* Democratic senator; the Policy Committee does not.

Figure 6 compares the number of times Johnson performed the dominant role in managing the floor debate on major legislation listed by Congressional Quarterly, Inc., in its weekly congressional boxscore during the Eighty-fifth and Eighty-sixth Congresses with the similar activity by Mansfield in the Eighty-seventh and Eighty-eighth. Although in many instances Johnson was not the official floor manager for the bill in question, that designation usually going to the chairman of the standing committee or subcommittee reporting the legislation, he nevertheless took active and visible control of proceedings on the floor by such actions as propounding unanimous consent requests to limit debate on the bill, allocating time for debate among senators under the terms of the unanimous consent agreement, recognizing senators to offer amendments, replying to opposition arguments, and delivering the closing statement prior to the final vote. In this sense he assumed the dominant if not controlling position on thirteen major bills in the Eighty-fifth Congress and on eight bills in the Eighty-sixth. Mansfield, however, performed this function only once in each of the Eighty-seventh and Eighty-eighth Congresses.

Johnson performed this role on a broad spectrum of legislation, including, among others, the Mideast Doctrine resolution, foreign aid, civil rights, federal pay raise, Hells Canyon authorization, reciprocal trade, creation of a space agency, housing, mutual security funds, corporate excise taxes, and increase of the debt limit. Mansfield took charge of the extension of the Civil Rights Commission and the ex-

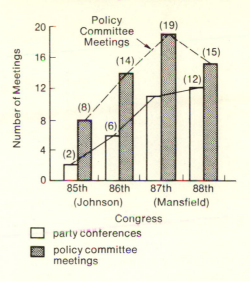

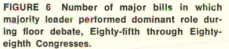

FIGURE 6 Number of major bills in which majority leader performed dominant role during floor debate, Eighty-fifth through Eighty-eighth Congresses.
Source: *Congressional Quarterly Almanac* (Washington, D.C.: Congressional Quarterly, Inc.), final congressional boxscore of major legislation for each session.

tended struggle to enact a constitutional amendment dealing with the apportionment of state legislatures.

Figure 7 portrays the increase in the percentage of amendments offered to major bills by first-term senators from the Eighty-fifth to the Eighty-eighth Congresses. In order to obtain a more meaningful comparison between the amendments offered under Johnson and Mansfield, these data *exclude* the amendments offered to the Communications Satellite bill in the Eighty-seventh Congress and the Civil Rights bill in the Eighty-eighth Congress. In both instances abnormally large numbers of amendments were introduced prior to cloture. Although Wayne Morse (Oreg.) qualified technically as a first-term Democrat when he switched parties in the Eighty-fourth Congress, his prior experience in the Senate and

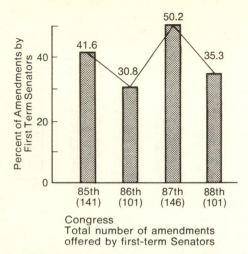

Congress
Total number of amendments
offered by first-term Senators

FIGURE 7 Percentage of amendments to major bills offered by first-term senators, Eighty-fifth through Eighty-eighth Congresses. Source: *Congressional Quarterly Almanac* (Washington, D.C.: Congressional Quarterly, Inc.), final congressional boxscore of major legislation for each session.

his restoration to seniority on committees by Johnson dictated that his amendments not be counted in the first-term category. Of special interest is the increase from 30.8 percent in the Eighty-sixth Congress under Johnson to 50.2 percent in the Eighty-seventh Congress under Mansfield. Although not included in Figure 7, the percentage for the *Democratic* first termers jumped from 20.2 percent in the Eighty-sixth to 27.5 percent in the Eighty-seventh, despite the advent of a Democratic president whose bills necessarily were the object of the Democrats' amendments.

These data support the earlier description of Mansfield's preference for remaining in the background during floor debate and Johnson's tendency to take charge. More than this, however, these figures also illustrate the greater opportunities for *all* senators, even first termers, to participate more actively under Mansfield in the process

of debating and amending major legislation on the Senate floor. To this degree, the *potential* for a decrease in leadership control also increased as the floor became more of an arena open to all senatorial party members. This also suggests the likelihood of committee chairmen becoming more dominant in making crucial decisions on the floor. This was, in fact, an additional result of Mansfield's strategy, since he relied heavily on committee chairmen for assuming the management of legislation up for debate. Finally, these data are consistent with the increased need for presidential or other executive branch assistance in executing certain routine but essential tasks of leadership, such as estimating voting strength and lining up votes of crucial senators. With a less visibly active majority leadership, the committee chairmen or the other senators managing a major bill generally welcomed whatever additional help they could get.

Performance of the senatorial party under Johnson and Mansfield

Despite their many differences, both the Johnson and Mansfield strategies of leadership were, in part, functional responses to the prevailing political environment. Were these responses successful?

One must first recognize the difficulty of identifying hard criteria to use in defending and justifying a more explicit analysis of the senatorial party's performance under a given strategy of leadership. What recognized guidelines exist for rating party leaders in the performance of their duties? How does one measure their impact on *any* legislative situation? What should one expect from a majority leader with a two-seat majority, such as Johnson had in the Eighty-fifth Congress, in comparison to a thirty-seat majority, which he acquired after the 1958 elections? And what should one expect from Mansfield with a two to one Democratic majority and a Democrat in the White House?

These questions are posed only to illustrate the highly tentative and generalized conclusions which must result from such an inquiry, given the multitude of variables and the lack of any recognized standards of judgment on which to anchor one's evaluation. But despite these reservations, two questions seem particularly relevant to raise in light of the decentralized and nondirective strategy followed so consistently by Mansfield: (1) Were there evidences of declining Democratic support for senatorial party programs during the period of this study, the Eighty-seventh and Eighty-eighth Congresses? (2) Were there measurable signs of other significant breakdowns in the structure or operations of the senatorial party in this period? Although it is impossible to establish a direct, causal relationship regardless of what the data may reveal, a decisive decline in the performance of the senatorial party in either category would, in combination with the earlier analysis of Mansfield's conduct, raise some serious doubts about the viability of his leadership strategy.

In considering the first question, Figure 8 reveals that on all "party unity" roll call votes, i.e., where a majority of one party opposed a majority of the other, the winning percentage for the Democrats rose significantly under Mansfield as compared to the levels achieved during Johnson's tenure. The thirty-seat majority stemming from the 1958 election was surely a major factor in the initial increase from 49.5 percent in the Eighty-fifth Congress to 69.8 percent in the Eighty-sixth. It also seems probable that Kennedy's victory in 1960 contributed to the 95.7 percentage

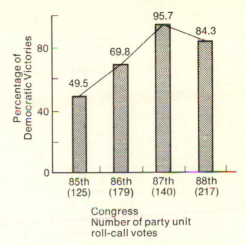

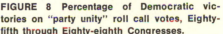

FIGURE 8 Percentage of Democratic victories on "party unity" roll call votes, Eighty-fifth through Eighty-eighth Congresses.
Source: *Congressional Quarterly Almanac* (Washington, D.C.: Congressional Quarterly, Inc.).

in the Eighty-seventh. But the major point is this: The votes *were* delivered under Mansfield.

The expected rise in the presidential support scores for both the party leaders and all Democrats is reflected in Figure 9.[24] But it is also noteworthy that during Mansfield's tenure the Democratic party leaders, as represented by the members of the Policy Committee, scored consistently higher than the party as a whole, suggesting that at least in relation to presidential legislative initiatives, Mansfield's deliberate decentralization of leadership functions did not produce among the beneficiaries of this policy any slackening in their willingness to support the senatorial party program. In other words, their greater freedom and responsibility did not go to their heads.

Stability of party structure is more difficult to evaluate by any quantitative measure. The index of cohesion, however, provides a simple tool for comparing relative unity of legislative parties or other groups. In this instance

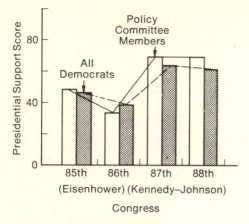

FIGURE 9 Composite presidential support scores for all Democrats and Policy Committee members, Eighty-fifth through Eighty-eighth Congresses.
Source: *Congressional Quarterly Almanac* (Washington, D.C.: Congressional Quarterly, Inc.).

the index measures, first, the difference between the percentage of all Democratic senators voting for and the percentage voting against a given motion. An exact split among the Democrats would produce an index of zero; the party would be completely divided. Unanimity on a roll call would produce an index of one hundred. Second, the index of cohesion is used to make a similar comparison of the Democratic party leadership, i.e., the members of the majority Policy Committee.[25]

Figure 10 portrays the mean indices among all Democratic senators and among Democratic party leaders for twelve key roll call votes selected by Congressional Quarterly, Inc. (CQ), for each of the Eighty-fifth through Eighty-eighth Congresses. These were the roll calls which, in the opinion of CQ, were of greatest significance in each Congress and, in most cases, were among the most controversial and bitterly contested. Marked divisions among all Democrats or the leaders on these votes would at least raise questions as

to the stability of the senatorial party during these Congresses.

The lowest figure of 26.2 for all Democrats recorded in the Eighty-fifth Congress stems primarily from the several key votes on the 1957 civil rights bill which sharply divided northern and southern Democrats. By the Eighty-sixth Congress, however, the increase of pro-civil rights senators resulting from the 1958 elections greatly offset the continued opposition among southern Democrats during the 1960 civil rights debate. Given the clear rise of Democratic cohesion on the key roll calls of the Eighty-eighth Congress, the negligible decline from the Eighty-sixth to the Eighty-seventh cannot be viewed as evidence of serious internal problems during Mansfield's incumbency, especially when the extremely high percentage of "party unity" victories achieved in the Eighty-seventh is also considered. Moreover, the greater co-

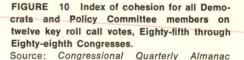

FIGURE 10 Index of cohesion for all Democrats and Policy Committee members on twelve key roll call votes, Eighty-fifth through Eighty-eighth Congresses.
Source: *Congressional Quarterly Almanac* (Washington, D.C.: Congressional Quarterly, Inc.).

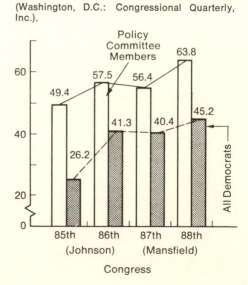

hesiveness among party leaders in comparison to all Democratic senators evident during Johnson's tenure continued under Mansfield. In sum, the key roll calls failed to reveal evidence of any serious breakdowns in the structure or operations of the senatorial party under Mansfield. Levels of cohesion comparable to those recorded during Johnson's incumbency were recorded in the Eighty-seventh Congress and surpassed in the Eighty-eighth. These results are in accord with the generally favorable reaction to the Mansfield strategy among party leaders and Democrats discussed earlier.

It is not necessary to establish a direct causal relationship between the legislative successes of the Democratic senatorial party and the operations of the Mansfield strategy of leadership during the Eighty-seventh and the Eighty-eighth Congresses. Indeed, given the fact of a vigorous Democratic president during these years and other elements of the prevailing political environment discussed earlier, such an effort to establish a direct linkage would not only be difficult to execute but probably misleading as well. It is, rather, sufficient to demonstrate that the Mansfield system operated functionally, that the party's two to one majority was used effectively on most crucial votes, that adequate levels of presidential support were maintained, and that the party and the leadership demonstrated adequate levels of cohesion on key roll call votes. The data suggests that these requirements were met: Despite the dispersal of many tasks of party leadership and the generally permissive if not at times passive attitude displayed by the majority leader in managing the legislative program, the senatorial party in the Eighty-seventh and Eighty-eighth Congresses functioned effectively, and its performance compared favorably with

and often surpassed the record compiled by the Eighty-fifth and Eighty-sixth Congresses under the driving and centralized leadership of Lyndon Johnson.

The Role of Senatorial Party Leaders: Some Propositions

Despite the differences between Johnson and Mansfield in the conception and execution of the majority leadership, there are nevertheless certain propositions about the role of party leadership per se which appear justified by the foregoing analysis:

1. The prevailing political environment will be a major factor in determining the content and success of a majority leader's strategy of leadership. Indeed, pressures within the senatorial party as well as the party affiliation and expected conduct of the president may even influence the choice of majority leader. The composition and expectations of the majority Democrats in 1961 made it difficult to conceive of their selecting a replacement for Johnson who would have continued his highly aggressive and centralized leadership. Johnson's conduct after the 1958 congressional elections, moreover, suggested that he would have made significant adjustments in his strategy if he had remained as majority leader in the Kennedy administration. As suggested by the marked differences between two leaders, however, there also exists latitude for the majority leader to devise a leadership strategy which takes into account his personal objectives and particular skills.

2. Regardless of the political environment or the personal objectives and skills of the majority leader, he will be faced with a deficit of institutionalized power which must be compensated for in some fashion if he is to establish

adequate control over the Senate's response to the president's legislative agenda. This deficit of leadership power can be traced fundamentally to the nature of the two-party system and the effect of the separation of powers on the standing of the Senate among the institutions of government.

3. In establishing adequate control over the Senate's response to the president's programs, the majority leader will likely give priority to methods which permit individual senators to serve their interests by the outcome. In his efforts to control the choices available to senators in a given legislative situation, Johnson gave priority to relatively short-term political or legislative objectives held by individual senators. Mansfield, on the other hand, was more concerned with appealing to the interests of senators in preserving the reputation of the Senate as a responsible and effective participant in the governmental process and in senators performing identifiable and self-satisfying roles in the legislative process.

4. Granting the impact which procedure can have on substantive decisions, the majority leader's position within the senatorial party makes him better equipped to control the *way* a decision is reached than to affect its substance. His use of his limited institutionalized powers and his methods for augmenting these powers will affect primarily his control over such matters as the scheduling and management of legislation on the Senate floor and the opportunity for other senators to participate in these procedural decisions.

5. If the majority leader is better equipped to affect the procedures of senatorial decision making, the president and the chairmen and members of the standing committees are more dominant in deciding matters of substance. For example, the president's legislative agenda, more than any other single factor, will define the issues likely to occupy the Senate and will establish a range of responses which the Senate is likely to make. Whether or not the committee chairmen choose to cooperate with the president on policy matters will be a major factor in determining the nature of this response, in addition to affecting the problems likely to be confronted by the majority leader.

6. Despite the president's dominance on questions of substance and the majority leader's influence on procedure, both are likely to consider activities on the Senate floor, the parliamentary dimension of Senate life, as more relevant and congenial to their respective objectives than the operations of the committee system, the working dimension of Senate life. Even for Johnson, the Senate floor was the place where his dominance could become visible and his capacity for control fully demonstrated. There exists an affinity of interest between the majority leader and the president to preserve the legitimacy of the floor as a place for reaching meaningful decisions. Moreover, the majority leader and the president will usually find it mutually profitable to bolster their respective abilities to influence procedure and substance, i.e., the majority leader can help the president by devising procedures which foster certain substantive results; the president can work for these ends in a way which makes the procedure possible to execute. There are, however, definite limits to which one can productively assist the other: The majority leader, in particular, cannot appear simply in the guise of presidential operative or apologist.

NOTES

1. The descriptions of leadership strategy of Lyndon Johnson and Mike Mansfield are compiled from various published sources, interviews, and, in the case of Mansfield, the personal observations of the author. The most useful published works include: Rowland Evans and Robert Novak, *Lyndon B. Johnson: The Exercise of Power* (New York: The New American Library, 1966); William S. White, *Citadel: The Story of the U. S. Senate* (New York: Harper and Brothers, 1956); Ralph Huitt, "Democratic Party Leadership in the Senate," *American Political Science Review,* Vol. 55 (June, 1961); Stewart Alsop, "Lyndon Johnson: How Does He Do It?" *Saturday Evening Post,* January 24, 1959, p. 13; William S. White, "The Two Texans Who Will Run Congress," *New York Times Magazine,* December 30, 1956, p. 5; Walter Lippmann, "Johnson and His Cities," *Washington Post and Times Herald,* July 9, 1959, p. A21; "Mr. Johnson's Leadership," *ibid.,* April 10, 1959, p. A12; F. W. Collins, "How To Be a Leader without Leading," *New York Times Magazine,* July 30, 1961, p. 9; "Why Kennedy's Program Is in Trouble with Congress," *U. S. News and World Report,* September 17, 1962, pp. 62–69; Mary McGrory, "Chaos in the Senate: Days without End," 109, *America,* 653; "I Am What I Am: Mansfield Answers Critics," *U. S. News and World Report,* December 9, 1963, p. 20; "Senate: A Crisis in Leadership," *Newsweek,* November 18, 1963, p. 21; "Interview with Hon. Mike Mansfield, U. S. Senator from the State of Montana," *U. S. Congressional Record,* 88th Cong., 1st Sess., 1963, 109, 22,862–65.

2. Johnson served in the House of Representatives from the seventy-fifth to the eightieth Congress (1937–48). Elected to the Senate in 1948, he was chosen in 1950 to succeed the defeated Francis Myers (Pa.), as majority whip. With the defeat of Majority Leader Ernest McFarland (Arizona) by Barry Goldwater in 1952, Johnson rose to the position of minority leader in the eighty-third Congress (1953–54) and became majority leader upon the Democrats' capture of the eighty-fourth Congress in the congressional elections of 1954; see *U. S. Congressional Directory,* ninetieth Cong., 2nd Sess., 1968, p. 417.

3. One should not, however, reach the erroneous conclusion that all southern Democrats performed in this fashion. Without much publicity or recognition by the general public, some southerners in these years were loyal and consistent supporters of the Democratic party program, e.g., Hill and Sparkman of Alabama, Scott of North Carolina, Johnston of South Carolina, Fulbright of Arkansas.

4. The majority leader's "right" of recognition rests solely on custom; the Standing Rules and precedents are silent on the matter, stressing instead that "the Chair should recognize the Senator who first addresses him, but the question of recognition is one within the province of the Chair from which no appeal will lie." But the fact that the practice does stem from custom makes it unlikely that any majority leader would attempt to abuse it. See Charles L. Watkins and Floyd M. Riddick, *Senate Procedure: Precedents and Practice* (Washington, D.C.: U. S. Government Printing Office, 1958), pp. 468–70.

5. In these years of Johnson's leadership the Democratic membership of the Senate stood as follows: eighty-third Congress (1953–54), 47; eighty-fourth Congress (1955–56), 48; eighty-fifth Congress (1957–58), 49; eighty-sixth Congress (1959–60), 64.

6. For example, in 1959 he noted that the Democrats "have, by our majority here, an obligation to lead. We do not have authority to command. . . .

Our mandate is a mandate for confident and creative leadership, beginning now, not two years hence. We shall honor that mandate. . . ." See
The New York Times, January 8, 1959, p. 14.

7. Among the more outspoken were Proxmire of Wisconsin, McNamara of
Michigan, Clark of Pennsylvania, Douglas of Illinois, Gore of Tennessee
and Carroll of Colorado. McNamara wrote the majority leader that Democratic conferences were too rare, and that this hampered the Democratic Party's capacity to deal with the issues facing the country. See
Evans and Novak, *op. cit.,* p. 197.

8. Among the principal Democratic and Republican party committees in the
Senate, only the Policy Committee has a statutory base. Stricken from
the Legislative Reorganization Act of 1946 at the insistence of Speaker of
the House Rayburn, the majority and minority Policy Committees were
created in the Senate by the party leaders inserting a line item in the
Legislative Branch Appropriations Act of 1947. *60 U. S. Statutes at Large*
(1947) 911. The other principal party committees, i.e., the Senatorial
Campaign Committees and the Steering Committee (Committee on Committees for the Republicans) are creatures of the Party Conference.

9. The Republicans limit membership on their Policy Committee to periods
of two years; members cannot succeed themselves but can be reap-
pointed after a lapse of two years; also the members are appointed by
the chairman of the Party Conference subject to its approval; the other
major party officers are ex officio members. The Democrats impose
no limitation on the number of years a senator may serve. See also
Hugh A. Bone, "An Introduction to the Senate Policy Committees," *American Political Science Review,* 50 (June, 1956), 339–59.

10. For a more detailed discussion of the Senatorial Campaign Committees
see Hugh A. Bone, "Some Notes on the Congressional Campaign Committees," *The Western Political Quarterly,* 9 (March, 1956), 134.

11. The Democratic whip, Earle Clements of Kentucky, held this chairmanship during the eighty-third and eighty-fourth Congresses, and, after his
defeat in 1956, continued to serve as Executive Director of the Committee. George Smathers of Florida assumed the chairmanship in the
eighty-fifth and eighty-sixth Congresses. *Congressional Quarterly Almanac, 1953* (Washington, D.C.: Congressional Quarterly, Inc., 1954), p.
17; *Congressional Quarterly Almanac, 1957,* p. 14.

12. See the excellent chapter, "Too Many Democrats," in Evans and Novak,
op. cit., pp. 193–224.

13. As quoted to the author by a participant at the Democratic Conference,
January 10, 1967.

14. In the opinion of Congressional Quarterly, the major items of the Democratic backlog which passed in the eighty-seventh Congress included
minimum wage legislation, distressed areas, social security benefits,
omnibus housing, water pollution, and public works. *Congress and the
Nation* (Washington, D.C.: Congressional Quarterly, Inc., 1965), p. 41.

15. But Johnson did on occasion preside over the Democratic Conference,
e.g., February 27, 1961, February 7, 1963; author's notes, July 18, 1967,
Washington, D.C.

16. This point was made frequently to the author in his interviews concerning
Mansfield's leadership strategy.

17. This view was expressed by Senator Clark of Pennsylvania in his well-
publicized speeches on "the Senate Establishment" delivered on the

Senate floor in February, 1963, following the Steering Committee's assignments for the eighty-eighth Congress. He charged that "when the Democratic steering committee met, it became obvious that in filling committee membership vacancies, the establishment would ignore seniority when to ignore it would strengthen the establishment's control, but would follow it when to do so would have the same result." *Congressional Record*, 109, *op. cit.*, 2,559.

18. For example, note the disorganization surrounding the votes on the Morton jury trial amendments during the debate on the Civil Rights Act of 1964. See Chapter VI, pp. 233–35.

19. The most publicized outburst was delivered spontaneously on the Senate floor by Thomas Dodd (D., Conn.), on November 6, 1963. He said (*Congressional Record*, 109, *op. cit.*, 21,247): "Mike Mansfield is a gentleman, Senators, we are of one mind about that. . . . But I worry about his leadership. He must assume it . . . he must behave like a leader. Because a leader is one who leads. . . ." He apologized the next day, noting: (*ibid.*, p. 21,372) "I felt this morning somewhat like a skunk at a lawn party . . . I fear I was harder than I meant to be last night toward him. . . ."

20. On November 27, 1963, Mansfield delivered on the Senate floor a strong defense of the Senate's record of accomplishment in the eighty-eighth Congress, at least partially motivated by the rising chorus of criticism directed against himself and the institution for its failure to pass major portions of the Kennedy program. He observed (*ibid.*, p. 22,862): "I shall not don any Mandarin's robes . . . in order that I may look like a majority leader or sound like a majority leader, however a majority leader is supposed to look or sound."

21. Truman, *op. cit.*, pp. 132–33; David Truman's conclusions as to the principal thrust of Policy Committee activities in the eighty-first Congress are relevant at this juncture; he writes: ". . . it may not be unreasonable to say that the Policy Committee is properly named. . . . Its importance rests principally upon its value as a center of communication and upon its connections with the Floor Leader's part in setting the Senate schedule, but in a group of this sort this may be far from trivial."

22. The ADAs annual ratings of members of Congress consist of selected roll-call votes which, in the opinion of that organization, raise issues of special concern for "liberals." Between ten and fourteen votes are generally chosen for each congressional session. The numerical scores are compiled on the basis of each senator's vote on these key issues. ADA ratings are also used in John G. Stewart, *op. cit.*, Chapter III to help analyze the Senate's reaction to efforts at restricting the body's prerogative of extended debate.

23. If one includes the number of party conferences called by Johnson in the eighty-third and eighty-fourth Congesses, the increase under Mansfield, as well as Johnson's change in the eighty-sixth Congress is even more striking. In the eighty-third Congress (1953–54), only two conferences were held; in the eighty-fourth Congress (1955–56), only one. Even Joseph Clark, persistent critic of the Democratic party leadership, acknowledges Mansfield's efforts to make the party conference more of a viable instrument of the senatorial party; he writes, "The Democratic Party has been resuscitated to some extent under the leadership of Senator Mike Mansfield." See Joseph S. Clark, *Congress: The Sapless Branch* (New York: Harper & Row, 1964), p. 120.

24. *Congressional Quarterly* computed its presidential support scores for each senator on the basis of their votes on roll calls, covering both foreign and domestic issues, on which the president took a public position. These numbered 155 roll calls in the eighty-fifth and 207 in the eighty-sixth under Eisenhower, and 249 in the eighty-seventh and 212 in the eighty-eighth under Kennedy and Johnson.

25. The index of cohesion was developed by S. A. Rice, *Quantitative Methods in Politics* (New York: Alfred A. Knopf, 1928), pp. 208–9.

6

ARTHUR VANDENBERG AND THE SENATE

DEAN ACHESON

It is not uncommon in societies ruled by aristocrats for the affairs of state to fall into the hands of men who in their later years adopt the gentle occupation of public reminiscence. Often enough, in these societies, a life of great states-manship is merely the prelude to a legacy of great memoirs. A quick glance at the writings (not to speak of the collected oratory) of American officials will in-dicate how far the United States is from aristocratic governance. We do require literacy of our public men—at least literacy sufficient to follow the spastic move-ments of a teleprompter or a neatly typed, double-spaced, one-page memoran-dum. But literary distinction of the quality that Dean Acheson parades in his memoirs is quite another matter. Fifty years ago he came from Harvard Law School to Washington to clerk for Mr. Justice Brandeis. Since then, as adviser to Democratic presidents, sometime high officer in the Treasury and State departments, senior partner in the capital city's most prestigious law firm, he has been at the center of our national life.

His account of the postwar Senate, with which, as President Truman's Secre-tary of State he had to deal, is a valuable evocation of those last days of relative calm and insularity before the Senate became an important staging area for the mounting of campaigns for the presidency.

The first time I worked with Senator Arthur H. Vandenberg was fairly early in the course of that change in his out-look on the world which one might call his long day's journey into our times. He had been, to use his own descrip-tion of himself, one of those "who had been so-called 'isolationists' prior to

"Arthur Vandenberg and the Senate" from *Sketches From Life of Men I Have Known* by Dean Acheson. Copyright © 1961 by Dean Acheson (pp. 123–132 originally appeared under the title "Journey Into Our Times" in *American Heritage Magazine*, February 1960. Copyright © 1960 by American Heritage Pub-lishing Co., Inc.). Reprinted by permission of Harper & Row, Publishers, Inc., and American Heritage Publishing Co., Inc.

Pearl Harbor." But "that day," he wrote later, "ended isolationism for any realist." The change in outlook was far advanced by January 10, 1945, when he took the floor of the Senate to urge an international organization with far-reaching powers to revise war settlements and to enforce peace.

This was a long road. Despite his dramatic words about Pearl Harbor —words of hindsight—Vandenberg's change of mind did not come in a sud-den flash like that other change on the road to Damascus. I have heard him ascribe it mainly to his work with Secretary Hull and the "Committee of

Eight," the special Senate committee on postwar plans. This group met for the first time on April 25, 1944. Here he was thrown, without prior experience or knowledge, into the most involved international problems since the Congress of Vienna. He was to spend the seven years of life which remained to him immersed in these problems. The experience brought out all his many and great talents. It led, too, to a unique service not only to his own country but, ironically enough, to peoples whose affairs and interests he had believed only a short time before to be no concern of his or of his country's.

My first work with the Senator began before the Committee of Eight had been formed. It was in the summer of 1943. Arthur Vandenberg was in a period of deep frustration. He was very much on the outside trying to look in; and he could see nothing. Suspicion consumed him—suspicion, in his own words, of "Executive dictatorship," "by-passing the Senate," "flouting of the Constitution"; suspicion, also, that our Allies were already using for their own ends the victory to which we were contributing so much, and that in doing so they would sow the seeds of another and more terrible war. Nothing is more frustrating than not to know what is going on; and the Republican minority in the Senate had not yet found a channel to the State Department.

His frustration led to a minor and now forgotten tempest in the summer of 1943. It is worth recalling because it hastened the "conversion," as he sometimes called it, of Arthur Vandenberg. The State Department was working on an international agreement, adopted that autumn, to deal with the first and most pressing of postwar problems, the relief and rehabilitation of war-torn countries. Within the De-

partment the task had fallen to me. At length a draft agreement had been prepared with some foreign consultation. Its form on our side was not that of a treaty requiring approval by the Senate, but of an agreement by authority of the President to contribute such funds for relief as the Congress should from time to time authorize and appropriate.

After the draft had been shown to the official leaders of the majority and minority in the Senate and the House, it was published to permit full consideration and discussion. Then the row started. The draft had not been discussed privately with the Senate or House foreign committees or their leaders. This was a mistake—though not so far as the House was concerned, since its rights over appropriations were preserved, and its members had no sympathy with the Senate's prerogatives in treaty making, from which the House was excluded. But in the Senate the publication of the draft set the cat among the pigeons. And it was Vandenberg who indefatigably kept them aflutter. He took the most horrendous view of what he thought was the shape of things to come. The draft he thought "pledged our total resources to whatever illimitable scheme for relief and rehabilitation all around the world our New Deal crystal-gazers might desire to pursue." Congress was to be "confronted with a 'fait accompli'" and there was to be "no interference with this world-wide prospectus as it might be conceived by Roosevelt, Lehman, Hopkins and Co."

Vandenberg would often be carried away by the hyperbole of his own rotund phrases. My father used to illustrate this very human characteristic by the example of a horse we owned years ago crossing the bridge over the Connecticut River at Middletown. She was gentle and well disposed. But as the buggy began to rumble across the bridge's planking, she would begin to prick up her ears and begin to move faster. More rumble brought more speed, until by the time the Portland shore was reached she was in full gallop and quite a lather. In the same way Vandenberg worked himself up to "a first showdown as to where President Roosevelt's treaty-making power leaves off and that of the Senate begins."

Secretary Hull and I found ourselves in the middle of this "showdown"; that is to say, we found ourselves before a Senate subcommittee appointed to investigate the suspected *coup d'état*. Hull, quite innocent of evil-doing, took umbrage at the vigor of Senator Tom Connally's examination of him and, after the first hearing, withdrew from the proceedings. It was left to Vandenberg and me to restore peace. This was not hard to do. As Vandenberg became informed about the extent of the relief problem and the way it was proposed to bring all friendly nations into the task of meeting it, he became convinced that the plan was a good one. A few changes in the text made plain what we had thought obvious, that the executive could not bind the Congress to make future appropriations and would seek congressional authorization. To a critic who thought that the result of all the fuss was a long way from the projected "showdown," Vandenberg replied, "I do not consider this to be the 'surrender'—I consider it to be the 'triumph' of constitutional procedure."

Well, it was not that, because the issue was never involved. But, nonetheless, the exercise was a valuable one. It resulted in Vandenberg's becoming the proponent and eloquent advocate of UNRRA [United Nations Relief and Rehabilitation Administration], after having first and publicly exorcised

from it all evil spirits. Without both, it might well have never been possible. And without this episode, much in our postwar history might not have been possible. For not only did this minor experience hasten the education of Arthur Vandenberg, but it was a forerunner of a ritual of statesmanship that I was to experience many times, and always with fascination.

Senator Vandenberg, faced with a proposal to take a step into the strange and frightening postwar world, invariably began by resisting the proposal. He declared the end unattainable, the means harebrained, and the cost staggering, particularly some mysterious costs which he thought were bound to occur but which the proposer had not foreseen because of faulty preparation. This first phase, the phase of opposition, usually lasted through one meeting and sometimes longer. All the while, Vandenberg was testing the proposal by attacking it; and he was learning a great deal in the process.

Then followed the period of gestation. The proposal grew and developed within him. This period had various manifestations, depending on the time available and the importance of the proposal. It could be, as we have seen with UNRRA, a fairly short time, a time of "assuming for the sake of argument that we go ahead with this, where will it lead and what will it accomplish?" This gave Vandenberg an opportunity to try out statements of the merits of the proposal and possible answers to arguments against it. He thought aloud; and his talk would proceed with mounting enthusiasm as conviction and confidence grew. But this period could take another and longer form, as it did in the case of the Marshall Plan. Senator Vandenberg was Chairman of the Senate Foreign Relations Committee when the Plan was considered in the committee and the

Senate. Upon his suggestion, committees were set up under Secretary of Commerce W. Averell Harriman and Julius A. Krug, Secretary of the Interior, to determine the capability of the country to carry out the plan and the economic consequences to it of doing so. This gave time for the country, the Republicans, and the Senator to get used to the idea and for the weight of supporting fact to have its effect.

At this stage Senator Vandenberg was convinced but not committed. Before that occurred, one further step remained to be taken. We called it, variously, "applying the trade-mark," or "determining the price." This meant either stamping the proposal with a Vandenberg brand or exacting from the administration a concession which he thought politically important. We have had one illustration in his insistence upon formal changes in the UNRRA draft. Let me give others just preceding the Marshall Plan.

When, in 1947, President Truman was discussing with congressional leaders his proposal for American aid to Greece and Turkey, he stressed that the attacks and pressures upon these countries were not, as surface appearances might suggest, merely due to border rows originating with their neighbors, but were part of a series of Soviet moves, which included stepped-up Communist party activity in Italy, France, and Germany. I can see Senator Vandenberg now, suddenly leaning forward on the sofa in the President's office and saying, "If you will say that to the whole country, I will support you." The presentation was put in this way, to the surprise and disapproval of some commentators.

Again, when the administration bill was introduced into Congress, no mention was made in it of the United Nations. Senator Vandenberg pounced on this and insisted that the bill should provide for cessation of United States aid if and when the United Nations should take charge of the situation. Both he and I knew that this event would never occur, since the Soviet Union would prevent it, but he was quite right in his point. The change was important, and provisions like this have been standard practice ever since. I agreed at once and offered to propose the change at the hearings on the bill. But he would have none of that. The change was proposed as the "Vandenberg Amendment." The brand had been applied; and fair enough it was.

In 1947–48, when the Marshall Plan was in the discussion stage, Senator Vandenberg, remembering the early New Deal, became obsessed with worry that the control of spending the billions of Marshall Plan dollars could give the administration such power as to decide the approaching election of 1948. While he himself had a healthy interest in preventing this, his concern was not due to mere political partisanship. For other Republicans could worry about the same thing and, since they controlled the Eightieth Congress, could doom the Marshall Plan, which Senator Vandenberg had now come to believe essential. To solve the problem the Senator turned to a plan of organization for administration of the Marshall Plan. The Brookings Institution of Washington was called in to give a detached and expert atmosphere to the deliberations; and finally, an "independent agency" form of organization was worked out, under, but not responding to, the President.

It is no matter that Senator Vandenberg's fears were unfounded. Under both the Truman and Eisenhower administrations, foreign aid has been administered within the regular hierarchy of government without being used for political patronage. The point I am making is that Vandenberg exacted as the price of his support a concession to the opposition which contributed to the acceptance of the proposal—whatever it did to its administration.

This attitude of Vandenberg's and my belief in its importance were to have a curious personal result before the Marshall Plan was fully launched. After the legislation was passed in 1948, the President spoke with me (I was then in private life) about his desire to send my name to the Senate as the administrator created by the act of Congress. I urged upon him, and he reluctantly agreed, that this would be unwise—not because Vandenberg had anything against me, but because, in view of my close relations with the President, the nomination would go a long way, in Vandenberg's mind, toward nullifying his efforts to establish an "independent" agency. This could well be disastrous. The act of Congress was still only an "authorization" for appropriations, a hunting license to go in search of them. The execution of the Marshall Plan still required the appropriation of billions of dollars by a Republican Congress.

The President wisely concluded that here, pre-eminently, was an occasion to seek the "advice and consent of the Senate," which, as a practical matter, meant to consult with Vandenberg. We speculated as to whom he would recommend, and concluded that it would be Mr. Paul Hoffman, a gentleman of the highest character and ability, wholly acceptable to the President. And so it turned out. Senator Vandenberg never knew what he escaped, but was greatly pleased that his advice had been sought and followed. He became more than ever committed to the support of the European Recovery Plan.

What I have said suggests a strong and practical mind rather than a subtle and original one. Arthur Vandenberg's mind was not original; but it was open.

He was not a creator of the ideas which he was eminently capable of receiving and using. A powerful advocate, he was not a great orator. His florid oratorical style, finding its emphasis in hyperbole and often in sheer lung power, had nothing like the range of Churchill's speeches. His importance lies not in brilliance of mind or speech, but—in equal parts—in himself, and in the time and place in which he lived and served. Without Vandenberg in the Senate from 1943 to 1951 the history of the postwar period might have been very different.

When in 1957 a committee of the Senate picked the five most "outstanding" Senators, whose portraits should hang in the Senate reception room, it did not include Vandenberg. The choice fell on Henry Clay, Daniel Webster, John C. Calhoun, Robert M. La Follette, and Robert A. Taft. Yet, in actual accomplishment, a good case can be made that Vandenberg's achievements exceeded those of any of the five, except Henry Clay; and that, as a symbol of his times in the Senate, Vandenberg stands for the emergence of the United States into world power and leadership; as Clay typified the growth of the country; Webster and Calhoun, the great debate of the antebellum days; and Robert M. La Follette, the turbulence of the Progressive Era.

Vandenberg, as I have said, did not furnish the ideas, the leadership, or the drive to chart the new course or to move the nation into it. But he made the result possible. What was needed was a national consensus, at a time when the hot war which had united the nation was over, and the full consequences of the disruption caused by the war were beginning to appear. How critical was the need can be judged by what happened after Vandenberg's death—I do not say because of it—when the consensus fell apart.

At the end of the war, the opposition of the business community, and its social adjuncts, to the Democratic administration—then in its fourth consecutive term—was ready to break into open revolt; as it did in November, 1946, but without the strength to win in 1948. Meanwhile the times called for action, drastic, unprecedented, and immediate. To those conversant with the situation there was not much doubt about what had to be done. How, by whom, and how soon were the questions. Without Arthur Vandenberg, solutions of these questions could not have been brought into action.

He had, as I have suggested, the capacity to learn and the capacity for action—rare gifts in themselves. As important as either, and giving both scope, he carefully maintained the preconditions for successful action. His prior history of isolationism was an asset which he never allowed to die. His relations with Senator Robert Taft were carefully maintained. Vandenberg's respect for Taft's proprietorship of Republican domestic policy led Taft to respect Vandenberg's position as Republican spokesman on foreign policy, so long as the latter's health and vigor remained. Vandenberg kept the friendship and respect of Senators Millikin of Colorado, Wherry of Nebraska, and Bridges of New Hampshire on the Republican Policy Committee. But, perhaps most important of all, he was in the very heart of the inner circle that ran the Senate.

Its membership did not coincide with the popular idea of importance in the Senate; some were much in the public eye; some were not. They were men of the type and character who, in a quiet way, are apt to dominate any male organization. The main ingredients of such men are force, likableness, and trustworthiness. Alben Barkley, Walter George, and Arthur Vandenberg were, perhaps, the *beaux idéals*. But Warren Austin, Joe Ball, Carl Hatch, Carl Hayden, Lister Hill, Richard Russell, Bob La Follette, Scott Lucas, Burnet Maybank, Bob Wagner, and Wallace White do not exhaust the list of the others. Many of them lunched together, more often than not in the office of Leslie Biffle, whether he was Secretary of the Senate or Secretary of the Minority. Party membership was a comparatively minor consideration. One had to be an adopted member of the group for quite a while to realize that anything was going on under the easy gossip and badinage. Then one discovered that almost everything was going on. The whole business of the Senate was being ordered and, in considerable part, decided.

A word about a few of these men, both in and out of the inner circle, may illuminate Vandenberg's problem in moving policies from hopes to action approved by the Senate. In this alchemy, eloquence on the Senate floor, though important, was not the major ingredient. The real work in shaping a Senator's vote was done off the floor. The height of success, of course, was to make it a favorable one. If that could not be done, a Senator might agree to be absent and unpaired; or, if a majority was pretty well assured, an opponent might be persuaded, while voting against the bill, not to support amendments which might seriously cripple it. Once, when I was Assistant Secretary of State for Congressional Liaison, I wrote a fiery speech against final passage of our bill for an important figure on the other side who agreed to be absent when amendments were considered in the committee and on the floor.

The most implacable opponents of the Truman administration in the

Senate, say from 1946 to 1950, prior to Senator [Joseph] McCarthy's emergence from obscurity, were Messrs. Robert Taft and Kenneth Wherry, both high in the Republican leadership. They believed that an opposition should oppose. Since they both totally lacked humor and possessed unlimited energy, their opposition was undiscriminating and ubiquitous. This helped to make it dull, scattered, and less effective than it could have been. Both were singularly obtuse in personal relationships. Bob Taft and I had for many years sat side by side on our university's governing body, the Yale Corporation. The temptation to tease him was too much for my power of resistance. At one meeting he arrived after discussion had already begun and asked me what the subject was. I replied that it was the condition of study and research in the natural sciences at Yale, which, it seemed, required improvement. Taft's critics were given to saying of him that he had an excellent mind until he made it up. However, he interrupted the speaker by announcing:

"Mr. President, *I* went through Yale without taking a single course in science."

While the Corporation was recovering in complete silence from this remarkable revelation, I was tempted and fell into sin. Addressing the President of the University, I said,

"Your Honor, the prosecution rests." The silence was broken; but the Senator was not amused.

With Wherry, too, I got into trouble. Late one afternoon in 1950 at a private hearing before the Senate Committee on Appropriations, Wherry was badgering me about some minor and dialectical point. He soon began shouting at me across the narrow table. While I was regretting the fate which required me to endure impassively such boring and boorish conduct, I began to wonder when I had last felt the purging sensation of fighting rage. To my horror I could not recall. It was lost in the mists of memory. Then I wondered whether I had lost even the capacity for rage, a chilling thought. So I began trying to work up a temper by murmuring hair-raising imprecations. To my delight I felt the blood rising along the back of my neck and my ears getting hot.

Just then the unhappy Wherry leaned across the table and shook his finger in my face. Without conscious volition on my part, I found myself standing, and, in a fair imitation of Wherry's raucous voice, shouting, "Don't you dare shake your dirty finger in my face!" He bellowed that he would; and he did. A rather inexpertly aimed and executed swing, which I launched at the distinguished Senator from Nebraska, was intercepted by Adrian Fisher, appropriately the Legal Adviser to the Department of State, and a former guard on the Princeton football team, who had accompanied me to the hearing for wholly different purposes. He now enveloped me in a bearlike embrace, murmuring, "Take it easy, Boss; take it easy."

By this time, quite cooled off and rather abashed by my unexpected capacities, I took a look at Senator McKellar of Tennessee, the Chairman of the committee, who was pounding away with his gavel and calling, "Gentlemen, Gentlemen," in a suspiciously choked voice. The secret was told by his ample stomach, which was shaking in uncontrolled glee. When comparative order was restored, Senator McKellar extorted mutual expressions of regret for, and withdrawal of, unparliamentary language from the principals.

The next morning I called on the old Chairman to apologize to him for turning his hearing into a brawl. But, still laughing, he would have none of it.

"Not at all, my boy, not at all," he said, beating his cane on the floor. "Funniest thing I've seen in thirty years on this Hill. I'll never forget Wherry's face when he saw the imperturbable Secretary aiming a haymaker at him. Do you know what I did after you left? I called Harry Truman and told him we could pay off the national debt by putting you two on the vaudeville circuit."

Needless to say, I did not experiment further with my emotions; but curiously enough my relations with Senator Wherry became much easier.

Another experience with Senator McKellar disclosed a coincidence perhaps worth mentioning. Discussions with Senators follow a distinctly Oriental pattern. The subject must not be approached directly and brusquely, but indirectly and leisurely, often by listening to a preliminary discourse by the Senator on how pressed and busy he is. On one occasion, my colleague, the co-Under Secretary of State, and dear friend, Will Clayton of Texas, and I were listening to a long tale by Senator McKellar of his brilliant conduct of a contested will trial in Tennessee a great many years ago. A devastating cross-examination of the widow was approaching its climax. "Then," said the Senator triumphantly, "I sprang the trap with this question," stating it.

Very quietly Will said, "Pardon me, Senator, but you didn't."

After a second of silent incredulity, McKellar burst out, "What the hell do you mean?"

"You see, Senator," Will went on, "I was the court reporter."

. . .

Another Senator who became a staunch supporter of our foreign policy and of Vandenberg's efforts was Senator Charles W. Tobey of New Hampshire. It all happened in a curious way, which illustrates the intensely personal quality of judgments and positions taken in the Senate. In selecting the United States delegation to the International Monetary Conference, held at Bretton Woods, New Hampshire, in July, 1944, Henry Morgenthau, Jr., Secretary of the Treasury, wisely wanted a Democrat and a Republican from both the Senate and House Committees on Banking and Currency, to which would be referred the recommendations of the conference. By all the time-encrusted rules of congressional propriety these positions were the perquisites of the chairman and ranking minority member of each committee and, in event of any declination, went to the next senior member of that party. Secretary Morgenthau, most unwisely, decided to skip Senator Tobey of New Hampshire, the senior Republican member, because of his isolationist record, and picked the next ranking Republican. When the Chairman, Senator Robert Wagner of New York, the father of the . . . Mayor of New York City, heard of this, he sent for me.

The Secretary's projected step, he told me, threatened to involve the whole complicated matter of the International Bank and the International Monetary Fund in a partisan political row which would go far to dim the chances of successful legislation. Not only would this discrimination strike at the whole oligarchical structure of Senate committees, in which every Senator had a present or future vested interest, but it would be regarded as a particularly mean partisan attack on Tobey, who was a very decent man even though overinclined to somewhat florid oratory. Tobey was running for re-election within four months, and due to intraparty difference was not yet assured of renomination. To subject him to public humiliation by excluding him from an international meeting to be held with considerable fanfare in his own state would be resented by the whole Senate as a foul blow and might well turn Tobey into a bitter and powerful enemy of the Bank and Fund.

I agreed and undertook to lay the matter before Morgenthau and the President. This was done and the plan was dropped. Since there are few secrets in Washington, thus began a friendship with Charlie Tobey which continued until his death. It even ripened further at Bretton Woods. We had barely arrived at the summer hotel, closed since the outbreak of the war, which was to house the delegates and their meetings, when the Fourth of July was upon us. This would necessitate a ceremony at which someone on behalf of our guests would felicitate and flatter us and a suitable response would be made by an American delegate. While the arrangements were still fluid, my new friend enlisted my help in obtaining for him the assignment to respond, pointing out that the intricacies of international finance were not apt to stampede New Hampshire voters, but that a good rousing Fourth of July speech by their local boy would reach throughout the State, and the nomination would be as good as his.

The Senator little knew how easy it was to gratify his wish. No other American delegate wanted to take the time from exacting homework and lengthy conferences to get up such a speech. So I was soon able to tell him that the honor was his, and felt no compulsion to minimize the undertaking. The speech was a great success and was widely reported through-

out New Hampshire. We were soon able to congratulate the Senator on obtaining the renomination of his party. As the days passed, he progressed from a passive delegate to an energetic, intelligent, and enthusiastic one.

Toward the end of the conference the Senator had one last request to which he attached the greatest importance. Would I do my best, he urged, to persuade Lord and Lady Keynes to come to a dinner which he wished to give for them in his home town, an hour or so away, where he would present to them the local dignitaries, who had never seen, much less met, an English lord. Again the task was not a difficult one. Maynard Keynes understood the political situation very well and knew, at once, that this by no means unpleasant effort would usefully grease the launching ways for his beloved Fund and Bank. But this time I raised the question whether the Senator was not now leading me into disloyalty to my party. It was one thing to be co-operative where the prize was the Republican nomination. But now the prize was the election. What about that? In a moment he had the answer.

"I know what we'll do," he said triumphantly. "I'll ask Democrats, too!" So we settled on that, though it by no means met the point. Lord and Lady Keynes came. The evening was not only a success for Charlie Tobey, but a pleasant one for his guests. I was one of the Democratic guests.

The Senator was re-elected. He proved a tower of strength in securing congressional approval of the Bretton Woods Agreement and United States participation in the Bank and Fund. Two years later, after the war had ended and death had put a new President in the White House, a political overturn and a Republican Congress made Senator Tobey Chairman of the Senate Committee on Banking and Currency. When the new Congress met in 1947, it faced a revolution in American foreign policy, as the nation found itself precipitated into leadership of the non-Communist world in the opening phases of the cold war. The administration found no more loyal and effective supporter than Senator Charles Tobey of New Hampshire. . . .

. . .

Even a short account of the postwar Senate would be incomplete without a mention of three giants, Senators Barkley of Kentucky, George of Georgia, and Tom Connally of Texas. Alben Barkley, who left the Senate for the Vice Presidency under Mr. Truman in 1949 and from then to 1953 was known as "The Veep," was not only the most popular man in the Senate, but easily the most popular in Washington. He was warm because he had a deeply affectionate nature and really liked people. In the rare cases where a person precluded even toleration, Barkley's courtesy took over. He was unborable. The problem of bearing fools gladly did not seem to arise for him, as he discovered endless amusement in them. Even a vigorous partisanship gave the impression of a genial and oratorical game which left no scars and led to happy libations in the clubhouse when the game was over. . . .

Warm, outgoing, the center of any group in which he found himself, one of the great raconteurs of his time, his gusto for life was enormous, with no shrinking desire for privacy preventing him from sharing his life. His romance when over seventy with a young and charming widow was followed with almost swooning enthusiasm by the whole country. . . .

Alben Barkley contributed very little to political thought and leadership in the United States. But he did contribute to the means by which that thought and leadership were translated into successful action. He did not belong on the General Staff; he was a good field commander.

Much the same was true of Senator George, except that he seemed to me less admirable in basic human qualities, less kindly, less generous, less outgoing, and more—much more—pompous. Senator George had immense influence. He was, so the phrase went, "a great constitutional lawyer.". . . "A great constitutional lawyer" is either a judge over a century dead, or a lawyer who interprets the utterances of the Supreme Court as one wishes them interpreted. Since most people who employ the phrase wish them interpreted to prevent innovation, "a great constitutional lawyer" is usually an ultra-conservative. Senator George met this test admirably.

I should say that he had no humor, but rather a regal geniality. He spoke slowly and ponderously, as he sipped a bourbon and water in Leslie Biffle's office before lunch, dispensing the benediction of a sentence here and there. But he was well worth a courtier's assiduous attention. A few days' attendance on him at his home in Vienna, Georgia, could result, as one Assistant Secretary of State played it, in the practical elimination of opposition to and any real debate of the Formosa Treaty and Resolution in 1955. Walter George was a powerful patron and a dangerous opponent.

Fate and temperament made Tom Connally and Arthur Vandenberg collaborators and rivals in the Senate. Since each was a *prima donna*, rivalry often got out of hand, even though they were agreed on fundamentals. Ranking members of their parties on the Committee on Foreign Relations, Connally was its Chairman, except during the Eightieth (Republican) Congress, when Vandenberg took his place from January, 1947, to January, 1949. But whether chairman or not, Vandenberg exercised great power. As I have pointed out, he was the key to indispensable Republican co-operation in obtaining legislative approval and support for policies and programs of the greatest magnitude and novelty.

In effect, sovereignty in the Senate over matters of foreign policy was a condominium; and we in the executive branch had to deal respectfully with both sovereigns. Tom Connally found this irksome, and all the more irksome because he felt that the press, to which he was far from insensitive, accorded Vandenberg an unwarranted and unfair pre-eminence. In a way it was unfair, just as it is unfair that there should be more joy in heaven over one sinner that repenteth than over ninety and nine just persons who need no repentance. Tom Connally shared the quite natural feelings of the prodigal son's elder brother. Connally had served long and faithfully; but the fatted calf was killed, so he thought, for a Johnny-come-lately.

In another way, however, the Senator from Texas contributed to the distasteful comparison. He was a greater debater than Vandenberg, but in a very different style. A master of sarcasm, irony, and ridicule, he would employ gestures and acting to evade the Senate rules and castigate an object of his scorn. "The position now taken by the distinguished Senator," he would say, "adds to his stature"—leaning over and measuring a distance about a foot from the floor—"and gives a true measure of the breadth of his mind" —holding up his hand with thumb and forefinger a quarter of an inch apart. His quick and stinging wit brought laughter and left wounds, all of which would be interspersed through a masterly exposition, or a dissection of the opposing position.

Unfortunately for Connally's public reputation, his appearances on the Senate floor, more often than not, amused the American public, but did not impress it. This public does not agree with Justice Holmes that one need not be heavy to be weighty. We like our public men to be ponderous, platitudinous, and pious, with a strong strain of sentimentality running through all. Vandenberg could exhibit all of these qualities and be a powerful advocate at the same time. Connally would make a noble start along these lines, but the imp of his wit and sense of the ridiculous would always get loose and give the game away. One night years ago at the annual dinner, a gay affair, of a club to which we both belong, I listened with sheer delight to Tom Connally imitate himself making a speech in the Senate. No other member of that body could possibly have done such a thing, or even thought of doing it.

Connally took pains to look like the stage version of a Southern Senator— black clothes, the coat cut in a style halfway between a sack coat and a morning coat, black bow string tie, white curls over his collar, a broadbrimmed black hat. . . .

Dealing with the two senior foreign relations Senators took a good deal of time. Here one had to make haste slowly. The simple thing would have been to talk with them together; but simplicity would have been, if not disastrous, at least hazardous. Connally loved to heckle Vandenberg. Vandenberg when aroused could respond in a way calculated to move Connally another notch toward disagreement for its own sake. So the procedure was first to see them separately, to get each so far committed that only the sheerest wilfulness could undo it. But which to see first? Here was a tricky decision. Both were fairly good about not leaking the content of our talks to the press. But each found it hard to resist leaking the fact of a private talk. Once this was done, the second to be seen knew that he was the second. With Connally this was instant cause for offense. We were members of the same party; he was loyal and proved; yet I turned to his rival first—if, indeed, I had done so. It was to him a poor explanation that Vandenberg was the Chairman of the committee, in the years in which he was.

This problem reached its height in early 1949, when the chairmanship had just changed to Connally and the North Atlantic Treaty was under negotiation. Three times a week, I met in the morning with the Ambassadors of the European countries to hammer out the operative words and in the afternoon with the two Senators to strengthen support among our ultimate partners in treaty-making on the Hill, and not such silent partners either.

Despite all the difficulties and minor pitfalls, the relationship worked. Great things were done; and both men carried the burden in the Senate. . . .

The characteristics of these men, powers in the Senate, I have said, were force, likableness, and trustworthiness —in varying proportions, as the list suggests. Was Arthur Vandenberg a likable man? Yes, he was. He had humor and warmth and occasional bursts of self-revealing candor. He was not among the "popular" Senators. His ego was too strong for that. Some regarded him, as Mr. James B. Reston of the *New York Times* concedes that he did for a time, as the "most pompous and prejudiced man in the United States Senate." But this was wrong. He was not that; but he took a bit of knowing. When I retired as Under Secretary of State, I wrote to thank him for a warm note which I described as "another of the long list of kindnesses which you have shown me," and "for your outstanding fairness and warm generosity." This was from the heart; he was a good friend.

All these gifts and qualities were what fitted Senator Vandenberg so preeminently to perform a service for which the country should be forever grateful: the service of bringing together in support of a foreign policy, dictated by the necessity of events, an administration which could carry it out and an opposition which could have prevented it from doing so. All the brilliance of Calhoun or the eloquence of Webster could not have performed this service. It called for what Arthur Vandenberg had, and was, and had spent a lifetime in acquiring and in being.

7

GOODBYE TO THE INNER CLUB

NELSON W. POLSBY

If this article is right, there have been significant changes in the risks and rewards of a senatorial career since the time that Acheson wrote. It is at least
arguable, in any event, that we are in the midst of a profound change in the role
of the Senate in the political system, from an intensely private and conservative
body to a very public and progressive one; from one focused on the virtues of
age and experience to one devoted to the young, the vigorous, and the ambitious.

At the opening of the 91st Congress in January, Senator Edward M. Kennedy (D-Mass.) challenged Senator Russell Long (D-La.) for the position of Senate Democratic Whip. Long, Chairman of the powerful Finance Committee and a Senator for 20 years, had held the Whip post nearly as long as Kennedy had been in the Senate.

The position is elective, by secret ballot in the caucus of Democratic Senators at the opening of each Congress, and, as readers of the newspapers could hardly avoid noticing, Kennedy won handily.

A few days later, Senator Robert P. Griffin (R-Mich.) left the Committee on Labor and Public Welfare for an opening on the relatively low-ranked Committee on Government Operations, and Senator Eugene F. McCarthy (D-Minn.) voluntarily left the prestigious Foreign Relations Committee to take up a place on the same committee. His public explanation of the move consisted of a Delphic quote from

Originally published in *The Washington Monthly*, (August, 1969), pp. 30–34.

Marshall McLuhan: "Operations is policy." When Senator Lee Metcalf (D-Mont.) removed himself from the Finance Committee that same week, in order to stay on Government Operations, he explained that the Finance Committee had become "just a rubber stamp for the House Ways and Means Committee. No matter what the Finance Committee or the Senate does," he said, "when we come back from conferences with the House we have given in to Wilbur Mills. He runs both committees." In part, Metcalf was protesting a decision of the Democratic Steering Committee, which had forced him to reduce his committee responsibilities from three to two while permitting more senior Senators to hold three assignments. The Steering Committee also reduced the size of the Appropriations and Foreign Relations Committees in a move widely interpreted as an attempt to staunch the flow of power from senior to junior Senators who might otherwise have been able to go a long way toward outvoting the chairmen of these two committees.

To a generation of followers of the U. S. Senate, these were peculiar goings-on. Whoever heard of Senators leaving important committees to go on unimportant ones—voluntarily? Or committee chairmen worried about uprisings of the peasants? Or an agreeable young man of negligible accomplishments, one eye cocked on the Presidency, knocking off a senior Southern chairman running for a job tending the inner gears of the institution?

If this sort of thing can happen in broad daylight these days on Capitol Hill, there must be something seriously the matter with the ideas that have dominated conversation about the Senate for the last 15 years. For at least since the publication of William S. White's *Citadel: The Story of the U. S. Senate* (1956), the common assumption has been that the Senate has been run by an "inner club" of "Senate types." "The Senate type," White wrote, "is, speaking broadly, a man for whom the Institution is a career in itself, a life in itself, and an end in itself." Although others might belong to the inner club, "At the core of the Inner Club stand the Southerners, who with rare exceptions automatically assume membership almost with the taking of the oath of office."

"The Senate type," White continued, makes the Institution his home in an almost literal sense, and certainly in a deeply emotional sense. His head swims with its history, its lore. . . . To him, precedent has an almost mystical meaning. . . . His concern for the preservation of Senate tradition is so great that he distrusts anything out of the ordinary. . . .

As the Southern members of the Inner Club make the ultimate decisions as to what is proper in point of manner—these decisions then infallibly pervading the Outer Club—so the whole generality of the Inner Club makes the decisions as to what *in general* is proper in the Institution and what *in general* its conclusions should be on high issues.

White conceded, of course, that the Senate had its "public men," who made their way by inflaming or instructing public opinion. But he argued that it was not these grasshoppers but rather the ants of the Inner Club who got their way in the decision-making of the Senate.

Since the publication of *Citadel*, commentators on Senate affairs have routinely alluded to the Inner Club as though to something as palpable as an office building. No senatorial biography—or obituary—is now complete without solemn consideration of whether the subject was in or out. Discussions of senatorial business can hardly compete with dissections of the Inner Club's informal rules, tapping ceremonies, secret handshakes, and other signs and stigmata by which members are recognized. One writer, Clayton Fritchey in *Harper's*, took the further step—in 1967—of actually naming names.

By far the most zealous promoter of the whole idea was someone whose opinion on the matter must be given some weight. This is the way Joseph S. Clark described a lunch that Majority Leader Lyndon B. Johnson gave for Clark's "class" of incoming freshman Democrats in 1957:

As we sat down to our steaks at the long table in the office of Felton M. (Skeeter) Johnston, Secretary of the Senate, . . . we found at our places copies of *Citadel: The Story of the U.S. Senate*, autographed "with all good wishes" not only by its author William S. White . . . but by the Majority Leader as well. During the course of the lunch, which was attended by the other recently re-elected leaders,

Senator Johnson encouraged us to consider Mr. White's book as a sort of *Mc-Guffey's Reader* from which we could learn much about the "greatest deliberative body in the world" and how to mold ourselves into its way of life.

These days, somehow, the mold seems to have broken. Ten years after the Johnson lunch, Clayton Fritchey's *Harper's* article named Russell Long as a "full-fledged member" of the Inner Club. Of Edward M. Kennedy, Fritchey said:

On his own, the amiable Teddy might some day have become at best a fringe member of the Club, but he is associated with Robert F., who like John F., is the archetype of the national kind of politician that the Club regards with suspicion. It believes (correctly) that the Kennedy family has always looked on the Senate as a means to an end, but not an end in itself.

And yet, only two years later, Kennedy unseated Long.

Power in the Senate

Some time ago, in *Congress and the Presidency*, I argued that the notion of an inner club misrepresented the distribution of power in the Senate in several ways. First, it vastly underplayed the extent to which *formal* position—committee chairmanships, great seniority, and official party leadership—conferred power and status on individual Senators almost regardless of their clubability. Second, it understated the extent to which power was spread by specialization and the need for cooperative effort. Fritchey's list bears this out; of the 92 nonfreshman Senators in 1967, he listed 53 as members or provisional members of the Inner Club. This suggests a third point:

the existence of an inner club was no doubt in part incorrectly inferred from the existence of its opposite—a small number of mavericks and outsiders. The Senate has always had its share of these, going back at least as far as that superbly cranky diarist, Senator William Plumer of New Hampshire, who served from 1803 to 1807. But the undeniable existence of cranks and mavericks—uncooperative men with whom in a legislative body it is necessary (but impossible) to do business—does not an Inner Club make, except, of course, by simple subtraction.

To dispute that there is an all-powerful Inner Club is not, of course, to claim that no norms govern the behavior of Senators toward one another, or that this body of adults has no status system. Any group whose members interact frequently, and expect to continue to do so on into the indefinite future, usually develops norms. All groups having boundaries, a corporate history, a division of labor, and work to do may be expected to have folkways and an informal social organization. What was opened to question was whether, in the case of the U. S. Senate, the informal social organization was as restrictive or as unlike the formal organization as proponents of the Inner Club Theory believed.

To these observations I would now add a number of others, the most important of which would be to suggest that the role of the Senate in the political system has changed over the last 20 years in such a way as to decrease the impact of norms internal to the Senate on the behavior and the status of Senators.

One possible interpretation of what went on at the opening of the current Congress is that the Senate today is far less of a citadel than when William S. White first wrote. It is a less insular body, and the fortunes of Senators are less and less tied to the smiles and frowns of their elders within the institution.

Why Operations?

What is the great attraction, for example, of the Committee on Government Operations? It reports little legislation, has oversight over no specific part of the executive branch. Rather, it takes the operations of government in general as its bailiwick, splits into nearly autonomous subcommittees, and holds investigations. In short, it has the power to publicize —both issues and Senators. It takes less of a Senator's time away from the increasingly absorbing enterprise of cultivating national constituencies on substantive issues.

The claim that lack of ambition for the Presidency distinguishes members of the Inner Club could not have been correct even 20 years ago, considering the Presidential hankerings of such quintessentially old-style Senate types as Robert A. Taft of Ohio, Richard B. Russell of Georgia, and Robert Kerr of Oklahoma. Today, Presidential ambition seems to lurk everywhere in the Senate chamber.

Over the course of these last 20 years, the Senate has obviously improved as a base from which to launch a Presidential bid, while other bases— such as the governorships—have gone into decline. There has certainly, since World War II, been a general movement of political resources and of public attention toward Washington and away from local and regional arenas. The growth of national news media— especially television—has augmented this trend. The impact upon the Presidency of this nationalization of public awareness has been frequently noted. To a lesser extent, this public aware-

ness has spread to all national political institutions. But of these, only the Senate has taken full advantage of its increased visibility. In the House, Sam Rayburn refused to allow televised coverage of any official House function, and Speaker John W. Mc-Cormack has continued this rule. The executive branch speaks through the President, or an occasional Cabinet member, and the Supreme Court remains aloof. Thus, only Senators have had little constraint placed on their availability for national publicity. Senate committee hearings are frequently televised. Senators turn up often on the televised Washington quiz shows on Sunday afternoons. House members, even the powerful committee chairmen, rarely do. National exposure does not seem to be as important a political resource for them.

As senatorial names—Kefauver, McCarthy, Kennedy, Goldwater—became household words, Governors slipped into relative obscurity. Where once the Governor's control of his state party organization was the single overwhelming resource in deciding who was Presidential timber at a national party convention, television and the nationalization of resources began to erode gubernatorial power. Early Presidential primaries, with their massive national press coverage, made it harder and harder for the leaders of state parties to wait until the national party conventions to bargain and make commitments in Presidential contests. Proliferating federal programs, financed by the lucrative federal income tax, were distributed to the states, in part as senatorial patronage. Governors were not always ignored in this process, but their influence was on the whole much reduced. Meanwhile, at the state level, services lagged and taxes were often inequitable and unproductive. Responsible Governors of both parties have often tried to do something about this problem, but it has led to donnybrooks with state legislatures, great unpopularity, and, on some occasions, electoral defeat.

This decline of Governors and the shift of public attention to national politics and national politicians goes some distance in explaining how the Senate, in its role as an incubator of Presidential hopefuls, seems to have made it increasingly hard for a Senate inner club to monopolize power. As the stakes of the senatorial game have changed, so has the importance of informal norms and folkways internal to the Senate, in the life space of Senators.

Two Accidents

In my view, two historical accidents also played a part. The first was the majority leadership of Lyndon B. Johnson. Ambitious for the Presidency, immensely skilled, Johnson sedulously perpetuated the myth of the Inner Club while destroying its substance.

If the idea of the Inner Club was collegiality among the fellowship of the elect, the essence of Johnson's Senate operation was the progressive centralization of power in the hands of the Majority Leader. By the time Johnson left the Senate, after eight years as Majority Leader, the "Inner Club" could command little of the power attributed to it. It had too long been merely a facade for Johnson's own activity—a polite and palatable explanation for the exercise of his own discretion in committee appointments, legislative priorities, and tactics. Under the loose rein of Majority Leader Mike Mansfield, the Senate has again become a much more collegial body whose corporate work has been pretty much determined by

Presidential programs and priorities. But it has not recaptured the sense of cohesion, community, and separateness that is supposed to have existed "in the old days." Younger men have come in, and in the last few years liberal majorities on legislation mobilized by the executive departments were by no means uncommon.

The second historical accident that shaped the contemporary Senate was the style of service hit upon by several post-war Senators, but most notably pioneered by the late Arthur Vandenberg of Michigan, and, in the 1950's and 1960's, brought to full flower by Hubert Humphrey. This new style combined the concerns over national issues—formerly attributed mainly to Senate outsiders—with patience and a mastery of internal procedure and strategy. Like Johnson, Humphrey entered the Senate in 1949. Unlike Johnson, Humphrey had a large and varied stock of interests in, and commitments to, public policy. These attuned him to demands from outside the Senate. Through his phenomenally retentive mind, insatiable curiosity, and unquenchable optimism, Humphrey could learn enough to hold his own on any issue. Invariably his name went on the bills that reached out for new national constituencies.

Much earlier than most members of his generation, Humphrey sensed the possibilities in the Senate for long-range political education. He spent the Eisenhower era incubating ideas that, in a better climate, could hatch into programs. In the early 1950's a flood of Humphrey bills (many of them co-sponsored by other liberal Senators) on civil rights, Medicare, housing, aid to farm workers, food stamps, Job Corps, area redevelopment, disarmament, and so on died in the Senate. A little over a decade later, most of them were law, and Humphrey had in the meantime become a political leader of national consequence.

By reconciling acceptance within the Senate with large public accomplishments, Humphrey set a new style— and it is a style that has grown in popularity among younger Senators as the role of the Senate as an appropriate place in the political system for the incubation of new policy and the building of national constituencies emerges more sharply.

8

FILIBUSTERS: MAJORITY RULE, PRESIDENTIAL LEADERSHIP, AND SENATE NORMS

RAYMOND E. WOLFINGER

Raymond E. Wolfinger's study of filibusters provides a useful corrective to the notion that the formal power that senators possess has nothing to do with the unwritten laws of senatorial status. Wolfinger is Associate Professor of Political Science at Stanford University.

Unlimited floor debate is a rarity among national legislatures and the glory of the United States Senate. The influence of filibusters on the fate of proposed civil rights legislation and attempts made by some senators to change the rules so as to weaken that influence have been a persistent subject in contemporary political history and have provided a basis for several generalizations about both the Senate and the American political system. In some important respects these generalizations are based on a misreading of the evidence, as I hope to show in this article.

Filibusters touch on several important and familiar themes: 1) They are a major weapon used by a parochial Congress to block presidential pro-

grams. 2) For a generation they were the means used to veto civil rights bills supported by legislative majorities. 3) They illustrate the importance of apolitical congressional norms, in this instance senatorial commitment to unlimited debate. As the following narrative demonstrates, all three of these generalizations are in need of revision.

– 1 –

Most Senate motions, including any to consider ("take up") a bill, as well as to pass it, are subject to unlimited debate unless cloture is imposed; and the Senate's Rule 22 requires a two-thirds vote for cloture. Weak as it is, Rule 22 has been on the books only for half a century. Until 1917 there were no limits at all on debate and thus a handful of determined senators could frustrate a majority's desire to pass a bill.[1]

From Raymond E. Wolfinger, *Readings on Congress* © 1970. Reprinted by permission of Prentice-Hall, Inc., Englewood Cliffs, New Jersey.

I am grateful to J. Vincent Buck, Nelson W. Polsby, and Leroy N. Rieselbach for comments on earlier drafts of this paper, which is a product of my participation in the Study of Congress sponsored by the American Political Science Foundation with the aid of a grant from the Carnegie Corporation.

From 1865, when the use of unlimited debate for this purpose became firmly established, until 1950, 36 proposed legislative measures were delayed or defeated by filibusters, most of which lasted only a few days.[2] All but eleven of these measures eventually were passed in some form. The exceptions —those bills totally defeated by unlimited debate—were almost all civil rights measures.[3] Numerous appropriations bills were also casualties of filibusters.[4] There is no way of knowing for sure how many other measures were shelved or modified by the threat of unlimited debate, but threatening to talk a provision to death is a commonplace Senate tactic, particularly in the closing days of a session when members are anxious to adjourn.[5]

Beginning with Henry Clay in 1841, many senators tried one means or another of limiting debate, but it was not until the emotional period just before our entry into the First World War that the Senate adopted any such restriction. Early in 1917 a dozen western progressives succeeded, by means of a very unpopular filibuster, in defeating President Wilson's bill to arm merchant ships. The infuriated Wilson uttered his famous denunciation of the filibusterers: "A little group of willful men, representing no opinion but their own, have rendered the great Government of the United States helpless and contemptible." He also called the Senate into extraordinary session. Three days later it adopted, by a vote of 76 to 3, an amendment to Rule 22 providing that debate could be limited by a vote of two-thirds of those senators present and voting; after cloture had been imposed, each senator could speak for one hour. This change in the rules was introduced by Senator Thomas S. Martin of Virginia. That a Southerner sponsored the cloture rule can be viewed either as an historical irony or

an illustration of the hollowness of pure principle as a motivation in any behavior concerning filibusters.

From the adoption of the Martin Resolution until 1964 there were 28 cloture votes, five of which passed. Four of these successful attempts occurred before 1928; the fifth, on the Communications Satellite (Comsat) Bill of 1962, is of special interest and will be discussed shortly. Cloture was not attempted on a civil rights bill until 1938; from then through 1962 there were eleven cloture votes on this issue, all unsuccessful.[6]

Over the years since 1917 various parliamentary rulings gradually had had the effect of barring cloture on procedural motions. Since these included motions to take up a bill, the 1917 change lost all meaning. This development was fully apparent in 1948 when, relying on precedents, Senator Arthur Vandenberg, the presiding officer, sustained a point of order against a cloture petition, observing that "in the final analysis, the Senate has no effective cloture rule at all . . . a small but determined minority can always prevent cloture . . . the existing Senate rules regarding cloture do not provide conclusive cloture."[7] The Senate did not vote on appeal of this ruling, which came during the post-convention special session.[8]

Soon after the new Congress convened in 1949 several liberal senators, cheered on by President Truman, moved for new rules to re-impose some control over unlimited debate. After weeks of argument on the floor they gained a provision applying cloture to procedural motions, but at a price dictated by the Republican–Dixiecrat coalition: motions to change the rules were exempted from cloture and the necessary majority was changed from two-thirds of those present and voting to two-thirds of the total membership.

(Both of these restrictions were removed ten years later.)

Four years later the opening of the 83rd Congress ushered in an era in which liberal attempts to strengthen Rule 22 became almost a biennial ritual. Down through the years there have been two proposals; the more moderate would change the required cloture majority from two-thirds to three-fifths; the other would provide for cloture fifteen days after a vote by a simple majority. None of the liberal campaigns against Rule 22 has been successful. But because the Senate's resolution of this question over the years reveals a good deal about its members' attitudes toward majority rule, a brief and selective chronicle of the fights over Rule 22 is useful.[9]

– 2 –

These controversies occur at the beginning of a Congress because otherwise motions to amend the rules unquestionably would be subject to unlimited debate unless restricted by a two-thirds vote. The liberals' goal was to bring a motion to revise Rule 22 to a vote under circumstances where a simple majority would suffice to change the rules. In introducing such motions at the opening of a Congress they argued that the Senate could not be bound forever by rules adopted by past Congresses; thus at the very beginning of a Congress the old rules would not be in effect unless they went unchallenged and in this state of nature general parliamentary rules would apply. In contrast to the Senate's rules, the latter regulations provide that a member can bring a pending motion to a vote by moving the previous question; this motion is not debatable and carries by a simple majority. The basis of the liberal case is Article I, Section 5 of the Constitution, which states that "each House may determine the rules of its proceedings." The defenders of Rule 22 point to Rule 32, which reads in part, "The rules of the Senate shall continue from one Congress to the next Congress unless they are changed as provided in these rules." The merits of the case, on which a great deal of talmudic argumentation has been displayed by both sides, are irrelevant to the concerns of this article.

In 1953, during the first of these fights, the liberals quickly learned that the champions of unlimited debate did not intend to apply the principle to proposals to change Rule 22. The 83rd Congress opened on January 3, 1953. On January 7 the Majority Leader, Robert A. Taft (R-Ohio), announced that the Republican Policy Committee had voted against a change in Rule 22 and moved to table a motion by Senator Clinton P. Anderson (D-N.M.) to consider new rules. The nondebatable tabling motion (dubbed "negative cloture" by some liberals) carried by a vote of 70 to 21. It was opposed by 15 Democrats, five Republicans, and Wayne Morse of Oregon, then an Independent in transition from the Republican to the Democratic party.

Much the same thing happened in 1957. Anderson again offered his motion on opening day and the Majority Leader—by now Lyndon B. Johnson—immediately moved to table it. Vice President Nixon issued various "advisory opinions" to the effect that Article I, Section 5 empowered each Congress to make its own rules and that, given the opportunity, he would so rule. This was no more than an informal expression of opinion, however, and in any event was beside the point, for Johnson's tabling motion carried, 55 to 38. All but six northern Democrats voted "no," but the Republicans were for it by a three-to-two ratio.

Two years later, following a landslide that produced fifteen freshmen Democrats, the liberals again prepared an assault on Rule 22. But Johnson took the initiative on opening day by offering proposals to extend cloture to attempts to change the rules and to relax the majority required for cloture to two-thirds of senators present and voting. The next day Johnson yielded the floor so Anderson could offer his familiar motion, then moved to table it and won by 60 to 36. After the liberals lost two more lopsided votes Johnson's palliatives passed handily and forestalled further action in 1959.

The 1960 election brought a new spirit of hope to liberals. Both party platforms in 1960 promised changes in Rule 22 and Kennedy's election suggested that the White House, which had eschewed any involvement during the Eisenhower years, might join the fight, thus making it more of a party issue and reinforcing the liberals with the prestige and pressure available to a newly elected president. Kennedy, who had opposed Rule 22 while in the Senate, promised an ambitious legislative program to "get this country moving again" and surely would want to remove one notorious obstruction to progressive legislation. With these hopes liberal senators—notably Paul H. Douglas (D-Ill.) and Joseph S. Clark (D-Penn.)—pressed Kennedy for a commitment to help. Clark met with the President-elect in December and professed to be satisfied with the outcome. A week later, however, Kennedy issued an Eisenhower-like statement to the effect that it was up to the members of both houses of Congress to work out their own rules. The reformers' campaign was further weakened when Kennedy's staff passed the word that he did not intend to ask Congress for civil rights legislation. Other developments were even more discouraging. Various liberal senators,

including Anderson, Hubert H. Humphrey (the new majority whip and previously an opponent of Rule 22), and Mike Mansfield (the new majority leader and also an opponent of Rule 22 in the past), all said or were reported to have said that the time was not ripe for an attack on the rule. Eventually, however, Anderson agreed to repeat his old role of proposing three-fifths cloture, Mansfield appeared to be neutral, and Humphrey, after vacillating almost until the opening prayer of the new Congress, finally joined the reformers.

Despite these and other disquieting signs and a general air of pessimism in the press, the liberals approached the beginning of the 87th Congress with outward optimism. The incoming administration seemed above the battle; Nixon, with two weeks to go as presiding officer, still maintained that each Congress could make its own rules by majority vote; and a head count showed that a probable majority was in favor of at least three-fifths cloture. The liberals planned to allow more than a week of debate and then move the previous question. Nixon was expected to rule that this motion was in order, the inevitable southern appeal of the ruling could be tabled without debate, the Senate could vote on the moving of the previous question and then on the proposed changes, beginning with the more extreme majority cloture and falling back to the Anderson proposal if the first one was rejected.

After a few days of debate Mansfield and the Republican leader, Everett M. Dirksen, said they would move to refer both proposals to the Rules and Administration Committee for "further study." Mansfield promised that the reform proposals would be reported to the floor "at a later date" and that "the minority leader join[s] with me in assuring the Senate that we shall do everything in our power to bring such a measure to a vote in this body." [10] Word soon spread that Kennedy favored the referral in order to dispose of an issue that otherwise would jeopardize his legislative program by antagonizing southern committee chairmen. The liberals argued desperately that postponement would cost them their procedural advantage; when the issue came before the Senate later in the session, debate on it could be limited only by a two-thirds vote. Furthermore, they would lose the help of a presumably sympathetic presiding officer, for Johnson, the new Vice President, had made no secret of his hostility to changing Rule 22. (Johnson was thought to have played an important part in the maneuvering on this issue in 1961.) Mansfield's motion carried by a vote of 50 to 46, with Democrats and Republicans evenly divided.

The "later date" for consideration of rules changes turned out to be very late indeed. Mansfield waited almost until the end of the session and then announced that the Anderson proposal, S. Res. 4, would be called up on Saturday, September 16, and that he would immediately file a cloture petition to avoid wasting time. The liberals, additionally handicapped by having to find a two-thirds majority for cutting off debate before there had been any debate, and doing so at the end of a session when everyone wanted to go home, pleaded for a delay until the next session began in January. Both party leaderships, supported by the ordinarily leisurely Southerners, insisted on handling the matter with dispatch. Cloture was rejected on the 19th by a vote of 37 to 43, again with both parties split evenly. Mansfield then moved successfully to table his motion to consider S. Res. 4, and the issue was dead until 1963.

In 1963 Johnson refused to rule whether a majority could cut off debate at the beginning of a Congress. Instead, he put the question to the Senate itself, saying that since 1803 such constitutional issues invariably had been decided by the members, not by the presiding officer. The question Johnson referred to the Senate was debatable and his action thus had the effect of requiring a two-thirds vote to end debate. Three days later the Senate approved a motion to table this question devised by Mansfield and Dirksen. The motion passed, 53 to 42, with all the Southerners, two-thirds of the Republicans and more than a third of the northern Democrats voting in favor. Five days later Mansfield filed a cloture petition. The 54–42 vote fell ten votes short, but the liberals at least had a majority, the first time since 1950 that this had happened on a cloture vote related to civil rights. The civil rights groups turned furiously on Johnson. One of their spokesmen claimed that the Vice President's ruling revealed that his first loyalty was to southern racists.

The successful cloture vote on the Civil Rights Bill of 1964 took some of the edge off the attempt to amend Rule 22 at the beginning of the 89th Congress. The customary two reform proposals were referred by unanimous consent to the Committee on Rules and Administration. Two months later they were reported back to the Senate, along with a five-to-four committee vote recommending against their adoption. No further action was taken. It seems likely that President Johnson's ambitious legislative program, none of which appeared threatened by a filibuster, led to a gentleman's agreement to forget about the issue.

In 1967 the liberals finally brought to a vote the question of whether a majority of senators could change the rules at the beginning of a session—and lost by more than 20 votes. George McGovern (D-S.D.) moved that the Senate vote immediately to end debate on a motion to take up a rules change proposal and then, if the motion carried by majority vote, proceed to further decisions on rules reform. Dirksen raised a point of order against McGovern's motion, calling it a violation of Rule 22. Vice President Humphrey said he would follow precedent and refer the question to the Senate for decision. But unlike Johnson in 1963, who referred the liberal motion to the Senate, Humphrey submitted this question: "Shall the point of order made by the Senator from Illinois be sustained?" [11] He also said that Dirksen's point of order was subject to a tabling motion and that if it were tabled, McGovern's motion would be in order and the way cleared to adopting a three-fifths cloture rule by a series of simple majority votes. Since a tabling motion is non-debatable and carries by a simple majority, Humphrey's action created a parliamentary situation diametrically opposed to the one produced by Johnson's seemingly similar ruling four years earlier: the rules could be changed by a simple majority.[12] At last the liberals stood at the threshold they had been seeking since 1949, and at last they learned the naked truth: confronted by a clear chance to amend Rule 22 uncomplicated by procedural distractions, a solid majority of senators went on record against majority rule. McGovern's motion to table Dirksen's point of order was defeated, 37 to 61; and the point of order then sustained, 59 to 37. On both roll calls only eight Republicans joined with just under two-thirds of the northern Democrats on the losing side. Mansfield, who supported Dirksen's point of

order, then brought the issue to a close by filing a cloture petition which, as expected, was rejected by 53 to 46, thirteen votes short of the necessary two-thirds. Nine Republicans and four northern Democrats who voted for cloture voted against tabling Dirksen's point of order, the key vote on this issue in 1967.

After the brutal reality of the 1967 votes the 1969 revival of the issue produced little more than an anticlimax. Humphrey's decision in 1967 had been widely interpreted as an example of his general betrayal of liberalism.[13] In 1969, having endured two more years of vilification on this theme, the lame duck Vice President made the ruling his radical critics had demanded, with results no different from the earlier outcome. Humphrey announced that if a simple majority voted for cloture on a motion to take up a rules change resolution, he would rule that the majority had prevailed; and that if this ruling were appealed, the vote on the appeal would give the Senate a chance to decide the constitutional question of whether a simple majority could amend the rules at the beginning of a new Congress. The vote on the cloture motion was 51 to 47; Humphrey ruled that cloture had been imposed; this ruling was appealed and reversed by a 45 to 53 vote.

This chronicle of unrelieved liberal defeats over Rule 22 contains important clues for understanding the role of unlimited debate in the Senate and in the national political system. The clearest conclusion to be drawn from these recurring episodes is that most senators consistently have opposed carrying the principle of majority rule so far as to weaken or abolish a minority's power to prevent the Senate from voting on a bill. Prior to 1967 it had been easier for many observers to believe that most senators disliked Rule

22 and would reform it if only a motion to do so could be brought to a vote. The outcome in 1967 exposed what the previous motions to table and refer to committee had obscured: most senators like Rule 22.

– 3 –

A second lesson from this history is that three presidents, who might be considered the natural enemies of the obstructive, sectional, anti-majoritarian, centrifugal filibuster, have been remarkably unconcerned by the threat it poses to their goals. They have, in fact, appeared much more disturbed by attempts to weaken the filibuster. It seems that neither Eisenhower, Kennedy, nor Johnson ever did anything to help amend Rule 22. Indeed, while firm evidence is elusive, it appears that at least the latter two covertly encouraged dropping the issue. (Harry S. Truman is an exception to this generalization. He was a vociferous advocate of reform in 1949, although there is no indication that his efforts went beyond advocacy. His public statements on this issue were quite maladroit, devoid of the necessary bipartisan spirit, and usually at odds with the efforts of the Democratic leadership, often to the point of being a hindrance rather than a help.) [14]

One school of political scientists, of whom James M. Burns has come to be the symbol, argues that this kind of behavior is unnatural, that by the very nature of things presidents should try to centralize power, and that when they do not, they are not only playing the role false but making a serious strategic error.[15] Since most presidents have made the same mistake, it might be useful to consider why they persist in behaving in such an apparently wrongheaded manner. The answer, I think, will also explain why most senators submit to minority rule.

One common explanation for the latter tolerance is that many senators anticipate a day when they may need to filibuster to protect some cherished interest of their own. It is said, for example, that the senators from Nevada oppose restricting debate because the gambling interests in their state, looking to future proposals for greater federal taxation or regulation, count on the filibuster for protection. This may be true, but it is also true that there are few Negroes and many ex-Southerners and Mormons in Nevada, and that the balance of constituent attitudes there is not favorable to civil rights. Moreover, it has been a long time since a liberal represented Nevada in the Senate.

I think it closer to the truth that filibusters essentially are for bills involving salient and emotional issues, of which the prime contemporary example is civil rights. Despite conservative filibusters to prevent elimination of Section 14(b) of the Taft–Hartley Act in 1965 and 1966 and liberal ones on Comsat and to preserve the Supreme Court's reapportionment decisions in 1964,[16] Rule 22 reform is almost wholly a civil rights issue. The familiar bloc of lobbyists institutionalized in the Leadership Conference on Civil Rights—including labor, liberal, and Negro organizations—takes the field on Rule 22 disputes just as it does on substantive bills. The hard core of senatorial votes in defense of Rule 22 is from the South, and the onslaught is led by the most liberal senators. The principal difference between voting on civil rights bills and on Rule 22 is that moderate Democrats and most Republicans other than the small liberal bloc tend to oppose rule reform, as do the leaderships of both parties.

The extent to which filibusters are reserved for civil rights legislation can

TABLE 1   Conservative Filibusters Against Liberal Legislation, 1960–68[a]

YEAR	BILL	CLOTURE VOTE	VOTES NEEDED	PRESIDENTIAL PRESSURE
1960	Civil Rights	42–53	64	Low
1962	Restrict Literacy Tests	43–53[b]	64	Low
1964	Civil Rights	71–29	67	High
1965	Voting Rights	70–30	67	High
1965	Repeal Section 14(b)	45–47	62	Low
1966	Repeal Section 14(b)	51–48[c]	66	Low
1966	Civil Rights	54–42[d]	64	High
1966	D.C. Home Rule	41–37	52	Low
1968	Open Housing	65–32[e]	65	High

[a] Includes only filibusters on which a cloture petition was filed and excludes non-legislative issues such as rules reform and the Fortas confirmation.
[b] On a second roll call a few days later the vote was 42–52.
[c] Two days later the vote was 50–49.
[d] A few days later the vote was 52–41.
[e] This successful vote was preceded by three unsuccessful ones.
Source (except for last column): *Congressional Quarterly Weekly Report*, January 17, 1969, p. 140.

be illustrated by examining the issues on which conservatives used this weapon against liberal bills in the Eisenhower, Kennedy, and Johnson Administrations. All such cases in which the threat of obstruction was sufficiently serious to lead to a cloture petition are summarized in Table 1. All concern civil rights except the unsuccessful attempt to repeal Section 14(b), which permitted states to adopt right-to-work laws. (President Johnson supported this measure, but without discernible enthusiasm, and the White House let it be known that the President would not push very hard for its passage.[17] It was generally felt that the bill's progress represented the Democratic party's debt to the labor movement rather than political calculations or ideological conviction.) The other seven cases all concern civil rights, which strongly suggests that filibusters are a realistic threat only to a narrow element of a president's program and often are directed at bills about which the president is not very enthusiastic. The table also shows quite a strong relationship between presidential involvement and failure of filibusters. The only deviant case, the Civil Rights Act of 1966, was passed two years later after a hairsbreadth cloture vote.

During the 1950s and early 1960s political observers often classified civil rights measures as part of a general liberal legislative agenda. In fact, however, the issue was something of a special category in the minds of many Democratic politicians, particularly those who prided themselves on their pragmatism. They calculated that significant civil rights legislation could not be passed, that attempts to do so would damage Democratic unity, and moreover that such efforts were politically unnecessary for national Democratic electoral success. Civil rights was thought to be something of an obsession of impractical liberals, and political leaders often expressed annoyance at the intrusion of the issue on their expectations. Thus during his period as majority leader Johnson complained: "I want to run the Senate. I want to pass the bills that need to be passed. I want my party to do right. But all I ever hear from the liberals is Nigra, Nigra, Nigra." [18]

In 1961 and 1963 President Kennedy helped defend Rule 22, not because he liked it, but because involvement in rule reform was not worth the price he would pay in party unity, since he had no intention of pressing Congress for action on the only issue likely to bring forth a filibuster. Much as his decision may have shocked liberal Democrats, they were unlikely to vote against his proposals, unlike the southern Democrats, who held the keys to his legislative success. The Kennedy Administration eventually did introduce and fight for significant civil rights legislation, but only after the Birmingham demonstrations in the spring of 1963 altered the political climate and forced a major policy shift in the White House.[19] Much the same pattern was followed in 1965. At the opening of the 89th Congress that January President Johnson had no plans to introduce civil rights legislation. The dramatic brutality marking suppression of demonstrations in Selma, Alabama, led Johnson to much the same rearrangement of his legislative program that his predecessor had made two years before, and again, with the Voting Rights Bill of 1965, civil rights legislation became an urgent White House goal.[20]

The narrow range of issues on which filibusters occur explains the durability of Rule 22, for if filibusters were more widely used, Rule 22 would not be so difficult to change. The Senate could not tolerate promiscuous filibusters in which any minority resorted to unlimited debate to avoid defeat. Filibusters do more than prevent just one bill from passing: they keep the whole Senate from functioning; committees cannot meet (except by unanimous consent), and the need to remain available for quorum calls keeps senators from tending to many other kinds of business. The filibusterers themselves must be organized and disciplined. For these reasons filibusters—as opposed to the use of unlimited debate for on-the-spot tactical purposes—generally are reserved for issues on which a minority of senators represent very intense and salient opinion. If they were used more often, or more capriciously, the Senate would amend Rule 22 so as to exert more control over its proceedings, with the president cheering it on.

This point—as it pertains both to the Senate and the president—can be illustrated by comparing the filibuster to another classic obstructive device, the House Rules Committee, and contrasting the new Kennedy Administration's behavior on the two procedural struggles that ushered in the opening of Congress in 1961, the Rule 22 fight and the enlargement of the Rules Committee. At the time of Kennedy's election the Rules Committee consisted, as it had for some years, of eight Democrats and four Republicans. Two of the Democrats, Chairman Howard W. Smith (Va.) and William M. Colmer (Miss.), were ultraconservatives who frequently sided with the four Republicans to make a six-to-six deadlock and thus block liberal legislation on a *variety of issues*. This obstruction did not, however, interfere with committee meetings, floor business, or House activity other than the blocked measure. Since the Rules Committee's obstructive potential was focused and thus less disruptive of the good order of the House than was the filibuster of the Senate's, it could be more widely used—and was. It was responsible for the death of several important liberal bills in the late 1950s. This is not to say that Smith could have stopped any legislation he disliked; if this were the case, the country's laws would be very different than they are.[21] But the

Rules Committee's potential for blocking Kennedy's legislative program was far more dangerous than the continuation of an unamended Rule 22. Since Kennedy had no plans for civil rights legislation, he had no cause to fear the filibuster and no incentive to inflame southern Democrats by trying to weaken it. But he did want to pass other social welfare legislation, some of which the Rules Committee had blocked in past years.[22] Therefore he leaped eagerly into the fight when liberal Democratic congressmen proposed enlarging the Rules Committee from twelve to fifteen so it would be composed of ten Democrats and five Republicans, replacing the old six-to-six deadlock with an eight-to-seven Administration majority. Rallying Speaker Sam Rayburn, he exerted every resource of his new administration in a tremendous campaign to enlarge the committee, succeeding by a margin of five votes.[23] The conclusion, I think, is clear: the filibuster is not used often enough on issues important to them to motivate either presidents or a majority of the Senate to weaken its power.

By itself this conclusion is not startling, but its implications do run counter to the widespread interpretation of American politics that sees the president (especially if he is a Democrat) and his legislative allies—representing modern, urban, majoritarian America —opposing a more conservative grouping based on traditional, rural, consensual ideas. This view is held by such diverse interpreters of the political scene as Burns and the late Willmoore Kendall.[24] Yet there are times when the President is not so much the advocate of liberal measures as their would-be undertaker, at odds with his presumed allies in Congress. In recent years the most important of these issues often has concerned civil rights,

and therefore in this respect the president has not been part of the coalition trying to make the policy-formation process more responsive to majority rule. In Burns' terminology, the president in these circumstances has been allied with the "congressional Democratic party," opposed to the goals supposedly pursued by the "presidential Democratic party."[25]

– 4 –

Readers familiar with some of the leisurely filibusters of the period before 1964 might think that my characterization of their disruptive impact on the Senate is exaggerated. This is a fair judgment, but it is important to note that these languid affairs were not "true filibusters" in which a determined minority balked a majority. Two conditions must be met before a particular filibuster could validly be judged a minority veto: 1) House passage of the bill being filibustered; 2) a majority vote for cloture.[26] In other words, there must be evidence that the bill would have passed but for the filibuster. On closer examination of the historical record, it appears that these conditions were met only once between the end of the war and 1964. The filibuster, then, does not deserve its fearsome reputation for defeating civil rights bills, but was instead a convenient scapegoat.

Of the eleven cloture votes on civil rights in this period, none came close to success. A simple majority was attained on only four of the eleven. The first of these four was a 48–36 vote in 1946 on a bill to establish a federal Fair Employment Practices Commission (FEPC). It is not at all clear that this was the true cause of the bill's death, however, for in the House an FEPC bill was bottled up in the Rules Committee.

In the same year a House-passed bill to prohibit poll taxes was stopped by filibuster, but won a simple majority in the cloture vote, 39–33. This is the only one of the four bills with simple majorities on cloture that also passed the House; that is, it is the only one that seemingly would have become law but for the filibuster. It is worth noting, however, that earlier in 1946 the Senate had tabled an attempt by Senator Wayne Morse to add this measure as a rider to another bill. This suggests that some of the votes for cloture were cast by senators fairly secure that they would not win.[27]

In 1950 two cloture votes on FEPC failed, 52–32 and 55–33. The latter was the closest approach to success on a civil rights cloture vote prior to 1964; it fell nine votes short. In this year an FEPC bill finally reached the floor of the House, but once there it was amended to remove all enforcement powers. Thus while a majority of the Senate favored an FEPC with power to enforce prohibitions against discrimination, a majority of the House was against it. Once again, the filibuster may have borne more than its proper share of guilt for the failure of FEPC.

Ten years passed before another cloture vote on civil rights legislation.[28] The cloture petition on the Civil Rights Bill of 1960 seems to have been more of a liberal grandstand play than a constructive attempt to strengthen the bill. The petition was filed even before a bill had reached the House floor, at least in part because of fears by the liberals in each party that the other party would appear the more dedicated to civil rights.[29] Cloture failed by 42 to 53, with Democrats split evenly and twelve Republicans in favor to 20 against. Neither party leadership nor the President supported cloture, and the bill eventually passed by

the House was subsequently accepted by the Senate without major damage.

Like other aspects of the 1962 bill restricting the use of literacy tests in voter registration, the filibuster against it was largely ceremonial. No action was taken by the House on this measure, nor did a simple majority of the Senate favor it. Although ostensibly it was an Administration bill, the White House and Justice Department barely went through the motions of supporting it. No serious attempt was made to exhaust the desultory southern filibuster before resorting to cloture which, as in 1961, was timed by the leadership to dispose of the issue as quickly as possible and thus minimize the Democratic split.

During the civil rights filibusters of the early 1960s the liberals were haunted by failure from start to finish. Their characteristic disorganization was less consequential than it might have been if the issue had ever been in doubt. Much of their behavior seemed to be for the sake of ceremony and Negro voters rather than constructive legislative purposes, as in 1960.

In short, from the war until 1964 only one civil rights bill was killed chiefly by unlimited debate, the anti-poll tax bill of 1946. During the Eisenhower and Kennedy Administrations no civil rights filibuster was strongly opposed by *either* party leadership or by the Executive Branch, and no cloture vote won even a simple majority. Thus while the filibuster is, as Dahl says, one of several governmental features that "provide a minority veto,"[30] it is a veto that is seldom exercised by a minority against a majority.

– 5 –

None of these judgments can be made of one other recent filibuster, against the Communications Satellite Bill of

1962, on which the Senate voted cloture for the first time since 1927. At issue was an Administration bill, already passed by the House, to authorize a private corporation to own and operate a commercial communications satellite system based on federally financed research. Some liberal Democratic senators denounced the bill as a giveaway of public resources and announced that they would filibuster it. The bill was debated for five days in June and again from July 26 to 31. On August 10 it came before the Senate for the third time and the next day the leadership filed a cloture petition. Cloture was invoked on August 14 by a vote of 63 to 27, three votes more than were needed.

The voting patterns made it quite clear that the principle of devotion to unlimited debate had its limits.[31] Every one of the 34 Republicans voted, and only the two most conservative, Barry Goldwater and John Tower of Texas, voted against cloture. Seventeen Republican senators who had never before voted for cloture on a civil rights or rules change measure in the 1960s voted for it on Comsat.

The behavior of the Southerners and their conservative northern Democratic allies is even more interesting. All of the eighteen inveterate southern filibusterers (those from all former Confederate states less Texas and Tennessee) supported the Comsat bill. Eleven of them voted against cloture, including their leader, Richard B. Russell of Georgia, who said, "I'll vote to gag the Senate when the shrimps start to whistling 'Dixie.' "[32] These eleven could afford their procedural principles, however, for the other seven filibusterers made cloture possible, two by voting for it and the other five by not voting.[33] Two other conservative Democrats who had never voted for cloture, Alan Bible of Nevada and

Robert Byrd of West Virginia, also abstained. If any five of these seven anti-cloture senators had voted, 65 votes would have been required to stop debate, two more than the Administration mustered. Undoubtedly two more conservatives could have been induced to vote for cloture at the cost of compromising their principles. All in all, ten Democrats failed to vote, eight of whom announced their opposition to cloture and voted for the bill on final passage.

Less conspicuous events after cloture shed light on the relative durability of one Senate norm—that every member should have his say—and the extent to which this courtesy is extended equally to different senators. According to the rules, each senator may speak for a total of one hour after cloture has been imposed. Together with quorum calls and a minimum of twenty minutes to complete a roll call on an amendment, this gives diehard filibusterers further chances to obstruct proceedings. The liberals intended to exploit these rules but quickly discovered that there were limits on the fabled Senate norms of respect for fellow members and opportunities for full discussion. As soon as a liberal offered an amendment, the leadership moved to table it, thus cutting off debate and forcing an immediate vote. The liberals lost every tabling motion and never mustered more than twenty votes. Most tabling motions carried by voice vote, which speeded up the proceedings even more. All in all, the liberals offered 122 amendments, some of which would have restored provisions in the bill the President originally had sent to Congress. Since many of these provisions had been amended in the House, restoring them in the Senate would have necessitated either House acceptance of the Senate amendments or a conference committee to compromise the differences in the two versions of the bill. If the bill went to conference, however, the motion that the Senate accept the conference committee report could be filibustered. Nevertheless, the leadership could have permitted debate on these amendments and then let the Senate "vote them up or down," since it clearly had the votes to defeat all amendments. Instead the leadership chose speed over comity and ruthlessly pressed on to final passage by moving to table every amendment offered after cloture.

Two years later, when cloture was imposed on the Civil Rights Bill of 1964, the leadership faced a similar problem: how to respond to the more than 500 amendments which the Southerners had filed and could call up one by one in order to delay the vote on final passage. At the meeting where this was discussed Senator Mansfield expressed his fears that the long controversy over the bill would end with the defeated Southerners deeply embittered and inclined to vent their feelings on other aspects of the Administration's program. Insisting "We've got to keep our party together," Mansfield was so solicitous of the filibusterers that he suggested trying to give each of them more than the allotted hour for speaking. Senator Clark objected and urged that amendments be tabled as they were offered and that no time be lost in bringing the bill to a final vote. But other senators shared Mansfield's concern for party unity, at which Clark bitterly asked, "Who worried about the liberals' feelings in the Comsat debate?" A conciliatory attitude prevailed, however, and the Southerners prolonged Senate proceedings for nine days after cloture by calling up and speaking for 104 unsuccessful amendments, all of which were the subject of roll call votes. Moreover, the leadership (in concert with Senator Dirksen) accepted several amendments offered by Southerners after private negotiations and, usually, redrafting.

The contrast between the leadership's behavior in 1962 and 1964 can be explained principally by the identity of the filibusterers in the two cases, and in part by the solidity of the pro-cloture coalitions. The Comsat filibusterers were mostly rather junior and none was a committee chairman at the time, while the 1964 filibusterers included ten of the Senate's sixteen standing committee chairmen, as well as the chairmen of seven of the twelve subcommittees of the Committee on Appropriations. The Southerners were bitter at losing the cloture vote and Mansfield, characteristically preoccupied with maintaining party unity in the long run, wanted to avoid any further possible annoyances. He was known to dislike the divisiveness of civil rights bills and to feel that southern chairmen took their revenge on this issue by delaying Administration legislation, particularly appropriations bills. The Comsat rebels, on the other hand, had neither the committee power of the Southerners nor their freedom to embarrass the Administration.

The leadership's willingness to accept amendments that were trifling or could be rendered harmless was motivated by a desire to be helpful to certain Southerners, for whom successful amendments were trophies to display at home. (One of them confided, "Down home, being against the bill isn't good enough; you've got to put in amendments, too.") Russell Long of Louisiana was most successful at this bargaining, principally because he was expected to succeed to the chairmanship of the Finance Committee fairly soon, and thus was a good man to propitiate.

Finally, there were fears that too

arbitrary a stance might inflame enough touchy senators to risk losing their support on important amendments, for some Republicans were dubious about various provisions in the bill. Indeed, the Southerners gathered enough Republican support on one damaging amendment to come within four votes of winning. Fears of provoking a reaction from their shaky coalition led the leadership to give the Southerners all the leeway they wanted and also to accept several trifling amendments from Republicans. (Three of these were from Jack Miller of Iowa, who kept banging out new amendments on a cloakroom typewriter while the debate was in progress.[34] Dirksen eventually tired of this and, when approached by Miller with yet another trivial amendment, thundered, "Enough of this cheese-paring, Jack.") There were no such problems on Comsat, where the filibusterers clearly had no chance to win any votes on amendments, and so could be treated less tenderly.

These events do not seem consistent with the picture of the Senate suggested by those writers—notably William S. White—who stress that body's weighty respect for prerogatives, courtesy, and deliberations.[35] These norms are by no means limited to Rule 22, of course, but provide that every senator should have his say, in contrast to the large and impersonal House, where bills are briskly debated and voted up or down. Now there is no doubt that the Senate displays far more respect for individual members' sensibilities than the House.[36] My point here is that this solicitude—an important and constant factor in the leadership's strategy throughout the 1964 filibuster —varies significantly with the exigencies of the legislative situation (which is not so surprising) and the charac-

teristics of those senators whose prerogatives are subject to violation. The contrasting post-cloture events in 1962 and 1964 suggest the existence of a Senate folkway that may take precedence over the norm of comity: some senators are more equal than others.[37]

White, the prototypical interpreter of senatorial norms, also offers a characterization of the Senate that seemingly accommodates my proposition: the "Inner Club."[38] But his argument about the "Club" differs from what I am arguing in two respects: 1) The advantages of being in White's Club are not that one then benefits from the norms of equality, courtesy, and so on. These, he implies, are universal save for the rare outcast. 2) Senators are in the Club by virtue of their conformity to role expectations, while the Southerners in 1964 were the beneficiaries of their formal institutional positions (their chairmanships), not their level of group acceptance.

– 6 –

To sum up the foregoing: 1) Filibusters have been so unthreatening to various presidents' legislative programs that the actual postwar occupants of the White House have remained aloof from attempts to curb this presumed impediment to their power or covertly helped defeat and distract such efforts. 2) With one possible exception, in no case between the war and 1966 was the filibuster responsible for the death of a civil rights bill supported by majorities in Congress. 3) Far from being the most devoted advocates of full and free discussion as a general principle, irrespective of politics, supporters of filibusters often have displayed uncommon zeal to deny their opponents unlimited debate, most notably when changes in the rules were proposed, when the votes to support such arbitrary treatment were assured, and/or when the squelched senators were relatively junior.

NOTES

1. During the Senate's first years its rules provided for ending debate by moving the previous question, but this provision was eliminated at the beginning of the 19th century. See William J. Keefe and Morris S. Ogul, *The American Legislative Process,* second edition (Englewood Cliffs, N.J.: Prentice-Hall, 1968), p. 256.

2. George B. Galloway, *Limitation of Debate in the U. S. Senate* (Washington, D.C.: Library of Congress, Legislative Reference Service, 1958), p. 29.

3. *Ibid.,* p. 30.

4. Galloway reports that there were 82 of these between 1876 and 1916 alone; *ibid.,* p. 3.

5. For a modern example of this tactic see Ralph K. Huitt, "The Outsider in the Senate: An Alternative Role," in Ralph K. Huitt and Robert L. Peabody, *Congress: Two Decades of Analysis* (New York: Harper & Row, 1969), 166–68.

6. *Congress and the Nation* (Washington, D.C.: Congressional Quarterly Service, 1965), p. 1415.

7. Galloway, *op. cit.,* p. 18.

8. A vote early in 1949 had the effect of affirming Vandenberg's ruling. See John G. Stewart, "Independence and Control: The Challenge of Senatorial Party Leadership" (Chicago: unpublished doctoral dissertation, University of Chicago, 1968), p. 92.

9. The principal sources are Galloway, *op. cit.; Congress and the Nation, op. cit.;* Howard E. Shuman, "Senate Rules and the Civil Rights Bill," *American Political Science Review,* 51 (December 1957), pp. 955–975; Alan Rosenthal, *Toward Majority Rule in the United States Senate* (New York: McGraw-Hill, 1962); and various issues of *Congressional Quarterly Weekly Report.*

10. Rosenthal, *op. cit.,* p. 23.

11. Quoted in *Congressional Quarterly Weekly Report,* January 20, 1967, p. 88.

12. Humphrey's ruling was carefully planned to allow the issue to be decided by majority vote and yet not violate the unbroken precedent that the presiding officer should refer constitutional questions to the Senate for its decision. This strategy had been planned in concert with the reformers. See Stewart, *op. cit.,* pp. 125–128. (Stewart was Humphrey's legislative assistant.)

13. See, e.g., Robert Sherrill and Harry W. Ernst, *The Drugstore Liberal* (New York: Grossman, 1968), p. 142.

14. Stewart, *op. cit.,* pp. 87–91. For Truman's failings in congressional liaison see Rowland Evans and Robert Novak, *Lyndon B. Johnson: The Exercise of Power* (New York: New American Library, 1966), Chapter 3.

15. For Burns' criticisms of Franklin D. Roosevelt on this score see his *Roosevelt: The Lion and the Fox* (New York: Harcourt, Brace, 1956), pp.

375–380. The closest nonacademic parallel to Burns is *The New Republic,* which habitually urges presidents to act more presidential.

16. Two other successful conservative filibusters, against home rule for the District of Columbia in 1966 and confirmation of Abe Fortas as Chief Justice in 1968, were motivated in part by racial considerations.

17. Eric F. Goldman, *The Tragedy of Lyndon Johnson* (New York: Dell Publishing Company, 1968), p. 334.

18. Quoted in Evans and Novak, *op. cit.,* p. 119.

19. David B. Filvaroff and Raymond E. Wolfinger, *The Civil Rights Act of 1964* (forthcoming).

20. Goldman, *op. cit.,* pp. 337, 376–377.

21. Nor does it mean that Smith did not eventually lose a good measure of his power as a consequence of exercising it too eagerly. In this connection see Charles O. Jones' important article, "Joseph G. Cannon and Howard W. Smith: An Essay on the Limits of Leadership in the House of Representatives," *Journal of Politics,* 30 (August, 1968), pp. 617–646.

22. *Ibid.;* James A. Robinson, *The House Rules Committee* (Indianapolis: Bobbs-Merrill, 1963); Frank J. Munger and Richard F. Fenno, Jr., *National Politics and Federal Aid to Education* (Syracuse: Syracuse University Press, 1962), pp. 132–136; Richard Bolling, *House Out of Order* (New York: E. P. Dutton & Co., 1965), Chapter 10; and Hugh D. Price, "Race, Religion, and the Rules Committee," in Alan F. Westin, ed., *The Uses of Power* (New York: Harcourt, Brace, and World, 1962), pp. 1–71.

23. There are many descriptions of the enlargement of the Rules Committee. See, e.g., Bolling, *op. cit.;* Milton C. Cummings, Jr. and Robert L. Peabody, "The Decision to Enlarge the Committee on Rules: An Analysis of the 1961 Vote," in Robert L. Peabody and Nelson W. Polsby, eds., *New Perspectives on the House of Representatives,* second edition (Chicago: Rand McNally and Co., 1969), pp. 253–281.

24. See James M. Burns, *The Deadlock of Democracy: Four-Party Politics in America* (Englewood Cliffs, N.J.: Prentice-Hall, 1963), Part III; and Willmoore Kendall, "The Two Majorities," *Midwest Journal of Political Science,* 4 (November, 1960), 317–345. I should add that neither of these authors explicitly states that presidents are deadly enemies of Rule 22.

25. *Ibid.*

26. It might be argued in rebuttal that votes on a cloture motion may reflect senators' views on the procedural issue of unlimited debate rather than their opinion of the bill being filibustered, and that therefore a significant number of senators voting against cloture on a bill might nevertheless vote for the bill itself if given the opportunity, and vice versa. The most that can be said for this argument is that it should be reformulated to state that, in given circumstances, senators' procedural preferences are more salient to them than their substantive views, when the two are in conflict. Even this proposition is not very important to the argument, however. As my discussion of the Comsat filibuster shows, procedural issues of this kind seldom keep senators from voting so as to further their policy preferences.

27. Although 15 Republican senators voted for cloture and seven opposed it, 16 others did not vote, which indicates either that the issue was not very salient to some Republicans or that they were staying away from the crucial vote as a means of ensuring the bill's defeat.

28. The threat of unlimited debate may have been responsible for the 52 to 38 vote to delete "Part III" (empowering the Attorney General to initiate suits to prevent denial of equal protection of the laws) from the 1957 Civil Rights Bill, but it is by no means certain that this was the decisive factor, in view of President Eisenhower's distaste for this provision. See Evans and Novak, *op. cit.,* pp. 124–140.

29. Statements about events in 1960 are based on my observations while a Congressional Fellow that year. Statements about civil rights politics in subsequent years are based on interviews with most of the politicians and lobbyists involved and my observations while a member of Senator Humphrey's staff in 1964.

30. Robert A. Dahl, *A Preface to Democratic Theory* (Chicago: University of Chicago Press, 1956), p. 55.

31. For a similar interpretation see Keefe and Ogul, *op. cit.,* pp. 259–260.

32. Quoted in the *1962 Congressional Quarterly Almanac,* p. 378.

33. The only known "principled" vote for cloture by an opponent of the bill was by Clark, who stuck to his belief that a majority of senators should be able to vote on an issue when they wanted to. Frank Moss of Utah voted against the bill and paired for cloture. The other nine senators who voted against the bill all voted against cloture.

34. The leadership was extraordinarily accommodating about granting unanimous consent to present amendments which had not been introduced before cloture.

35. The standard work is William S. White, *Citadel: The Story of the U. S. Senate* (New York: Harper, 1956).

36. For a useful discussion and demonstration of this point and its implications see Lewis A. Froman, Jr., *The Congressional Process* (Boston: Little, Brown, 1967), pp. 6–15.

37. A more explicit discussion of Senate folkways is in Donald R. Matthews, *U. S. Senators and Their World* (Chapel Hill: University of North Carolina Press, 1960), Chapter 5; and Huitt, *op. cit.* For both these writers folkways or norms are individual role expectations, while I have broadened the terms to apply to leadership behavior, or collective senatorial decisions. This somewhat different usage is one of the reasons why my discussion of "unequal norms" is not directly at variance with Matthews, although it is not in consonance with his picture of the Senate.

38. White, *op. cit.,* Chapters 7–10. For a strong critique of the Inner Club theme see Nelson W. Polsby, *Congress and the Presidency* (Englewood Cliffs, N.J.: Prentice-Hall, 1965), pp. 32–43.

THE HOUSE

In order to understand the Senate, it is necessary to understand senators. In order to understand the House, it is necessary to understand how the House is organized. The House has 435 members. They must in some fashion be mobilized, subdivided into work groups, and assembled into majorities in order to accomplish their work together. The ways in which this is accomplished and the responses of congressmen to these varying processes is the theme of many of the essays that follow.

9

THE FRESHMAN CONGRESSMAN: HIS VIEW OF THE HOUSE

RICHARD F. FENNO, JR.

The reactions of two freshman congressmen from New York to the House of Representatives give Richard Fenno an opportunity to make several important points about the nature of the House as an institution. Fenno is Professor of Political Science at the University of Rochester, and the author of *The Power of the Purse,* the authoritative study of congressional aspects of the appropriations process.

"A man has to learn to be a Representative just as he must learn to be a blacksmith, a carpenter, a farmer, an engineer, a lawyer or a doctor." This comment by former Speaker Champ Clark is accepted wisdom in the United States House of Representatives. And every two years, the learning process begins for a new class of "freshman" Congressmen. Since January 3, the "Class of 1965"—67 Democrats and 19 Republicans—has been passing through its orientation period on Capitol Hill. Barber B. Conable, Jr., Republican of Alexander, and James S. Scheuer, Democrat of the Bronx, are two able, observant New York members of the class. Through their experiences and their reflections we can discover how Speaker Clark's education process works and, at the same time, get a revealing perspective on one of our most important political institutions.

The historic meeting of the Democrat caucus, which voted to deprive

Printed by permission of the author.

two southern Democratic Goldwater-supporters of their seniority, brought an early revelation for Representative Scheuer, a forty-four year old businessman-lawyer.

John Blatnik presented the motion in about five minutes, asked for one additional minute, and sat down. The southerners and their supporters talked for over an hour and their theme was that ours is a heterogeneous party in a pluralistic society and that it is big enough for all points of view. What I wanted to say was, "Well, if this is such a broad heterogeneous party in a pluralistic society how come you left it?" I was dying to make that speech! I leaned over to Blatnik and I whispered, "Why doesn't someone get up and say thus and so?" He whispered back, "When you've got the votes, you don't need to make speeches." And that's one lesson I've learned about legislative politics.

For forty-two year old Representative Conable, his legislative lessons had begun two years earlier in the State Senate. Contemplating the crucial business of his assignment to a congressional committee, he recalled,

When I first went to the Senate, I was the victim of some bad advice. I went around to see Walter Mahoney, the Republican leader, and he asked me what committees I wanted. Following my advice, I named the three most important ones—Finance, Judiciary, and Codes. Mahoney's eyes popped out, then they rolled around in his head for a whole minute and he finally said, "Well!"—and he changed the subject. Needless to say, the conversation didn't help my committee assignments. This time I'm not going whistling up a rain spout after top committees like Appropriations. The main thing I've told Gerry Ford is that I want to go on a working committee where I can learn the business of legislation.

No matter how imposing their achievements or their reputation in the outside world, Representatives Conable, Scheuer and their freshmen colleagues must begin all over again in the House of Representatives—a strange institution populated by people they do not know, run by people they rarely meet, in accordance with rules and customs they do not understand. During the first of four freshmen orientation sessions held the first week in January, for example, Scheuer rose to inquire, "Are there any rules about where new Members sit in the chamber? Do they have to sit in the back?" (Answer: No.) The next day, Conable, clutching his very first bill in his hand and walking from his office to the House floor to introduce it remarked, "I don't even know where I'm supposed to put this thing." (Answer: In the "hopper" at the House Clerk's desk.) Minor matters, of course; but the point is that every experience for the freshman is a new experience from which there is much to be learned.

Not only must the newcomer absorb a multitude of lessons, he must learn them quickly—especially if he aspires to become influential in the chamber. The committee assignments he receives, the friendships he acquires, the groups he joins, the impressions he makes on others—all during these first weeks on Capitol Hill—can spur or impede his rise to influence. Representatives Conable and Scheuer have been apt pupils precisely because they prize their membership in the House and are unabashedly ambitious for long-term careers there.

"A western New York Congressman has to face the fact that the way our state is set up, he can't run statewide," says Conable who represents one-half of the City of Rochester, some of its suburbs and four rural counties to the south and west. "The House represents a real opportunity for service— an opportunity few people get. And I can be a more effective Congressman down here if I'm not trying to chase will-o'-the-wisps."

Representative Scheuer had been president of a private corporation building urban housing projects in eight cities under the federal urban renewal program.

Some of my friends thought the job of a Congressman was downgrading after what I have been doing. But I disagree. I'll be satisfied to make the House my career, to accumulate seniority and perhaps become a committee chairman sometime. That way you can have a lot of influence over the areas in which you are interested.

Although their ambitions are similar, the two young freshmen cannot be expected to follow identical paths to positions of influence in the House. They do not share the same party affiliation, the same constituency background, the same social philosophy or the same immediate legislative goals.

Representative Conable, a lawyer with a degree from Cornell, represents the relatively stable, ethnically homogeneous and reasonably prosperous 37th Congressional District. He has deep roots in and strong attachments to "Western New York," where he (following several generations of his family) was born, raised and had a law practice. "We're all decentralists back home," he says. "We don't always trust the impersonal government way off in the distance somewhere. We believe in the diffusion of power and we like our local institutions."

A pragmatic conservative, he does not carry a pocket full of proposals for new federal programs. By conviction and by circumstance, he is more interested for the moment in establishing good two-way constituency relations than he is in promoting legislation. "I'll have to postpone my statesmanship for a couple of years at least. With the tiny minority we Republicans have here, there won't be much opportunity for that anyway."

Representative Scheuer, a graduate of Columbia Law School, has served on city, state, and national commissions and has participated in four United Nations conferences concerned with housing and inter-group problems in metropolitan areas. His 21st Congressional District, carved out of the Bronx along the lower Harlem River, is a typically urban constituency—polyglot, densely populated and relatively poor. "My district is a declining area," he says, "and it needs help from all levels of government if it is to become an attractive residential area where people enjoy the amenities of life. We need housing. We need schools. We need playgrounds and parks."

His own philosophy, the needs of his constituents, and the huge Democratic majority propel Scheuer, a Reform Democrat, toward a creative legislative role. He supports a wide range of new federal assistance programs; and he hopes to make some contributions to them himself. "I know there won't be any Wagner Act with my name on it during my first term. But if I can get these ideas of mine in here or there, I'll be satisfied."

During their early weeks on Capitol Hill, Representatives Conable and Scheuer have been going their separate ways—indeed, they have not even met each other. Yet they have been absorbing the same kinds of legislative knowledge and acquiring the same picture of the House as an institution. And herein lies the significance of Champ Clark's educational process. It is the process by which a heterogeneous group of new Members becomes sufficiently homogenized and sufficiently attuned to the ways of the House to guarantee its stability. The teaching of the young is vital to the survival of every human society. And so it is for the House. Though their specific experiences have been different, the two New York newcomers already agree in making the three fundamental observations about the institution which follow.

The House Is a Hierarchy

A perceptive freshman realizes almost immediately that a vast gap in experience, information and influence separates him from those senior members who effectively run the House. "I know I've got a great deal to learn," said Conable to Speaker John McCormack when the two first met at a picture-taking ceremony. The Speaker's solicitous rejoinder ("I'm still learning, too.") was indicative of that Member to Member friendliness which both freshmen have noted. But it hardly diminished the sense of being "junior" which a man at the bottom of the House ladder feels when he confronts the man at the top. Nor does it alter the brute fact conveyed to Scheuer by another elder statesman of the House, "The 89th Congress is not going to go down in history as the Scheuer Congress."

One factor which gives a hierarchical cast to life in the chamber is the pervasiveness of seniority rules—in filling such powerful positions as committee chairmen and in distributing such perquisites as office space, Capitol Hill patronage and seating arrangements on social occasions. "The organizational concept of the House is seniority," says Scheuer. "They don't hand out marks each month and then divide up responsibility. Your responsibilities are assigned on the basis of seniority." "It's the committee structure that makes the House seem hierarchical. That's where you really feel junior," observes Conable. "But it's partly because you're trying so hard to find out what they are talking about." It is not, therefore, just the rules of seniority that put the image of a House ladder in the mind of a freshman; it is the acknowledged differences in experience and information as well.

The first critical decision in every freshman's career involves his assignment to one of the House's twenty standing committees. And no decision is better calculated to impress the idea of hierarchy upon him. He can campaign for the assignment he wants, and usually does, but his fate rests almost entirely in the hands of a few senior Congressmen. Each party has its own Committee on Committees, and New York has a member on each—Representative Eugene Keogh for the Democrats and Representative Howard Robison for the Republicans. These committees (particularly the member from one's home state) plus the elected leaders of the respective parties plus the most senior party member of the committee involved decide the fate of each freshman. Representatives Scheuer and Conable were assigned to their first-choice committees—Scheuer to Education and Labor, Conable to Science and Astronautics. Both described themselves as "very pleased and very lucky."

"My first choice was Education and Labor. Its work is vital to the interests of New York," explained Scheuer.

I wrote to Gene Keogh, listed the committees I wanted in order and put myself in his hands. I also talked to Adam Powell (Chairman of the Committee). He wanted me on his committee and pushed aggressively for me. The AFL–CIO leaders let the House leaders know they looked upon my application with favor. I talked to the party leaders. From their point of view I had excellent connections with liberal groups, I had a solid background in business and banking institutions, and I had been active in civil rights. I guess I had something that pleased everybody.

"I didn't come down here with any particular committee preference," says Conable.

I talked to a lot of people about it and decided that Science and Astronautics was a good one that I might have a chance to get on. I put that first on my list, but I told Howie Robison I would trust his judgment. Howie went to Gerry Ford and said he had no committee assignment for me. Gerry asked him what my first choice was and said maybe they could get it. Apparently the minority leader threw his weight behind it. I was told later that he went to bat and really helped me. I'm not sure why, and I haven't gone around to ask.

The House Is an Oligarchy

Though the principle of hierarchy pervades the relationship between the senior old-timer and the junior newcomer, a closer inspection of the House reveals not one monolithic pyramid but many smaller pyramids. A few weeks of experience make it clear to the freshman that each of these lesser hierarchies bestows influence on its leaders and that it is these leaders—forty or fifty of them—who manage the affairs of the chamber. In practice, then, the House of Representatives is an oligarchy; and the committee chairmen, the subcommittee chairmen and the party leaders are its oligarchs. The ambitious freshman must still climb to a position of influence. But the oligarchical structure of the House means that he will be climbing several medium-sized ladders instead of a single ladder 435 rungs high.

Since most of the day to day legislative work of the House is done in its committees, it is here, more than any place else, that the freshman will make or break his House career. Influence inside the chamber rests heavily on expertise, and expertise rests in turn on specialization in the field of one's committee or subcommittee. Once assigned to their committees, Representatives Conable and Scheuer began their careers with the search for information —on space problems and education problems respectively.

"The Committee Chairman called the nine new members together the other day," said Conable.

He told us, "you fellows will be helping to pass on a 5 billion dollar budget for NASA, and the hearings begin in two weeks. I want you at least to have seen the installations where the bulk of the money is spent. You can't visualize what's going on in the field unless you've had some experience. I'm going to ask you to make yourselves available to go south this week to Huntsville, Cape Kennedy and the Mississippi Test Facility." He ordered us to go—well, you don't order a Congressman—but he put it in strong terms that we should go.

"I've been assigned to three subcommittees," said Scheuer,

but they haven't met yet. So I've been sitting in on the hearings of the subcommittee on aid to education. I'm not a member, but I've been acting like one. I've asked some questions and I've helped them to get a quorum once or twice. The chairman has welcomed my participation and we're going six days a week.

Nearly all decision-making in the House is organized, if not actually conducted, by the two parties. Every freshman, therefore, stands on a party as well as a committee ladder. He will not of course be admitted to the councils of his party leaders; but he will talk constantly with other members of his party about the business of the House and the issues of the day. Much of this intra-party communication is *ad hoc* and fragmentary, but some of it is organized. And it is through the lesser party organizations that cluster beneath the top leadership that a freshman gets his best opportunity to participate in party activity and pursue a party career.

As soon as he arrived in Washington, Representative Scheuer joined the Democratic Study Group, an unofficial organization of 140 or so liberal Democratic members. It was this group, for example, which pressed hardest for disciplinary action against the two southern Goldwater supporters and engineered House rules changes early in the session. Scheuer views the DSG as a group of experienced teachers, as a communications conduit and as "a special avenue through which I can express myself politically."

"They are a thoughtful, responsible liberal group," he says enthusiastically. "From a purely informational point of view they have made the seasoned experience of several first class members available to me. If I hadn't associated myself with the DSG and if I hadn't known people like Bill Phillips (its staff director) and Dick Bolling (one of its important members) for many, many years, I wouldn't know what was going on around here." As a member of the DSG's committee on civil rights, Scheuer recently joined 14 other Congressmen on an informal fact-finding trip to Selma, Alabama. His DSG activities have given Scheuer the feeling that he is participating in as well as observing the work of the 89th Congress.

On his side of the aisle, Representative Conable was one of two freshmen to be invited to join the informal SOS club—an "in-group" of 18 Republicans, including such official party leaders as Melvin Laird and Bob Wilson—which meets regularly to exchange information and discuss policy. He has also busied himself helping to launch "the 89th Club," an organization comprised of all Republican freshmen. "Communication is obviously a problem around here. So we meet every Monday in the office of one of the members to swap experiences, discuss evolving legislative issues and make common cause if we can. Usually we have a guest speaker too—last week it was Senator Thruston Morton, Senate Campaign Committee Chairman." Membership in these party groups promises to fill one freshman's need to communicate and participate. And, says Conable, "Devices like the SOS Club and the 89th Club increase your effectiveness without any doubt."

The House Is a Community

A great deal of what the freshman learns sums up to this—that the House is a little world of its own and that legislative careers are shaped primarily by what happens in that world. The House has its own traditions, customs and rules. It has its own formulas for success, its standards of judgment and its ways of punishing nonconformity. For four days early in January, a group of eight experienced Congressmen in conjunction with the American Political Science Association conducted orientation seminars for the Class of 1965. Speaker McCormack set the major theme of those sessions when he advised his listeners to "learn the rules of the House" and to "work hard in Committee" because by so doing "you will enlist and secure the confidence of your colleagues."

Again and again, the freshmen were told that "the House is the best judge of its members"; "we measure each other"; "the House is the greatest jury in the world"; "we spend a lot of time sizing each other up"—especially, of course, within committee and party groups. The seminar leaders passed along their standards of judgment in the form of advice—"work hard," "specialize," "do your homework," "be in attendance on the floor," "don't speak 'till you know what you are talking about," "follow your committees," "if you want to get along, go along," "learn parliamentary procedure," "be courteous to your colleagues," etc. The Member who follows these canons of behavior stands the best chance of being judged favorably. And with favorable judgment comes the most enduring basis for influence in the House —that is, the "confidence," "respect" and "trust" of one's fellow Members.

There is little doubt but what the two New York freshmen feel that they are, indeed, members of a little community. "Even seniority isn't ironclad," observed Scheuer.

You still have to command the respect of your colleagues. If you don't—if you work for a fast headline instead of doing the serious, anonymous kind of work that is expected of you—the seniority system can be circumvented. It can be bent to reflect the collective judgment of the House on a Member.

"I haven't made any speeches," says Conable.

I know a man's effectiveness is not measured by the amount of his palaver on the floor. I'm still studying my manual trying to match up the different Members' pictures, faces and names. That's important.

You can't do anything all by yourself around here. It's a collective operation.

It requires a feat of imagination to remind ourselves that fifteen, twenty or even thirty years ago the present leaders of the 89th Congress underwent an identical learning process. But they did. By the time of the 96th or 97th Congress, Representatives Conable and Scheuer may well be among the oligarchs of the House. Before their ultimate ambitions are satisfied, however, each must solve for himself the greatest of all problems facing a first-term Congressman—how to become a second-term Congressman.

10

SIX LETTERS TO CONSTITUENTS

CLEM MILLER

The duties of a member of Congress are manifold and varied. He must badger —or supplicate—the bureaucracies in behalf of wronged or bewildered or importunate constituents. He must understand, worry about, and protect the interests of his district, state, and region. He must think of the national welfare and learn to grapple with complex issues of public policy. He must monitor the political climate in which he exists: his committee, his state delegation, his party leaders, his allies, his opposition, in Washington and back home. These are complicated tasks; at stake is his own career and the fate of public policy. It is rare to see a member of Congress who does many of these things superlatively well. Some do become craftsmen, of course. It was well worth a trip to Capitol Hill to watch Robert Taft or Paul Douglas in debate, each a master of lucid, spare, and powerful exposition. No one who hears Wilbur Mills argue a tax bill can doubt his total command of that intricate business. Some congressmen have less visible talents: It was hardly possible to follow the energetic, behind-the-scenes generalship that gave Lyndon Johnson his grip on the Senate in the 1950s. The force of intellect and character that made Walter George and Richard Russell of Georgia, each in his time first among southern Democrats, was rarely visible from the Senate gallery, though from the House Gallery one could scarcely doubt the rocklike integrity displayed on Speaker Rayburn's Mount Rushmore-like countenance.

In his way, Clem Miller was as impressive as any of these better known figures. In two terms of service, he did not rise far in the House of Representatives, although his easy, approachable manner, intelligence, and varied background made him agreeable company, and he was marked by his seniors as very promising. Miller came from a well-to-do Delaware family, the son of a civil engineer, grandson of a governor of Delaware, nephew of a congressman. He was educated at Lawrenceville School, Williams College, and Cornell University, and easily held his own among eastern Establishment types. He was by preference an outdoorsman, by occupation a landscape consultant, after some years as a labor-relations expert, and he represented a predominantly rural district in Northern California—extending from the north shore of the Golden Gate to the Oregon line. Many of his legislative interests lay in the field of conservation and just before his death he had the satisfaction of seeing President Kennedy sign into law his bill—which he nurtured through the legislative process from his arrival in Washington—to make Point Reyes Peninsula, in his district, a national seashore.

But where he shone was as an educator. A great obligation of public officials in a democracy is to educate the people. It is mostly an unmet obligation.

When American officials go to the people, it is to mobilize support, or opposition, to plead for votes, to divine which way the wind is blowing. But rarely do they attempt to spread understanding of how things are done or why. Clem Miller was a great exception. His letters went out regularly, to friends and supporters in his home district, not merely describing, but evoking the experience of Congress for the people back home who had helped send him to Washington. No one who received the letters could fail to see what Congress was about. Friends of friends and colleagues of Miller's who learned about the letters passed old copies from hand to hand and asked to be put on the mailing list. Many of them were collected in his *Member of the House* (edited by John W. Baker and published by Charles Scribner's Sons in 1962). A week after the book was published, Clem Miller lay dead, at forty-six years of age the victim of the crash of a light private airplane in which he was campaigning through his 300-mile long district in search of a third term in Congress. A month later the people of his district reelected him posthumously, a salute believed to be without precedent in the history of the House. The selection below consists of six unpublished letters from Clem Miller to his constituents. They capture the voice of one of the finest, most effective teachers ever to speak or write about the House of Representatives.

June 15, 1961

Dear Friend:

It is difficult to vote against your friends, against your party. Even admitting that there is a group which does it regularly, it is as a group. They are friends, knitted together by a deeply held conviction.

As I have had occasion to remark, conformity is a most powerful force in Congress. The major battles are so protracted, and so much of all but the essence has been squeezed out of an issue before it arrives on the Floor, that it must be a powerful conviction to stand against your friends when the showdown comes.

I recall watching Fred Marshall of Minnesota stand against the Democrats in the Public Works Bill veto override vote in 1959. Only five other Democrats were with him on this, five from the most entrenched part of the Deep South. The vote was so close that a single vote did make a difference and the Democrats were hungry for their first victory over an Eisenhower veto. Fred sat in his usual seat, inert and immobile as the party guns worked him over in relays. With his hands folded in his lap, and only his eyes registering fire, he turned each man away with a jerk of his head.

When it comes to voting, each Member is his castle. It is not good form to question a Member's vote, no matter how curious

Copyright © 1970 by Katherine Johnson, and Katherine Johnson and Wells Fargo Bank, trustees u/w Clement W. Miller.

you may be. Even among friends, Members are resentful of having their vote challenged after it is cast, no matter what has been said earlier. There have been bitter words when a Member casting discretion to the winds, does make some challenging remark at the close of a vote. It is as though their good faith, their integrity or their judgment were challenged. They have voted—that is the end of the matter.

This does nothing to soften the silent reproof when one goes the other way. There are a lot of votes where sectionalism, industrialism, ruralism are bound to prevail. This is readily comprehended. It is "voting your District." But constituting a force of one or two or three, standing against your friends, that sticks in the memory of others. It lingers in the back of the mind for a long time. It adds a factor to the continuing catalog one makes of all his fellow Members.

Teller votes are the most difficult, it seems. Teller votes are not recorded votes. The "yeas" walk up the center aisle to be counted by the tellers, then the "nays." There is a great milling around in the well of the House. There is some self-conscious banter and cat calling. It is a time of maximum exposure. You feel physically exposed. You feel very vulnerable. It is trying to troop up the aisle, in absolute opposition to those seated who watch intently.

This is so even when you are allied with your own. It is doubly true when you are allied with the opposition. Then, the other side is very courteous, very solicitous. They stand aside and urge their temporary ally to go first—which the ally promptly accepts. The Southern bolters are truculent and defiant; they march up the aisle very boldly. This is a familiar road for them, and they are braced for it. Others are more apologetic, evasive.

Just a few days ago we had one such teller vote. Many of our friends simply ducked rather than go through the gauntlet. This is a perfectly accepted manner of indicating repudiation of the bill without repudiating your friends. It was a close vote. The private power lobby was against the amendment, long an issue with Democrats. Certain coal Congressmen and New Englanders, feeling the pinch of industrial competition elsewhere, were torn between the tradition of their party and regional prejudice or interest as they see it. Their discomfiture was obvious, even though they were quite resolute.

It is curious to watch. Before a teller vote the standers waiting to vote banter with those who are seated. "What's the matter, chicken?" "Come on, get up and vote with the man." "Tired of sitting? Let's take a walk together." But after the vote, as they return to their seats, the bantering is gone. No one says anything. It's over and done. The memory alone is there, part of the constant evaluating everyone does of everyone else, a summing up over a long period, now charitable, now harsh, forgiving and stern, weighing frailty and self-interest and courage against party and loyalty.

Very sincerely,
Clem Miller

September 15, 1961

Dear Friend:

Summertime is vacation-time, and for hundreds of thousands it includes a trip to the National Capitol. Hordes of travellers pour through the halls and corridors, ogling and listening, scrambling in behind the guides, queuing up anywhere and everywhere. On the eastern entrance to the Capitol, one small revolving door handles all the traffic and teems with humanity. The pinched, cramped hallways contrast oddly with the glistening grandeur of the façade.

Congressmen on the way to a roll-call must wedge by as best they can, assisted by phalanxes of police seeking to make way for them. They have come from their rooms in either of the two office buildings. Elevators are everywhere to expedite the movement of the Congressmen hurrying to the Floor. There are 12 in the Old House Office Building alone, regulated to carry traffic swiftly. The short walk from office to Capitol is a beautiful one. The sidewalks are serpentine through an avenue of old, well-cared-for trees. The great dome of the Capitol looms overhead in a constantly changing pattern.

Congress convenes at noon. Curious as it may seem, this has justification. The morning has been spent with mail from home, committee meetings, and so on. As the House begins its routine, the Congressman can combine his lunch with activities on the Floor. From the restaurant, he can mount the stairs immediately at hand for a roll-call, or other matters, then return.

The business of the House goes forward with prescribed rules and forms, with continuity, agenda and purpose. Only the names of the participants and details of the subject matter change. Generally speaking, if it is not a matter of his immediate concern, the congressman will not be present. Through the *Congressional Record,* the various calendars, and by telephonic inquiry, he knows what is going to be brought up, and he presents himself accordingly when it is necessary.

This is difficult for our throngs of visitors to understand. They came to Washington to see their legislators at work. Work to them is the debate—in the manner of Daniel Webster and Robert Y. Hayne. They are ushered into the visitors' galleries flanking three sides of the House Chamber in blocs of 25 or 50. I see them walk down the gallery rows, sit for five minutes, and arise on signal to march stolidly out. Among the gallery visitors there are those who are there with specific purpose to see a certain bill through. There are others who develop a knowledge of the crabbed procedures of the House, and, like any connoisseur, come to love its operations.

These visitors from everywhere look down on a vast Chamber, 139 feet long by 92 feet wide, which seats more than 400. Their eyes light on 30 to 50 members, scattered about without any apparent design, and they hear voices drone back and forth. "I have an amendment at the desk." "Third reading. A motion to recommit is laid upon the table." "Mr. Speaker, I move to take from the desk." It may as well be in another language. Yet, in its own manner, the business of our country is being conducted. This is the routine.

Upon occasion the orderly routine business of the House will erupt into high excitement. It is difficult to believe that this Chamber which is so still one moment can seethe with such a ferment in the twinkling of an eye. These moments are rare, perhaps four or five times in a session. The Members jam the Chamber, listening, and jumping up for recognition in clusters, finger pointed, and the cries rise like the wind. The excitement is electric.

Such a moment came last month with the Saund amendment to the Foreign Aid Bill. This is a moment of drama as distinguished from mere activity and motion, say on a roll-call. Congressmen hurry through the streets, work their way through the halls, packing into elevators, disgorging and rounding the corner into the Speaker's Lobby going full tilt, past banks of bystanders waiting to talk to members—till they burst on the Floor in a flood, then stand stock-still to catch the rhythm of the roll-call. "Abitt, Abernethy, Adair, Addabbo, Addonizio . . ." The hubbub of the moment is disconcerting. "Garmatz, Gary, Gathings, Gavin, Giaimo . . ." Roll-calls may come on major matters or on thoroughly insignificant bills. It is largely a matter of policy and strategy. For various reasons, the Leadership may not want a roll-call. Then the bill will go through on a voice vote. On the other hand, if a quorum is not present at the time of the vote any congressman making the point of order can force an automatic roll-call. That is why a listing of the bills on which votes are recorded reads curiously.

As the call continues, knots of members gather to get the word—what's the vote? Others cock an ear to catch the responses of trusted friends. Rushing in late, they may grab the committee report on the bill and wait for the second round. "Young, Younger, Zablocki, Zelenko . . ." In all the hurly-burly and noisy confusion, it is rare that a Member makes a mistake in casting his vote. If he should, he can go to the well of the House at the conclusion to change his vote. Generally, a little checking, a sharp question or two, and one is ready. "May, Meader, Merrow, Michel . . ."

Very sincerely
Clem Miller

October 15, 1961

Dear Friend:

The legislative year is a long one, and as the complexity of government becomes greater, it gets still longer. Those who have been here a while understand the measured pace of legislation through Congress. But, for many, the delays are incomprehensible, and a fertile source of journalistic speculation.

Great legislation is scarce. There are only a half dozen or so bills of overriding importance in a session. This very process of selection takes up an impressive block of time each year. Much of the preliminary jockeying for position and priorities is quite complicated. Is the bill of prime rank? Is it more important than another bill? Should it be considered at all, at least right now?

Through July, August and September such a dispute for priority went on between the Disarmament Agency Bill and the Peace Corps Bill. All were agreed that the Foreign Aid Bill came first. Huge energies were expended on this great bill, of primary rank, and there was no time in the Foreign Affairs Committee to devote to the remaining two until the big one was enacted. Their proponents stood in the wings dickering for clearance through the legislative chutes. Last year, vital legislation was at a standstill in the Education and Labor Committee while the full talents of its Members were engaged in the titanic battle over what became the Landrum–Griffin Bill.

It would be fair to say that much of the legislative energies of Congress goes to the assignment of priorities. This is no inconsiderable function.

Then, when we get down to *The* Bill, there remains the further task of reaching a consensus. This also takes time. Sometimes it may take a decade or longer; at the very least it takes months. Major legislation simply will not move through Congress if it is encrusted with too many debatable issues. The base of support erodes away. A great part of the work then, in committees, is to establish a general area of agreement, and to point up *The* Issue of *The* Bill on which it will go to the test.

Ever since January the Foreign Aid Bill has been in travail. There were many issues at the start. When the bill arrived on the Floor only one real issue remained—that of Treasury borrowing authority, known widely as back-door spending. It was on this that the key vote of the bill came—on the Saund Amendment. The moment in the House Chamber was electric. Months of bitter feeling, reams of memos and reports, all came to a resolution at this moment. When this vote was taken by tellers, 197–185, the Foreign Aid Bill was laid to rest as a partisan issue. There was some more oratory; some of it in strong terms, but it really was all over.

This was the ground President Kennedy had selected to make a fight on, and the ground he had asked his lieutenants to dig in upon. All spring, estimates of strength were cast up again and again. For it is axiomatic that you can only ask politicians to do what is possible. Trying to arrive at what is possible—what will your people accept that is as close as possible to the rejection point of the other side—is a fine point, but essential to the calculation.

So now that the President stands beaten, the second-guessers are at work. It is true one could tell, sitting in the Chamber at the moment the Saund Amendment was offered, that the President did not have a chance. There was real steam, real emotion, a real coalition of forces, behind Judge Saund that could not be stopped. It was easy to observe at the time, but hard to have foreseen accurately. Everyone knew Treasury borrowing was in trouble but did not know where or exactly how the action would come about. It may be likened to a general infection, distributed through the system, which suddenly localizes in an organ.

The successful art of congressional politics is to know the disease, localize it early and have the specific remedy ready at the time required. If this cannot be done, the bill will fail. A good example is this year's Aid to Education Bill, badly beaten in a bob-tailed version, 169 to 242. There were too many things going against it. The religious issue. The constitutional issue. The spending issue. The population issue. The Federal vs. local government issue. Rich state vs. poor state. Attrition sets in. On each of these, votes drop away.

Generalship in cases of this sort consists in narrowing your objectives, lowering your sights and pulling in your horns. This is what they sought to do on the Education Bill: make it modest enough to attract a consensus. The chairman of the Subcommittee on Housing, Congressman Albert Rains, uses another strategy, the red-herring technique. He uses public housing as the herring in the Housing Bill. It draws all the fire, while the rest of this monumental bill marches by. It is worth noting that he also uses sweetening as a primary device. Don't take anything out of the bill, just add something which will make it palatable—

"I don't like the bill, but I'm going to have to vote for it because
. . ." "I don't like the Farm Bill" (for instance), "but I'm going to
have to vote for it because it includes apples." (peanuts) (corn)
(cotton).

One may have the best bill in the world but if there is no broad
consensus, that bill is usually finished or very dormant. Take the
Wilderness Bill. It is a good bill. The foresters from the big
companies will tell you so. But the proponents can't get a consensus, an agreement of where to draw the line on the acreage to
be included as wilderness. Stubbornly, over a period of 12 years,
the wilderness proponents have been slowly and reluctantly giving way in the hopes of getting agreement. One of these days,
the right formula will be found and onlookers will gasp at the ease
with which it will sail through Congress. Although passed by the
Senate last session, right now the deadlock in the House looks
hopeless. But the antagonists continue to search for the formula.*

Much of committee work is the process of finding this consensus between the parties. A bill of importance is introduced
and heard in committee. The hearing may be window-dressing.
It may also, and usually does, reveal more about what the committee members are thinking than what the witnesses are telling
them. Armed with this knowledge the chairman will direct the
staff to find out what minimum terms would be acceptable to the
minority party. Working from this base the real issue, on which
there can be no agreement, or in which other issues pale into
insignificance and are lost, is developed and sharpened for later
resolution in a vote on the Floor. Alternatively, the chairman may
adopt the minimum terms of the Minority as his own. The consensus may be broad. In this sort of situation, the real issue is
too insignificant to argue about. So, the bill appears on the Consent Calendar or Suspense Calendar cleared for immediate passage by consensus.

This is what the legislative year is all about and why it takes
nine months. When we read of the violence of inter-party dispute,
we must realize that the gap between the two must be narrow
enough to be bridged in one jump. Arriving at this point of consensus on any particular bill may have taken many months or
many years. It does not mean brilliance or inventiveness on the
part of the principals. It means, as I have said before, that patience and persistence are the invaluable attributes of a congressman.

Very sincerely,
Clem Miller

* The National Wilderness Preservation Act was enacted in 1964.

June 1962

Dear Friend:

One of the major responsibilities of a Congresman is meeting with his constituents when they come to Washington. Constituents are a key part of his congressional daily life.

One of our most familiar public images is of our Capitol with the thronging of citizens in wait for beleaguered office holders. It comes down to us as a central fact of political life from the times of Andrew Jackson.

Now is the season for visitors to the Capitol. Most usually, they arrive in great caravans of buses, festooned with placarded slogans and place-name identifications, having covered many miles to see the sights. In greater or lesser number they troop through the corridors, disciplined by their leaders in files of two, or straggling along in curious, unruly bunches. They are on their way to the office of "their" congressman.

They will crowd into the congressman's office spilling out into the hall. The meeting may be confined to a few formal words from the congressman, or a very social function with chicken box lunches, chairs out into the hall, while the congressman passes from one to another chatting and talking.

In almost every office the door is always open, the welcome sign is out, and the staff fully organized to rally at a moment's notice. Office entertaining for the 1st District of California is considerably different than the 1st District of Maryland, where the contrast is individuals versus throngs.

From the West Coast there is a consistent pattern of callers. Each individual who comes to the office is seen. No matter what I am doing, it is put aside for the visitor. For the constituents, it is an occasion. Greeting them is part of the life of the representative in Congress. Most people seem genuinely pleased to talk for a few moments with their representative in Congress. It may be a family with several sons or daughters, who sit in varying degrees of enthusiasm or "coolness" but always armed with cameras.

The talk is like conversation everywhere. "How is the life here?" "How do you like being congressman?" "Is your family with you?" "Five girls, you say?" "How often do you get home?" There may be a question or two about the operation of Congress, about a bill. The courteous and friendly visit of those from home, obeying the conventions.

There are others too. The man from California who is "touching-base" or sounding you out on a bill, or alerting you to a mortal peril. He wants five minutes, or ten. The Canners League, the County Supervisors Association, a county engineer. A few minutes of quick, purposeful talk, a brochure to read, and a prompt exit.

Visitors come in all sizes and packages. Overseas-assigned officials, college students, PHD paper writers, veterans, labor representatives, business executives, bank presidents, mosquito abatement officers, leagues of women voters, lottery supporters. There are the callers, the seekers and the dispensers; those who call, and those who call to get something done. You listen and you talk, slowly embellishing your personal tapestry of political life, weaving here, matching there, weighing the values, drawing the tentative conclusion upon which you will act.

The visits continue in the Capitol itself. A card is brought to you on the Floor of the House by a page, and the meeting with the constituent ensues at the West Door of the House Chamber. At any time, with the House in session, the West Door is a cluster of people, waiting for their representative or talking to him in animated terms. This is hallway discussion, different and distracting, but the best the occasion offers. Members lean against the walls, or the statue of Thomas Jefferson, or in the corner niche reserved for some absent statuary, seeking as best they may to avoid the busy traffic humming to and fro. It is catch-as-catch-can conversation, trivial, perhaps, or intense and purposeful.

Until this time, there was no place to take constituents for private conversation. One could go to the House restaurant which has been refurbished after years of dingy crampedness. Table cloths and a fine painting of Washington crossing the Delaware add new lustre to the proper entertainment of guests. The anteroom is jam-packed with congressmen and their guests waiting while the major domo, with an impeccable memory, keeps track of where everyone is on the waiting list.

A fresh addition this year is a reception room off the Floor of the Chamber. Decorous to a degree, with its brand new Chippendale chairs, its fluted wooden Corinthian columns, and floor-length red damask drapes, it affords measured contrast to the crowded halls. This tranquil backwater seems to emphasize the hurly-burly of traffic passing by in the hallway outside. Most passers-by pause a moment, open-mouthed, to absorb the interior. It is as though they are estimating, with this glance, the life of the congressman.

Outside, a few steps away, on the broad marble steps that lead two floors (45 steps) down from the grand, marbled portico to the ground, groups of school classes, 4-H clubs, Boy Scouts, fraternal organizations stack up four and five rows deep as the Capitol photographers, working in relays, shoot away, framing the glistening, newly-painted Capitol dome in the vista, complete with smiling congressman.

This is the world of the to-and-fro. You easily acclimate yourself to the constant going and coming. It is part of your very life. Perhaps the efficiency expert would find it a questionable use of time.

It is a difficult choice, to get on with the work at hand, or to linger over folks from home. They have come a long way. This trip to Washington may be one of the great events of their lives. So, you debate with yourself—the degree of pressure you are under at that time. Weighing these factors, you must make the choice. A few minutes in the office? A trip to the Members' gallery to explain how Congress works right on the spot, pointing out the arrangements for debate and naming the participants?

It is the same for all. Many times I have stood open-mouthed as a crusty senior Member displays an unexpected winsomeness before the visitor from home. On one occasion, a rare visit to the Senate, I found an august senior chairman of that body showing two strangers from home the office of the Vice-President. I was invited to go along while he displayed a detailed knowledge of the wall picture, the desk and the flags.

Inefficient, perhaps, but the human, connecting link between the serious, frequently deadly work of the Chamber, and the people who send us to Washington to represent them.

Very sincerely,
Clem Miller

January–February 1962

Dear Friend:

Congressional experts have not recorded that the House of Representatives is particularly democratic in its modes and procedures. Most congressmen start their career with the understandable hope that it might be found so, but inevitably tend to accept its autocracy. Resentfully, or not, they learn to abide by this rule as the sole means of controlling the violent pluralism of its members. Since he submits to endless petty chaffering, each congressman hopes that he will serve under a Speaker who will share some of his hopes and treat him kindly. Thus, interest in the recent selection of a Speaker of the House took on a personal overtone even though the Law of Succession was as unruffled and secure as it might be at Westminister Abby.

There was no surprise that John McCormack of Massachusetts became Speaker. Since 1940, he had been Majority Leader under Speaker Sam Rayburn. The Majority Leader's job is to do battle for the Ins, fine season or foul; to place a protective shield over legislation of all sorts; and to protect members of the Majority Party—good ones, bad ones, little ones and big ones. Every Democrat from Georgia to California enjoyed watching John McCormack at his work as Majority Leader—stabbing the air with his great curved forefinger repeating the symmetry of his astringent features. The relish John McCormack brought to his job of playing up Democrats and belaboring Republicans brought joyous cries from his side of the aisle, and even the spiteful silence from the other side seemed to redouble the good spirits. Time and again, amidst the bitter acrimony of the final moments, John McCormack's appearance heralded the same tumult and clamor one might expect of a school yard. Yet, with all of this it was equally true that John McCormack was the Big Gun who did the final cannonading on every bill. Leadership of this sort and over this long period gave to him every initial advantage in the contest for a new Speaker.

These were factors, but certainly there must be others to continue the Law of Succession that has put eight of the last nine majority leaders in the Speaker's chair. Why has this been the case?

The Speaker is elected by the membership of the House. In practice this means a solid, party-line vote from amongst two nominees, one selected from the Majority Party in caucus, the other from the Minority Party by the same means. In this instance the 248 members of the Democratic Party sounded the name "McCormack" and 166 Republicans dutifully responded "Halleck."

The Democrats then proceeded with the task of filling the official and unofficial leadership jobs in the House, the Republicans, the Minority spots. To occupy the position of Majority Leader, Mr. Carl Albert of Oklahoma moved up from Party Whip. For Party Whip, Mr. Hale Boggs of Louisiana moved up from Deputy Whip. The new Deputy Whip was Mr. John Moss of California, who had been Regional Whip.

It thus appeared to some that the Law of Succession would now apply to the whole leadership family, not only the Speakership. Some noted the dynastic overtones in the fact that while the Speaker and Majority Leader are elected, the whips are appointed. This set off a wave of speculation. Leadership selection by appointment rather than election could make the democratic procedures of the House more attenuated than ever, as control over the Leadership, even indirectly, appeared to recede somewhat.

Of course, to many private citizens, the reasons for a Law of Succession are not at all obvious. Observing the national legislative process in the same way that they look at all sporting events, everything is seen as a rugged onset, with clashes and tilting in abundance; strangers as from another ward or another county meeting head on in mortal political combat.

The natural conclusion does not mirror the leadership struggles within the House of Representatives. The Members are not suspicious strangers, but essentially associates, comrades-in-arms, with all the personal feeling this implies. These Congressmen know their fellows over long years of scrutiny, evaluation, understanding and sympathy for the unique problems common to all in congressional politics.

There is bound to come with this association a feeling of moderation, tolerance, and, as well, an acceptance of a hieratic, almost monarchical order of things. As an integral part of this attitude is a requirement that the candidate for leadership has substantial seniority, say at least six terms, more probably eight or ten. This shuts out the commonly held belief that a newcomer by sheer ability or strength can topple the wily veteran. It is not this way in the House.

There are other factors of intra-House political struggles which vary from the public expectations. These concern the way a member will bid for Power. Who has the organization (such as it is in the House of Representatives)? Who has a prominent, identified base of support? How is the timing?

Any contender is going to make a realistic appraisal of the complexities of the House. He is not going after Power unless his chances of success are reasonable.

With his associational ties, and with experience, he sees a long and bleak future for himself if he should try and then fail.

There are few Congressmen who could provide themselves with a personal base of support sufficient to challenge Mr. McCormack. Further, the timing was not right for a challenger. Neither did anyone have the time nor the personal organization even if he should choose to attempt it. Mr. McCormack had these things. Aside from the comforting tradition of the Law of Succession, he fell heir to the interior lines of communication in the House when Sam Rayburn fell ill. This organization is extensive and consists of all the machinery for the administrative functioning of the House of Representatives. It includes the Doorkeeper of the House, who is a power in his own right, the Clerk of the House, a host of others.

This organizational base of support in the House administrative staff became crucial because of the particular moment in time that the Speakership vacancy occurred.

It was vacated during a recess when congressmen were scattered to the four winds. Hence, whatever organization there was in the House was among the staff. Because of the benign onset of Speaker Rayburn's illness in late summer, there was promise of recovery. It would have been unthinkable for any congressman to have organized for succession at a time when members were in attendance during the active session of Congress. Then, when Congress adjourned, the machinery of the House was firmly in the hands of the Majority Leader, Mr. McCormack. Stopped from organizing while the Members were in Washington, it would be a bold man to take on Mr. McCormack at the time of the vacancy, and the man with initial strength to do it would be gambling everything, winner-take-all. As we have had occasion to remark previously, the traditions of the House do not encourage boldness or bravery. Above all, in the House, one must *last*. If one does last, influence will accrue, but this power is diluted with any defeat. So a congressman, however strong or senior, does not commit himself carelessly. He waits.

Consider Congressman Carl Albert. Easy and friendly, his accessibility has a Rhodes-scholar backup. His home state is Oklahoma, his district solidly Democratic. He presents to the House the same attractive combinations of a Sam Rayburn with one foot in the South, a keen tolerant view of the North and West.

Mr. Albert could have mounted a campaign for Speaker—if he had wanted to. Geography and other factors would have given him a base of support too large for reprisal and perhaps large enough even for victory, at the least for bargaining; but he chose the surer path by promotion from Party Whip to Majority Leader.

The South with its 100 or so votes is always a factor, but the word is that a Southerner could not be elected Speaker. The leaders in the South are out to alter this. If they can combine their solid power base with the tradition of the Law of Succession perhaps this can be reversed. Their man has come to be Mr. Hale Boggs of New Orleans, who has a liberal voting record and who carries himself with magisterial presence on the Floor. He was Deputy Whip. He moves to Whip. Should the time come around, it seems that the South, with its realistic approach will back him down the line. From other members he will be receiving the meticulous appraisal granted to all who are moving along the ladder. Members of Congress, high and low, quickly become expert in the subtleties of political evaluation. It often seems Floor debate is not so valuable for its exposition of the particular issue under consideration as it is for evaluating leadership qualities. Those who fit the measure will then be granted, *for the future,* and for legislation as yet unheard, the trust to proceed under their own discretion.

For the hard present, however, we had a situation in which no one with the eight or nine terms of seniority necessary had the base of support nor the means of organizing it and most certainly not at the time it might have been effective. Thus, when the Democratic Caucus was called to order on January 9, 1962—the day before the convening of Congress—the nomination and election of John McCormack was settled in every detail.

Very sincerely,
Clem Miller

April, 1962

Dear Friend:

A few weeks ago in a discussion about Washington, I was asked by a visitor, "How do you organize your day?" My answer was, "I have very little to do with organizing my day. It is pretty well organized for me." While people readily comprehend an answer of this sort as it applies to their personal experience, they seem to expect differently of Congress.

It should not be so unlikely. Congressmen are subjected to continuing diversion which begins as soon as they arrive at the office, keeps up steadily until they leave, and frequently beyond. There are congressmen who succeed in insulating themselves against this impact. There are others who seek to minimize the effect of pressure by ruses, strategems and sundry devices. These are only partially successful. One is satisfied to get any sort of ordering of priorities amidst the helter-skelter.

Congress is intensely "here and now." Logical development, coordinated action, "follow-through" all seem most difficult. One feels like the survivor of a river raft upset, fishing out his belongings at a sandbar. He must decide in an immediate and transient fashion what to save or let go. This leads almost inevitably to handling matters as they float by, large or small, big or little, important or less so.

Telephone calls follow one another in a steady procession, from federal departments, constituents, fellow Congressmen. An incoming call seems to touch off a train of outgoing calls as a matter of course. All the while, visitors are being sandwiched in here or there as the opportunity provides.

There are points about which a Congressman will pivot—a meeting of his committee, a gathering of the state delegation. But even in these cases attention is constantly diverted by importunate demands which cannot be turned aside.

No matter what schemes may be devised to channel the handling of mail and telephone calls, or employing his staff as a protective shield, the day is a series of disconnected interruptions. While this becomes a way of life that must be acclimated to, most congressmen seem affected by it to a greater or lesser degree. To many, the interminable prospect of being unable to concentrate blocks of time and of being constantly behind in their work is oppressive.

This furnishes a sort of backdrop for the second question asked by my visitor, "How do you develop your ideas on legislation? How do you develop knowledge about an issue, remember your argument and arrive at a decision?" This question indicates a presumption that there is an intellectual, contemplative approach to political problems. I do not think it exists.

First of all, most of the legislative issues are in the air for a long time before they come down to the voting stage. Thus, there is quite a time span to absorb a background view. This roots itself more deeply than the congressman would even admit to himself. The background is conditioned from the very start— partisan attitudes of each party guide the decisionmaking proc- ess of the individual congressman.

These ideas or attitudes are brought along by discussion rather than literary, contemplative research. The time for de- cision all too often arrives with the suddenness of a thunderclap. One realizes the bill has been around for some time, but in the hurly-burly it is forgotten. All of a sudden it is right before you. The process seems intensely pragmatic, intuitive. It has a hap- hazard air, but it is amazing how well the intuition will stand the test of a more considered judgment in hindsight.

Suppose we were to start out with a very vague idea of a bill, say the Trade Expansion Bill. The tariffs question has been around for a long time as a great political issue. You begin with only the notion that vigorous trade would be helpful to our country for a number of reasons, and is possibly a necessity in our modern world. The need for more precise reasoning is given urgent focus by a concerted appeal for assistance from a substantial group of constituents who see themselves in jeop- ardy. Their demands for answers to very real problems jolt you loose from traditional attitudes. The point is that while many congressional issues can be tremendously complicated, or broad in scope, an individual Member's decision-making is customarily in general terms, unless a specific issue is raised, as for example, the treatment of California specialty crops by our country's trade-agreement negotiating teams. If California agriculture, largest in the Nation, were to be mistreated under the bill, it would be serious for all of us.

Interestingly enough, the key to the farmers' complaints was alleged to be contained in a 72-page report which each con- gressman was supposed to have received three months before. How the other copies got lost might be a subject for inquiry, but only one congressman had the report, and he had not read it. Even when emergency copies were distributed, no one read it in entirety, and most did not read it at all.

In times past, I would have had an extensive folder or two full of information in addition to 3 x 5 cards packed with data. The insistent flow of life in Washington has made these issue files literally impossible to keep up and less possible to delve through. In another time, I would certainly have visited the li- brary to bone up on the subject. I would have read the bill and any reports around.

Not in the life of the present. Rather, my first step was to call several Congressmen in my state delegation. I discovered that they were perplexed. One of them knew a real expert in the Agriculture Department. Our first move was to get together with the "expert." The next step was to call other "experts" in the State of California. In the meantime, all of us, separately, were reaching out with discussions with farmers and industry representatives whom we knew.

Then, we checked back with one another, seeking to arrive at a specific point in the bill where we might offer a constructive amendment. Also, we were in touch with members of the committee of jurisdiction, in this case Ways and Means, to get a line on the general direction of the bill, how it was faring, what the real possibilities were for amendment, and so forth.

Finally, we collated some suitable language. It was circulated among us, back to our constituents, then to our California member of the Committee, and, finally, to the Chairman, Mr. Mills of Arkansas. Based on this amendment, this resolution of our problem, our decision on the bill became relatively fixed.

From this sketchy account, one can perceive the outlines of the decision-making process in Congress. The circumstances and the factors may change, but the essential point here is that decision-making and decision-changing is essentially a people-to-people arrangement.

One begins with general ideas as a background. This view, oriented to the position of your party and your own District's interests, usually holds right through to a vote. It is unnecessary to go further unless there ensues a reaction by constituents, or by committee members with a circular letter, or by the Administration. These special arguments buttress and make palatable, or alternatively make objectionable, the basic bill. One uses "the expert" to bring the issue into better focus. At the same time one keeps on a course in line with political realities by checking with the committee, fellow congressmen, and with the White House downtown, for this process takes place within the framework of the two-party system.

The difficulty is that none of this can be done sequentially or in an orderly fashion. All of these actions must be inserted between the other demands on your time. Thus, what could be readily accomplished in a half a day or several days, must languish over a period of weeks. It must be this way for any public person who must be available to many people and pressures and influences at any given time.

Very sincerely,
Clem Miller

P.S. I would like to emphasize that I am here considering one aspect of the decision-making process, and as space allows will consider others, in future letters.

11

COMMITTEE ASSIGNMENTS

NICHOLAS A. MASTERS

The organization of 435 members of the House of Representatives into work groups is an intensely political process. In part it is simplified by the seniority system, which decrees that every member may retain his committee assignment from year to year and move up the ladder as more senior men fall by the wayside. But in order to fill vacancies and place new members, each party convenes Committees-on-Committees, and, within these committees, the initial work assignments are bargained out. Nicholas A. Masters, Professor of Political Science at Southern Illinois University at Edwardsville, has written this authoritative description of the process.

Any attempt to understand the legislative process, or to reckon how well it fulfills its purported functions, calls for a careful consideration of the relationships among congressmen. The beginning weeks of the first session of every congress are dominated by the internal politics of one phase of those relationships, the assignment of members to committees. Since congressmen devote most of their energies—constituents' errands apart—to the committees on which they serve, the political stakes in securing a suitable assignment are high. Competition for the more coveted posts is intense in both houses; compromises and adjustments are necessary. Members contest with each other over particularly desir-

able assignments; less frequently, one member challenges the entire body, as when Senator Wayne Morse fought for his committee assignments in 1953.[1]

The processes and patterns of committee assignments have been only generally discussed by political scientists and journalists. Perhaps the reason for this is too ready an acceptance of the supposition that these assignments are made primarily on the basis of seniority. Continuous service, it is true, insures a member of his place on a committee once he is assigned, but seniority may have very little to do with transfers to other committees, and it has virtually nothing to do with the assignment of freshman members. On what basis, then, are assignments made? Surely, not on the basis of simple random selection.

A recent student sees the committee assignment process as analogous to working out a "giant jig saw puzzle" in which the committees-on-committees observe certain limitations. These committees

Reprinted from *American Political Science Review*, LV (June, 1961), 345–57. Copyright © 1961, The American Political Science Association. This study was made possible by the support of the Ford Foundation and Wayne State University. Neither of them, of course, is responsible for any errors of fact or interpretation.

... must, of course, be guided by the number of vacancies and by the number of applications for transfer. Care is taken to attain geographical distribution, if not balance. Attention is paid to group desires and to the experience and training of individual legislators. And balance among the various factions of the party is sought. Beyond these more or less objective factors, being in the good graces of the party leader is certainly important in getting on major committees.[2]

This statement leaves significant questions unanswered. What, for example, is meant by geographical distribution or balance? Is every section or region represented in each party on each committee? Or does the committee's subject matter jurisdiction guide the type of geographical representation the committee-on-committees considers? Is the number of assignments allotted to a state party delegation on particular committees restricted? Do state party delegations develop a "vested interest" in certain committees and attempt to maintain continuous representation on them? What groups actively seek representation for their interests on the various committees by campaigning for an individual congressman to fill a vacancy? How influential are they? The study of committee assignments should also throw light on party factionalism, the differences between the parties in performing this organizational task, and the importance attached to the professional and group backgrounds of legislators.

As a step toward answers to these questions this study looks into the formal and informal processes of committee assignments in the House of Representatives.[3]

The special hazards of this study deserve mention. No attempt was made to sample the House. The information derived from each Congressman must be used with caution, for legislators view events from a variety of perspectives. And finally, in all likelihood, some of the subtleties and nuances of the process have escaped observation. Despite these limitations, relatively crude techniques of analysis can yield significant results. For what sometimes frustrates our understanding of the most unique part of the American legislative process—the committee system—is the lack of organized data and the failure to analyse readily available data.

I. The Committees-on-Committees

In one of the more notable features of the reorganization of Congress in 1911, each party created a committee-on-committees to distribute committee assignments, on the theory, still asserted, that a party committee offers at least an opportunity for all party members to receive suitable assignments. Such a committee would go a long way toward eliminating the arbitrary judgments of the Speaker who, in the past, had used committee assignments as rewards and punishments, to help insure his control of pending legislation.

Though both parties use a committee for this purpose, their methods of selecting its members differ. Each committee therefore needs separate treatment, with comparisons from time to time.

Democrats

By custom the Democratic members of the House Ways and Means Committee, together with the Speaker and Majority Floor Leader (or the Minority Floor Leader when Democrats are in the minority), have constituted the committee-on-committees since 1911. This arrangement is evidently an outgrowth of the former practice of selecting the chairman of Ways and Means as the Majority Floor Leader. Because the Democratic members serve in this dual capacity, and although they are formally designated by the Democratic caucus, they are in fact self-perpetuating. The Speaker and Majority Floor Leader participate extensively in the Committee's deliberations and, of course, have considerable influence on the decisions.

The method of organizing the work of the Committee-on-committees in the 86th Congress was typical. Each member of the Committee was assigned a geographical zone within which his own district lies. (See Table 1.) All zones except two were geographically contiguous. Requests for committee assignments coming from members were handled by their respective zone committeeman. For example, Representative Aime Forand from Rhode Island was responsible for the assignment and re-assignment requests of all Democratic representatives from districts within his zone, which includes, in addition to his own state, Connecticut, Maine, Massachusetts and Vermont. As can be seen from Table 1, each zone representative served an average of approximately 18 members.

Although committee deliberations are closed, the procedure followed is well known among most House members. Each zone representative, speaking in order of seniority, nominates candidates from his zone for the various committee vacancies, usually with supporting arguments. Thereupon the Committee votes on each of the vacancies, and the nominee receiving the highest number of votes is designated to fill it.

The volume of work before the Committee varies, depending chiefly on the changes resulting from the preceding election. Almost always, however, there are more applications than vacancies; in the 86th Congress 124 applications were made for 75 places to be filled. The major committees were naturally most in demand; applications exceeded vacancies for all committees except District of Columbia, House Administration, Merchant Marine and Fisheries, Post Office and Civil Service, and Science and Astronautics—all regarded as lesser committees. Applicants usually list their order of preference, taking into account not only their personal desires but also advice from other members and their own assessments of where they stand the best chance to land at least an acceptable assignment. Without encouragement from above, an applicant, however much he might prefer to be on the Appropriations Committee, say, would hardly bother (or venture) to ask for what he realizes he has virtually no chance of getting.

Much more than committee structure and manner of procedure is involved in making assignments. Animating and guiding these formal mechanisms are the norms and customs observed when assignments are sought. The pervasive seniority rule, for example, works in a manner not commonly appreciated. Members seeking assignments, and particularly freshmen, channel their requests through the "dean" or senior member of their state party delegation. In negotiations between the Committee-on-committees and the applicants he plays a crucially important role in securing assignments. It is his special responsibility to see that his members receive adequate representation on the various committees. In performing this task, he tries to protect or maintain the delegation's place on a major committee when a vacancy occurs and the seat has previously been held by a member of the delegation; he consults with, and advises, the members of his delegation seeking assignments as to what their chances are, and which committee assignments he will support for them. The dean's decisions must be made in consideration of the needs of his state, the qualifications of his own members, and the necessity for adjusting the requests among his members to prevent duplication on committees. It falls to his lot also to discourage and dissuade members who have unrealistic designs on the major committees—Appropriations, Rules, and Ways and Means.

The importance of the deans of the state delegations may be illustrated negatively. Connecticut, for the first time since 1936, elected six freshmen Democrats in 1958. Since the entire delegation was composed of freshmen, no senior member could serve as the dean and apparently there was no time or forethought to form an agreement to become part of an area delegation. So when the committee assignments were made, only one of the six, Chester

TABLE 1   House Democratic Committee-on-Committees and Zone Assignments, 86th Congress

COMMITTEE MEMBER	ZONE	DEMS. IN STATE DEL.	FRESH-MEN	COMMITTEE MEMBER	ZONE	DEMS. IN STATE DEL.	FRESH-MEN
Mills (Ark.)	Ark.	6	(1)	Herlong (Fla.)	Fla.	7	(0)
	Del.	1	(1)		Ga.	10	(0)
	Kans.	3	(2)			17	(0)
	Okla.	5	(0)	Ikard (Texas)	Texas	21	(1)
		15	(4)		N. Mex.	2	(1)
Forand (R.I.)	R.I.	2	(0)			23	(2)
	Conn.	6	(6)	Frazier (Tenn.)	Tenn.	7	(0)
	Me.	2	(1)		N.C.	11	(1)
	Mass.	8	(1)			18	(1)
	Vt.	1	(1)				
		19	(9)	Machrowicz (Mich.)	Mich.	7	(1)
King (Calif.)	Calif.	16	(4)		Ind.	8	(6)
	Alas.	1	(1)		Ohio	9	(3)
	Ariz.	1	(0)			24	(10)
	Nev.	1	(0)	Metcalf (Mont.)	Mont.	2	(0)
	Utah	1	(1)		Colo.	3	(1)
		20	(6)		Idaho	1	(0)
O'Brien (Ill.)	Ill.	14	(4)		Nebr.	2	(2)
	Wis.	5	(2)		N. Dak.	1	(1)
		19	(6)		Ore.	3	(0)
Boggs (La.)	La.	8	(1)		S. Dak.	1	(0)
	Ala.	9	(0)		Wash.	1	(0)
	Miss.	6	(0)			14	(4)
		23	(1)	Green (Pa.)	Pa.	16	(4)
Keogh (N.Y.)	N.Y.	19	(2)		N.J.	5	(2)
		19	(2)			21	(6)
Harrison (Va.)	Va.	8	(1)	Watts (Ky.)	Ky.	7	(2)
	S.C.	6	(0)		Md.	7	(3)
		14	(1)		W. Va.	5	(2)
Karsten (Mo.)	Mo.	10	(0)			19	(7)
	Iowa	4	(3)	Total		283	(63)
	Minn.	4	(1)				
		18	(4)				

Bowles, felt that he had been given as good representation as he was entitled to. Bowles got the assignment of his choice, Foreign Affairs. Frank Kowalski was assigned to Armed Services because of his extensive military experience although it was not an assignment he wanted. The remaining four were given committee places they did not prefer, namely Science and Astronautics, Education and Labor, Government Operations, and a dual appointment to the District of Columbia and Post Office and Civil Service Committees. Several dissatisfied Connecticut congressmen complained, two of them quite bitterly, that their committee positions would not help them to be reelected—that they had received the "left over" assignments. These assignments had not been made from any desire to penalize them, but apparently because they were orphans with no dean or senior member to fight for their preferences or look after their interests.

If the Democratic Committee-on-committees is judged as a system of collective responsibility among men of equal status, then it is clear that the use of members of a permanent standing committee for this purpose has had almost the opposite effect. Each member does not carry equal weight on the committee. The status and rank of each Democratic member of Ways and Means are carried over to the Committee-on-committees. The ranking Democrat serves as chairman and the status of the other ranking members is unquestionably enhanced by the fact that they also serve as Ways and Means subcommittee chairmen when the Democrats are in the majority. These are the senior members in an institution that respects seniority. Ways and Means members have had considerable congressional experience prior to their assignment. For the period 1913 to 1958, only five of 86 assignments to this Committee were given to congressmen without any seniority; and each of these five had had previous, but interrupted, congressional service. On the average, members have served at least three consecutive terms prior to being placed on the Committee, and the average is closer to five terms if computations are based simply on prior, rather than continuous, service before selection. The stability of the Committee's membership is also increased by the fact that, although a congressman may sometimes shrink from its responsibilities, only one member has ever left the Committee by his own request. What turnover there is results from death, resignation, or loss of party control, rather than from transfers or election defeat.

For a key functioning unit of the Democratic party's legislative apparatus, so much continuity in the Committee-on-committees makes it ill-designed for flexibility and responsiveness to electoral changes and public-opinion trends. Rather, it is more analogous to a firmly entrenched bureaucracy, not completely immune but well insulated, and capable of considerable resistance to any pressures placed upon it.

Republicans

The Republican Committee-on-committees is specially set up for its function and is responsible for no other. It is composed of one member from each state having Republican representation in the House; thereby, a lone Republican from any state is automatically included. Each state delegation determines its member on the Committee. This method might be thought to provide an opportunity to select a new member for each new Congress, but the normal pattern, on the contrary, is for the senior member of the delegation, usually the dean, to assume membership on the Committee and hold it as long as he desires or remains in Congress. Table 2 shows the membership of the Republican Committee-on-committees for the 86th Congress.

The point is sometimes argued that the Republicans make it possible for each state delegation to assume a greater share of the organizational responsibility than the Democratic committee assignment process allows, and consequently that the decentralized Republican method is much more responsible to electoral changes. Actual Re-

publican practice tends to contradict this argument. For the Republicans allow each representative on the Committee-on-committees to cast as many votes as there are Republicans in his delegation. This concentrates the power over committee assignments in the hands of the senior members from the large state delegations. In the 86th Congress, members from seven states —California, Illinois, Michigan, New Jersey, New York, Ohio, and Pennsylvania—controlled 97 of the 153 committee votes.

Not to mask the realities of power, the Republican committee assignments

TABLE 2   House Republican Committee-on-Committees, 86th Congress

STATE	MEMBER	VOTES	STATE	MEMBER	VOTES
Arizona	John J. Rhodes	1	New Jersey	Frank C. Osmers	9
California	James Utt	14	New York	Mrs. K. St. George	24
Colorado	J. Edgar Chenoweth	1	North Carolina	Chas. R. Jonas	1
Florida	William C. Cramer	1	North Dakota	Don L. Short	1
Idaho	Hamer Budge	1	Ohio	Clarence J. Brown	14
Illinois	Leo E. Allen	11	Oklahoma	Page Belcher	1
Indiana	E. Ross Adair	3	Oregon	Walter Norblad	1
Iowa	Charles B. Hoeven	4	Pennsylvania	Richard Simpson	14
Kansas	Edward H. Rees	3	South Dakota	E. Y. Berry	1
Kentucky	Eugene Siler	1	Tennessee	Howard H. Baker	2
Maine	Clifford G. McIntire	1	Texas	Bruce Alger	1
Massachusetts	William H. Bates	6	Utah	Henry A. Dixon	1
Michigan	Clare E. Hoffman	11	Virginia	Joel T. Broyhill	2
Minnesota	H. Carl Anderson	5	Washington	Jack Westland	6
Missouri	Thomas B. Curtis	1	West Virginia	Arch A. Moore	1
Nebraska	Phil Weaver	2	Wisconsin	John W. Byrnes	5
New Hampshire	Perkins Bass	2	Wyoming	E. Keith Thomson	1

Total 153

SUBCOMMITTEE APPOINTED BY MINORITY LEADER

STATE	MEMBER	VOTES	SENIORITY
California	James Utt	14	4 consecutive terms
Idaho	Hamer H. Budge	1	5 consecutive terms
Illinois	Leo E. Allen	11	14 consecutive terms
Michigan	Clare E. Hoffman	11	13 consecutive terms
New Jersey	Frank C. Osmers	9	7 non-consecutive terms
New York	Katharine St. George	24	7 consecutive terms
North Carolina	Charles Raper Jonas	1	4 consecutive terms
Ohio	Clarence J. Brown	14	11 consecutive terms
Pennsylvania	Richard M. Simpson	14	7 consecutive terms

Total 99

are handled by a Subcommittee which, in the 86th Congress for example, was composed of the senior members from these seven states and two others, with one vote each, evidently added to give a voice to large geographical areas (intermountain and southern) that would otherwise have gone entirely unrepresented. Together the Subcommittee members controlled about two-thirds of the full committee's votes. None of them had served less than four terms in Congress. By custom the Subcommittee is appointed by the Minority Leader (or Speaker, as the case may be) on the authority granted by a resolution of the full Committee. The resolution leaves the membership of the Subcommittee apparently at the discretion of the party leader, but the example just given shows how far he is hemmed in by the practice of appointing the same members from the larger delegations each time a new Congress convenes. The change in the minority leadership in the 86th Congress had no discernible effect on this part of the organizational process.

The Subcommittee receives and considers *all* applications for assignment and transfer, and the full Committee invariably accepts all of its recommendations. Subcommittee sessions are informal and each member is free to speak for or against any assignment. Information on newly elected members is obtained from the Republican Congressional Campaign Committee and the party leaders pride themselves on having extensive knowledge not only of the professional and personal backgrounds of their colleagues, but also of the constituencies they represent. Members of the full Committee who are not on the Subcommittee are entitled to participate in the determinations if they desire, but they seldom do.

Republicans from small states sometimes object that as a result of the system of proportional voting and large-state domination of the Subcommittee they have no real voice in committee assignments and are often overlooked for assignments to the better committees. Along the same line they complain that the Republican procedure allows no mechanism whereby the small state delegations can combine their voting power in the Committee-on-committees. The critics point to the Democratic practice of letting smaller state delegations select a joint dean in order to be able to negotiate for committee assignments from a position of strength.

Actually, the principal difference between Republican and Democratic practice in formal organization is that the Republicans have built into their system a voting formula that rewards heavy Republican areas; the Democrats offer no comparable leverage to the large delegations. Nor is it likely the Democrats would even consider such a plan as long as the seniority system prevails. For it would only lessen the power of the Southern Democrats by putting more control over committee assignments into the hands of the larger northern, midwestern, and western delegations, with their very different traditions and interests.

There is little to distinguish the manner and procedure followed by an individual Republican or Democratic congressman in securing an assignment. Republican freshman members also work through the deans of the state delegations, but the deans, unlike their Democratic counterparts, are usually members of the Committee-on-committees.

Despite these differences the arrangements in both parties for handling committee assignments have one basic feature in common. Both committees-on-committees are so constituted as to be virtually immune to immediate pressures brought about by electoral changes. This is no accident. Its justification rests on a number of considerations congenial to the norms and customs of the entire body. If junior or freshman members had the responsibility for making committee assignments, they would immediately be thrust into difficult and delicate positions, particularly in deciding on transfer requests from senior members. Such decisions might well be controversial enough to damage permanently a junior member's career within the legislature and possibly outside of it. In private as well as public life, organizations seldom allow the newcomer—unfamiliar with the subtleties and the institutional trappings of the process—to make important personnel decisions; and committee assignments are party personnel decisions of the most crucial importance. Senior members simply would not willingly tolerate decisions made in this way. If forced to do so, the pressures, roadblocks and penalties they could evoke might be so severe and difficult to overcome that order in the whole legislative process might be endangered. The system has evolved as it has for these reasons, as well as for more positive benefits, such as the desire to rely on the more knowledgeable judgments of those with greater experience in the legislature.

Finally, the system is intended to give the process a tone of moderation and detachment. Members with seniority are less threatened by an election two years hence, being less subject to the vicissitudes of a competitive district. After years of experience in a collective body, senior members are readier to recognise the need for compromise and adjustment if work is to be done. Although competitive ambitions among members may be intense, prolonged debate over committee assignments would delay the conduct of legislative business which is already too long delayed by the employment of existing institutional and parliamentary devices.

The role of party leaders

The role of the party leaders in making committee assignments is difficult to define; no simple definition fits all the realities. Generally speaking, the leadership of each party in the House is formidable and independent to a great degree, though the leaders' power varies with their personal relations with the other members. David Truman explains the dependence of the rank-and-file upon the party leaders as follows:

The machinery of the House and of its parties is normally available to the ordinary member only, so to speak, on its own terms, because the source of its strength is also the source of its disabilities, namely, numbers. In a House of 435 or in a body roughly half that size, as one of the parties, there is a tendency . . . for the real and formal leadership closely to coincide. A formal, standardized system of communication and control is indispensable to the conduct of affairs in a body of that size. . . . This standardization of the communication structure implies that initiative tends to be centralized or at least that there are central controls on the flow of business. These the rank-and-file member cannot command or, as sometimes happens in the Senate, supplant. Hence, excepting some aspects of his own voting decisions, the independence of the ordinary member is restricted.[4]

The Democratic and Republican leaders not only play the principal role in the selection of the members of their respective committees-on-committees, but their personal judgments also tend to become the norm for major committee assignments. In practice, the leadership of both parties is directly involved in assignments to all the major committees, though the leaders do not usually concern themselves with applicants to lesser ones.

The party leaders use their power over committee assignments variously, to reward members who have been loyal and cooperative, and to reinforce the strength of their own positions by rewarding members whose loyalty may be suspected but whose strength may no longer be safely disregarded. Party leaders working with the committee-on-committees have in a number of instances offered important committee positions to members with demonstrated followings who were regarded as prospective threats. Such offers are made for the obvious purpose of securing cooperation, and so are frequently labelled as "sell-outs" or "the buying-off process" by some discontented members. Value judgments on particular cases will vary with individual viewpoints, but it must be recognized that Congress is not the only place where adjustments in the power structure are designed to accommodate or to absorb potentially strong rivals.

A specific example may be offered from the 86th Congress. Prior to the opening of the first session a group of liberal Democrats announced their intention to mobilize forces in the House in order to bring about the passage of legislation they favored. While the movement was underway—letters were being sent to the new Democratic members, as well as to incumbents sympathetic to their cause—Speaker Rayburn intervened, promising to use his influence to prevent the Rules Committee from blocking their bills. The Speaker, working with Chairman Wilbur Mills of the Ways and Means Committee and Majority Leader John McCormack, in order to demonstrate his willingness to cooperate with the

group, offered one of their leaders, Lee Metcalf of Montana, an appointment to the Ways and Means Committee. Contrary to expectations, Metcalf said he did not want the assignment; he contended that he preferred to be on Interior and Insular Affairs—important for Montana. The leaders insisted, however, that he had a responsibility to his party to accept the post, and he finally did. Metcalf was the logical choice in a move to head off a possible revolt, because his previous behavior had satisfied the party leaders that he was a "responsible" legislator—a concept that warrants further examination presently.

II. Criteria for Committee Assignments

The committees-on-committees have rules to govern them in assigning members to the twenty permanent standing committees. The Legislative Reorganization Act of 1946 limited members of the House to service on a single committee, but this provision has since been amended as follows: (1) Three committees are *exclusive*—namely, Appropriations, Rules, and Ways and Means. A member who serves on any of these can serve on no other committee. An occasional exception is made, however. (2) Ten committees are *semi-exclusive;* members may serve on any one of them and any one of the seven non-exclusive committees. The ten are: Agriculture, Armed Services, Banking and Currency, Education and Labor, Foreign Affairs, Interstate and Foreign Commerce, Judiciary, Post Office and Civil Service, Public Works, and Science and Astronautics. (3) Seven committees are *non-exclusive*. A member may serve on any two of these seven, or any one of them and any one of the ten semi-exclusive committees. The seven are: District of

Columbia, Government Operations, House Administration, Interior and Insular Affairs, Merchant Marine and Fisheries, Un-American Activities, and Veterans' Affairs.

The 1946 Act also fixes the total membership of each committee, although changes can be and are made for the duration of a Congress by means of a House resolution. Party ratios on the Rules and Ways and Means committees are fixed by agreement among the party leaders, while the ratios on other committees ordinarily reflect the House division.[5]

Beyond these ground rules, experience has developed other criteria used in determining committee assignments. In discussing them here, the exclusive committees are treated separately first, because of the special attention given to filling vacancies on them. I will then turn to the variables that affect assignments to all of the committees.

Assignments to major committees

The three exclusive committees, Appropriations, Rules, and Ways and Means are regarded by all in both parties as being of special importance. Other committees—among them Agriculture, Armed Services, and Public Works—deal with issues that affect vital congressional and national interests, but none can lay continuous claim to the power and prestige of the top three. As one Congressman stated, "If you get appointed to one of the top three, you have 'arrived.'"

Although the manner of attaining positions on these committees varies, each nominee must fit a bill of particulars. In practice, as indicated earlier, these lesser leaders are selected by the party leaders in consultation with the members of the committee-on-committees, rather than the other way around. A nominee's name may be first brought up by the party leaders, a committee

member, or even by someone not involved in the mechanics, but whatever the technical circumstances surrounding the introduction of his name, if the nominee is assigned, he bears the party leaders' stamp of approval. This is true in both parties.

The principal factors involved in selecting members for a major committee may be grouped under three broad headings: (1) legislative responsibility, (2) type of district represented, and (3) geographical area represented.

(1) Legislative Responsibility. The most crucial test is whether a candidate is a "responsible" legislator, as the leaders of both parties use that term. What does a member have to be or do—or avoid—in order to be regarded as a responsible legislator?

According to the party leaders and the members of the committees-on-committees, a responsible legislator is one whose ability, attitudes, and relationships with his colleagues serve to enhance the prestige and importance of the House of Representatives. He has a basic and fundamental respect for the legislative process and understands and appreciates its formal and informal rules. He has the respect of his fellow legislators, and particularly the respect of the party leaders. He does not attempt to manipulate every situation for his own personal advantage. In the consideration of issues, he is careful to protect the rights of others; he is careful to clear matters that require clearance; and he is especially careful about details. He understands the pressures on the members with whom he cannot always agree and avoids pushing an issue to the point where his opponents may suffer personal embarrassment. On specific issues, no matter how firm his convictions and no matter how great the pressures upon him, he demonstrates a willingness to compromise. He is moderate, not so much in the sense of his voting record and his personal ideology, but rather in the sense of a moderate approach; he is not to be found on the uncompromising extremes of the political spectrum. Although the notions of those interviewed were somewhat vague on this point, a responsible legislator is apparently one who does not believe that the Congress is the proper place to initiate drastic and rapid changes in the direction of public policy. On the contrary, he is more inclined to be a gradualist, and to see public policy as a sort of "synthesis of opposing viewpoints." In short, a responsible legislator is politically pliant, but not without conviction.

A legislator can demonstrate his responsibility in many ways: how he manages a major bill; what he contributes in committee work; the sort of testimony he presents before other committees, the nature of his remarks on the floor—all these are tests of his responsibility. If he behaves properly in these settings and refrains from criticizing the party leadership—and gets reelected at home—his chances of being selected for a major committee post are very good. In the interviews, both Democrats and Republicans emphasized repeatedly the attention paid to the past performance of major-committee applicants. For the major committees are "closed corporations," and their membership is composed only of those who have served their "apprenticeships" on lesser committees for considerable periods of time. Even in an instance in which party leaders feel compelled to appoint a member of a dissident wing of the party in order to gain greater cooperation, they will tend to select the member who most closely conforms to the norms of responsibility.

When the question was raised how Southern Democrats, who might be regarded as uncompromising on many questions, yet were appointed to major committees, the interviewees immediately pointed out how the Southerners differ from many of their "uncompromising" northern colleagues: they never denounce the legislative process as ill suited for public policy formation, they are never frustrated by its intricacies; rather, they master its techniques and use them skillfully and artfully to support their positions. "After all," one Congressman commented,

the southerner usually joins this body free from the pressures many of the rest of us face and is usually eager to make his mark. Membership in Congress is the highest political office he is likely to attain and he will devote full time to the legislature. Other members often entertain higher political ambitions or may have to devote the majority of their time to keeping things running smoothly in their districts.

(2) *Type of District Represented.* It would be rare indeed for a member to earn regard as "responsible" in only one or two terms. No freshman has been assigned to the Rules Committee since the Legislative Reorganization Act was passed and only 14 have been assigned to the larger Appropriations Committee and two to the Ways and Means Committee (Table 3). So the concept of responsibility is connected with an element beyond the member's personality, an element that takes into account the nature of his district. The members of the committees-on-committees have something more in mind here than simply a particular member's ability to be reelected. Long tenure by itself is an obvious objective fact, and common sense proof that a district is "safe"; but this is not enough.

It is not necessarily to the point either that the member's district may be safe for the incumbent but not for any one else. The essence of the criterion lies in the terms on which the member is returned rather than in the fact of his return alone. The committee-on-committees wants to feel that his district will not only reelect him but also allow him to operate as a free agent, enabling him to make controversial decisions on major policy questions without constant fear of reprisals at the polls. His district must not be one that forces him to take definite, uncompromising positions, for this would jeopardize his usefulness in committee work. In the terminology of Eulau, Wahlke *et al.*, the district should be one that elects its members as a "trustee" or a "politico" and not as a "delegate."[6] This requirement is of special importance in considering assignments to the Rules Committee; many members would not relish being on this committee despite its power, simply because it is inevitably involved in practically every issue before the Congress.

TABLE 3   Committee Assignments to Freshmen, House of Representatives, 80th–86th Congresses

COMMITTEE	NUMBER OF FRESHMAN ASSIGNMENTS	
	REPUBLICANS	DEMOCRATS
Exclusive Committees		
Appropriations	8	6
Rules	0	0
Ways and Means	2	0
Semi-Exclusive Committees		
Agriculture	13	11
Armed Services	1	11
Banking and Currency	15	20
Education and Labor	17	27
Foreign Affairs	4	10
Interstate and Foreign Commerce	8	10
Judiciary	15	14
Post Office and Civil Service *	22	35
Public Works	20	20
Science and Astronautics †	0	8
Non-Exclusive Committees		
District of Columbia	13	8
Government Operations	24	26
House Administration	11	19
Interior and Insular Affairs	17	28
Merchant Marine and Fisheries	24	26
Un-American Activities	6	1
Veterans' Affairs	33	30
Totals	253	310

* Reams of Ohio, Independent, assigned to Post Office and Civil Service in Eighty-second Congress.
† Created by Eighty-sixth Congress.
Source: Data from *Congressional Directory*, 1st Session of each Congress. Includes only Representatives with *no* previous service at any time. Some Representatives received double assignments, so totals shown are higher than the total of freshmen in each Congress.

A related reason for the "safe" district requirement is based on the idea that important committee posts should belong to the professional, the veteran politician who has earned his way up the ladder—the "politico" in preference to the "trustee." A politician from a safe district has fought and won enough political battles to nail down a district and thus help his party maintain control of the House. In short, he is a sure vote in the battle for control and he should receive the rewards of the system.

Members of the committees-on-committees felt no compulsion to explain away or camouflage this requirement. On the contrary, they argue that a realistic appraisal of the factors operating in our political system reveals that if a member sits on a congressional committee in which compromises must continually be made on matters of major policy, he cannot come from a district that does not allow him flexibility.

(3) *Geographical Area.* A legislator who is responsible and who comes from a district that allows him considerable independence on issues still has no guarantee that he will be selected to fill a major committee vacancy. He simply has a better chance than others. A third factor serves to narrow the range of choice. For both party committees tend to follow the practice of selecting a member from the same state party delegation as the member who vacated the seat, in order not to disturb the existing geographical balance. For example, upon the death or defeat of three members of the Ways and Means Committee, the Kentucky, Michigan, and Pennsylvania Democratic delegations asserted a prescriptive right to have members from their respective delegations chosen to fill the vacancies. Moreover, this prac-

tice sometimes extends to other committees. The Ohio Republican delegation, for example, insists that it should have one of its members on the Public Works Committee at all times.

Along this line, each party attempts to have every section of the nation represented on the Appropriations and Ways and Means committees. These are the only two committees, however, on which geographical balance is regarded as especially important. Actually the only geographical rule applied to all committee assignments provides that no state party delegation shall have more than one representative on any committee, except for the largest state delegations where strict application of the rule would be impossible.

General criteria for all committee assignments

The most important single factor in distributing assignments to all other committees is whether a particular place will help to insure the reelection of the member in question. So although it might abstractly seem desirable and logical to place an urban congressman on the Agriculture Committee to protect consumer interests, there is little operative political warrant for such an assignment. Not only do congressmen from urban areas usually refrain from applying for such vacancies when they occur, but the committees-on-committees also insist that members coming from predominantly agricultural areas have first call on them in order that they may use the assignments to protect their tenure in office. Both parties take it for granted that wheat, cotton and tobacco areas should have the majority of representation on the committee. The leaders know from previous experience that assignment of an urban congressman to the Agriculture Committee would only make him "fair game" for each of the farm lobbies.

The same general reasoning applies to other committees as well. Assignments to Public Works, Interior and Insular Affairs or Merchant Marine and Fisheries are usually based on the ecological make-up of the members' districts, so as to allow them to serve their constituent interests and protect their incumbency. For example, South Dakota Democrat George McGovern's application for transfer to the Agriculture Committee from the Education and Labor Committee was approved primarily on the grounds that his former assignment handicapped his effectiveness in providing service to his constituents and was a disadvantage to him since it had become a major campaign issue in his farm district.

When two or more members stake a claim to the same assignment, on the ground that it is essential to their electoral success, both party committees usually, if not invariably, will give preference to the member with longer service. Members have often maneuvered for a position on a particular committee long before a vacancy existed, and sometimes even long before other applicants were first elected. But open importunity may be self-defeating, for no one likes a pest.

Some special cases

The assignment of members to the Education and Labor Committee—with jurisdiction over the explosive issues of school aid, segregation and labor-management relations—has called for the most careful attention to the constituencies of applicants. As the party committees have seen it in recent years, this assignment is no place for a neutral when there are so many belligerents around. Their assign-ments have produced a standoff between antagonists,[7] and a suggestion during the 86th Congress, dropped in the end, for a partition of the Committee as an alternative to the prospective accession of Adam Clayton Powell of New York to its chairmanship upon the retirement of Graham Barden of North Carolina. Apart from the Southerners and a handful of others from districts safe enough to allow them comfortable independence, Democrats have felt that only members who can afford politically to take an outright pro-labor position—i.e., who get union support for election—should be assigned to this committee.

Members from farm or middle-class suburban districts are discouraged from applying. Service on this committee by a member whose district is relatively free of labor-management or segregation conflicts would only result in raising issues in his district that could prove embarrassing and even politically fatal to the member.

Republicans appear to have concluded, too, that it is impossible to take a moderate position on labor-management issues. They also dissuade members from applying for this committee when it might impair their chances for reelection. Republican assignees, however, are more likely to take a pro-management or non-labor view for the obvious reason that fewer Republicans receive overt political support from organized labor; more have close ties with management groups.

For the Democratic Committee-on-committees, a special issue affects assignments to what has been commonly described as an unimportant committee, the District of Columbia Committee. Southern legislators attach a great deal of importance to their efforts to maintain representation on that committee and to control it. The objective is to block home rule for the

District, with all the implications of extensive Negro participation in District political affairs.

More generally, southern congressmen have a more or less collective understanding that in order to maximize their influence on the legislative process they need to spread their strength over all the committees. This involves maneuvering for positions on the "housekeeping" committees. Although *a priori* calculations might seem to argue that dispersing members over twenty committees would weaken rather than strengthen southern control of the House, in actual practice the seniority rule vindicates their strategy. Collectively, congressmen from the South build up more seniority than any other sectional contingent and reap their rewards in committee and sub-committee chairmanships when the Democrats are in the majority.

Organized interest group participation

All members of the committees-on-committees recognized that organized groups outside Congress take a hand in the assignment process from time to time. The influence of such groups is thought to be important, but little evidence is available on its nature and extent. Sometimes, though not often, organized groups formally endorse a nominee for a committee vacancy. For example, Representative Harold B. McSween (Dem., La.), when applying for assignment to the Agriculture Committee, had letters of endorsement from American Farm Bureau representatives placed in his application file. Democrats attempt to placate organized labor by placing pro-labor representatives on the Education and Labor Committee, while Republicans attempt to satisfy the National Association of Manufacturers by appointing pro-business members to the same committee.

The most widely publicized groups connected with assignments to the Ways and Means committee are spokesmen for the oil interests. Democratic members and staff personnel frequently mentioned in interviews that a nominee's acceptability for assignment to this committee often hinged on whether he demonstrated a willingness to oppose any attempts to reduce the oil depletion tax allowance.

Nevertheless, organized groups, with occasional exceptions, appear to refrain from direct intervention in committee assignments; overt intrusion is apt to be resented and so be self-defeating. Rather, they have certain "expectations" about the type of person who should be selected for the vacancies on committees which affect their interests. Each group usually counts several members "friendly" or responsive to their needs. Organized interests do not often concern themselves too much with the selection of a particular member of the "friendly" group so long as one of them is eventually chosen.

Other considerations

The proposition is sometimes advanced that geographical balance is a deliberate objective in distributing assignments to all committees. If so, it has a low priority. There is no evidence of systematic effort to provide each section with representation on the various committees proportional to its representation in the House. The Appropriations and Ways and Means committees may be considered as exceptions, but even here a much more pressing consideration is representation for the large tax-paying states. An examination of the membership of the Interior and Insular Affairs Committee clearly shows that geographical balance is not necessarily a primary goal for all committees. Of the 19 Democratic members of this committee in the 86th Congress, 17 were from districts west of the Mississippi, and of the twelve Republican members six were from western states. Both committees-on-committees will, indeed, listen sympathetically to an applicant who argues that his section of the nation has no representation on the committee of his choice, but this argument is not a compelling reason for making the assignment. Ordinarily, applications are based on district and state delegation, not regional, considerations. Republican New Englanders, for instance, do not approach committee assignments from the viewpoint that each committee should have a New Englander on it. A notable exception to this generalization sets the Southern Democrats apart; as stated earlier, they regularly try to have Southern representation on all committees.

Party factionalism is a more serious concern than geographical balance. Republicans and Democrats alike, who were responsible for making committee assignments, vigorously denied the existence of factions within their parties; but readily admitted that their respective groups harbored members with widely divergent viewpoints. Occasional alignments emerge, they acknowledged, but these are regarded as fleeting in character. They asserted that no committee's party representation should be composed exclusively of members who view political issues from the same perspective and claimed to have made a reasonable effort to see that divergent viewpoints within each party find expression on each committee. We have already noted, however, that members on the extremes of the political spectrum are usually passed over for vacancies in the major committees; and a member's location on

the spectrum is assessed by the party leadership and the committee-on-committees. It is a matter of opinion, therefore, how well founded is the frequent claim that party representation on each committee is balanced ideologically.

Unfavorable assignments, of little political value to the recipients, are sometimes deliberately given by the powers that be as a mark of disapproval, or for reasons that might be described as "for the good of the order." In one recent instance Dale Alford, Democrat from Arkansas, was said to have been assigned to the Post Office and Civil Service Committee because some members of the Committee-on-committees felt that he had violated the "rules of the game" in his campaign that displaced former Representative Brooks Hays, a widely respected member, in the wake of the Little Rock controversy. Two years later, after he had voted with the leadership to "pack" the Rules Committee, he was given a place on the Appropriations Committee. Also, there was surprising agreement among those interviewed that the original Democratic transfers to the newly created Science and Astronautics Committee— not taken seriously in the House at its founding—were made in order to provide the transferees with sinecures, and so to remove some of the less qualified members from the other committees. The transfer offers were made attractive to senior members by promises that they would receive subcommittee chairmanships, which would provide them opportunities to build their niches within the legislative bureaucracy.

The professional background of an individual legislator is seldom in and of itself the controlling factor in his assignment. However, some general rules relating to the professional backgrounds of legislators are followed by both parties. Almost without exception, lawyers only are appointed to the Judiciary Committee. Members with outstanding experience in international relations or with extensive military service are regarded as excellent choices for the Foreign Affairs and Armed Services committees respectively. Other things being equal, former bankers and financiers may be given a slight edge over competing applicants for such committees as Appropriations, Ways and Means, and Banking and Currency. The same holds true for farmers who apply for the Agriculture Committee and for members closely identified with the labor movement who apply for the Education and Labor Committee. But all agreed that holding elective office, particularly a state legislative office, outweighed any other type of professional experience as a qualification for any committee assignment. Holding elective office is regarded as a profession by members of the committees, and they feel that the rewards of the system should go to the professionals. Although the patterns of committee assignments tend to document the importance of professional background, it would be a mistake to assume that the committees-on-committees seek out applicants on this ground. Normally, the reverse is true. Applicants tend to apply for assignments where they think their professional skills can be used to best advantage.

The manner in which a congressman campaigns for a committee is an important factor in the outcome. For example, a member seeking an assignment often solicits the support of members already on the committee. Another technique is to obtain the support of influential political leaders, such as endorsements from the governor, senators, or members of the state legislature. If an individual is comparatively unknown in national politics, he may attempt to familiarize the members of the Committee-on-committees with his background and training as it relates to the type of service he can give on the committee he desires. All these tactics, properly employed, can go a long way toward helping a member get favorable consideration by his party. He must be careful, however, to avoid giving the impression of exerting undue political pressure on the members of the Committee-on-committees. For example, if the committee tells him that a vacancy has already been promised to another, he is *expected* to accept this decision. Attempts to challenge either committee's decisions are generally regarded as serious departures from the norms of conduct in the House.

Religious considerations are not ignored in judging the qualifications of applicants. Most Democratic members interviewed conceded that it was important, when possible, to have at least one Roman Catholic on the major committees, and particularly on the Ways and Means and Education and Labor Committees. Republicans, on the other hand, contended that religious factors had no bearing on their assignments.

Racial and ethnic factors also enter into the calculations occasionally. For example, the Democratic committee-on-committees thought it made sense to appoint Charles Diggs, Democrat and Negro from the 13th District in Michigan, to the House Foreign Affairs Committee because of his race and because of the emerging prominence of Africa in international affairs. In his letter of application to the Committee, Diggs argued on these grounds. Republicans denied considering racial factors as they denied the relevance of religion.

Finally, a few committee assignments are made virtually at random. Usually a handful of lesser places are left over after the committees-on-committees have argued and settled all the applications. These may be handed out more or less indiscriminately to freshman members. At least two circumstances contribute to this result. One occurs when members fail to make their preferences known or to attract any advance support for their applications. This may stem simply from a freshman member's innocence of the process, or, as in the case of the Connecticut Democratic delegation, from the absence of any senior spokesman in their behalf. A second arises when the committee-on-committees members, along with the party leadership, have too many prior commitments to give serious considerations to each applicant's stated preference. These commitments may extend to members who are obviously less qualified than those who were passed over.

III. Summary and Conclusion

Committee assignments in the House of Representatives involve all the complexities of an organization whose members "are not automatons but reasoning men and women acting in a setting in which they are subject to a bewildering barrage of conflicting or, at the least, inconsistent, demands— from within their constituencies." [8] Caution is consequently in order in formulating generalizations to describe the assignment process. In this study I have not tried to go beyond an assessment of the factors taken into account at the time the assignments were made, by those who made them. Whether the behavior, then or later, of those who were assigned is consistent with the reasons given for the assignments, or vindicated expectations expressed,

is outside the scope of my endeavor.

From the data, several conclusions can be advanced as hypotheses for future studies:

(1) Despite some important differences in the formal structure, both the Democratic and Republican committee assignments are handled by small groups composed of senior members appointed and greatly influenced by the party leaders.

(2) Party leaders, working in conjunction with their committees-on-committees, use assignments to major committees to bargain with the leaders of party groups or factions, in order to preserve and fortify their leadership positions and conciliate potential rivals, as well as to reward members who have cooperated.

(3) Assignment to the major committees is restricted, with some exceptions, to members who have served two or more terms, who are "responsible" legislators, and who represent districts which do not require them to take inflexible positions on controversial issues.

(4) Although a number of factors enter into committee assignments— geography, group support, professional background, etc.—the most important single consideration—unless it can be taken for granted—is to provide each member with an assignment that will help to insure his re-election. Stated differently, the most impressive argument in any applicant's favor is that the assignment he seeks will give him an opportunity to provide the kind of service to his constituents that will sustain and attract voter interest and support. In distributing assignments the party acts as a mutual benefit and improvement society, and this for the obvious reason that control of the House depends on the re-election of party members.

(5) With minor differences, both

parties apply the same criteria for making committee assignments. This does not necessarily imply that there are no differences between Republican and Democratic assignees. It does show that both parties tend to empha-size factors beyond the ideological commitments of the members, and that calculations of party advantage lead them both to substantially the same criteria.

NOTES

1. Ralph K. Huitt, "The Morse Committee Assignment Controversy: A Study in Senate Norms," *American Political Science Review,* LI (June 1957), 313–329.

2. George Goodwin, Jr. "The Seniority System in Congress," *American Political Science Review,* LIII (June 1959), 412–436.

3. Data have been derived from unstructured interviews with members and staffs of the various committees, personal letters and similar papers, official documents of various types, and personal observations. I interviewed members of the committees-on-committees, deans of state delegations, and other members affected by the decisions. The survey covered the 80th through the 86th Congresses, with special attention to the 86th.

4. David Truman, *The Congressional Party: A Case Study* (New York, 1959), p. 195.

5. In the 87th Congress a serious conflict arose over the Rules Committee ratio. There was newspaper talk of "purging" the ranking Democratic member, William Colmer from Mississippi, who had supported the Dixiecrat presidential candidacy of Mississippi's Governor Barnett in the 1960 campaign, and who regularly voted with Chairman Howard Smith in the coalition of southern Democrats and conservative Republicans that controlled the Rules Committee. But Speaker Rayburn, in order to break the "stranglehold" the coalition would have over the impending legislation of the Kennedy Administration, advocated instead an increase in the Committee's size. The conflict was resolved in Rayburn's favor by a narrow margin with the entire House participating in the vote. The subsequent appointments, however, were made along the lines suggested in this article.

6. "The Role of the Representative: Some Empirical Observations on the Theory of Edmund Burke," *American Political Science Review,* LIII (September 1959), 742–756.

7. *Cf.* Seymour Scher, "Congressional Committee Members as Independent Agency Overseers: A Case Study," *American Political Science Review,* LIV (December 1960), 911–920.

8. Truman, *op. cit.,* p. 279.

12

THE GROWTH OF THE SENIORITY SYSTEM IN THE U. S. HOUSE OF REPRESENTATIVES[*]

NELSON W. POLSBY, MIRIAM GALLAHER, AND BARRY SPENCER RUNDQUIST

Seniority in the House is like filibusters in the Senate—very frequently complained of, thought to control much behavior, but not much studied. The following article is an effort to bring together widely scattered information about the growth of the House seniority system and to account for its causes. Miriam Gallaher, a staff member at the Center for Advanced Study in the Behavioral Sciences, and Barry Spencer Rundquist, now Assistant Professor of Political Science at the University of Illinois, gathered and organized much of the data on which this study was based.

I. The Significance of Seniority

Popular discussions of the internal management of the U. S. House of Representatives in the present era generally give great weight to the ubiquity and arbitrariness of the seniority system as a significant determinant of outcomes there. Careful attention to the scholarly literature, however, should long since have modified this view. For it appears that except for relatively unimportant matters such as the allocation of office space on Capitol Hill,[1] the criterion of seniority is generally intermingled in House decision-making with a great many other criteria of choice, and the business of choosing is not automatic, but remains in the hands of persons having some considerable discretion. This, apparently, is the case with respect to such decisions as the allocation

Reprinted from *The American Political Science Review*, Vol. LXIII, No. 3 (September 1969), 787–807.

* The study of which this article is a part was made possible by the generosity of the Rockefeller Foundation, the Institute of International Studies and the Institute of Governmental Studies of the University of California, the Social Science Research Council, Wesleyan University, the Center for Advanced Study in the Behavioral Sciences, and the Carnegie Corporation of New York, the latter through its grant to the American Political Science Association for the Study of Congress. After this article was largely drafted, we were able to read Michael Eckstein Abram, "The Rise of Modern Seniority System in the U. S. House of Representatives" (unpublished Harvard honors thesis, April, 1966). Though based on a more restricted sample of data than the present report, the main lines of Mr. Abram's findings are gratifyingly similar to our own. They are reported also in Michael Abram and Joseph Cooper, "The Rise of Seniority in the House of Representatives," *Polity* I (Fall, 1968), 52–85. We are grateful for the creative assistance of Paul Sniderman, Robert vom Eigen, Joan McLaughlin, and Sam Kernell.

Capitol Hill patronage,[2] the initial assignment of Representatives to committees,[3] the distribution of responsibilities within committees,[4] and the choice of party leaders.[5] The one important area in which seniority seems to play a role of overwhelming significance is in the matter of succession to the chairmanship of committees; this is in turn governed by the custom (not a formal rule) of seniority that guarantees members reappointment to committees at the opening of each new Congress, in rank order of committee service. It is the growth of this method of selecting committee chairmen in the House that is the subject of this paper.

The importance of a committee chairmanship varies, to be sure, with the importance from session to session of the legislation considered by the committee. It is also significantly modified by committee customs and practices, since formally, committee chairmen are subject to the will of committee majorities. Committees vary in the discretion they leave to their chairmen, and many examples exist of committee chairmen who were bypassed or defeated in specific controversies when they had gone "too far"—or not far enough.[6] Nevertheless, it would be foolish to deny that committee chairmen, on the whole, have enormous power over the activities of their committees, and over the ultimate output of Congress. It is generally the chairman who sets the pace that determines the total workload of the committee, the chairman who hires and fires staff, the chairman who forms subcommittees and assigns them jurisdictions, members and aides. It is generally the chairman who manages the most important bills that are assigned to his committee, and at his own option oversees the endless tinkering with the substance of major bills that goes on in committee, on the floor, and in conference. All this is common knowledge; it provides a backdrop for the continuing interest of scholars and men of affairs in the people who become committee chairmen, and in the process that selects them.

Parliamentary bodies differ in the extent to which they divide labor and decentralize power. The two are, moreover, not precisely synonymous, since an efficient division of labor can be effected while retaining centralized control. Such is the case, for example, in the Italian Parliament, and the Japanese Diet where strong committee systems are combined with strict party government.[7] Decentralization of power without division of labor leads to Parliamentary ineffectiveness such as in Colombia and Ecuador.[8] [See Figure 1.]

A more familiar pattern than either, one congenial to the classic British parliamentary features of ministerial responsibility and strict party regularity, is the centralization of power in the hands of party leaders and a division of labor in the legislature that is rudimentary at the very most. Thus Bagehot's magisterial classification of the 19th century House of Commons as an "electoral chamber" that passes upon the legitimacy of the sitting government but engages not at all in policymaking.[9] At the opposite extreme is a legislature where labor is divided and where power is likewise decentralized, such as in the case of the contemporary U. S. House of Representatives.

Operational indices of these characteristics can be suggested, and in so doing, the importance of seniority can be clarified. Briefly, the strength of a division of labor can be defined as the extent to which legislatures rely upon standing committees to conduct their business. When committees are not

Division of Labor

	Strong (Strong comittees)	Weak (Weak committees)
Centralized (Strong party leadership)	Italian Parliament Japanese Diet	British House of Commons
Decentralized (Weak party leadership)	U.S. House of Representatives	Columbian and Ecuadorian Legislatures

Power over Policy

FIGURE 1   Relationships between the division of labor and the centralization of power over substantive policy in legislatures

relied upon, centralization of power can be observed in the extent to which the initiation and modification of policies eventually enacted by the legislature is concentrated in a few hands (normally the hands of party leaders) or dispersed into many. When committees are relied upon, whether they are populated by automatic or discretionary means, and whether discretionary means are at the discretion of few or many members, is an acceptable test of the centralization or decentralization of power.

From these stipulations, we can deduce that an automatic means of assigning members to committees is a sufficient, though not a necessary, condition for decentralization of power, to the extent that committees are heavily relied on in legislatures. A seniority system is automatic. Therefore, in the U. S. House of Representatives, where committees are strong, the seniority system is sufficient to explain the decentralization of congressional power.

The extent of a seniority rule's application may be said to constitute a measure of the allocation of discretion and hence of power as between party leaders and committee chairmen. Previous commentators have agreed upon this even when they agreed on little else.[10] It is of course not the only such measure imaginable, but it is an important one. Committee chairmen subject to the selection of party leaders stand in a different relation to the leadership than chairmen selected by an impersonal process in which the leadership is powerless to interfere. Thus, like pregnancy, seniority is for most purposes a dichotomous variable. When seniority operates as a partial influence upon decision-making rather than as an automatic determinant of committee rank, political influence flows to those empowered to vary the application of the diverse criteria of choice—normally party leaders. When seniority is sovereign and inviolate, power is decentralized to those accordingly protected.

II. When Did Seniority Begin?

There is disagreement in the literature about how well-entrenched decision-making by seniority has been in the House, and for how long. Numerous anecdotes exist, testifying to the violation of seniority in the selection of committee chairmen in former times.[11] Nowadays, the year 1910, which marks the revolt against Speaker Cannon, is often mentioned as the effective beginning of the system. George Galloway says: "Seniority in point of service has been the prevailing principle governing both committee assignments and the selection of chairmen since . . . 1910 in the House."[12] However, James K. Pollock maintains, "From early years the rule that has been generally followed in the appointment of committees is the so-called seniority rule. It has made no difference whether Republicans or Democrats controlled Congress; the method of selection has been the same. . . . The practice . . . is a universal one."[13] Chang-wei Chiu shows that in the four Congresses just prior to 1910 (the 58th to 61st), with respect to ten important committees, many appointments were made at the discretion of the Speaker, but "more than four-fifths of the members . . . were appointed under the seniority rule."[14] Writing in 1884, Woodrow Wilson says: "The Speaker is expected to constitute the committees in accordance with his own political views [and he] generally uses his powers as freely and imperatively as he is expected to use them." But he also writes: "by custom, seniority in Congressional service determines the bestowal of the principal chairmanships."[15]

These writers seem to be reporting upon a situation in which seniority figured as a criterion of choice, but where discretion was left to party leaders. Hence they are describing a period preceding the advent of a seniority *system* such as operates today. Earlier, in 1865, there seems to be no doubt or ambiguity about the locus of power to allocate committee chairmanships. W. R. Brock writes

The Speaker was a man of considerable influence and much depended upon him. He appointed members of committees, acted in effect as majority leader in the arrangement of business, recognized or failed to recognize would-be participants in debate, interpreted the rules of the House, and dealt with the numerous points of order. . . . A good deal of power rested with the chairmen of committees, though perhaps less than in more recent times. . . .[16]

Likewise, in 1871, the Speaker constituted the committees. A member of Speaker Blaine's household wrote in a family letter,

Your father sits here at the table toiling away over his committees. . . . As fast as he gets them arranged, just so fast some after-consideration comes up which disarranges not one, but many, and over topples the whole row of bricks. It is a matter in which no one can help him. . . [He] had wool and cotton manufacturers to meet in Boston, dinners, breakfasts, and lunches . . . to give and take in New York, and, over and above all, pressures, to resist or permit, of Congressional committees.[17]

There is much other commentary on the wide discretion of the Speaker before 1910. George Rothwell Brown observed, "The right of the Chair to delay making committee assignments for long periods was recognized, Mr. Reed, for example, refraining from appointing the committees in the 55th Congress for 131 days."[18] James Bryce, in the revised edition of *The American Commonwealth* (1905), says: "In America the Speaker has immense political power, and is permitted, nay expected, to use it in the interests of his party . . . His most important privilege is . . . the nomination of the numerous standing committees. . . ."[19] Alexander, writing just after the 1910 revolt against Cannon, says: "The Speaker's greatest power has its source in his authority to appoint committees." [20]

There is, obviously, an important empirical question to be settled which these quotations, taken all together, raise. This has to do with the extent to which seniority was actually followed in the assignment of committee chairmanships before a hard and fast seniority system was established. The answer to this may, in turn, raise questions about the processes by which seniority came to be established as an inflexible norm in the House of Representatives.

The data we shall presently consider consist of a report on the selection of all chairmen of House standing committees, by Congresses, from the 47th to the 88th Congress (1881–1965). This information was gathered from *The Congressional Directory* for each Congress. From the 75th to the 88th Congress, committee memberships are listed and the party affiliations of members designated in the *Directory*. Prior to the 75th Congress, the *Directory* lists committee members without designation as to party. However, from the 74th back through the 55th Congress, the committee lists were, with a few discrepancies, columnized by party affiliation. After an unsystematic but reasonably thorough cross-check in the *Biographical Directory of the American Congress*,[21] these columnizations were followed. From the 54th to the 47th Congress, a systematic and complete checking of names in the *Biographical Directory* enabled us to establish party designations.

The Congressional Directory was published for each Congress we studied; but its publication schedule has been erratic. The most common practice seems to have been for the *Directory* to appear once for each session of every Congress, that is, annually. However, in some years, the first edition of the *Directory* appeared before committee lists were established. Since we proposed to sample committee lists only once per Congress, we adopted the policy of consulting the first edition of the *Directory* available to us for each Congress that contained full listings of committee members. Thus, changes in chairmanships within Congresses may have been lost to us.[22]

The *Directory* is neither a wholly uniform, nor a strictly official source; much superior would be the committee lists appearing in the *Journals* or the assignments as they are recorded in the verbatim accounts of debates, currently entitled *The Congressional Record*. However, the former of these sources is not widely available, and the latter is not indexed under the rubric "Committee Assignments." Hence both are exceedingly cumbersome for the purposes of research and, in any event, would in all probability disclose only the most insignificant variations from the *Directory*.

Our most important finding can be summarized in a single table which shows for each Congress the number of times that seniority was and was not followed in the appointment of committee chairmen for each of 40 Congresses from 1881 to 1963. When a committee chairman met the following conditions he was classified as a chairman by virtue of seniority: In the preceding Congress he was the chairman, or if his party was in the minority, the ranking member, or he had been on the committee in the previous Congress and all those listed above him for that Congress were no longer serving in Congress. If a chairman could meet none of these conditions, he was classified as having been designated by some method other than seniority. These simple rules of classification yielded Table 1.

The general trend, over the 80-year

TABLE 1   The Growth of Seniority 1881–1963 Violation of the Seniority of Chairmen, by Committee, U. S. House of Representatives, by Congress

CONGRESS	YEAR	SPEAKER	PARTY	SENIORITY FOLLOWED	SENIORITY NOT FOLLOWED	TOTAL COMMITTEES*
47	1881	Keifer	R	2	37	39
48	1883	Carlisle	D	8	30	38
49	1885			21	19	40
50	1887			20	21	41
51	1889	Reed	R	20	27	47
52	1891	Crisp	D	12	35	47
53	1893			25	24	49
54	1895	Reed	R	13	39	52
55	1897			36	16	52
56	1899	Henderson	R	42	15	57
57	1901			49	8	57
58	1903	Cannon	R	43	11	54
59	1905			51	8	59
60	1907			45	13	58
61	1909			42	18	60
62	1911	Clark	D	25	27	52
63	1913			33	20	53
64	1915			50	6	56
65	1917			45	10	55
66	1919	Gillett	R	35	22	57
67	1921			44	15	59
68	1923			40	17	57
69	1925	Longworth	R	37	22	59
70	1927			43	1	44
71	1929			38	7	45
72	1931	Garner	D	27	18	45
73	1933	Rainey	D	38	7	45
74	1935	Byrns/Bankhead	D	32	13	45
75	1937	Bankhead		42	4	46
76	1939	Rayburn	D	37	9	46
77	1941			39	7	46
78	1943			34	11	45
79	1945			37	9	46
80	1947	Martin	R	9	4	13
81	1949	Rayburn	D	19	0	19
82	1951			18	0	18
83	1953	Martin	R	17	1	18
84	1955	Rayburn	D	19	0	19
85	1957			19	0	19
86	1959			19	0	19
87	1961	Rayburn/McCormack	D	20	0	20
88	1963	McCormack		20	0	20

* Total equals the number of committees in the Congress minus the number of new committees and the number of committees in which the three top members in the previous Congress are absent in the present Congress. The latter are excluded because we have no data on men below the number three position in the previous Congress.

period, is toward the increasing use of seniority as a determinant of committee chairmanships, as Figure 2 shows. Several different kinds of seniority violation are summarized in Table 1. Some members of Congress who by our criteria should have been committee chairmen were demoted. Others stayed at the same rank but were jumped by members from below them on the list or from elsewhere. Others left their committees. Some of these received new committee assignments; others did not. Of those who received new assignments, some did as well or better than if they had stayed put.[23]

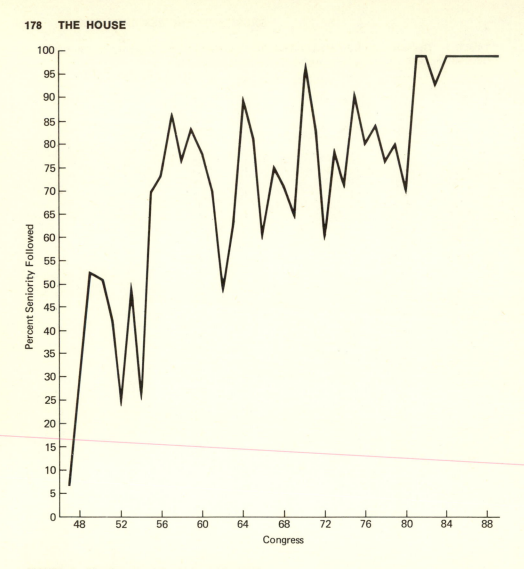

FIGURE 2 **The Growth of Seniority (1881–1963)**
Percentage of Committees on which Seniority was followed in the Selection of Chairman, by Congress*

* Percentages were calculated as follows: Seniority (from Table 1), divided by total committees (from Table 1) for each Congress.

Finally, some members who otherwise might have become, or remained, chairmen were found to hold chairmanships of other committees, or party leadership positions. Thus Table 2 distinguishes instances where potential chairmen whose seniority was violated seem to have been compensated in the appointment process from instances where no such compensation is visible.

Compensation was not fully in the discretion of House leaders. A senior

TABLE 2   Compensated and Uncompensated Violations of Seniority *

CONGRESS	YEAR	VIOLATIONS COMPENSATED	UNCOMPENSATED (NUMBER)	UNCOMPENSATED (PERCENT)	TOTAL VIOLATIONS
47	1881	12	25	68	37
48	1883	16	14	47	30
49	1885	7	12	63	19
50	1887	12	9	43	21
51	1889	19	8	30	27
52	1891	22	13	37	35
53	1893	15	9	38	24
54	1895	30	9	23	39
55	1897	11	5	31	16
56	1899	13	2	13	15
57	1901	5	3	38	8
58	1903	7	4	36	11
59	1905	5	3	38	8
60	1907	10	3	23	13
61	1909	8	10	56	18
62	1911	21	6	22	27
63	1913	13	7	35	20
64	1915	6	0	0	6
65	1917	7	3	30	10
66	1919	19	3	14	22
67	1921	15	0	0	15
68	1923	16	1	6	17
69	1925	20	2	9	22
70	1927	1	0	0	1
71	1929	7	0	0	7
72	1931	16	2	11	18
73	1933	7	0	0	7
74	1935	13	0	0	13
75	1937	4	0	0	4
76	1939	9	0	0	9
77	1941	6	1	14	7
78	1943	10	1	9	11
79	1945	9	0	0	9
80	1947	4	0	0	4
81	1949	0	0	0	0
82	1951	0	0	0	0
83	1953	1	0	0	1
84	1955	0	0	0	0
85	1957	0	0	0	0
86	1959	0	0	0	0
87	1961	0	0	0	0
88	1963	0	0	0	0

* Uncompensated violations of seniority occur when members eligible to be chairman are not, and meet one or more of the following conditions: Demoted, jumped, received no new assignment, or held a chairmanship on a less desirable committee.

Compensated violations occur when potential chairmen receive or hold better assignments, or equal or better chairmanships or are elected to party leadership. For rankings of committees, see Note 23.

member who picked between chairmanships was not necessarily in the debt of the Speaker. Appointments to new positions as good or better than a relinquished chairmanship were undoubtedly negotiated through the party leadership of the majority party (and, after Speaker Cannon established the custom, for minority members in negotiation with the leaders of the minority party) but it is difficult to interpret compensations as entirely within the

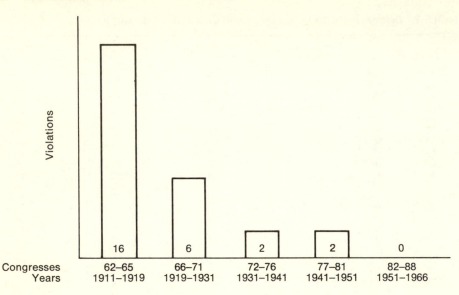

Congresses	62–65	66–71	72–76	77–81	82–88
Years	1911–1919	1919–1931	1931–1941	1941–1951	1951–1966

FIGURE 3   Compensated and uncompensated violations of seniority, 1881–1963

Speaker's control, since it was necessary for the Speaker to use the appointment power to build a coalition that would support him in office by rewarding his allies and mollifying the leaders of rival factions within his party.[24]

Uncompensated violations of seniority can be interpreted as purer examples of central leadership, since they represent instances where the committee assignment process was used by party leaders to intervene in the careers of members but where no payment in kind can be detected. As Figure 3 makes clear, this sort of intervention declined rapidly over the years surveyed, barely surviving after the 1911 rules changes vesting the Speaker's jurisdiction over committee assignments in party committees on committees.

Compensated violations of seniority, however, survived well into the 20th century. Table 3 demonstrates that most of these violations occur on committees whose chairmen had become

chairmen of committees of equal or greater importance. Less significant numerically are potential chairmen of insignificant committees who take up appointments instead on more important committees. Before 1911, these appointments to new committees were not necessarily at the bottom; committee rank was assigned at the Speaker's discretion—although this was not frequently used to disturb committee ranks orders.

Seniority is now strictly observed in the placement of new members, which means that the costs of transferring from a chairmanship to membership on a better committee have risen over the years. Even so, a compensated violation of a chairman's seniority can be recorded for the 91st Congress. In the waning days of the 90th Congress Omar Burleson of Texas gave up his chairmanship of the moribund Committee on House Administration to fill a vacancy on the Ways and Means Committee—where he ranked below Democrats

TABLE 3   Compensated Violations

CONGRESS	YEAR	CHAIRMAN OF EQUAL OR BETTER COMMITTEE (NUMBER)	(PERCENT)	BETTER NEW ASSIGNMENT (NUMBER)	(PERCENT)	TO LEADERSHIP (NUMBER)	(PERCENT)	TOTAL COMPENSATED VIOLATIONS
47	1881	8	67	3	25	1	8	12
48	1883	15	94	1	6	0	0	16
49	1885	7	100	0	0	0	0	7
50	1887	8	67	4	33	0	0	12
51	1889	12	63	7	37	0	0	19
52	1891	13	59	9	41	0	0	22
53	1893	6	40	9	60	0	0	15
54	1895	25	83	5	17	0	0	30
55	1897	8	73	3	27	0	0	11
56	1899	10	77	3	23	0	0	13
57	1901	3	60	2	40	0	0	5
58	1903	2	28	4	57	1	14	7
59	1905	1	20	4	80	0	0	5
60	1907	8	80	2	20	0	0	10
61	1909	5	62	3	38	0	0	8
62	1911	9	43	10	48	2	9	21
63	1913	7	54	6	46	0	0	13
64	1915	3	50	3	50	0	0	6
65	1917	5	71	2	28	0	0	7
66	1919	10	53	8	42	1	5	19
67	1921	10	67	5	33	0	0	15
68	1923	13	81	3	19	0	0	16
69	1925	18	40	2	10	0	0	20
70	1927	1	100	0	0	0	0	1
71	1929	6	86	1	14	0	0	7
72	1931	11	69	4	25	1	6	16
73	1933	5	71	0	0	2	28	7
74	1935	10	77	2	15	1	8	13
75	1937	3	75	0	0	1	25	4
76	1939	6	67	3	33	0	0	9
77	1941	5	83	1	17	0	0	6
78	1943	9	90	1	10	0	0	10
79	1945	8	89	1	11	0	0	9
80	1947	4	100	0	0	0	0	4
81	1949	0	0	0	0	0	0	0
82	1951	0	0	0	0	0	0	0
83	1953	0	0	1	100	0	0	1
84	1955	0	0	0	0	0	0	0
85	1957	0	0	0	0	0	0	0
86	1959	0	0	0	0	0	0	0
87	1961	0	0	0	0	0	0	0
88	1963	0	0	0	0	0	0	0

far junior to him in House service. For obvious reasons, this is not a frequent occurrence.

Almost as infrequent, indeed, is the transfer of any member from the middle or top range of any committee to the bottom of any other, no matter what the disparity in the prestige of the two committees. When such a transfer does take place, it is generally at the request either of party leaders or of the leaders of a particularly large and cohesive state delegation that can find no other or more satisfactory way of exercising its option to occupy a seat on a key committee.

Compensated violations, in short, do not reflect the concentration of political power in any reliable way, since they may occur as the outcome of bargains between party leaders and members, but more often involve a choice between chairmanships. Uncompensated violations, on the other hand, disclose more about options available to party leaders. The sharp decline in the frequency of this sort of violation during the period covered by our investigation suggests that these options were somewhat circumscribed and could hardly have been exercised whimsically or without cost. A closer look at patterns of violation before 1911, to which we now turn, may suggest ways in which party leaders managed and conserved their options in the committee assignment process.

III. How Speakers Managed: Patterns of Violation Before 1910

Until the 1910 revolt against Cannon, Speakers held the formal power to name committees from top to bottom, majority and minority. They were expected to use this power to enhance their ability to lead their party to legislative success. Their allies expected to be favored, their rivals to be placated. The extent to which Speakers fulfilled these expectations is reflected in the pattern of uncompensated seniority violations before 1910.

The Speaker's discretion in the appointment of committee chairmen was not a free good. It had to be employed carefully. Thus, instead of tearing up committee rosters root and branch at the opening of each Congress, Speakers concentrated on relatively few appointments on only a few committees. Pollock mentions a tabulation by Representative Luce showing "that in the seven appointings that took place from 1896 to 1910, about 407 chairmen were named. Of these 265 were reappointments, 93 were promotions of men already on the committees, and only 49, or an average of seven for each appointing, were new men brought to chairmanships from outside the ranks of the respective committees." [25] Our figures, tabulated on a slightly different

base (since we were limited as indicated in the note to Table 1) and classifying as violations instances where potential chairmen were jumped from within the committee as well as cases where they were replaced from outside, are nevertheless confirmatory: for the same seven Congresses (55th through 61st) 304 out of 397 appointments (77%) involved no violations of seniority at all. Only 34 of the 397 (8.5%) were uncompensated violations. For the longer period, 1881 to 1910, 133 of the 750 appointments to chairmanships were uncompensated violations of the seniority principle.

The strategies available to Speakers in the appointment process before 1911 varied according to easily described external conditions. There was, first of all, the problem of creating a coalition, when a new Speaker took control of a new majority after an election which brought a new party to the control of all committees. Under these circumstances a new Speaker had new friends to reward and rivals to neutralize, and so it is not surprising that violations of seniority in these circumstances were higher than in years when the Speaker was new but the majority was not, or when there was no change in leadership. This is the finding expressed in Table 4.

Speakers under these circumstances were also able to replace incumbent chairmen (as contrasted with the more vulnerable men newly eligible for chairmanships) to a degree not possible when there had been no party turnover, as Table 5 shows.

When Speakers replaced incumbents, they preferred to move the chairman off the committee rather than keep him on looking over his successor's shoulder; this was less necessary for nonincumbents, as Table 6 suggests.

Table 7 shows a sharp contrast between the treatment of incumbent

TABLE 4   When There Is a New Speaker and a New Majority, Seniority Violations Are Frequent, 1881–1910

	NEW SPEAKER, PARTY TURNOVER		NEW SPEAKER, BUT NO TURNOVER		NO TURNOVER	
Seniority Followed	25%	[55]	77%	[83]	69%	[287]
Seniority Violated	75%	[168]	23%	[26]	31%	[127]
	100%	[223]	100%	[109]	100%	[414]

TABLE 5   When There Is Party Turnover, the New Speaker Can Violate the Seniority of Incumbent Chairman Without Compensation, 1881–1910

	NEW SPEAKER PARTY TURNOVER		NEW SPEAKER NO TURNOVER		NO TURNOVER	
Incumbent	58%	[40]	17%	[1]	26%	[14]
Nonincumbent	42%	[29]	83%	[5]	74%	[40]
	100%	[69]	100%	[6]	100%	[54]

TABLE 6   When an Incumbent Chairman's Seniority Is Violated, He Is Moved to Another Committee Rather Than Demoted

	UNCOMPENSATED VIOLATIONS			
	CHAIRMAN		NONCHAIRMAN	
Demoted	20%	[11]	61%	[45]
Moved	80%	[44]	39%	[29]
	100%	[55]	100%	[74]

TABLE 7   In Years Where There Is No Party Turnover, the Power of Chairmen to Resist Demotion Is Increased

	TURNOVER YEARS				NO TURNOVER YEARS			
	CHAIRMAN		NONCHAIRMAN		CHAIRMAN		NONCHAIRMAN	
Demoted	25%	[10]	39%	[11]	7%	[1]	53%	[24]
Moved	75%	[30]	61%	[18]	93%	[14]	47%	[21]
	100%	[40]	100%	[29]	100%	[15]	100%	[45]

chairmen and others in years when there is no party turnover. Party turnover, in other words, appears in our data as a strong force, legitimizing activities that in more "normal" circumstances were not permitted to Speakers.

Even though new Speakers taking control of new majorities violated the seniority of chairmen and potential chairmen much more often than was true for most new Congresses, the ratio between compensated and uncompensated violations remained at

TABLE 8   Compensated and Uncompensated Violations Remain Constant, Regardless of Changes in Majority Party, 1881–1910

VIOLATIONS	NEW SPEAKER PARTY TURNOVER		NO PARTY TURNOVER	
Compensated	59%	[99]	61%	[93]
Uncompensated	41%	[69]	39%	[60]
	100%	[168]	100%	[153]

TABLE 9   New Speakers Without New Majorities Compensate When They Violate Seniority

VIOLATIONS	NEW SPEAKER NO NEW MAJORITY		OTHER CASES	
Compensated	77%	[20]	58%	[172]
Uncompensated	23%	[6]	42%	[123]
	100%	[26]	100%	[295]

about 3 to 2. That is, more violations were compensated than not, even when twice as many chairmanships changed hands by means other than seniority. This is shown in Table 8.

Clearly, creating a coalition differs in its effects upon committee assignments from situations where a new Speaker inherited a coalition or acted to maintain a coalition. When there was a new Speaker but no party turnover, Speakers moved cautiously: these were the circumstances in which there were the fewest violations of seniority, as Table 4 indicates, and in which violations, when they occurred, were overwhelmingly of the compensated type. This is shown in Table 9.

Thus we can conclude that by far the most leeway existed for Speakers when they came fresh to office on the heels of a party victory establishing a new majority in the House. Violations of seniority in other circumstances were much less frequent, and much more subject to compensation.

This suggests that for the period 1881–1910 a number of small but significant constraints upon the Speaker's

de jure options were developing. They can be noted in the restraint which seems to have been exercised in the violation of seniority when Speakers acted without a party turnover to legitimize their manipulation of assignments to committee chairmanships.

IV. Speaker Cannon: A Transitional Figure

Speaker Joseph Gurney Cannon (1903–1911) more often than any other Speaker is responsible for exceptions to the patterns we have been describing. This is consistent with an interpretation of the committee assignment process as a method—undoubtedly the most important method before 1911—by which Speakers maintained a supportive coalition in the House in behalf of policies favored by the majority party. When the Progressive movement became powerful at the Republican grass roots, as it did in the 1890's, it was only a matter of time before this was reflected in party insurgency in the House of Representatives.

House chroniclers make it clear that

the insurgents' successful challenge to Cannon's leadership in 1910 laid heavy stress upon his arbitrary use of the Speaker's power of appointment. George Rothwell Brown quotes Representative Nelson of Wisconsin:

"Have we not been punished by every means at the disposal of the powerful House organization? Members long chairmen of important committees, others holding high rank—all with records of faithful and efficient party service to their credit—have been ruthlessly removed, deposed, and humiliated. . . ."

Brown continues:

The House knew as it listened to this merciless indictment of the speakership that it was true. Members were there who had been removed from their committee places, because they had displeased the organization, through the exercise of power which had raised the speakership of Mr. Cannon to an unprecedented height.[26]

George Norris, a Congressman in that era, wrote long afterward:

Every two years the members knew they were confronted with the appointment of the various standing Committees; and one man, the Speaker, possessed absolute authority to do what he pleased in these selections. He held in his hands the political life of virtually every member. He could reward the faithful, and he could punish the "guilty." I doubt if any Speaker in the history of Congress was as ruthless as Joe Cannon sometimes was.[27]

Booth Mooney says, "[Cannon] stacked the key committees with men who would unquestioningly support everything he favored and oppose everything he was against. He arbitrarily took chairmanships away from members who tried to flout his authority."[28]

Cannon may indeed have been the most ruthless Speaker in House history, but these and other complaints[29] about his "ruthlessness" are hard to substantiate with a casual look at the figures we have. Of the six Speakers between 1883 and 1910, Cannon ranks next to lowest in his over-all violations of seniority. (See Table 10.) What the data provide are indications of important differences in the timing of his violations of seniority as compared with those of his predecessors. Cannon became Speaker after Speaker Henderson, also a Republican, for somewhat mysterious reasons decided to retire from Congress. While Speakers customarily rearranged committee chairmanships after party turnovers, as we have seen, the custom when there was no party turnover was pretty much to maintain the existing arrangements. In his first term, Cannon succeeded the retired Henderson as chairman of the Rules Committee,

TABLE 10   Violations of Seniority by Speaker, 1881–1910

SPEAKER	VIOLATIONS	VIOLATIONS AS A % OF ALL APPOINTMENTS
Keifer (1881–83)	37	92%
Carlisle (1883–89)	70	59%
Reed (1889–91)	27	57%
Crisp (1891–95)	59	61%
Reed (1895–99)	55	53%
Henderson (1899–1903)	23	20%
Cannon (1903–1911)	50	21%

TABLE 11   Cannon Committed a Higher Proportion of Violations After His First Term Than Any Other Speaker

	NUMBER POST FIRST TERM VIOLATIONS	TOTAL VIOLATIONS DURING SPEAKERSHIP	POST FIRST TERM VIOLATIONS AS % OF TOTAL
Carlisle	40	70	57
Crisp	24	59	41
Reed	16	55	29
Henderson	8	23	35
Cannon	39	50	78

a procedure which violated the seniority of John Dalzell (who under Cannon became second ranked member of Ways and Means as well as of Rules) but which was well in keeping with House custom. Then he committed one violation on a semi-exclusive committee, Post Office and Post Roads, and four violations on minor committees. This constitutes the most restrained first term performance of any Speaker, including Henderson, although the latter restricted his eight first term violations to minor committees. In his second term Cannon transferred two incumbents and skipped over three non-incumbents—all on minor committees.

In Cannon's last two terms, there began an increase in factionalism in the Republican Party that solidified into the Progressive and Farmer–Labor insurgent movements. This split in the Republican Party found a focus in hot legislative battles over tariff and conservation measures. Cannon responded in part [30] by *increasingly* tinkering with committee chairmanships. (See Table 11.)

What Cannon did involved a number of innovations as compared with his immediate predecessors. He compensated potential chairmen less often (Table 12). Although he deprived incumbent chairmen without compensating them to about the same degree as his predecessors (Table 13), he violated seniority without compensation to a much greater extent after his first term (Table 14). He deprived many potential chairmen of major and semi-exclusive committees (Table 15) and did so after his first term to an unprecedented extent (Table 16).

TABLE 12   Cannon Committed a Higher Proportion of Uncompensated Violations After His First Term Than Any Other Speaker

	NUMBER POST FIRST TERM UNCOMPENSATED VIOLATIONS	TOTAL UNCOMPENSATED VIOLATIONS DURING SPEAKERSHIP	POST FIRST TERM UNCOMPENSATED VIOLATIONS AS % OF TOTAL
Carlisle	21	35	60
Crisp	9	22	41
Reed	5	14	36
Henderson	3	5	60
Cannon	16	20	80

TABLE 13   Violations by Speaker of the Seniority of Incumbents Without Compensation (by percentages)

	UNCOMPENSATED VIOLATIONS OF INCUMBENTS	UNCOMPENSATED VIOLATIONS	% 1 OF 2
Keifer	13	25	52
Carlisle	12	35	34
Reed	5	8	62
Crisp	12	22	55
Reed	6	14	43
Henderson	0	5	0
Cannon	7	20	35

TABLE 14   Cannon's Uncompensated Violations of Incumbents' Seniority Occurs After His First Term as Speaker

	POST FIRST TERM VIOLATIONS OF INCUMBENTS	TOTAL VIOLATIONS OF INCUMBENTS	% 1 OF 2
Carlisle	4	12	33
Crisp	3	12	25
Reed	1	6	17
Henderson	0	0	0
Cannon	6	7	86

TABLE 15   Uncompensated Violations of Seniority on Major and Semi-exclusive Committees by Speaker

	UNCOMPENSATED VIOLATIONS ON MAJOR AND SEMI-EXCLUSIVE COMMITTEES	TOTAL UNCOMPENSATED VIOLATIONS	MAJOR AND SEMI-EXCLUSIVE AS % OF TOTAL
Keifer	5	25	20
Carlisle	10	35	29
Reed	3	8	38
Crisp	7	22	32
Reed	7	14	50
Henderson	0	5	0
Cannon	7	20	35

Bolles says,

Cannon drove his advantage home in the House by dismissing the most obstreperous progressives and other insurgents from the committees where they could do him harm. Cooper lost his chairmanship of Insular Affairs, and Norris lost his membership on Public Buildings and Grounds. Cannon removed Fowler as chairman of Banking and Currency, and he dropped Lindbergh from Indian Af-

TABLE 16 Uncompensated Violations on Major and Semi-exclusive Committees After Speaker's First Term By Speaker

	MAJOR AND SEMI-EXCLUSIVE COMMITTEES AFTER FIRST TERM	TOTAL UNCOMPEN-SATED VIOLATIONS ON MAJOR AND SEMI-EXCLUSIVE COMMITTEES	% POST FIRST TERM
Carlisle	6	10	60
Crisp	3	7	43
Reed	0	7	0
Henderson	0	0	0
Cannon	5	7	71

fairs. He put Lenroot to one side by assigning him to the inane Committee on Ventilation and Acoustics.[31]

In the Sixtieth Congress (1907) he removed four incumbent chairmen from nonexclusive committees, giving them no new committee assignments. These four removals of incumbents after a Speaker's first term were unprecedented. (See Table 14.) At the same time Cannon skipped over John A. T. Hull on Militia and Gilbert Haugen on War Claims—both men from progressive Iowa, to reward Helvor Stienerson (Minn.) and Kittredge Haskins (Pa.) with chairmanships on these two committees. He also transferred Stevens Henry (Conn.), about to become chairman on Agriculture, to a low ranking position on Merchant Marine and Fisheries and gave Henry's chairmanship to Charles Scott (Kansas).

Insurgents opposed Cannon's reelection to the Speakership in the first session of the 61st Congress (March, 1909), and supported Democratic leader Champ Clark's attempt to change the rules and sharply curtail the powers of the Speaker.[32] Cannon fought back with the main weapon at his disposal. He made John Weeks (Mass.) chairman of semi-exclusive Post Office and Post Roads, thus violating John J. Gardner's seniority, replaced vacant

chairmanships with low ranked members on Banking and Currency and Interstate and Foreign Commerce, and deprived three incumbents and five non-incumbents of their chairmanships on minor committees.

In sum, after a cautious beginning, Cannon committed more violations on major and semi-exclusive committees after his first term than any Speaker (Table 16), more post-first-term violations of the seniority of incumbents than anyone (Table 14), and more uncompensated violations after his first term than anyone. These irregularities became entwined with Cannon's legislative conservatism in the insurgents' ideology of anti-Cannonism.

Ultimately Cannon's maneuvers were not enough to stem the Progressive revolt in his party. This demonstrated that there were limits to the Speaker's ability to maintain his leadership position by depriving his opponents of chairmanships and awarding them to supporters. Cannon's problem seems to have been that he took over a relatively unified party and had little need at first to build a special supportive coalition. When the party began to split apart in his third term, he responded by attempting to maintain a workable coalition by dumping insurgent chairmen and rewarding loyal Republicans with chairmanships. In so doing he deprived more incumbents

TABLE 17   Uncompensated Violations in Speakers' First and Later Terms *

	SPEAKER'S FIRST TERM			AFTER SPEAKER'S FIRST TERM		
TYPE OF VIOLATION	(1) ALL SPEAKERS	(2) CANNON	% 2 OF 1	(1) ALL SPEAKERS	(2) CANNON	% 2 OF 1
Demotions or Jumps	23	3	13	19	6	32
Transfers to Other Committees	52	1	2	34	10	29

* Note that Cannon not only contributes disproportionately to the number of uncompensated violations of seniority in general after speakers' first terms, but also contributes disproportionately to the number of demotions and jumps.

and chairmen of major and semi-exclusive committees than had previously been done in the House. Cannon also resorted disproportionately after his first term to the strategy of demoting chairmen or jumping over potential chairmen, rather than moving them to other committees. (See Table 17.) It is costlier to deprive an incumbent than a nonincumbent, a member of an exclusive committee than a minor committee. Likewise, it is costlier to demote than to transfer, and given the customary practice of previous Speakers, costlier to violate seniority after the Speaker's first term. Thus the costs of Cannon's efforts to maintain a supportive coalition are clear and his failure more understandable. It seems likely then, that it was not the sheer number of his seniority violations that earned Cannon his notoriety as the House's most ruthless Speaker, but how and when they occurred.

Before 1911 each newly elected Speaker enjoyed a period in which he could build a supportive coalition, to maximize his party's legislative success or his own popularity or longevity as Speaker. During this period he could gain supporters by pursuing relatively low-cost strategies. He could violate the seniority of fewer incumbents than non-incumbents, fewer members of exclusive committees than minor committees, and make fewer changes by internal shifts than transfers. After the initial phase, support became more costly. For each increment of support the Speaker had to expend more resources to employ each possible strategy. The longer the Speaker waited to form his coalition, the more probable it became that he could not afford to do so. Therefore the greater the likelihood he would either have to rely on seniority and give in to the legislative preferences of committee chairmen, or resist their preferences and risk losing party support.

Similarly, the earlier a Speaker could build his coalition, the more he could rely on seniority in subsequent terms. Thus, even during the pre-1911 period, seniority had gained a foothold in the House of Representatives.

V. After 1911:
Growing Decentralization

After 1911, the power of appointment was taken from the Speaker and vested in party committees on committees, subject to the ratification (which was pro forma) of the whole House. For most of the first decade after this sweeping change, the appointment of chairmen was the business of the Democratic party, as the majority party in the House.

The revolt against Cannon did not immediately result in the decentralization of power in the House. Rather, power was shifted from the Speaker to the majority leader, Oscar Underwood, who chaired the House Committee on Ways and Means, the Democratic committee on committees, and led the Democratic caucus. George Rothwell Brown remarks:

. . . The authority to name the committees of the House when taken from the Speaker was lodged theoretically in the most important committee of the House, but actually in the chairman of that committee. The Ways and Means Committee appointed the Committee on Rules, and the caucus adopted a resolution that no man should serve on more than one of the fourteen major committees.[33]

The Republican caucus had been destroyed by the revolt against Cannon, but not the Democratic caucus, with its two-thirds rule. In the 62nd Congress, rules changes were put through by the Democratic caucus vastly weakening the powers of the Speaker, with Speaker Clark's consent, but not decentralizing power in the House. The caucus was run by the Ways and Means committee, its chairman, and President Wilson. As American involvement in World War I increased, Wilson took more and more initiative and came to dominate Congressional activity.[34]

A recent study of the period observes:

The emergence of the Democratic caucus as the real source of legislative power in the Congress was particularly galling to the insurgents. . . . Far from supplanting the caucus, Wilson relied upon it as his prime instrument of legislative power. Agreements on administration programs were hammered out in the Democratic congressional caucuses and then steamrollered through Congress by solid Democratic majorities. In the standing committees Republican Congressmen and Senators, whether progressives or conservatives, were rarely allowed to play any significant part in the legislative process.[35]

The continued centralization of power in the first decade after the revolt against Cannon is reflected in our data as well. Table 18 shows a sizeable number of uncompensated violations of seniority in this first decade. When a potential chairman moved to a better committee, we interpreted the decision as also reflecting the influence of centralized power, since the shift had to be negotiated through the committee on committees. These two outcomes of seniority violation are contrasted in Table 18 with situations where members chose between chairmanships or themselves became party leaders, which we interpret as reflecting decentralization of discretion over the appointment process. The long-term trend toward decentralization is, of course, clear, and it emerges most strongly first in the decade of Republican dominance after the Wilson era, and continues on into the present day.

In 1919, decentralization took a major leap forward. In the election of 1918 the Republican party regained control of the House but was badly split between two leaders, James R. Mann of Illinois, a protégé of Cannon (who was still serving in the House and active in party affairs), and the more progressive Frederick H. Gillett of Massachusetts. Gillett was elected Speaker on the first ballot, but did not fare so well in the Republican caucus on the matter of committee assignments, as the *New York Times* account indicates:

At 12:30 o'clock this morning it was announced that the Mann forces had routed the Gillett faction in the matter of the selection of the Committee on Committees. . . . Mr. Mann offered a [motion] providing that each of the Republican states

TABLE 18   How Decentralization in Committee Assignments Grew. Violations of Seniority, by Period

	47–61 1881–1911 BEFORE REVOLT AGAINST CANNON	62–65 1911–1919 DEMOCRATIC CAUCUS DOMINATES	66–72 1919–1932 REPUBLICAN ERA	73–79 1933–1946 F. D. R. ERA	80–88 1947–1963 SINCE REORGANI- ZATION ACT
CONGRESS: YEAR:					
Centralized Decision-Making					
1. Uncompensated Violations	40% (129)	25% (16)	9% (9)	4% (2)	0
2. Potential Chairmen Awarded Better Assignments	18% (59)	33% (21)	22% (23)	14% (8)	20% (1)
	58%	58%	31%	18%	20%
Decentralized Decision-Making					
1. Member Chose Between Chairmanships	41% (131)	38% (24)	67% (69)	75% (46)	80% (4)
2. Member Joined Party Leadership	1% (2)	4% (2)	2% (2)	7% (4)	0
	42%	42%	69%	82%	80%
Total Violations	(321)	(63)	(103)	(60)	(5)

having representation in the House . . . should elect a member of a Committee on Committees [and providing that] the members of this committee should each respectively have a voting power equal to the State's pro rata Republican membership in the House.

The duties of the proposed new form of Committee on Committees will be to elect the Republican members of the standing committees in the next House, to elect a Steering Committee of five, a Republican whip, and also a floor leader who should be ex officio Chairman of the new Committee on Committees, and likewise a Chairman of the Steering Committee.

The adoption of the Mann substitute was interpreted as indicating that the movement [for] breaking down and overthrowing the domination of House committees under the rule of seniority of service has been blocked and defeated. The Mann substitute was probably adopted because the members who are holdovers and who have worked their way toward the top of the Republican side of the various committees want to retain the benefit of the rule of seniority. The adoption of the Mann substitute was interpreted as meaning that the House committees would be organized and their Chairmen picked in virtually the same old way, after the manner that put Southern men at the top of most of the important committees in both House and Senate in the [outgoing] Congress.[36]

Save for slight differences in the prose style, this passage, now nearly 50 years old, might have been clipped from the *New York Times* of today. In the decades that followed, the split in the Republican majority led to the formation of a legislative coalition with increasingly dissident southern Democrats. Party cohesion and majority rule through the caucus gave way to majority rule based on a powerful cross-party alliance which sup-

TABLE 19   After 1910 Uncompensated Violations Take Place on Minor Committees

	1881–1910		1910–1963	
Major	8%	(10)		(0)
Semi-exclusive	22%	(29)	4%	(1)
Minor	70%	(90)	96%	(26)
	100%	(129)	100%	(27)

FIGURE 4   Most Uncompensated Violations of Seniority After 1910 Take Place During the Period of Democratic Caucus Centralization

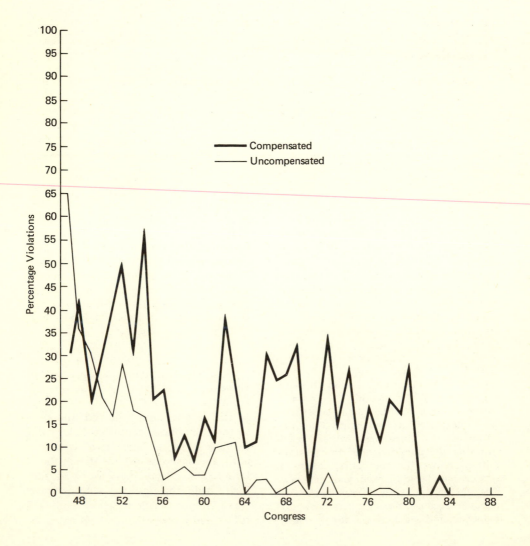

ported and maintained the seniority system.

The great profusion of minor committees up until 1946 gave party leaders a small amount of room for maneuver, however. Table 19 demonstrates that virtually all uncompensated violations of seniority in the period after 1910 involved the chairmen of minor committees. But even these, as Figure 4 shows, occurred predominantly during the first decade, when power was still centralized in the Democratic caucus.

The year 1946 marks the passage of the Legislative Reorganization Act, which reduced the number of committees from 48 to 19, principally by consolidating or abolishing minor committees and, in the process, liquidating large numbers of minor chairmanships. Since 1946, the seniority system has been virtually untouched, and chairmen have stayed put. The exceptions over two and a half decades are Omar Burleson, whom we mentioned earlier, and Adam Clayton Powell, who was deprived of his chairmanship in 1967 in the course of proceedings which led to his exclusion from Congress altogether.[37] If 1911 signals the decline of uncompensated violations, 1946 marks the virtual demise of exceptions to the seniority system, as Table 20 illustrates.

But even before 1946, most exceptions to seniority reflected decentralized choices rather than the manipulations of party leaders. Here is a brief listing of the circumstances surrounding the eleven most recent vio-

lations of the seniority of a committee chairman in the House of Representatives, aside from the cases of Powell and Burleson.

(1) In the Republican-controlled 83rd Congress (1953–55), A. L. Miller of Nebraska became chairman of the committee on Interior and Insular Affairs. The ranking Republican member in the previous Congress, Fred Crawford of Michigan, failed to be renominated to Congress. The second ranking Republican, Dean P. Taylor of New York, whose seniority was violated, transferred to the Judiciary committee. Miller was third in seniority.

(2) In the 80th Congress, Richard Welch of California became chairman of the Public Lands Committee. He had been ranking member of three other committees in the previous Congress, two of which (Labor and Insular Affairs) ceased to exist in the 80th Congress when, under the reorganization of that year, they were combined with other committees. Welch's third committee in the 79th Congress was Merchant Marine and Fisheries, which he left to become chairman of Public Lands.

(3) In the 80th Congress, on the Committee on Merchant Marine and Fisheries, Fred Bradley of Michigan, second ranked Republican, became chairman when the ranking member, Richard Welch, took the chairmanship of Public Lands instead.

(4) In the 79th Congress the chairman of the Committee on Elections (Number 3) gave up his chairmanship and became ranking member. He took

TABLE 20   The Decline of Uncompensated Violations

	1881–1910	1910–1946	1946–1963
Compensated	59% (192)	88% (204)	(1)
Uncompensated	41% (129)	12% (27)	(0)
	(321)	(231)	(1)

the chairmanship of the Committee on Territories instead.

There were seven other violations of seniority in the 79th Congress, involving the following committees: Election of the President and Vice President (previous chairman transferred to Agriculture); Irrigation and Reclamation (previous chairman, a congressman from silver-rich Idaho, transferred to the chairmanship of the Committee on Coinage); Memorials (previous chairman, retaining five other committee assignments, transferred to UnAmerican Activities); Enrolled Bills (a freshman member became chairman, violating the seniority of Mary T. Norton, who chose instead to become Chairman of Labor. She retained her position on Enrolled Bills as ranking Democrat rather than move up to the Chairmanship); Expenditures in the Executive Departments (ranking Democrat failed to move up); and Indian Affairs (previous chairman and ranking Democrat failed to return to Congress; third-ranking man, Samuel Dickstein of New York, moved up to second place but did not take the chairmanship. Dickstein was at the time chairman of the Committee on Immigration and Naturalization; no doubt there were more immigrants than Indians in his lower east side Manhattan constituency).

Thus seniority violations after 1919 appear to reflect not Speaker's discretion, or the discretion of a leadership committee, but rather the application of a norm that no member should chair more than one committee. The exercise by members of their preferences in this connection was capable of setting off chain reactions reshuffling large numbers of committee chairmen; this accounts for the fact that even after 1919 there was a sizable number of seniority violations. However, the main mechanisms at work

before 1911, from 1911 to 1919 and thereafter seem quite different.

Party leaders did retain some room for maneuver, even in the post 1911 situation, owing to the large number of minor committees. When vacancies on important committees opened up, party leaders could offer senior men on minor committees the vacancy and thereby manipulate minor committee chairmanships. This option was effectively closed by the Legislative Reorganization Act of 1946, which reduced the number of committees and also vastly cut down on the number and diversity of manipulable vacancies available at any one time.[38] And, of course, as the number of committee places diminished, the committee assignments of individual members were limited in most cases to only one committee.[39]

VI. Conclusions

What caused seniority? Historically, the answer seems to have been a split in the grass roots of the Republican party that ultimately produced a strong but unstable Democratic–Insurgent Republican majority coalition in the House—strong enough permanently to weaken the prerogatives of the Speaker, unstable enough to preclude the election of a strong Speaker of its own.[40] One of the consequences of this split was the reinforcement of weak preexisting norms favoring continuity of chairmanships and limiting in practice the freedom of Speakers to appoint chairmen when there was no party turnover. After the Democratic Insurgent coalition weakened the power of the Speaker and of the Republican caucus, only the Democratic caucus was left as a centralizing force in the House. The Democrats lost control of the House in the 1920's, and in time a conservative cross-party

AT GRASS ROOTS

IN CONGRESS ⟶

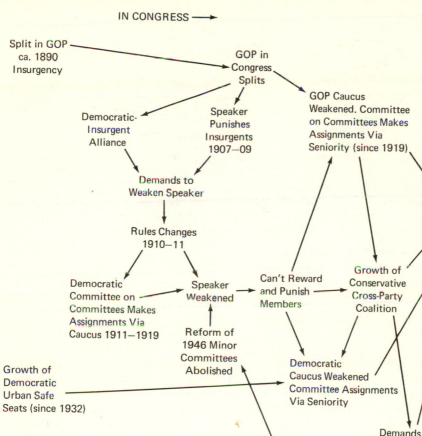

FIGURE 5   Historical causes of seniority system

coalition undermined the Democratic caucus.[41] Meanwhile, longer-term pressures for routinization and specialization were having marginal effects. This is the complexly interrelated set of historical "causes" of seniority as it exists today that we have attempted to diagram in Figure 5.

Seniority is also an ongoing social process that helps to maintain itself by creating conditions favorable to its own perpetuation. Our speculation as to the important causal relations in this process and their connections with the processes that established the system are diagrammed in Figure 6.

To summarize, we believe that our data show the effects of four main influences upon the growth of the seniority system in the U. S. House of

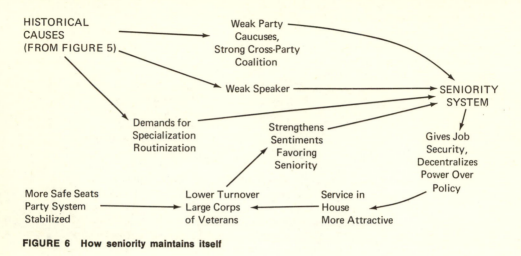

AT GRASS ROOTS   IN CONGRESS

FIGURE 6   How seniority maintains itself

Representatives. In the period between 1881 and 1911, a large number of committees and a discretionary system of appointment in which seniority and political considerations played a part produced a pattern of relatively frequent violations of seniority. Many of these were responsive to the necessity for new Speakers, after a party turnover in the House, to organize a majority coalition in the committees. After 1911 the system responded at first to the centralized decisions enforced by the Democratic caucus, and later to piecemeal bargaining and tinkering, as Representatives with many committee assignments adjusted their workloads with respect to a large number of narrowly focused committees. This produced some violations of seniority, but within a context providing much less power and discretion for party leaders in the House. After 1946, both the discretionary rights of leaders and the rich array of minor committees disappeared with the "streamlining" of the committee system, and thus from 1946 onward, the rule of seniority is virtually never breached. From a situation where seniority is one of a number of criteria determining committee chairmanships, then, we move through two intermediate periods, where centralized coordination of appointments is first undermined in the Republican party (1910) and later (after 1919) in the Democratic. Finally, the House moves after 1947 to a situation where there exists a full-blown seniority *system*, in which seniority is the single, automatic criterion determining the chairmanships of all committees, and the application of this criterion is not subject to the discretion of any body short of the relatively inactive full party caucuses.

These results are compatible with the argument that power in the House has decentralized rather than concentrated over time. They also reflect a general trend, discussed elsewhere, toward impersonal, automatic, and universalistic methods of conducting internal business, a characteristic pattern in the development of social organizations as they move from tentative, informal, and less complex stages toward institutional maturity.[42] It is an interesting anomaly that these two phenomena, progressive decentralization of power and institutionalization, are not normally associated, and that "ideal types" describing the natural history of organizational development typically presume a movement toward, rather than away from, concentration of power. The House of Representatives may be the exception that proves the rule, or it may serve as an occasion for the reconsideration of at least one small branch of organization theory.

NOTES

1. The Speaker has executive responsibility for the House side of the Capitol, including the three House Office Buildings, which he exercises through his chairmanship of the House Office Building Commission. The rules currently in effect on the allocation of office space are: Each member is entitled to the space he currently occupies. Vacancies as they occur are allocated to claimants in order of their seniority. Entering freshmen members are ordered by lot and given their choice of the remaining office space at a predetermined time at the beginning of each Congress. Any extra office space over and above members' suites and rooms set aside for the offices of specific committees are allocated at the discretion of the Speaker. See Donald G. Tacheron and Morris K. Udall, *The Job of the Congressman* (Indianapolis: Bobbs-Merrill, 1966), pp. 41–43, 277–279.

    Until the opening of the Rayburn building, the third House Office Building, in 1965, no clear patterns of preference for office space were discernible. Some members liked to be near the Capitol; others preferred more remote locations, away from the crowds of tourists. Many members had their offices near the rooms of the committees to which they were assigned, which were spotted through both "old" buildings. Some members preferred the more modern facilities of the Longworth Building (opened, 1926). Others agreed with Clem Miller:

    I don't care for it. Low ceilings, panelled walls smacking of a 1925 corporation lawyer. . . . I am in the Old Office Building [built 1909], a huge square with a hollow center, wide corridors, high ceilings. Old-fashioned railroad-car carpeting. High-backed leather chairs. If you take away the electric typewriters, you move right into the world of William Howard Taft.

    For Miller's remarks, see John W. Baker, ed., *Member of the House* (New York: Scribner's, 1962) p. 27.

    The Rayburn building has changed some of this: about half of the House, including most of the senior men, are in it. Rayburn building offices are larger and more commodious; the much greater inconvenience in getting from the Rayburn building to the Capitol is somewhat offset by the installation of a Toonerville trolley in the subway that runs between this building and the Capitol building. The two older office buildings are being remodeled to provide more or less equal space for everyone once again.

2. There are a number of kinds of Capitol Hill patronage. Employees of the Capitol fall under the control of the majority party. Major employees at the level of Clerk of the House, Sergeant at Arms, Parliamentarian, Door-

keeper and Postmaster are formally selected by party caucus, in fact are usually appointed by the Speaker, and are elected by vote of the whole House. These are more or less permanent career jobs, and most have minority counterparts built into the organization. When party control of the House shifts, the permanent top bureaucrats of the House exchange jobs with their minority "shadows." When a vacancy occurs, the Speaker appoints what amounts to a permanent member of the Congressional bureaucracy. Jobs at the middle level such as assistant doorkeepers, assistant parliamentarians, folding room superintendent, reading clerks, recorders of debate, and so on are also regarded as career jobs, and require the initial sponsorship of Congressmen of the majority party. These jobs also come under the purview of the Speaker. Low level jobs such as elevator operator, mail room employee, page are also handled by a system of sponsorship and cleared through a committee of the majority party appointed by the Speaker. An informal quota system based in part upon the seniority of members determines the entitlement of members to sponsor candidates for these jobs.

A second form of patronage is provided by the Congressional campaign committees of each party which allocate funds to House incumbents running for reelection. Seniority as such plays little part in the distribution of these funds. See Michael J. Kirwan as told to Jack Redding, *How to Succeed in Politics* (New York: MacFadden, 1964), pp. 9–11; and Hugh A. Bone, *Party Committees and National Politics* (Seattle: University of Washington: 1958), pp. 120–165, esp. p. 147.

3. See Nicholas A. Masters, "Committee Assignments in the House of Representatives," *American Political Science Review,* 55 (June, 1961), pp. 345–357. Masters gives the following desiderata for appointments to committees: the candidate must show "legislative responsibility," i.e., personal characteristics of flexibility and willingness to follow norms of predictability, reciprocity and courtesy; his district should allow him flexibility in major matters—which means that norms internal to the House must be allowed to weigh heavily in his committee decision making; the geographical balance of committees must be preserved; and the appointment should bear some relationship to the member's chance of being reelected. In addition to these criteria, Masters says: "When two or more members stake a claim to the same assignment, on the ground that it is essential to their electoral success, both party committees usually, if not invariably, will give preference to the member with longer service." State delegations sometimes but not always use seniority as the criterion determining which among their members will lay claim to a seat on a major committee that the state is thought to be "entitled" to. On the whole, large state delegations are much more successful than small states in getting the committee assignments they want for their members. This is true for both parties, and it operates without regard to the seniority of individual members.

4. Seniority is generally followed pro forma in the granting of subcommittee chairmanships, but not always. Neither Adam Clayton Powell nor Phil M. Landrum received subcommittee assignments, much less chairmanships, when they were each ranking member of the Education and Labor Committee. This was an unusually frank recognition of estrangement between them and their respective committee chairmen. Ordinarily, senior men out of favor with the chairman receive the recognition of a subcommittee chairmanship, but since the membership and the substantive responsibili-

ties of subcommittees are more or less discretionary with the chairman, it is quite easy for the committee to circumvent a subcommittee chairman he dislikes or mistrusts. Thus the operation of seniority in the organization of subcommittees does not necessarily mean very much. See e.g. Richard F. Fenno, "The House of Representatives and Federal Aid to Education," in Robert L. Peabody and Nelson W. Polsby, eds., *New Perspectives on the House of Representatives* (Chicago: Rand McNally, 1963), pp. 195–235.

5. Seniority in a strict sense does not enter in as a criterion for party leadership. To be eligible for consideration as a party leader, a member must have served long enough to be well known; but Carl Albert was tied with nine others for 30th in seniority on the Democratic side of the aisle when he was elected majority leader in a 1962 Democratic caucus. The Republican caucus has twice, in recent years, removed a more senior man from the party leadership and replaced him with a more junior one. Factors of personality, sectionalism and ideology seem to matter most in the choice of party leaders—including chairmen of the caucuses, whips, assistant whips, and Congressional campaign committee chairmen. See Nelson W. Polsby, "Two Strategies of Influence in the U. S. House of Representatives: Choosing a Majority Leader, 1962," in Peabody and Polsby, *op. cit.,* pp. 237–270; Robert L. Peabody, "The Ford–Halleck Minority Leadership Contest, 1965" *Eagleton Institute Cases in Practical Politics,* No. 40 (New York: McGraw-Hill, 1966); and Robert L. Peabody, "Party Leadership Change in the United States House of Representatives" *American Political Science Review,* 61 (September, 1967) pp. 675–693.

6. Examples would include the following: There was a revolt against Chairman Dan Reed of the Committee on Ways and Means in 1953. See Raymond A. Bauer, Ithiel de Sola Pool and Lewis Anthony Dexter, *American Business and Public Policy* (New York: Atherton, 1963) p. 33; a revolt against Chairman Clair Hoffman of Government Operations in the same year; a number of small-scale rebellions against two successive chairmen of the Committee on Education and Labor (see Fenno, *op. cit.*); two major rebellions against Judge Smith of the Rules Committee, one in 1961 that packed the Committee against him, and one in 1965 that established the 21-day rule; in 1965–1966 and again in 1967 a revolt against Chairman Wright Patman of the Banking and Currency Committee; and in 1967 a revolt against Chairman William Colmer of the Rules Committee. Both these latter revolts eventuated in important changes in committee rules.

7. See Giovanni Sartori, ed., *Il Parlamento Italiano, 1946–1963* (Naples: Edizioni Scientifiche Italiane, 1963), esp. pp. 246–248; Robert E. Ward, "Japan" in Robert E. Ward and Roy Macridis, eds., *Modern Political Systems: Asia* (Englewood Cliffs, N.J.: Prentice-Hall, 1963) pp. 92–94; Hans H. Baerwald "Parliament and Parliamentarians in Japan" *Pacific Affairs,* 37 (Fall, 1964) pp. 271–282; Chitoshi Yanaga, *Japanese People and Politics* (New York: Wiley, 1956) p. 255; and Nobutaka Ike, *Japanese Politics* (New York: Knopf, 1957) pp. 181–182.

8. See James L. Payne, *Patterns of Conflict in Columbia* (New Haven: Yale University Press, 1968); and George Blanksten, *Ecuador: Constitutions and Cavdillos* (Berkeley: University of California Press, 1951), pp. 100–119.

9. Walter Bagehot, *The English Constitution* (London: Collins, 1963, first published in 1867), p. 150.

10. See, for example, on one hand, James K. Pollock, Jr., "Seniority Rule in Congress," *The North American Review,* 222 (1925), pp. 235–245; and on the other, the testimony of George H. E. Smith in the Hearings, Senate Committee on Expenditures in the Executive Departments, *Evaluation of Legislative Reorganization Act of 1946* (80th Congress, 2nd Session; Washington, D.C.: U. S. Government Printing Office, 1948), pp. 61, 71–73, 184–185. These are collected in Walter Kravitz, "Seniority in Congress," Library of Congress Legislative Reference Service, November 7, 1961 (mimeographed).

11. See, for example, Chang-wei Chiu, *The Speaker of the House of Representatives Since 1896* (New York: Columbia University Press, 1928), pp. 64–68; George B. Galloway, *History of the U. S. House of Representatives* (House Document 246, 87th Congress, 1st Session; Washington, D.C.: U. S. Government Printing Office, 1962), pp. 62–63; Pollock, *op. cit.*

12. George B. Galloway, *Congress at the Crossroads* (New York: Crowell, 1946), p. 187. See also George Goodwin, "The Seniority System in Congress," *American Political Science Review,* 53 (June, 1959) p. 417.

13. Pollock, *op. cit.,* pp. 235–236.

14. Chiu, *op. cit.,* p. 71.

15. Woodrow Wilson, *Congressional Government* (New York: Meridian, 1956), (first published in 1884), p. 85, p. 82.

16. W. R. Brock, *An American Crisis* (New York: St. Martin, 1963) pp. 58–59.

17. Gail Hamilton, *Biography of James G. Blaine* (Norwich, Connecticut: Henry Bill, 1895), pp. 260, 263. A slightly garbled version is in DeAlva Stanwood Alexander, *History and Procedure of the House of Representatives,* (Boston: Houghton Mifflin, 1916), p. 69.

18. George Rothwell Brown, *The Leadership of Congress* (Indianapolis: Bobbs-Merrill, 1922), p. 109.

19. James Bryce, *The American Commonwealth* (New York: Macmillan, 1905) Vol. I, pp. 138–139.

20. Alexander, *op. cit.,* p. 67.

21. *Biographical Directory of the American Congress,* 1774–1961 (Washington, D.C.: U. S. Government Printing Office, 1961).

22. We doubt that this would make much difference in our findings. Paul DeWitt Hasbrouck says: "Even Speaker Cannon did not go so far as to remove a committeeman in the middle of a Congress." See his *Party Government in the House of Representatives* (New York: Macmillan, 1927), p. 50.

23. In classifying committees by order of importance (and therefore desirability) we relied upon two sources: Chang-wei Chiu's listing of important committees (*op. cit.* pp. 68–69) for the early period, and the sorting of committees into three classes by the Amended Legislative Reorganization Act of 1946, which provided that (1) Three committees are *exclusive*— namely Appropriations, Rules, and Ways and Means. A member who serves on any of these can serve on no other committee. (2) Ten committees are *semi-exclusive:* members may serve on any one of them and any one of the seven non-exclusive committees. The ten are: Agriculture, Armed Services, Banking and Currency, Education and Labor, Foreign Affairs, Interstate and Foreign Commerce, Judiciary, Post Office and Civil Service, Public Works, and Science and Astronautics. (3) Seven committees are *non-exclusive.* A member may serve on any two of these

seven, or on any one plus one of the ten semi-exclusive committees. The seven are: District of Columbia, Government Operations, House Administration, Interior and Insular Affairs, Merchant Marine and Fisheries, Un-American Activities, and Veteran Affairs. Chiu mentions four committees not listed above as having some importance in the period (1896–1928) covered by his study. These are committees on Military Affairs, Naval Affairs, Post Offices and Post Roads and Rivers and Harbors. For our purposes, we considered these four semi-exclusive committees.

A total of 57 standing committees other than the ones mentioned in our sources also existed at some point in the period covered by our study. These were added to the non-exclusive committees for our purposes. In general, changes in the total numbers of committees over the years (until the major consolidation of 1946) reflect changes in the number of minor committees.

24. For examples, see Abram and Cooper, *op. cit.,* pp. 63 ff.

25. Pollock, *op. cit.*

26. Brown, *op. cit.,* pp. 158–159.

27. George W. Norris, *Fighting Liberal* (New York: Macmillan, 1946) p. 111.

28. Booth Mooney, *Mr. Speaker* (Chicago: Follett, 1964) p. 109.

29. See, e.g., Victor Murdock, "After Cannonism, What?" *The Independent,* September 22, 1910, pp. 622–625; George B. Galloway, *History of the United States House of Representatives, op. cit.,* pp. 51–52; Hasbrouck, *op. cit.,* p. 48.

30: Charles O. Jones describes a number of the powers available to a Speaker in this era which could be used as strategic resources:

> He could appoint committees—including the chairmen, determine the schedule of business, recognize members on the floor, appoint members to conference committees, dispense favors of various kinds. Particularly significant was Speaker Cannon's power as chairman of the Committee on Rules. . . . Speaker Cannon was not above delaying the appointment of committees until his wishes on legislation had been met. In the famous 61st Congress, he appointed the important Rules and Ways and Means committees on March 16, the second day of the session. Most of the remaining appointments had to wait until the Payne–Aldrich tariff bill was in the conference committee—nearly five months after the session began.

See "Joseph G. Cannon and Howard W. Smith: An Essay on the Limits of Leadership in the House of Representatives," *Journal of Politics* 30 (August 1968), 617–646. See also Hubert Bruce Fuller, *The Speakers of the House* (Boston: Little Brown, 1909), p. 256 ff.

31. Blair Bolles, *Tyrant From Illinois* (New York: Norton, 1951), p. 195.

32. See Hasbrouck, *op. cit.,* pp. 4–6.

33. Brown, *op. cit.,* pp. 175 ff.

34. *Ibid.,* pp. 175–187. See also Wilder Haines "The Congressional Caucus of Today," *American Political Science Review,* 9 (November, 1915) pp. 696–706. The corresponding story in the Senate is told by Claude G. Bowers, *The Life of John Worth Kern* (Indianapolis: Hollenbeck, 1918) pp. 287–295.

35. James Holt, *Congressional Insurgents and the Party System 1909–1916* (Cambridge: Harvard University Press, 1967), pp. 84–85.

36. *New York Times,* February 28, 1919.

37. Seniority has also been pretty much inviolate since 1946 for committee rank and file as well as chairmen. There are only two exceptions. It

took an elaborate warning procedure followed by a fight in the full caucus of the House Democratic party in 1965 to impair the seniority of two southern House Democrats, neither of them chairmen, who had campaigned actively for Republicans in the election of 1964. One of these Democrats promptly resigned his seat and was reelected to Congress as a Republican. The other quit the House soon thereafter and became Governor of Mississippi. Under a rule of the Democratic caucus, the so-called Byrnes Rule, the Democratic committee on committees' assignments are subject to review by the caucus. In practice, however, except for these two cases, there has been no review. The overwhelming liberal Democratic majority of 1965, mobilized by the Democratic Study Group, was able to threaten a review and thereby opened the question of the seniority of these two members.

38. It also increased the difficulty for any member of attaining a chairmanship. Richard Brooks shows a tremendous contrast in the average number of years a member had to serve before becoming a committee chairman before and after 1946. From 1889–1910 the average wait was 6.1 years. From 1911–1946 the average wait was 7.5 years. From 1947 to 1954 chairmen served in the ranks an average of 16.6 years. See Richard Stephens Brooks, "The Sectional and Seniority Bases of the Standing Committee Chairmanships on the U. S. House of Representatives, 1889–1954" (unpublished Ph.D. dissertation, University of Oklahoma, 1956), p. 89.

39. See Lewis C. Gawthrop, "Changing Membership Patterns in House Committees," *American Political Science Review,* 60 (June, 1966), pp. 366–373.

40. Holt, *op. cit., passim* makes this argument very persuasively.

41. On the present-day weakness of the Democratic caucus, see Clem Miller's *Member of the House,* John W. Baker, (ed.), (N.Y.: Scribner's, 1962), pp. 88–89, 92.

42. See Nelson W. Polsby, "The Institutionalization of the U. S. House of Representatives," *American Political Science Review,* 62 (March, 1968), pp. 144–168. The present discussion supersedes, and in some respects corrects, the preliminary findings on seniority offered on pp. 160–161.

13

JOSEPH G. CANNON AND HOWARD W. SMITH: AN ESSAY ON THE LIMITS OF LEADERSHIP IN THE HOUSE OF REPRESENTATIVES *

CHARLES O. JONES

Charles O. Jones' essay contains the useful reminder that leaders as well as freshmen legislators operate within a context that limits their autonomy as well as grants them opportunities. From the standpoint of rank-and-file members, the central problems of political organization have to do with representation and accountability. From the standpoint of leaders, the problems are more likely to be in obtaining enough power to do the job, putting together (or preventing) majorities, enacting policies, or preventing their enactment. Both Cannon and Smith were conservatives in their time, and so the acts which limited their leadership were bound to be more dramatic, entailing positive acts rather than the manifold failures to act which constrain progressive leaders. The general point is still a useful one—that constraints of some kind operate everywhere in congressional politics. Charles O. Jones is Falk Professor of Political Science at the University of Pittsburgh.

That the House of Representatives is characterized by bargaining has been well established by many scholars of that institution[1] and suggests that leaders of that body must be skilled negotiators. Ultimately each representative, even the freshman, has some bargaining power (at minimum—his

Reprinted from *The Journal of Politics*, **30** (August 1968), 617–646, by permission of the author and publisher.
* Financial support for this study was provided by the American Political Science Association's Study of Congress, Professor Ralph K. Huitt, Director, and the Institute of Government Research, University of Arizona. I wish to acknowledge the comments of Richard Cortner, Conrad Joyner, John Crow, Phillip Chapman, and Clifford Lytle.

vote). It is on this basis of bargaining that the "middle-man" thesis of congressional leadership has been developed.[2] Rightly or wrongly House leaders must attend to their majorities.

Two types of majorities in the House are of interest here—procedural and substantive. Procedural majorities are those necessary to organize the House for business and maintain that organization.[3] They are formed at the beginning of the session. Leaders are selected and provided with a number of bargaining advantages so that the House may perform its functions in the political system. Normally, membership of procedural majorities and minorities coincides with that of the two political parties.[4]

Substantive majorities are those necessary to pass legislation in the House. Whereas procedural majorities are relatively stable in membership, the make-up of substantive majorities may well differ issue to issue, since many substantive measures cut across party lines. Leaders are expected to build substantive majorities—employing the many bargaining advantages provided by their procedural majorities. They are not expected, nor do they normally have the power, to force members into substantive majorities.

House leaders must take care not to lose touch with any sizeable segment of their procedural majorities. On most issues they will find the basis for substantive majorities in their own party. Obviously, party members have views on the substantive matters before the House. If he wishes to remain in office, a leader must hold himself accountable to his procedural majority when building substantive majorities and accommodate important substantive changes among segments of his procedural majority. House leaders have latitude in their behavior, to be sure, and the process of defeat and/or reform is often painfully slow, but the leader who maintains himself in a responsible position of authority over a long period of time must be adaptive, communicative, accommodating, and accountable.

What if a House leader fails to behave in this way? In the short run, it probably will not make much difference. In the long run, however aberrant behavior is bound to cause trouble for the leader with segments of his procedural majority. If it is a case of a leader exceeding the authority given to him, or failing to meet the expectations of his followers, he may simply be removed. But what if he has developed sources of power which make him independent of his procedural majority? That is, he is exercising authority which is real—it is incorporated into the position he holds —but is contextually inappropriate because it violates the bargaining condition in the House. Under these circumstances removing the leader is not the whole solution. One may expect some House members to be concerned enough about the potential of divorce between the procedural majority and its leader to press for reform. One may further expect that in these situations the House will define the limits of leadership in that body as it debates reform.

There are two spectacular cases of "excessive leadership" in the House in this century. Joseph G. Cannon, as Speaker, had become an exceptionally powerful figure in American politics. He had a wide variety of sanctions available and he used them all. Nearly 50 years later, Howard W. Smith, as Chairman of the Committee on Rules, also had an impressive array of prerogatives—all of which he used to his advantage. The purposes of this essay are to examine the authority of these two men, how they exercised this authority in relationship to their procedural majorities, and the reaction and ultimate loss of their majorities. The findings not only tend to support the "middle-man" hypothesis but provide a clearer indication of its meaning as defined by the members themselves.

The Case of Uncle Joe Cannon

The House leadership situation in 1910 should have satisfied many of the responsible party scholars. There was no question that the Speaker was responsible for leading the House. Since his election in 1903, Speaker Joseph G. Cannon had enjoyed rather substantial procedural majorities and due to the growth of the speakership and Cannon's interpretation and use of his powers, a procedural majority carried with it awesome authority. He could appoint committees—including the chairmen, determine the schedule of business, recognize members on the floor, appoint members to conference committees, dispense favors of various kinds.

Cannon's exercise of power

Particularly significant was Speaker Cannon's power as chairman of the Committee on Rules. The Committee was small—never over five members prior to 1910. The three-to-two edge of the Republicans was potent, however, since the Speaker appointed the members carefully—insuring that they agreed with his views.[5] Champ Clark's view of the Committee was widely shared:

I violate no secret when I tell you the committee is made up of three very distinguished Republicans and two ornamental Democrats. [Laughter] . . . there never would be a rule reported out of that committee that the Speaker and his two Republican colleagues do not want reported.[6]

During Speaker Cannon's reign, four Republicans served on the Committee on Rules in addition to the Speaker himself—John Dalzell, Pennsylvania; Charles Grosvenor, Ohio; James S. Sherman, New York; and Walter I. Smith, Iowa. These members had considerable seniority (overall the average number of terms served by Committee members was approximately three times that of other House Republicans) and therefore also were high ranking on other important standing committees.

A second center of power which the Speaker dominated was the Committee on Ways and Means. It was the custom to have the Chairman of Ways and Means serve as the majority floor leader. Sereno Payne, New York, served Cannon in these two important posts during his speakership. There was considerable overlapping membership between Rules and Ways and Means. Between 1903 and 1907, Dalzell and Grosvenor were second- and third-ranking Republicans on Ways and Means. Dalzell remained in both positions throughout Cannon's speakership.[7]

The list of grievances against Cannon and his lieutenants on Rules and Ways and Means lengthened with each year of his speakership. A frequent complaint was that Speaker Cannon abused House Rule X, which gave him the power to appoint the standing committees. He had made some spectacular appointments and adjustments prior to 1909—selecting Tawney, Minnesota, as Chairman of Appropriations in 1905, even though Tawney had never served on that committee; Overstreet, Indiana, as Chairman of Post Office and Post Roads in 1903, even though Overstreet had never served on that committee; and Scott, Kansas, as Chairman of Agriculture in 1907 over Henry, Connecticut (whom Cannon removed completely from the Committee) and Haugen, Iowa. In 1909, however, Speaker Cannon appeared to shift assignments about at will. Though seniority was not an inviolable rule at this time, it was relied on as a significant factor in committee assignments.[8] Twelve Republicans had not voted for Cannon for Speaker in 1909 and seniority was certainly no protection for them. Table 1 provides some examples of actions taken by the Speaker in the 61st Congress.

Speaker Cannon was not above de-

TABLE 1   Examples of Violations of Seniority Principle in Committee Assignments, 61st Congress

MEMBER	COMMITTEE AND RANK, 60TH CONGRESS	COMMITTEE AND RANK, 61ST CONGRESS	COMMENTS
Cooper, Wisc.	Insular Affairs, Chmn.	Elections #3, 2nd Foreign Affairs, 10th	Cooper had been Chairman since 56th Congress.
Fowler, N.J.	Banking & Currency, Chmn. Reform of Civil Service, 2nd	Insular Affairs, 11th Reform of Civil Service, 2nd	Fowler had been Chairman since 57th Congress. Vreeland, N.Y., made Chairman. Not on Banking & Currency before. Was lowest on Appropriations in 60th.
Haugen, Iowa	Agriculture, 2nd War Claims, 2nd Expenditures in Interior Dept., Chmn.	Agriculture, 4th War Claims, 3rd	Haugen had been passed over in 60th in Agriculture. In 61st two lower-ranking members moved ahead of him. Same on War Claims—thus denying him Chairmanship.
Lovering, Mass.	Coinage, Weights & Measures, 4th Interstate & Foreign Commerce, 5th	Coinage, Weights & Measures, 4th Manufacturers, 4th	Lovering had previously been removed from Banking & Currency (59th).
Morse, Wisc.	Indian Affairs, 10th War Claims, 9th	War Claims, 4th Manufacturers, 6th Private Land Claims, 4th	
Murdock, Kans.	Post Office and Post Roads, 9th	Post Office and Post Roads, 12th	Six new members plus one who was below Murdock in 60th, were placed ahead of him.
Norris, Nebr.	Election of Pres., V. Pres. & Repres., 3rd Public Bldgs. & Grounds, 6th Labor, 7th	Coinage, Weights & Measures, 7th Private Land Claims, 2nd Revision of the Laws, 6th	

Source: Various volumes of the *Congressional Directory* and Paul D. Hasbrouck, *Party Government in the House of Representatives* (New York: Macmillan, 1927).

laying the appointment of committees until his wishes on legislation had been met. In the famous 61st Congress, he appointed the important Rules and Ways and Means Committees on March 16, the second day of the session. Most of the remaining appointments had to wait until the Payne–Aldrich tariff bill was in the conference committee— nearly five months after the session began.[9]

Joe Cannon did not limit himself to managing committee appointments.

He also managed the output of the House. George Norris describes one of his early experiences on the House Committee on Public Buildings and Grounds. The Committee discussed drafting a public building bill and Norris soon learned that the Speaker would ultimately decide whether the Committee should proceed or not.

The senior Democratic member of the committee, Representative Bankhead of Alabama . . . actually made a motion that the chairman of the committee should seek a conference with the Speaker and ascertain whether or not we should be allowed to have a public building bill at that session.[10]

There were many examples of the frustrations of the insurgents in dealing with Speaker Cannon's Committee on Rules during the debate in 1910 to remove the Speaker from that Committee. One involved a first-term congressman from New York, Hamilton Fish. He had unsuccessfully sought to get a hearing before the Committee on a resolution which called on the Committee on Post Office and Post Roads to inquire into the feasibility and the desirability of establishing a parcel-post system. The colloquy between Fish and Walter I. Smith, Iowa, a member of the Committee on Rules, is worth recording here as an example of how various senior members would treat a freshman.

Mr. Smith: I deny that a hearing has ever been refused.

Mr. Fish: Mr. Speaker, I have the evidence in writing that I asked a hearing and none has been granted me.

Mr. Smith: Well—

Mr. Fish: I will ask the gentleman, in the six weeks that the resolution has been before the Committee on Rules why he has not answered my request and given me the privilege of a hearing?

Mr. Smith: Does the gentleman ask that question?

Mr. Fish: Yes; why have you not given me a hearing?

Mr. Smith: I wrote the gentleman in person that while I did not approve of a parcel post myself I was opposed to suppressing any measure, and that I was willing to give him a hearing and report the bill adversely.

Mr. Fish: I would ask the gentleman, then, why he did not give me a hearing?

Mr. Smith: The gentleman never appeared and asked for a hearing.

Mr. Fish: But I have written time and time again asking for it.

Mr. Smith: Oh, written— [11]

Fish's subsequent question to John Dalzell, also a member of the Rules Committee, regarding how a member extracted a bill from a committee which did not wish to report it, went unanswered.

Managing the work assignments of congressmen, managing their work, and managing the rules by which their work would be done—such were the powers of the Speaker. Yet still other sanctions were available to him. Speakers have always had a number of temporary and honorary appointments which they can make. In some cases these are much sought after—for publicity, prestige, or for some other special purpose. Norris reports one such appointment which he sought. William C. Lovering, Massachusetts, a close friend of Norris and an early insurgent congressman, died February 4, 1910. Norris wished to be appointed to the committee representing the House at the funeral.

I hoped the Speaker, recognizing my close ties with Mr. Lovering, would accord me the privilege of paying my respects to a very dear friend, as a member of the House committee. Without seeing the Speaker about it personally, I had one or two friends approach him; and they reported he refused absolutely to approve my selection. It was a long time before the deep resentment which this aroused in me disappeared.[12]

This awesome list of powers exceeded that exercised by any previous Speaker. It was exceedingly difficult for the insurgent members to "force" the Speaker to accommodate their views because (1) he had so many sanctions available and could discipline not only them but any members who might otherwise be enticed to join them, and (2) the insurgent Republicans did not want to defeat Cannon so as to elect a Democratic Speaker, who would likely be no more accommodating to their views. Thus, Cannon had a considerable advantage and could ignore the changes occurring within his own procedural majority—he had developed a certain amount of independence from that majority.

The warning signals

Speaker Cannon and the regular Republicans had ample warning of the unrest among their more progressive brethren during the 60th and 61st Congresses. In fact, members made no effort to hide their dissatisfaction in speeches on the House floor. Twelve insurgents refused to vote for Cannon for Speaker at the opening of the special session in 1909, called by President Taft to consider the tariff. And a combination of insurgents and Democrats defeated the motion to adopt the rules of the preceding Congress. Minority Leader Champ Clark followed this victory with a resolution which would have increased the size of the Committee on Rules, removed the Speaker from the Committee, and taken from the Speaker his power of appointing all committees except Ways and Means. With insurgent support, the stage was set for revolution at that moment, but John J. Fitzgerald (D-New York) and 22 bolting Democrats voted with the majority of Republicans to defeat Clark's move and Cannon was saved. Fitzgerald then offered a compromise motion of his own which established a unanimous consent calendar, a motion of recommital (for use by the minority), and increased the majority necessary to set aside Calendar Wednesday.[13]

Calendar Wednesday itself had been adopted at the close of the 60th Congress and though it did not meet the reform standards of the insurgents, there were strong hopes that it would limit Cannon's power. These hopes were dashed rather soon and rather decisively. A call of standing committees every Wednesday allowed committee chairmen to take bills which had been reported off the calendar for House consideration. With the changes as a result of the Fitzgerald compromise, the procedure could be dispensed with only by a two-thirds majority. A variety of devices was used to neutralize the procedure—adjournment required only a simple majority and was used to avoid Calendar Wednesday; bills of great length and complexity were called up and debated on successive Calendar Wednesdays (all nine Calendar Wednesdays were devoted to one bill in the third session of the 61st Congress).[14]

The Consent Calendar was more of a victory for the rank-and-file. There was an unanimous consent procedure in existence wherein any member could move consideration of a bill. The Speaker, theoretically, had no greater power of objection than any other member. In practice, however, the Speaker required advance notice of a unanimous consent request before he would recognize it. Thus, members had to clear such requests with Cannon before they could even be recognized on the floor.[15] The rules change created a Calendar for Unanimous Consent. The Speaker's consent was no longer required for a unanimous consent motion.

It was unlikely that these reforms would satisfy those members who were increasingly alienated from their own party. The 1908 elections resulted in a further reduction of the size of the

House Republican majority. Cannon had a slim 29-vote majority in his first term as Speaker. Roosevelt's election in 1904 brought with it a 114-vote majority for Republicans in the House. This was reduced to 58 in 1906 and to 47 in 1908. Many of the new Republicans elected in 1906 and 1908 were from states in the Middle West and were soon to join veteran insurgents like Henry Cooper, Wisconsin; Gilbert Haugen, Iowa; and George Norris, Nebraska. Thus, not only was Cannon's majority being reduced but regular Republicans were being replaced by members who were potential threats to Cannon's leadership. The result was that if enough members absented themselves on crucial votes, the insurgents would hold the balance of power. For the insurgents the time had come. Speaker Cannon would be taught some fundamental lessons about leadership in the House of Representatives. Though he had developed impressive power as Speaker and found that he didn't have to make accommodations to a changing procedural majority in the short run, there were other alternatives available to the insurgents. They could always take their one bargaining advantage—the vote—and join the Democrats to curb the powers of the Speaker.

The revolt

The full-scale revolt against Cannon began on March 16, 1910. Though the details of the revolt are adequately recorded in a number of sources,[16] a brief resumé of pertinent facts is necessary. March 16 was Calendar Wednesday. Mr. Crumpacker (R-Indiana) called for the consideration of House Joint Resolution 172 on the 1910 census.[17] Mr. Fitzgerald (D-New York) made the point of order that a call of the committees was in order, under the Calendar Wednesday procedure. Speaker Cannon overruled the point of order, noting that

a certain class of business, like election cases, like matters arising in impeachment, and like legislation relating to apportionment or the taking of the census as to the population, have invariably been admitted as involving *constitutional privilege*, presenting a privilege higher than any rule of the House would give.[18] (Emphasis added.)

Fitzgerald appealed the ruling of the chair to the House. Crumpacker moved that the matter be postponed until Thursday—thus postponing the appeal to the chair as well. Fitzgerald objected. Cannon overruled his objection but the House supported Fitzgerald and refused to allow the matter to be postponed. After some debate, the appeal to the House was voted on and Cannon was defeated, 112 to 163, as 42 Republicans voted with the Democrats. Cannon then made the dramatic announcement: "The decision of the Chair does not stand as the decision of the House."[19]

On March 17, Crumpacker again attempted to bring his resolution before the House. Cannon refused to rule. He put the question to the House: "Is the bill called up by the gentleman from Indiana in order as a question of constitutional privilege, the rule prescribing the order of business to the contrary notwithstanding?"[20] The House, in no mood to let the Speaker snatch victory from defeat, responded negatively. The House then passed the following revised version of the question, as put by Oscar W. Underwood (D-Alabama): "Is the House joint resolution called up by the gentleman from Indiana in order now?"[21] Note that no mention was made of the Constitution in the Underwood resolution. It simply asked if the Crumpacker resolution were in order "now." William R. Gwinn, in his account of the overthrow, observes that the House had "endorsed the proposition that his [Crumpacker's] resolution was privileged under the Constitution . . ."[22] and, as is discussed below, George Norris later so argued. Technically, however, the House never did rule that the Crumpacker resolution was privileged.

Following the debate on House Joint Resolution 172, Norris pulled from his pocket a resolution to change the rules of the House. In his autobiography, Norris observes:

. . . I had carried it for a long time, certain that in the flush of its power the Cannon machine would overreach itself. The paper upon which I had written my resolution had become so tattered it scarcely hung together.[23]

Norris announced: "Mr. Speaker, I present a resolution made privileged by the Constitution." In Crumpacker's effort to have his census resolution considered on Calendar Wednesday, Norris found a way to circumvent the House Committee on Rules for effecting a rules change. His "privileged" resolution would reorganize the Rules Committee by increasing its size, having members selected by groups of state delegations, and removing the Speaker from the Committee. Norris argued that his resolution was privileged under the Constitution because in Article I, Section 5, paragraph 2, it stated "Each House may determine the rules of its proceedings." The Speaker ordered the clerk to read the resolution. "The moment the reading clerk saw it he smiled, for he recognized the fact that the great fight on the rules of the House was on."[24]

The turnabout was a strange one indeed. Speaker Cannon had ruled that Crumpacker's resolution was privileged but was overruled by the House.

Norris had voted against the Speaker. On March 17, the House *voted against* Cannon's question which explicitly stated that the resolution was in order *under constitutional privilege* but voted in favor of the more ambiguous motion which simply stated that the Crumpacker resolution was in order. Norris waltzed through all of this with the head-spinning logic that his resolution was privileged because the Crumpacker resolution was in order. And there was no difference between the two resolutions resulting from the fact that Crumpacker's had been in committee and Norris' had not (a critical fact if his resolution was to survive).

If it [Crumpacker's] was privileged it was privileged because the Constitution made it so, and having decided that it was privileged, because the Constitution made it privileged, its privileged character was not added to by the fact that it had been referred to a committee and a report made by the committee.[25]

As indicated here, there is considerable doubt that Crumpacker's resolution *was* ruled by the House to be privileged. If it was not, then Norris and Cannon might well be faced with a complete reversal of positions—Cannon denying Norris' request because the House had not allowed the Crumpacker resolution to be privileged matter, and Norris arguing that the Crumpacker resolution had been ruled as privileged, even though Norris had not agreed that it should be.

Cannon, in his book written by L. White Busbey, argues that Norris was right. Not because Norris' resolution was as privileged as Crumpacker's but rather because:

The House having made itself ridiculous in the space of two days and publicly declared that it was bound by no rules and had no regard for logic or consistency, why should it not continue to maintain the record? [26]

The Cannon forces stayed with their original position, however—that the Crumpacker resolution was privileged. They then proceeded to argue that the Norris resolution was not. The difference was in the wording of the two relevant sections of the Constitution. "The actual enumeration *shall be made* . . ." (Article I, Section 2, Clause 3) but "Each House *may* determine the rules. . . ." One was interpreted to be compelling, and thus privileged; the other was a right, could be accomplished at any time, and was not privileged.

Thus began the debate which was to terminate on March 19 with important rules changes that would have a serious impact on party government in the House of Representatives. There were six unsuccessful attempts to recess throughout the evening, on into the night, and the next morning. At 2:02 P.M. on March 18, a motion to recess until 4:00 P.M. was finally approved. The House had been in session over 26 hours. The House again recessed at 4:00 P.M. until March 19 at noon. Speaker Cannon then ruled that "the [Norris] resolution is not in order." Norris appealed the decision of the chair and the Speaker was overruled (162 Republicans supporting Cannon and 34 Republicans voting with 148 Democrats against him). An amended version of the Norris resolution then passed the House 193 to 153. A total of 43 insurgent Republicans crossed over on this key vote to defeat the Speaker. Speaker Cannon then invited a resolution which would declare the Speakership vacant and call for an election. Such a resolution was introduced by Burleson (D-Texas) and was overwhelmingly defeated. Only eight insurgents voted against Cannon.

Defining the limits of leadership

In debate the Cannon forces set forth the following argument—basically a party responsibility position with important modifications. The people had elected a majority of Republicans to the House of Representatives. That majority had selected a leadership group which acted for the party and therefore for the country. There is a necessary coincidence between electoral majorities, procedural majorities, and substantive majorities which must not break down. That is, no member may leave the majority without severe penalty. Those members who reject the party leadership are rejecting the Republican party and its mandate from the people to manage the House and its work. The leadership would provide mechanisms whereby individual members could make their opinions known. Mr. Fassett of New York spoke for the Cannon forces:

We are robust partisans, every one of us. . . . I take it that no Democrat was elected to cooperate with our party nor was any Republican elected to hand over the Republican control of this House to our political opponents. . . . A man ought to have opinions and convictions. He ought not to be a political chocolate eclair. . . . In my judgment, the place to adjust differences of opinion on unimportant questions, and on important questions of public policy and party policy is not in public, where one minority uniting with another minority may make a temporary majority; but in the family caucus . . .[27]

Mr. Gardner of Michigan noted the importance of two parties which put the issues before the people in debate and the threat caused by actions of the sort contemplated by Norris.[28] Mr. Nye of Minnesota observed that "Parties are a necessity, and the great power and effectiveness of the Republican party has been largely its cohesiveness. Its followers have stood shoulder to shoulder and fought the battle against a political foe." [29]

But it was left to Speaker Cannon, following his defeat, to summarize the position most eloquently.

The Speaker. Gentlemen of the House of Representatives: Actions, not words, determine the conduct and the sincerity of men in the affairs of life. This is a government by the people acting through the representatives of a majority of the people. Results cannot be had except by a majority, and in the House of Representatives a majority, being responsible, should have full power and should exercise that power; otherwise the majority is inefficient and does not perform its function. The office of the minority is to put the majority on its good behavior, advocating, in good faith, the policies which it professes, ever ready to take advantage of the mistakes of the majority party, and appeal to the country for its vindication.[30]

After his defeat, Cannon surprised both his friends and his enemies by entertaining a motion to declare the office of Speaker vacant so that the new majority could proceed to elect a new Speaker. It was a perfectly consistent maneuver on his part—consistent with his notion of party leadership in the House of Representatives. If a new majority had formed, and the recent vote indicated to him that such was the case, then that new majority "ought to have the courage of its convictions, and logically meet the situation that confronts it." Though Cannon's action was consistent with his notions of party leadership, it is likely that this move was less honest consistency than it was impressive strategy. If he felt strongly about the logic of his theory of party leadership, he could have easily resigned. He did not resign, however, because, in his words, he declined "to precipitate a contest

upon the House . . . a contest that might greatly endanger the final passage of all legislation necessary to redeem Republican pledges . . ." and because resignation would be "a confession of weakness or mistake or an apology for past actions." [31] Neither reason is convincing. A lengthy and divisive contest could as easily ensue as a result of declaring the office vacant. Cannon himself noted that he was entertaining the motion so that the new majority could proceed to elect another Speaker. There was no reason to think that Cannon would be the only nominee. Further, if Cannon was consistent with the party responsibility theory, he would have resigned, not because of his analysis of his personal weakness or strength or because of his view of whether he had made mistakes or not, but due to the simple fact that on a paramount issue, *he had been defeated.* Other considerations were irrelevant.

In short, Cannon, and probably his cohorts, believed more in strong, personal party leadership with limited accountability to party membership, let alone the nation as whole, than they did in the classic party responsibility position. There is abundant evidence for this interpretation in their behavior before 1910, in the actions of the cabal before the debate in 1910, and in the Cannon maneuver following his defeat. He chose the strategy of entertaining the motion to declare the office vacant so that he might regain control of the situation. At the time, it looked very much as though he might succeed. As he proudly notes in his autobiography: "I was given more votes than at the beginning of Congress and when I went back to resume the Chair I received a demonstration from both sides such as the House has seldom witnessed." [32]

It was precisely this "limited accountability" interpretation of party leadership in the House which defeated Cannon. It was not, and is not, consistent either with the structure of the House as noted above or the "middle-man" concept of leadership which is fostered by this structure. The insurgents articulated an interpretation much more consistent with the structure of the House. Whether theirs was a good or bad theory; whether it was well articulated or not; these are not relevant to the present argument. Though their position was much less tidy, and required considerable painful unraveling in the 1910 debate, it was more in the mainstream of the traditions of party leadership in Congress.

The insurgents argued that Cannon and his supporters had simply gone too far. Each congressman is an individual who is potentially part of a majority—procedural or substantive. On substantive issues, the insurgents argued, the Republican leadership was not attuned to new attitudes among Republicans. Leaders were using sanctions provided by procedural majorities to force—rather than build—substantive majorities. Leaders who do not attend to new opinions, and recognize their force, must face the consequences of losing their procedural majorities. Mr. Lindbergh of Minnesota argued the case for the insurgents as follows:

. . . when I look back over the proceedings of this House, and when I know, and the entire country knows, that by indirection the will of this House has been thwarted time and time again, then I say, when we have a resolution before us, which proposes to do by direction the will of the House, it is time now and here on this occasion to manifest our power, to enforce the rule of the majority, in the language that has frequently been expressed by the able Speaker of this House. I say now and here, in the light of what

has occurred over and over again, in defeating, in holding back, in preventing bills that have been introduced in this House, which were in accord with the wish of the entire country at large—I say, when those bills have time and time again been pigeonholed by select committees, that now . . . the House can by a direct vote do directly the will of the House . . .[33]

John Nelson of Wisconsin also stated the insurgents' case vigorously. He observed that their duty was unpleasant —but that theirs had been an unpleasant experience in the House for some time. They had foregone the many privileges of the "regulars"—e.g., patronage and power—for the sake of principle. Their punishment was severe for failing to "cringe or crawl before the arbitrary power of the Speaker and his House machine." Nelson then discussed the problems of majorities, rules, leadership, and representation.

The eloquent gentleman from New York [Mr. Fassett] says the majority must control, but what is the majority? Speaker Reed emphatically said:
"There is no greater fallacy than this idea that majority and minority are predicated on political parties only."
Why should the subject of the rules be a party matter? At what convention did the Republican party adopt the present rules of the House? The Speaker says he represents the majority. But how? He and his chief lieutenants—favorites or personal friends, a small minority within the majority—call themselves the party and then pass the word on to the rank and file of the Republican membership to line up or be punished. What is the controlling force? Party principles? No. The Speaker's power under the rules. . . . We are no less Republicans because we would be free Members of Congress. We do not need to be kept on leading strings. We are free representatives of the people, and we want freedom here for every Member of every party.[34]

It seems quite clear that Nelson's remarks may be interpreted in line with the analysis suggested here. Cannon's exercise of power was inconsistent with the bargaining condition in the House and therefore "free representatives" would form a new majority which would change the sanctions available to the Speaker.

The argument of the Democrats was very much like that of the insurgents. Oscar W. Underwood was led to conclude that leadership in the House should not be centered in the speakership—at least as it was exercised by Cannon. The Cannon "system" had to be overthrown.

We are fighting a system, and that system is the system that enables the Speaker, by the power vested in him, to thwart and overthrow the will of the majority membership of this House. We recognize today that there has to be leadership; that some man must be the leader of the majority and some man must be the leader of the minority, but we say the place for that leadership *is not in the Chair*.[35] (Emphasis added.)

In summary, the insurgent Republican members were led to take the drastic action of leaving their party to join the Democrats on a major procedural change because they were convinced that the Speaker's authority had allowed him to ignore segments of his procedural majority. They were unable to reach him directly in pressing for representation of their views. As their numbers grew, they merely waited for the right moment—primed to take action sometime to make the Speaker more accountable. Mr. Norris' resolution served as the catalyst for action.

The Case of Judge Smith

In 1961, the House voted 217 to 212 to enlarge the Committee on Rules from 12 to 15 members. By this action, the House took the first of a series of steps to curb the power of the Committee and its chairman, Howard W. Smith of Virginia. The Committee had, since 1937, developed an anti-administration nature. Southern Democrats and Republicans joined to defeat presidential proposals. There was considerable evidence to suggest that these actions more often than not had the tacit support of a bipartisan majority in the House. As Lewis J. Lapham concluded:

. . . it is perfectly true that a very good case can be developed for supporting the proposition that the Rules Committee, though out of sympathy with the majority party program as defined by the President and his supporters, did in fact faithfully represent majority sentiment in the House.[36]

Adolph Sabath (D-Illinois) chaired the Committee every Congress, except the 80th, between 1939 and 1952. Though he personally supported Democratic presidents and their programs, he was extremely weak and ineffective as Chairman. Lapham observed that "the *Congressional Record*, since 1939, is replete with candid admissions by Mr. Sabath that he was 'helpless' in the face of an obstinate majority on the Committee which he could not control."[37]

In 1953, conservative Republican Leo Allen (Illinois) again chaired the Committee, as he had in the 80th Congress. And in 1955, after the Democrats recaptured control of Congress in the 1954 elections, Howard W. Smith became chairman. Smith had been influential on the Committee before his accession to the chairmanship. He and Eugene E. Cox of Georgia were the principal leaders of the Southern Democratic–Republican coalition during Sabath's long tenure as chairman. Smith was first appointed to the Committee in 1933—over the objections of the then-Speaker, Henry T. Rainey of Illinois. As chairman, Smith was free to exercise his considerable powers to stifle legislation which he and his southern Democratic and Republican colleagues opposed. In some cases the legislation was part of President Eisenhower's program—in other cases attempts by the Democratic majority in the House to enact their own legislation.

Smith's procedural majority was of a different sort than that provided Speaker Cannon. Whereas Cannon was elected to office, Smith achieved his position of leadership through seniority. Thus, in accepting seniority as a procedure for committee chairmanships, the Democrats had to accept Howard W. Smith as chairman of the Committee on Rules. To "defeat" Smith, the Democrats would have to strike a blow against the whole seniority system. Thus, Smith, like Cannon, had a considerable advantage. He had a certain amount of independence from his procedural majority. Up to a point, he could afford to ignore it in exercising the considerable reservoir of power in the Committee on Rules. He proceeded to do just that.

Chairman Smith's exercise of power

How did Smith develop and use his powers? Two careful students of the House Committee on Rules, James A. Robinson and Walter Kravitz, have examined the influence of the Committee on legislation during this period.[38] Both indicated the wide variety of powers available to the Committee at the height of its influence. The more overt actions were to refuse to grant a hearing for a rule and to refuse to grant the rule. During the 84th Congress, Robinson found that only four requests for hearings were refused and 11 rules

were denied. During the 85th Congress, 20 requests for hearings were refused and 9 requests for rules were denied. In addition to these more obvious exercises of power, the Committee could force changes in the legislation as a condition for granting a rule, they could delay granting a rule until the mood of the House changed for some reason, they could grant a rule with conditions for debate which the authors did not want, they could threaten to refuse a rule. All of these tactics were relied on during the 84th and 85th Congresses. And, as is indicated by both Robinson and Kravitz, the legislation which was affected was often important legislation—the doctors' draft, housing, statehood for Alaska and Hawaii, aid to education, civil rights, depressed areas aid, presidential disability, absentee voting, appropriations measures, federal judgeships.

Warning signals again

In 1958, the Democrats won a sweeping victory throughout the nation. They increased their margin in the House by 49 seats and their margin in the Senate by 17 seats. A number of Democratic liberals in the House went to the Speaker and proposed that the party ratio on the Committee on Rules be changed from eight Democrats and four Republicans to nine and three. They further pressed for the return of the 21-day rule. Speaker Rayburn convinced them that they should not press for the changes. He assured them that legislation would be brought out of the Committee.[39]

The 1958 elections were of considerable importance to Chairman Smith and his power base. It was at this time that his procedural majority began to change drastically. There were 48 congressional districts in which Democrats replaced Republicans. What was the significance of this trade for Chairman Smith? The *Congressional Quarterly* provides economy support and opposition scores for the 85th Congress and for the first session of the 86th Congress.[40] The 48 House Republicans who were replaced by Democrats in 1958 had an average economy score of 42.9 and an average economy opposition score of 42.0 in the 85th Congress. Their Democratic replacements in the 86th Congress, 1st session, had an average economy score of 9.3 and an average economy opposition score of 86.3. Obviously this new group of congressmen was considerably more liberal than the Republicans who left Congress in 1958, and markedly less dependable for Chairman Smith.

If Chairman Smith wished to retain his position of power in the long run, several developments made it evident that he would have to make some accommodations during the 86th Congress. Speaker Rayburn had given the reformers his assurance that important legislation would not be delayed and thus had put his prestige on the line. The new Democrats were anxious to develop a legislative record for the 1960 presidential elections. Criticism of the Chairman and his committee had continued to mount during the 85th Congress. And, the new Democrats had served notice of their intentions with their reform suggestions during the early days of the 86th Congress (much as the progressive Republicans had placed Speaker Cannon on notice 50 years earlier).

The record shows, however, that Chairman Smith continued to block legislation. He relied on the same techniques as before, despite the fact that a new, restive majority was emerging in the House—a majority which ultimately could deprive Chairman Smith of much of his influence through procedural changes. During the 86th Congress, the Committee on Rules denied 31 requests for hearings and 11 requests for rules. As before, the Committee was a major factor in practically all significant legislation to come before the House—either by preventing its consideration on the floor or by influencing the substance of the legislation. But the most controversial action of the Committee was that taken in 1960 to defeat the first broad scale federal aid to education bill since the Morrill Act of 1862. Following the passage of the bill in both houses, the Committee on Rules invoked its power to deny the request for a rule allowing the House of Representatives to agree to a conference so as to resolve the differences between the House and Senate versions of the bill. The result, of course, was to kill the bill. By this action, the Committee on Rules seemed to place itself above majority action by *both* the House and the Senate. It became obvious to the liberal and moderate Democrats that Chairman Smith was not going to make accommodations. They concluded that their only alternative was to curb the power of Chairman Smith and his Committee on Rules.

The limits of leadership reemphasized

The 1960 elections brought to the White House an energetic young President of the twentieth century. He had campaigned on a platform of "action." Though his majority in the House was 20 less than the Democratic majority of the 86th Congress, it was still sizeable and it was made up of many members who were extremely critical of the Committee on Rules. If the President's program was to receive favorable consideration in Congress, it would have to receive favorable consideration in the Committee on Rules.

TABLE 2   Sequence of Events in Decline of Power of House Committee on Rules, 1961–65

EVENT	DATE	VOTE
Enlargement of Committee from 12 to 15 for 87th Congress	January 31, 1961	217–212 GOP-22–148 Dem-195–64
Permanent Enlargement of Committee from 12 to 15	January 9, 1963	235–196 GOP-28–148 Dem-207–48
Reinstitution of the 21-day rule and transfer of power regarding sending bills to conference *	January 4, 1965	224–201 † GOP-16–123 Dem-208–78

* The second change permitted the Speaker to recognize a member to offer a motion to send a bill to conference.
† On a motion to close debate. Rules changes actually passed by voice vote.

Unless changes were made, it was unlikely that the Committee would be so cooperative.

The results of the power struggle between the young President, his Speaker, and Chairman Smith have been well chronicled and thus only the sequence of events needs repeating here.[41] Our interest is not in the details of what happened but rather in the arguments which were made, since these arguments should provide clues in defining the limits of power for leaders in the House. A brief sequence of events is provided in Table 2.

As might be expected there are parallels between the debate in 1910 and the debates during the 1961–1965 period (of which the 1961 debate was the most crucial). As in 1910, those who pressed for change in 1961 argued in favor of leadership accountability to the majority. The Committee on Rules was a roadblock to the majority. It was not allowing the House to vote on measures which a majority in the House wished to vote on. Despite the fact that the majority party had a 2 to 1 majority on the Committee, Chairman Smith and second-ranking Democrat, William Colmer (Mississippi), would frequently vote with the four Republicans on important legislation to prevent it from coming to the floor.

John A. Blatnik (D-Minnesota), head of the Democratic Study Group, and therefore a principal leader in adopting the rules changes, stated the case as follows:

My constituents did not cast a free ballot for the office of U. S. Representative to Congress to have the functions of that Office limited by one or two or even six other Members. They understand that in a body as large as this the majority shall be established in caucus and put forward in the form of legislation by the leadership chosen by the majority. It is difficult to explain to them how 2 members of the majority [Smith and Colmer] can desert the majority's program, join with 4 members of the minority and among them determine the course of action of 431 other Members of this House. . . . Does their judgment supersede the cumulative judgment of the legislative committees? Do they have some inherent right . . . to determine the course of legislation . . . ? It would appear that they at least think so.[42]

Thus, though Blatnik, and others who pressed for change, agreed that any leader or any leadership committee had latitude in exercising power, they also agreed that there should be limits beyond which leaders are not permitted to go. To the reformers, the Committee on Rules ultimately should be a part of the majority leadership. That meant something very specific. For example, to Paul J. Kilday (D-Texas), it meant that:

. . . the Committee on Rules is an arm of the leadership of the majority party. . . . one who assumes membership on the Committee on Rules must be prepared to exercise a function of leadership. His personal objection to the proposal is not always sufficient reason for him to vote to deny the membership of the whole House the opportunity to express its approval or, equally important, the opportunity to express its disapproval.[43]

Speaker Rayburn expressed much the same sentiment:

I think that the Committee on Rules should grant that rule whether its membership is for the bill or not. I think this House should be allowed on great measures to work its will, and it cannot work its will if the Committee on Rules is so constituted as not to allow the House to pass on those things.[44]

Frequent references to 1910 were made. At the time "too much control was centered in the Speaker. . . ." "Today . . . we fight a system which has deposited too much power in the Committee on Rules . . ."[45] according to Sidney R. Yates (D-Illinois). What is the definition of "too much power?" It is that situation when leaders have been permitted to exercise greater authority than was intended by the procedural majority in the House.

The limited accountability theory restated

The arguments of Smith and his supporters also bore the characteristics of the 1910 debate. Speaker Cannon believed in limited accountability and so did Smith. Though their positions of leadership were different, and there-

fore one would not expect exact parallels between the two situations, the two had similar views of leadership and accountability. To Chairman Smith, the whole effort to enlarge the Committee was both unnecessary and premature. In a series of circumlocutions (some of which were contradictory), Smith and his cohorts argued as follows:

1. The Committee has been wrongly charged—it does not block important legislation which requires "emergency action." As Clarence Brown (R-Ohio), ranking Republican on the Committee on Rules, and close colleague of Chairman Smith, noted: "In my nearly a quarter of a century of service here, I have never known of a single instance, when the House leadership desired a bill to be brought to a House vote, that such measure was not voted upon."[46]

2. The committee will delay on measures which are not "emergency" measures but "nothing is lost and much is gained by delay. . . . 'haste make waste' . . . John Nance Garner . . . once was reported to have said, 'The country never suffers from the things that Congress fails to do.' "[47]

3. The majority can always work its will—it can go around the Committee on Rules by relying on Calendar Wednesday, discharge petition, and suspension of the rules.

4. Much more legislation is killed in other standing committees than in the Committee on Rules.

5. How can the president know that his program will not be enacted? He has just arrived on the scene. It would be better to leave the "packing" resolution on the calendar for two years and then assess the situation when the evidence is in.

6. The Chairman is willing now to insure that "no obstacles" would be interposed "to the five major bills that the President has publicly announced as his program for this session."

This example of a Smith accommodation is very revealing and brings us to an analysis of his broader view of his position of leadership. He did not consider it necessary generally to work with his party leaders and membership in passing legislation but he was willing to allow five major bills to reach the floor. This offer was considered "audacious" by the reformers. Blatnik expressed their views:

Who else would have the audacity and arrogance to even suggest that in exchange for our agreeing to the status quo they would permit us to consider five pieces of legislation said to be the cornerstone of the new administration's domestic program? This offer was an insult to the House and its Members. The fact that it was a bona fide and sincere attempt only heightens the frightening picture of two men telling a nation that they will permit five bills to pass if they can reserve their right to kill off any others that do not meet with their approval.[48]

How could this type of proposal be offered by Smith? Clearly, he saw it as a definite concession. "All of the five bills which the President has announced as his program for this session . . . are five bills that I am very much opposed to. . . ."[49] Smith did not consider that he had an obligation to support his party's legislation just because he chaired the committee which scheduled that legislation.

When I made this pledge to the Speaker and to the Members of this House, it is a pledge I made when I first became chairman of the Rules Committee. That is, *I will cooperate with the Democratic leadership of the House of Representatives just as long and just as far as my conscience will permit me to go.*[50] (Emphasis added.)

The convenience of holding oneself accountable to "conscience" is that only the individual himself is involved in defining accountability. This self-interpretation was the very thing that was objected to by the reformers. It meant that the majority could not be assured of cooperation from one of their leaders. Speaker Rayburn, among others, expressed his concern.

The gentleman from Virginia says that he is not going to report anything that violates his conscience and then winds up his talk on the floor by saying you have nothing to fear from the action of the Committee on Rules.[51]

In 1963 the Committee on Rules was permanently expanded to 15 members. Many of the same arguments were invoked but the political situation had changed. The reformers could now defend their experiment—pointing out that the dire predictions of those opposed in 1961 had not come true. Even the Republicans seemed to accept the 15-member committee, though they tried to have the party division changed from 10 Democrats and 5 Republicans to 9 Democrats and 6 Republicans. The best the opponents of a 15-member committee could do was to reiterate their earlier arguments and note that the committee's performance in the 87th Congress was little different than before—it, too, blocked legislation.[52] For Judge Smith's part, he focused his attention on southern Democrats, warning that:

. . . this matter of packing the Rules Committee affects more closely our area of the country than anywhere else. . . . I hope that none of my southern friends are going to be complaining around here when certain measures come up, and come up quite promptly, if the Committee on Rules is packed again. . . . I hope that at least those members who voted against the packing before will see fit to do the same thing again, because I believe *it is vital*

to the interests of their States. . . .[53]
(Emphasis added.)

The Chairman also addressed the new members of the 88th Congress. He warned them that unwise fiscal legislation would soon be introduced.

Are you going to yield up every little leverage or every little weapon you may have to defeat measures so unsound? Are you going to yield some of your prerogatives and privileges here today that are going to adversely affect your people for the next 20 years? If you do, *that is your business and none of mine.*[54] (Emphasis added.)

Howard W. Smith proved himself to be an unintentioned prophet. By a margin of 39 votes (see Table 2), the House did make an attempt to clarify the distinction between its business and that of Judge Smith. Thus occurred the second important increment in the decline of the chairmanship of the Committee on Rules.
The third increment came in 1965. With very little debate, the House re-invoked the 21-day rule[55] and took away the Committee on Rules' power, when any member of the House objected, to grant rules to send a bill to conference (or to agree to the Senate version). In both instances, the powers of the Speaker were increased. To Clarence Brown (R-Ohio) this raised the spectre of the all-powerful Speaker before 1910. In a colloquy with Speaker McCormack, he observed:

You are too nice a fellow. But I am thinking about some dirty dog that might come along some other time and say here is a nice little wrinkle in the rule which we can use to block this legislation.
In other words, should we give that power to every Speaker in the future? We gave that power to "Uncle Joe" Cannon and Tom Reed as the gentleman recalls. We gave them too much power.[56]

Ironically, Brown failed to perceive that his colleague, Howard W. Smith, also had been given more power than was compatible with the structure, organization, and composition of the House of Representatives. Smith had developed independence from those who ultimately had provided him with this position of authority. Smith's refusal to heed the warning signals of substantive shifts in his procedural majority resulted in changes which forced him to be more dependent on this majority or face a serious loss of influence in the process of building substantive majorities.

Conclusions

In 1910 and 1961 the House of Representatives acted to curb the power of two generally well-loved and admired leaders—Joseph G. Cannon and Howard W. Smith. These men had realized the full potential of the authority inherent in their respective positions in the House. Though in different ways, they both had become virtually independent of their procedural majorities. Defeating them would not have solved the problems raised by their exercise of power. Thus, the House took the more drastic action of making procedural changes to guarantee the predominance of the condition of relatively free bargaining, with leaders acting as "middle-men."
Though it is not possible as a result of this inquiry to set forth a handbook for successful leadership in the House, it is possible to draw some inferences concerning the limits which must be observed by the "middle-man" type of leader. First, the procedural majority is of major significance for House leaders since the sanctions it allows determine the limits on leaders in forming or thwarting substantive majorities.

In order to protect his position, the House leader must be exceptionally protective of this procedural majority —developing techniques which will inform him as to substantive changes which have occurred within various segments of the majority, and making a requisite number of adaptations.

Second, there are cases, as noted here, where leaders have developed, over a period of time, the authority of the position to the extent that they seemingly are independent of the procedural majority. Their exercise of power eventually leads some members to the conclusion that procedural changes are necessary to prevent a recurrence of such independent action. If there are enough members of the majority who perceive violations of bargaining behavior on the part of leaders over a period of time, they may take extreme action to force compliance with their expectations. These instances are of major significance for the study of the House since they provide important clues as to how that body defines leadership for itself.

Third, all House leaders have considerable latitude in using the sanctions provided by procedural majorities in building substantive majorities. In the short run, therefore, leaders thwart the emergence of new majorities. Furthermore, leaders are normally given ample warning of dissatisfaction before action is taken. If the leader persists in ignoring these signs (or in simply failing to read them properly), he will be defeated. If, in addition, he has assumed so much power that he is protected from his procedural majority, the reform condition is set and changes will be made eventually.

Fourth, both cases cited here suggest that leadership positions of great, absolute authority in the House of Representatives are contextually inappropriate. Congressional political parties are coalitions of members, each of whom has some bargaining power. Thus, conditions in the House are not conducive to the exercise of power with such limited accountability to major segments of the procedural majority, as in the two cases cited here.

Fifth, one is inevitably led to inquire whether Speaker Cannon and Chairman Smith could have avoided the consequences which ultimately developed. If the analysis of this essay is accurate, the answer must be "yes." They could have avoided the reforms by accepting the conditions of leadership in the House and behaving accordingly. Had they been more flexible, they would likely have not only avoided being "reformed" but also have preserved more power for themselves in the long run. Speaker Sam Rayburn, the model "middle-man," could have counseled them both on such matters.

NOTES   1. For a sample of this literature see: David B. Truman, *The Governmental Process* (New York: Knopf, 1951); Bertram M. Gross, *The Legislative Struggle* (New York: McGraw-Hill, 1953); Robert L. Peabody and Nelson W. Polsby, eds., *New Perspectives on the House of Representatives* (Chicago: Rand-McNally, 1963); and particularly Robert L. Peabody, "Organization Theory and Legislative Behavior: Bargaining, Hierarchy and Change in the U.S. House of Representatives," unpublished paper delivered at the Annual Meeting of the American Political Science Association, New York, 1963.

2. The "middle-man" thesis of congressional leadership is discussed in David B. Truman, *The Congressional Party: A Case Study* (New York: Wiley, 1959). See also Samuel C. Patterson, "Legislative Leadership and Political Ideology," *Public Opinion Quarterly,* 27 (Fall, 1963), 399–410.

3. Richard F. Fenno, Jr., has eloquently discussed the organizational problems of the House in his essay in David B. Truman, ed., *The Congress and America's Future* (Englewood Cliffs, N.J.: Prentice-Hall, 1965).

4. Lewis A. Froman, Jr., and Randall B. Ripley note that the two parties maintain the highest level of cohesion on procedural questions. See "Conditions for Party Leadership: The Case of the House Democrats," *American Political Science Review,* 59 (March, 1965), 52–63. Much of this essay tends to support their general argument.

5. Cannon allowed the Democrats to select their members, though he did not have to make this concession. He did so because he thought that by giving the minority leader this power, the Democrats would fight over committee assignments. See William R. Gwinn, *Uncle Joe Cannon: Archfoe of Insurgency* (New York: Bookman Associates, 1957), p. 97.

6. *Congressional Record,* 61st Cong., 2d sess., March 17, 1910, p. 3294.

7. Cannon also preferred to have his whip on Ways and Means. James Tawney (Minnesota), James Watson (Indiana), and John Dwight (New York), all were on that Committee while serving as Whip under Cannon.

8. For discussions of seniority and its development, see George Goodwin, "The Seniority System in Congress," *American Political Science Review,* 53 (June, 1959), 596–604; George B. Galloway, *History of the House of Representatives* (New York: Crowell, 1961); and particularly Nelson W. Polsby, "The Institutionalization of the U.S. House of Representatives," *American Political Science Review,* 62 (March, 1968), 144–168.

9. See Paul D. Hasbrouck, *Party Government in the House of Representatives* (New York: Macmillan, 1927), p. 37.

10. George Norris, *Fighting Liberal* (New York: Macmillan, 1945), p. 109.

11. *Congressional Record,* 61st Cong., 2d sess., March 17, 1910, p. 3300.

12. Norris, *op. cit.,* p. 144.

13. Hasbrouck, *op. cit.,* pp. 4–6.

14. The principal student of these changes is Joseph Cooper. See "Congress and its Committees," unpublished Ph.D. dissertation, Harvard University, 1961. See also Chang-wei Chiu, *The Speaker of the House of Representatives Since 1896* (New York: Columbia University Press, 1928), Chapter VI. Actually, for rather complicated reasons, the insurgents hadn't voted for Calendar Wednesday, see Cooper, Chapter II.

15. Hasbrouck, *op. cit.,* p. 126.

16. One can consult any number of sources on the 1910 revolt. Those highly recommended include: Hasbrouck; Chiu; Gwinn; Norris; Kenneth Hechler, *Insurgency* (New York: Columbia University Press, 1941); George R. Brown, *The Leadership of Congress* (Indianapolis: Bobbs-Merrill, 1922); Charles R. Atkinson, *The Committee on Rules and the Overthrow of Speaker Cannon* (New York: Columbia University Press, 1911), plus the several biographies and autobiographies of those who participated. For a listing of the latter see Charles O. Jones and Randall B. Ripley, *The Role of Political Parties in Congress: A Bibliography and Research Guide* (Tucson: University of Arizona Press, 1966).

17. Gwinn suggests that this move was prearranged between Crumpacker and Cannon. See p. 206. Gwinn, *op. cit.,* p. 206.

18. *Congressional Record,* 61st Cong., 2d sess., March 16, 1910, p. 3241.

19. *Ibid.,* p. 3251.

20. *Congressional Record,* 61st Cong., 2d sess., March 17, 1910, p. 3287.

21. *Ibid.,* p. 3289.

22. Gwinn, *op. cit.,* p. 207.

23. Norris, *op. cit.,* p. 126.

24. *New York Times,* March 18, 1910, p. 1.

25. *Congressional Record,* 61st Cong., 2d sess., March 17, 1910, p. 3292.

26. L. White Busbey, *Uncle Joe Cannon: The Story of a Pioneer American* (New York: Holt, 1927), p. 254.

27. *Congressional Record,* 61st Cong., 2d sess., March 17, 1910, p. 3302.

28. *Ibid.,* p. 3305.

29. *Congressional Record,* 61st Cong., 2d sess., March 19, 1910, p. 3430.

30. *Ibid.,* p. 3436.

31. *Ibid.,* p. 3437.

32. Busbey, *op. cit.,* p. 266.

33. *Congressional Record,* 61st Cong., 2d sess., March 17, 1910, p. 3300.

34. *Ibid.,* p. 3304.

35. *Congressional Record,* 61st Cong., 2d sess., March 19, 1910, p. 3433. Interestingly, Underwood later became the principal leader of the House during the 62nd Congress as majority leader. The Democrats were in a ticklish spot. They wanted to emphasize the internal divisions in the Republican Party so as to win the 1910 elections, but did not want the Republicans either to get credit for reform or to reunite after reform. One news story suggested that the Democrats wanted Cannon to win, so as not to lose an issue in 1910 (*New York Times,* March 19, 1910). The Democrats also had to consider the problems for themselves of a drastic change in the Speaker's power, should they gain control of the House in 1910.

36. Lewis J. Lapham, "Party Leadership and the House Committee on Rules," unpublished Ph.D. dissertation, Harvard University, 1954, p. 137.

37. *Ibid.,* p. 123.

38. See James A. Robinson, *The House Rules Committee* (Indianapolis: Bobbs-Merrill, 1963); and the several useful unpublished research papers on the House Committee on Rules produced by Walter Kravitz of the Legislative Reference Service, Library of Congress. See also, Christopher Van Hollen, "The House Committee on Rules (1933–1951): Agent of Party and Agent of Opposition," unpublished Ph.D. dissertation, Johns Hopkins University, 1951.

39. See Congressional Quarterly, Inc., *Congress and the Nation,* p. 1425. See also William MacKaye, *A New Coalition Takes Control: The House Rules Committee Fight 1961* (New York: McGraw-Hill, 1963).

40. *Congressional Quarterly Almanacs,* Vols. 14 and 15.

41. Note in particular, in addition to Robinson and MacKaye, the two articles in Peabody and Polsby—one by Peabody and one by Peabody and Milton C. Cummings, Jr.; and Neil MacNeil, *Forge of Democracy: The House of Representatives* (New York: MacKay, 1963), Chapter 15.

42. *Congressional Record,* 87th Cong., 1st sess., January 31, 1961, pp. 1582–1583.

43. *Ibid.,* p. 1574.

44. *Ibid.,* p. 1579.

45. *Ibid.,* p. 1581.

46. *Ibid.,* p. 1575.

47. *Ibid.,* p. 1577.

48. *Ibid.,* p. 1583.

49. *Ibid.,* p. 1576.

50. *Loc. cit.*

51. *Ibid.,* p. 1580.

52. Particularly noted was the defeat of the federal aid to education bill in the Committee in 1961. Though a bargain had been struck between pro- and anti-parochial school aid members, the parochial aid proponents were not convinced that they would get what they wanted. Thus, a liberal, Democratic, Catholic member of the Committee on Rules, James Delaney of New York, voted with the conservatives to kill the bill. See H. Douglas Price, "Race, Religion, and the Rules Committee," in Alan F. Westin, **ed.,** *The Uses of Power* (New York: Harcourt, Brace, 1962); and Robert **Bendi**ner, *Obstacle Course on Capitol Hill* (New York: McGraw-Hill, 1964).

53. *Congressional Record,* 88th Cong., 1st sess., January 9, 1963, p. 18.

54. *Loc. cit.*

55. The 21-day rule had been implemented during the 81st Congress and abandoned in the 82nd Congress. It has since been abandoned in the 90th Congress.

56. *Congressional Record,* 89th Cong., 1st sess., January 4, 1965, p. 22.

THE PARTY WHIP ORGANIZATIONS IN THE UNITED STATES HOUSE OF REPRESENTATIVES *

RANDALL B. RIPLEY

Party leadership in Congress is necessarily constrained by the character of those led. Congressmen are not centrally recruited or screened, but rather are nominated by the parties in their home districts and separately elected from constituencies that vary enormously in their composition, needs, and preoccupations —though not in their size. There are many kinds of Democrats. There are at least four kinds of southern Democrats, for example: modern liberals from urban and working-class areas of the "New South," old-style populist-liberals from poor, subsistence-crop rural areas, courthouse conservatives from areas controlled by plantation-economy or businessmen's elites, and wool-hat conservatives whose election was the result of their own organizational efforts and popular appeal. Naturally, some southern Democrats defy classification and others are mixtures. The variety of northern Democrats is equally great: Some were nominated and elected by urban machines, others by ethnic minorities, others by labor unions, still others by country club liberals.

The problem therefore arises: How should such a disparate group be led? Upon what measures can they find agreement? The purpose of the party whip system is not so much to lead as to discover whether leadership in any given area is possible or can be effective. The whips monitor floor attendance and provide a few routine informational services to members in exchange for which members are obliged to be pleasant—though not necessarily informative—when asked how they are disposed toward legislation. Randall Ripley, whose study of the Democratic whip's office during a period of recent history where it was unusually effective, follows, is Associate Professor of Political Science at Ohio State University.

Reprinted from *The American Political Science Review*, LVII (September 1964), 197–225, by permission of the author and publisher.

* The research for this article was conducted while the author was an intern in the Office of the Democratic Whip in the United States House of Representatives, from April to September, 1963. The research was financially sponsored by a Brookings Institution Research Fellowship. In addition to the printed sources this article is based on interviews and correspondence with members and former members of the House, employees of the House, and various staff members; and on files of the Office of the Democratic Whip.

I am especially indebted to Congressman Hale Boggs and his Administrative Assistant, D. B. Hardeman, for cooperating in many ways in the research for this article. I am also grateful to John Bibby, Lewis A. Froman, Jr., Theodore Lowi, Robert Peabody, and H. Douglas Price, as well as Hardeman, for their careful critiques of an earlier draft.

The findings and conclusions are those of the author and do not purport to represent the views of the Brookings Institution, its trustees, officers, or other staff members.

In the literature on political parties in the United States Congress two points are usually stressed. First, it is said that the political party label lacks a precise programmatic content because "party government" in the British sense is absent in the American Congress.[1] Second, however, it is contended that the party label is the single most important and reliable attribute in predicting the voting behavior of a Senator or Representative.[2]

Between these two contentions lies a sizeable area of unexplored territory. If party is the best predictive device in analyzing voting behavior in Congress then, despite the lack of "party government," the party machinery in both houses must have effects that deserve study. Professor Huitt has suggested the necessity and importance of this kind of study:

. . . the preoccupation with reform has obscured the fact that we have no really adequate model of party leadership as it exists in Congress, and that none can be constructed because we lack simple descriptions of many of the basic working parts of the present system.[3]

Huitt himself and a few others have filled some of these gaps.[4]

An important office of party leadership that has received no sustained treatment is that of whip. Only two moderately long articles have been specifically devoted to it, and neither analyzes the relation of the whips to rule by the majority party.[5] Other works on Congress mention the whips, but only in passing.[6]

This article proposes to (1) recount briefly the 20th Century history of the whips in the House of Representatives, (2) describe the whip organizations in the House, (3) analyze the role played by the House Democratic whip organization in the Second Session of the 87th Congress (1962) and the First Session of the 88th Congress (1963), and (4) suggest the broader importance of the whips in the House.

– 1 –

Champ Clark, Speaker of the House for eight years (1911–19), called the whips "the right hands of the two leaders," and described the principal duty of a whip as "to have his fellow political members in the House when needed."[7] His comments are still accurate, although the functions performed by the whips have become more diversified in recent years. The whips are (1) responsible for the presence of their fellow party members, but they must also (2) transmit certain information to them, (3) ascertain how they will vote on selected important pieces of legislation, and (4) guide pressure to change the minds of the recalcitrant and stiffen the wills of the wavering.

Most of these functions have been performed at least haphazardly in the House since 1789, although the name "whip" was not formally applied to a party official in the House until the end of the 19th Century.[8] Throughout most of the 19th Century members functioning as whips were in evidence only in connection with important legislation and only when the division between the parties was close enough to necessitate a device that would help gain a high degree of party regularity.[9] Many of these whips were volunteers for a given floor fight only.[10] Both parties began to designate their whips formally for an entire Congress around the turn of this century. Table 1 lists them and summarizes their House careers.

The Republicans

The exact method of Tawney's initial appointment as Republican whip in

TABLE 1   Party Whips in the House

NAME, STATE, YEARS OF SERVICE AS WHIP	HOUSE CAREER		
	YEARS BEFORE BECOMING WHIP	YEARS AS WHIP	YEARS AFTER BEING WHIP
Democrats			
Oscar W. Underwood, Alabama, 1900–01	5	1	14
James T. Lloyd, Mo., 1901–08	4	8	8
Thomas M. Bell, Ga., (1913–15?) †	?	?	?
William A. Oldfield, Ark., 1921–28	12	8	—
John McDuffie, Alabama, 1929–33	10	4	2
Arthur Greenwood, Indiana, 1933–35	10	2	4
Patrick Boland, Pa., 1935–42	4	7	—
Robert Ramspeck, Ga., 1942–45	12	3	—
John Sparkman, Alabama, 1946	9	1	—
John McCormack, Mass., 1947–49; 1953–55	18	4	13*
Percy Priest, Tenn., 1949–53	8	4	4
Carl Albert, Okla., 1955–62	8	7	2*
Hale Boggs, La., 1962–	17	2 *	
Republicans			
James A. Tawney, Minn., 1897–1905	4	8	6
James E. Watson, Indiana, 1905–09	8	4	—
John W. Dwight, N.Y., 1909–13	6	4	—
Charles Burke, S.D., 1913–15	12	2	—
Charles M. Hamilton, N.Y., 1915–19	2	4	—
Harold Knutson, Minn., 1919–23	2	4	26
Albert H. Vestal, Indiana, 1923–31	6	8	—
Carl G. Bachmann, W.Va., 1931–33	6	2	—
Harry L. Englebright, Cal., 1933–43	6	11	—
Leslie C. Arends, Ill., 1944–	9	20*	

* As of the end of 1963.
† Bell served in the House from 1905 until 1931.

1897 is obscure. Speaker Cannon ended it by appointing him Chairman of the Appropriations Committee in 1905, although he had never previously served on that Committee. Watson, who succeeded Tawney,[11] resigned from the House in 1908 to run for the governorship of Indiana; he later served 16 years in the Senate. Though he had left the House, Cannon consulted him as a personal assistant in the 1910 rules fight.[12] The third Republican whip, Dwight, began to organize a more extensive system and develop modern techniques—particularly the use of a systematic poll prior to an important vote.[13]

During Wilson's presidency Burke and Hamilton were understandably less active than Dwight had been. In 1919, with the Republicans again in control of the House, the post of whip resumed its importance to them. In that year, reflecting other changes in party practice after 1910, the power of appointing the Republican whip was transferred from the Speaker (or Minority Leader, depending on electoral fortunes) to the Republican Committee on Committees.[14] The Republican Conference (caucus) could ratify or reject the Committee's recommendation. Except in 1919 itself the normal practice has been for the Conference automatically to adopt it.[15]

Knutson, who later became Chairman of the Committee on Ways and Means, was whip for four years.[16] He was followed in turn by Vestal, Bachmann, Englebright, and Arends. The last three in particular developed, expanded, and solidified the organizational structure of the Republican whip.

The Democrats

The first Democratic whip, Underwood, later became floor leader in the House, and still later, the same in the Senate. Underwood offered the resolution at the 1900 Democratic Caucus—going into a campaign year—which formally created the posts of whip and assistant whip. The Minority Leader then announced Underwood's appointment as whip.[17] The method of appointment for Democratic whips has never changed. The floor leader, aided by Democratic Speakers, has appointed all the Democratic whips.

Lloyd succeeded Underwood and served until he resigned to become Chairman of the Democratic Congressional Campaign Committee in the crucial election years of 1908, 1910, and 1912.[18] The identity of the Democratic whip in the period from 1909 until 1921 is obscure. Bell was the whip during at least the 63rd Congress (1913–15). He may have been whip for the entire 12 years, or there may have been others, as yet unidentified, who served part of that period.[19]

Oldfield was whip for eight years, serving until his death. McDuffie followed him for four years, resigning after an unsuccessful race for Speaker against Henry Rainey in the 1933 Democratic Caucus. Greenwood also ceased to be whip after an intraparty struggle which resulted in the election of Joseph Byrns to the Speakership. He was replaced by Boland, an important Byrns supporter. Greenwood and Boland built the modern Democratic whip organization in the House in the course of coping with the exigencies of New Deal legislation.

The party whip organizations were initially the product of the close, hard-fought party battles of the late 19th Century. By the late 1920s and the beginning of the party battles that predated the New Deal struggles the whips became even more prominent in the House. Both parties were eager to maintain disciplined lines either for or against far-reaching legislation. The top-heavy Democratic majorities of the 1930's began to be plagued by dissenting Southerners and Westerners; defection increased the need for machinery aimed at a high degree of party unity in voting. Republicans desired to produce a united opposition, and needed discipline to participate effectively in their recurrent coalitions with Southern Democrats. By 1963 the Democratic whip had a reasonable expectation of succeeding to the floor leadership and even the Speakership.[20]

Gradually the House began to recognize not only the importance of the individuals serving as whips but also the importance of the whips as institutions. From 1911 until the present the Republican whip has had an office in the Capitol, unless he chose to operate from his congressional office. The Democratic whip had an office in the Capitol in the 63d Congress (1913–15) and has had an office there continuously since 1919.[21] Since 1913 the House has provided for at least limited staff help to be appointed by the whips.[22] The sum was to be used for a messenger for each whip until 1947, when provision was also made for two clerks. In 1953 the party whips were given administrative assistants.[23] By 1963 the office of each whip had a budget of about $40,000.[24]

– 2 –

The whip organizations of the parties grew in size and complexity through the years of this century. By 1963, on both sides they were large, formal organizations that performed a variety of tasks.

The Republican organization

John Dwight in 1909–1913 was apparently the first Republican whip to have assistants.[25] There is no evidence that any Republican until Carl Bachmann in 1931 again used assistant whips. Bachmann organized the Republican whip system on essentially the same basis that is still in use. He divided the country into two divisions and appointed Joseph Martin of Massachusetts to be in charge of the Eastern division and Harry Englebright of California to be in charge of the Western division. He also designated a "key man" in each state with Republican members. When a poll of the Republican members was necessary Bachmann asked Martin and Englebright to get reports from the key men about their state delegations.[26] When Englebright became Republican whip in 1933 he retained the pattern of assistant whips (increasing them to three in number) and "key men" in the state delegations.

The Republican whip from 1944 to the present, Les Arends of Illinois, formalized and expanded the key man system. By 1963 he had a deputy whip, three regional whips, and 12 assistant whips. After the chief whip is chosen he has a free hand in appointing all of his assistants. The Republican organization in the First Session of the 88th Congress is summarized in Table 2.

The Republican whip organization performs the four functions already mentioned, involving attendance, information, polling, and pressure. The Republican whip keeps records of Republican members' voting on teller votes as well as on roll calls. This the Democratic whip does only informally and sporadically, without notes or records being kept.

The Republicans have developed a different pattern of leadership succession. Joe Martin had been an assistant whip before becoming Minority Leader and then Speaker, but no whip has yet become the Republican floor leader. Similarly, when a Republican Speaker has been forced to become Minority Leader the Republican whip has kept his job, rather than surrendering it to the former Majority Leader. Thus Arends remained as whip in both 1949 and 1955 while Halleck lost any formal leadership title.[27] So long as Arends is content to continue indefinitely as whip, without contesting for the Speakership, the succession ladder simply bypasses him. This may be a temporary accident of personality; the test will come after his retirement, when it is seen whether his successor proves to be an aspirant for the Speakership or whether the post has become permanently neutralized.

The Democratic organization

On the Democratic side Underwood had an assistant whip in 1900. But in the 1921–1928 period Oldfield had no assistant whips. John McDuffie (1929–1933) had two assistants. The great expansion in the whip organization, which had come in 1931 in the Republican Party, came in 1933 for the Democrats under Arthur Greenwood. He

TABLE 2   Republican Whip Organization, 1963
Whip: Leslie C. Arends, Illinois
Deputy Whip: Charles Hoeven, Iowa

Regional and Assistant Whips

NAME AND STATE	STATES IN ZONE	NO. OF GOP MEMBERS
Regional Whip: Katherine St. George, New York		
William Bates, Mass.	Conn., Mass., N.J., Me., N.H., Vt.	19
Carleton King, N.Y.	New York	21
William Curtin, Pa.	Pa.	14
Regional Whip: Jackson Betts, Ohio		
Elford Cederberg, Mich.	Michigan	11
Jackson Betts, Ohio	Ohio	18
William Van Pelt, Wisc.	Wisc., Minn., Iowa	16
Robert Michel, Ill.	Illinois	14
Richard Roudebush, Ind.	Indiana, Ky., Tenn.	12
Regional Whip: Catherine May, Wash.		
Walter Norblad, Ore.	Ore., Colo., Mont., Utah, Wash., Wyo.	13
Hjalmar Nygaard, N.D.	N.D., S.D., Nebr., Kans., Okla.	13
John Baldwin, Cal.	California	14
William Cramer, Fla.	Fla., Ariz., Md., N.C., Tex., W.Va.	12

organized a system of 15 assistant whips, each responsible for the Democrats in a specific zone. The zones were identical with those established for the Democratic Steering Committee, which was also created in 1933.[28] The Steering Committee withered quickly but the whip zones remained. The initial 15 zones were similar in composition to the present 18 zones.

Greenwood's successor, Pat Boland of Pennsylvania, worked diligently to perfect the functioning of the organization. During his 7-year tenure the press and other Democratic leaders began to take public notice of his operations.[29]

The Democratic deputy whip, who is especially active on the floor in checking attendance and voting, is appointed by the whip.[30] The Democratic assistant whips are either appointed by the dean of the delegations for which they are responsible or they are elected by members of those delegations.[31] Table 3 summarizes the Democratic whip organization in the First Session of the 88th Congress.

The assistant whips are responsible for a small number of Democrats, averaging between 14 and 15. The whips, or staff members designated by them, make the regular contacts with all of the Democratic members' offices. When the Democratic leadership in the House wishes to transmit information to all Democrats—or elicit information from them—the chief whip's office contacts the 18 assistants. In this way all Democrats can be alerted to come to the floor in 15 to 20 minutes. The leadership can ascertain the sentiments

TABLE 3   Democratic Whip Organization, 1963
Whip: Hale Boggs, Louisiana
Deputy Whip: John Moss, Calif.

Assistant Whips

NAME AND STATE	STATES IN ZONE	NO. OF DEMS.	METHOD OF SELECTION
Torbert Macdonald, Mass.	Mass., Conn., R.I.	14	Election
Abraham Multer, N.Y.	N.Y.	20	Election
George Rhodes, Pa.	Pa.	13	Election
Peter Rodino, N.J.	N.J., Del., Md.	14	Election
Thomas Downing, Va.	Va., N.C.	17	Appointed
John Flynt, Ga.	Ga., S.C.	16	Appointed
James O'Hara, Mich.	Mich., Minn., Wisc.	16	Election
Winfield Denton, Ind.	Indiana	4	Election
Harley Staggers, W.Va.	W.Va., Ohio	10	Election
Robert Everett, Tenn.	Tenn., Ark., Ky.	15	Election
Gillis Long, La.	La., Miss.	13	Election
Don Fuqua, Fla.	Fla., Alabama	18	Election
Frank Karsten, Mo.	Mo., Iowa	9	Election
Dan Rostenkowski, Ill.	Illinois	12	Appointed
Jack Brooks, Tex.	Texas	21	Appointed
Ed Edmondson, Okla.	Oklahoma	5	Election
Thomas Morris, N.M.	N.M., Ariz., Alaska, Colo., Ida., Hawaii, Mont., Nev., Ore., Wash.	17	Appointed
John McFall, Calif.	California	23	Appointed

of virtually every Democrat in the House on a given bill in a day or two.[32]

– 3 –

The purpose of this section is to analyze the functioning of the Democratic whip organization in the Second Session of the 87th Congress (1962) and the First Session of the 88th (1963),[33] years of great activity for it. The Democratic whip organization, be it remembered, has worked as an arm of the majority party in the House ever since 1933, except for two two-year periods (1947–49 and 1953–55). In the 1930s, as noted above, Boland had greatly expanded its use. Rayburn, on the other hand, who was a strong leader and had never been whip himself, used it less than the weaker

Speakers of the 1930s. For example, the whip who served for the longest period under Rayburn, Carl Albert, employed his top staff member on congressional business rather than on whip business.[34]

But in 1962 and 1963 the new Speaker, John McCormack, began to use the whip organization for a greater number of formal polls. McCormack had been whip, as had the new Majority Leader, Albert. Hale Boggs, the new whip, had been deputy whip under Albert. Thus the three top Democrats in the House all appreciated the potentialities of the whip organization—both formal and informal. These three men, joined by D. B. Hardeman, Administrative Assistant to Boggs, and the deputy whip, John Moss, functioned as a small, close-knit group dedicated to attaining the most favorable voting outcomes on Administration bills. This group—not, conspicuously, including the chairman of the Rules Committee—met with White House and Departmental officials on legislative matters throughout 1962 and 1963.

The Office of the Democratic Whip was composed of four people—Boggs, Hardeman, a secretary, and an intern—during the entire period studied. The office had a contact—generally a staff member—in the office of each of the 18 assistant whips. Information on poll requests was transmitted by telephone between the whip's office and the offices of the assistant whips. Occasionally the whip's office made contact with all Democratic members of the House directly, either on substantive legislation matters or on attendance needs.[35] The whip's office, located in the Capitol, served as a meeting place for White House and Departmental congressional liaison officials interested in the success of a particular bill.

The whip during these two years was Hale Boggs of Louisiana, a loyal Administration supporter on most matters. The deputy whip, John Moss of California, was even more consistently loyal.[36] The assistant whips, the primary direct contacts with rank and file Democratic members, varied considerably in their voting loyalty to the Administration. Table 4 shows the

TABLE 4   Voting of Democratic Assistant Whips and Members of Their Zones, 1962–1963

Part I: Per Cent Support of Administration on 17 Key Roll Calls

	1962		1963	
STATES IN WHIP ZONE	ASSISTANT WHIP	ALL ZONE MEMBERS	ASSISTANT WHIP	ALL ZONE MEMBERS
	(%)	(%)	(%)	(%)
Mass., Conn., R.I.	100	95	100	97
N.Y.	100	95	100	97
Pa.	100	98	90	95
N.J., Del., Md.	100	92	100	99
*Va., N.C.	43	53	60	56
Ga., S.C.	86	62	89	74
Mich., Wisc., Minn.	100	97	100	97
Ind.	100	96	100	97
W.Va., Ohio	57	83	100	93
Tenn., Ky., Ark.	71	81	90	90
*Miss., La.	86	41	100	53
*Alabama, Fla.	67	62	78	70
Mo., Iowa	100	80	100	81
*Illinois	100	98	100	98
*Texas	29	51	100	70
Okla. (Kan. & Mont. in 1962)	100	78	90	90
Wash., Ore., Alaska, Hawaii, Ariz., N.M., Utah, Colo., Ida., Nev. (Mont. in 1963)	67	86	100	92
California	100	98	100	97
Average	84	70	94	85

* Assistant whip changed during the two-year period.

Part II: Per Cent Support of Specific Legislation

YEAR AND LEGISLATION	SUPPORT BY ALL ASSISTANT WHIPS	SUPPORT BY ALL DEMOCRATS
1962:	(%)	(%)
Urban Affairs	61	55
Tax Bill	94	86
Debt Limit	89	84
Farm Bill	78	81
Trade Expansion Act	89	83
Public Works	89	82
U.N. Bonds	87	81
1963:		
Rules Committee	83	81
Public Works Appropriation	94	86
Medical Student Loans	95	87
Feed Grains Program	93	88
Debt Limit (May)	100	87
Area Redevelopment	83	77
Debt Limit (August)	100	93
Tax Bill	100	90
Debt Limit (November)	100	85
Cotton Bill	93	79

support they gave the Administration on the 17 votes chosen for analysis here,[37] together with the support given by all Democrats in each whip zone on these same votes. In general, the assistant whips tend to be more loyal to the Administration than all Democrats, and variations in their individual loyalty tend to reflect the normal variations by zone.[38]

The problem of "disloyal" assistant whips is troublesome. The power to appoint and replace them rests exclusively with the Democratic delegations involved. But even if the whip had the power to remove assistant whips the roll-call voting record of the assistants would not be an infallible test. For example, in 1962 one assistant whip supported the Administration only rarely and yet did an excellent job as assistant whip, not only in reporting accurately but also in indicating the weak point of each member

through which he might be induced to change his mind and support the Administration on a given bill. Loyalty is less important than accuracy and thoroughness. The Democratic assistant whips are expected to perform the functions involving attendance, information, and polling but they have a great deal of discretion in deciding whether they also wish to pressure their zone members to vote the Administration position.[39]

An analysis of how the Democratic whip organization performed these four main functions in dealing with the major legislation the House acted on in 1962 and 1963 will form the bulk of this section. "Major legislation" here indicates those measures on which the House leadership decided a poll should be taken, on which the poll was taken and completed, and on which the House acted either favorably or unfavorably by roll-call vote. This definition includes seven bills in 1962 and ten in 1963.[40] The 17 votes include 14 which the Administration won (11 by close margins) and three which the Administration lost (two by close margins).[41]

The first function of the whip organization is to insure maximum Democratic attendance on the floor when critical votes are taken. Getting this is a matter both of keeping the members in Washington and getting them to the House chamber when the vote comes. To this end, the whip's office uses a variation of a poll called an attendance check. In this procedure the assistant whips simply ask the members if they will be in town "next Wednesday" or "next Wednesday and next Thursday." Answers to these questions tell the whip which members should be asked to change their plans and stay in town. Or, if the leadership has a choice in scheduling it can estimate on which one of two or three days the attendance and absence situation will work most in the Administration's favor.

On the day of a vote on the floor the whip's office checks its attendance poll against the absentees on the first quorum call of the day to indicate what members need to be called or may need pairs. The whip's office is particularly anxious to arrange live pairs—whereby an anti-Administration vote actually present is nullified by an absent pro-Administration vote. As the time of the vote or votes approaches, whip calls go out from the whip's office, specifying what is being voted on and indicating that the Speaker, Majority Leader, and whip desire the member's presence on the floor.[42]

The whip's office goes to great lengths to guarantee the presence of members on crucial votes. In April, 1963, votes on a medical student loan provision and on the feed-grains program were scheduled for the same week. The whip's office called one Democratic member who was on the West Coast to make a long-scheduled speech and arranged for her to fly back for the votes. It reached another member touring his district with the Argentine Ambassador and asked him to return to Washington. In the May, 1963, fight over increasing the limit on the national debt the whip's office was instrumental in arranging for two Democrats to attend the session in wheel chairs. Occasionally, faulty timing lost a vote. In the June, 1963, vote on the Area Redevelopment Act amendments, a member was told that the vote would be taken about two hours later than it actually came. Consequently he was at the Washington Airport when his vote was needed.

The promotion of optimum attendance can also involve some selectivity. On the day of the Area Redevelopment vote in 1963 the Air Force was scheduled to take 19 members to an air show in Paris. The whip's office called the Air Force to get assurances that the plane would not leave until one hour after the final vote on the bill. Then it got word to the six Democratic members known to be friendly to the bill who were also scheduled to go on the trip and let them know this, so as to insure their presence on the floor.

In the August, 1963, debt-limit fight the whip's office was especially active in working on attendance. Democrats friendly to the bill and not answering the quorum call on the day before the vote received telegrams from Boggs urging them, in the Speaker's name, "to make every effort to be present Thursday . . ." for the vote. On the day of the vote the whip's office called the offices of 15 Democratic members who had not answered the quorum call that morning. Despite the previous stress on attendance seven of these members had absented themselves without informing the leadership.

In late August, 1963, there was a long, bitter floor fight over the foreign aid authorization bill. The whip organization made a concerted effort to get all Democrats to the floor and keep them there; a series of teller votes was anticipated on Wednesday and Thursday. On Tuesday a meeting held in the whip's office was attended by all but one of the assistant whips (or their representatives), the Democratic House leadership, Executive liaison personnel, Undersecretary of State Harriman and AID Administrator Bell. Harriman and Bell explained the provisions of the bill and the necessity of defeating crippling amendments. The leadership stressed that all assistant whips should be on the floor during the entire voting period (which consumed 10 to 12 hours) and should keep track of the members from their zones. The appeal was effective to the extent that all 18 assistant whips were on the floor during both days of teller votes. Yet two early votes were lost because of absentees and thus a whip call directed at friendly assistant whips (15 of the 18 on this issue) stressed the necessity of winning the first teller vote on the next day.

The attendance in voting on the tax bill in 1963 was almost perfect. On the most important vote (on the Republican recommittal motion) only one Democrat was unexpectedly absent. The other four Democratic absentees had been identified for several days; three of them were in the hospital. Special efforts were made to get everyone else. For example, two Democrats flew back from a conference abroad specifically for the vote.

No statistical measure can judge *precisely* the effect of the Democratic whip organization on attendance for roll call votes. Yet some inferences can be drawn from a few figures.[43] On the 17 bills in these two sessions on which the whip organization was fully active total Democratic voting attendance was 94 per cent. This can be compared with the Democratic attendance on all roll calls: 83 per cent in 1962 and 84 per cent in 1963.[44] This higher attendance was partially a function of the importance of the bills. Yet the specific instances recounted above suggest that the whip organization had some marginal effect in producing a high voting turnout.

The second function of the whip's office is providing information to Democratic members on pending measures. At the most mechanical level the whip's office is responsible for informing all Democrats what is scheduled for floor action week by week. But the office also provides information more directly related to legislation which is highly important to the Administration and to the House leadership. In May, 1963, during the struggle over the increase in the debt limit the whip organization distributed sheets of information on what the defeat of such an increase would mean to the country and to all Democratic members. A more neutral communication was sent to all Democrats directly from the whip's office with reference to the June, 1963, Area Redevelopment amendments. The content of this letter was an outline explanation of the provisions of the bill. A similar letter —signed by Albert and Boggs—was sent in connection with the cotton bill late in the 1963 session.

In 1963, prior to the passage of the foreign aid authorization bill, an effort at informing the assistant whips on specific features of the program was made at the meeting described above. As a result of the meeting, AID prepared two memoranda which were then distributed to the assistant whips through the whip's office.

Before the voting on the tax bill in 1963 the whip's office was instrumental in helping Chairman Mills distribute a short summary of the bill to all Democratic members. It was accompanied by a brief letter urging support for final passage and defeat of the recommittal motion because "this bill is essential to our national well-being." The letter was signed by Mills, the Speaker, Albert, and Boggs.

The third function of the whip's office is to ascertain how the Democratic members of the House will vote on certain pieces of legislation central to the Administration's program.[45] The principal device used to get this information is the poll. The whip's office does not take a poll until the leadership decides one is needed. This comes usually some time after the bill has been reported from the committee and before it is scheduled for floor action. Ordinarily, then, the poll must be completed within a period lasting from two days to two weeks. Naturally the longer time periods produce greater accuracy in results. Likewise, the more clear and specific the question asked of the members the more accurate the result. If the legislation is extremely complex a simple response for or against the bill may hide important feelings about amendments. The most effective assistant whips probe the sentiments of their membership about specific provisions. If a current of opinion develops against a certain feature, the legislation may be changed in time to save it from defeat. In 1963 a poll was started on a bill extending the Export-Import Bank and allowing it to continue direct or "backdoor" borrowing from the Treasury. The

initial poll results revealed a strong feeling against backdoor financing and the Banking and Currency Committee changed the bill to eliminate it.

The question the assistant whips are to ask members is precisely framed, since ambiguous questions produce ambiguous answers. It is not always on the final passage of the legislation. Often it is on the recommittal motion to be offered by the Republicans, if the "instructions" in this motion can be discovered in advance of the vote. At other times a specific amendment is the subject of a poll.

The results of the poll are supplemented by and checked with officials from the White House and the Executive Department involved, and occasionally group lobbyists provide some information. Without a sensitive and knowledgeable interpreter of the poll data the results could be highly misleading. Fortunately for the Democratic leadership such an interpreter was in charge of the office during the period studied. He could tell when a report from a member was of dubious validity and when it could be accepted at face value.[46] He had a "feel" for contacting the proper members.

How accurate were the final poll results which were submitted to the leadership? Accuracy is important because decisions about provisions in the bill, scheduling the bill for floor action, and attempts to change Democratic votes are based partially on these results. To judge the accuracy of the whip poll the final complete poll presented to the leadership usually two days before the vote—which still left time for any of the actions indicated above—was checked, individual by individual, against the final roll call embodying the issue on which the poll had been taken. The results are summarized in Table 5, to show the percentage of members reported correctly

TABLE 5   Accuracy of Democratic Whip Polls, 1962--1963

	PER CENT CORRECT	NUMBER CORRECT	NUMBER INCORRECT	NUMBER UNKNOWN
1962:	(%)			
Urban Affairs	87	226	15	19
Tax Bill	81	212	26	23
Debt Limit	90.5	237	18	7
Farm Bill	82.5	216	36	10
Trade Expansion	92	241	15	6
Public Works	87.5	228	23	10
U.N. Bonds	87	227	24	10
1963:				
Rules Committee	97	247	2	8
Public Works Approp.	91	233	8	15
Medical Student Loans	94	240	0	16
Feed Grains	84	214	16	26
Debt Limit (May)	93	239	9	8
Area Redevelopment	91	232	17	6
Debt Limit (August)	85	218	32	6
Tax Bill *	96	246	6	4
Debt Limit (Nov.)	92	235	19	2
Cotton Bill	84	214	34	8

* Not formally a whip organization poll. See footnote 40, *supra*.

by the poll and also the number reported correctly and incorrectly and the number whose positions could not be ascertained. Evidently the whip's office increased in accuracy in 1963 as compared with 1962. Apparently the refinement of techniques and the lessons of experience were put to good use.

Probably the most important use for the poll results is in helping the leadership determine where to apply pressure. Meetings of the Speaker, Majority Leader, whip, Administrative Assistant to the whip, deputy whip, White House and Departmental liaison officials, and the relevant Committee Chairman begin during a period between three weeks and three days before a bill comes to the floor. At these meetings a division of labor is made, on the basis of the whip poll. Thus a more thorough and accurate poll produces fewer wasted contacts and

enhances the probability that the contacts that are made will be with members who may be persuaded.

This fourth function of the whip's office—that of directing pressure—is, in some ways, the most important of the four. The goal of the office is, after all, to produce votes for the President's program. There is no precise systematic or statistical way of charting the effectiveness of this whip-guided pressure, since the ultimate test would compare what happened with what might otherwise have happened.[47] But an indication of some incidents involving the legislation studied in this article will give a sample of the work done and its effectiveness.

The whip's office was effective in 1962 in identifying the trouble spots on the tax bill of that year. One particularly dangerous area was the New York delegation, which was finally brought into line, with the loss of only three votes. Several Southern delegations were initially opposed to the bill but a caucus of the North Carolina delegation, together with the effective work of the assistant whip for Texas, helped hold Southern losses on the bill to 15 votes. At the last minute, during the floor debate, the secretary in the whip's office discovered that some of the members from a midwestern state might be wavering in their support for the bill. This message was transmitted to Boggs on the floor and he proceeded to escort one of the delegation's members to the Speaker's office where both the Speaker and the President (on the telephone) convinced him that he should support the bill.

During the 1962 prelude to the vote on increasing the national-debt limit the whip's office was instrumental in enlisting Francis Walter of Pennsylvania to use some of his credit with the Southerners to convince one major Southern delegation to vote for the bill. As a result, only three Democrats from that state voted nay.

During the week of June 25, 1962, the whip poll began to show that the Republican motion to recommit the trade bill with instructions to continue the reciprocal trade agreements program for another year might attract as many as 80 Democratic votes. Frantic activity on the part of the President, Chairman Mills of the Ways and Means Committee, Secretaries Goldberg and Hodges and Undersecretaries Wirtz and Price, the Speaker, Majority Leader, whip, and others on Tuesday and Wednesday of that week reduced the eventual Democratic losses on the recommittal motion on Thursday to 44.

During the 1963 Rules Committee fight, after the whip poll was relatively complete, the Speaker, Majority Leader, and whip each took a list of doubtful members to call. Of the 17 called about their vote seven finally voted with the leadership.

The events leading up to the passage of the debt-limit increase in May, 1963, provide another illustration of the use made of the information supplied by the whip poll. At a meeting five days before the vote the results of the poll were discussed. During this meeting the Speaker, Majority Leader, and Larry O'Brien of the White House called and talked to several members about either their opposition or their possible absence. Those members still considered doubtful or open to persuasion were divided among the leadership for further work. Chairman Mills asked that the latest whip poll be given to him the day before the vote so that postponement of the bill could still be announced if it appeared that defeat were likely. A week before the final vote the Speaker had seen an early version of the poll and, on the basis of that, persuaded six members reporting doubtful to commit themselves to voting for the bill. By the time of the floor action the poll indicated that the vote would be extremely close. Armed with that information the leadership secured promises from 13 Democrats who were planning to vote against the legislation that they would vote for it if their votes were needed to change defeat into victory.[48]

The passage of the second debt-limit increase of 1963, in August, was the occasion for a substantial amount of whip-directed activity. The Secretary of the Treasury persuaded one Southern Democrat to vote for the increase after the whip poll had shown him to be vacillating. The Speaker contacted 15 wavering Democrats directly and, as a result, persuaded 10 of them to vote for the bill. Chairman Mills was especially effective in getting Southerners to vote for the bill. Again, as in May, the leadership had ten "pocket votes," that is, men who preferred to vote nay but would vote aye if necessary to pass the bill.[49]

In summary, the whip's office performs its four functions in such a way as to enhance the chances of Democratic victories on floor votes in the House. No absolute figures can be given on votes won that would otherwise be lost. Yet the weight of evidence is that the efforts to insure a maximum attendance, to inform the Democratic membership of undesirable effects on the country if an Administration proposal is defeated, to ascertain voting expectations with great accuracy in advance, and to direct pressure to the precise spots where it will do the most good, result in some small, yet definite, net gains for the Democratic majority in the House.

– 4 –

David Truman has commented that "the persistent reality of party in the functioning of the [House] chamber is unmistakable."[50] Julius Turner stated that "Party pressure seems to be more effective than any other pressure on congressional voting."[51] Yet neither they nor any other commentators on Congress using primarily statistical indices based on roll call votes have been able to be more specific about the nature of party activity in the House. The indices describe the *results* of the activity. But the *activity itself* —the "reality" of Truman or the "pressure" of Turner—cannot be caught by indices of votes.

The whip organizations are at the core of party activity in the House, particularly on the Democratic side. Thus the data here presented on the

whip organizations are also data on parties in the House. They can be analyzed to provide a considerable range of generalizations about party activity in the House. Some of the generalizations which follow are quite speculative and demand much more research. Others come closer to being fully supported by the data on the whips.

1. The Democratic whip organization has become the focus of a corporate or collegial leadership in the House. Truman concluded that the evidence provided by record votes shows no collegial leadership,[52] although he indicated that the individual elective leaders in each party showed somewhat more unity. But observation of the Democratic whip organization suggests that the pattern of leadership in 1962 and 1963 was for the Speaker, Majority Leader, whip, deputy whip, and relevant committee chairman to work closely together in the effort to pass a given piece of legislation. To expect a greater degree of corporate leadership—including *all* major committee chairmen on every separate piece of major legislation—is unrealistic. Each chairman has time to be concerned only about the legislation produced by his committee. The major missing participant during the period of this study, whom one would expect to find in a collegial leadership because he has a legitimate interest in all major legislation, is the Chairman of the Committee on Rules.[53]

2. Truman found that the voting structure of the parties in Congress "was focused upon one or a pair of positions: the Floor Leaders, joined at times, particularly on the Democratic side, by the Whips and, among the House Democrats, impliedly by the Speaker."[54] For House Democrats the operation of the whip organization

helps explain why this focus is not mere coincidence. Even if the assistant whips do not uniformly "pressure" the members of their zones they do inform them of the voting preferences of the Speaker, Majority Leader, and whip. This information, as universally distributed to all Democrats, is one of the "triggers" which Bauer, Pool, and Dexter discuss.[55]

3. Truman suggests that the majority party has a natural basis for greater coherence than the minority party.[56] The Democratic whip organization, coordinated with the leadership offered by the President, helped the House Democrats to cohere on the major votes in 1962–1963. Similarly, the whip organization is an important institutional device for helping the House leadership perform a mediating role between the President and the rank and file Democratic membership. The elected legislative leaders of the President's party have a stake in his success in the House. The whip organization has a similar stake and also provides machinery for improving the President's chances.[57]

4. An important function of the Democratic whip organization is the carrying and recording of various bargains struck between party members on legislative matters. Within whip zones and even between whip zones both explicit and implicit bargains[58] are made between individual members. The whip organization then provides a framework for channeling the information on the bargains to a more central location—either the whip's office or the relevant Committee Chairman or one of the leaders individually. The transmission of information is incomplete but it is more complete than totally unorganized gossip.

5. The operations of the Democratic whip organization, especially of the sort noted in points 2 and 4 above,

suggest that information can be as important and as effective as "pressure" of the classic mold. Information about legislation and about the intentions of individual legislators can be used to cue voting behavior favorable to the President and the leadership.[59]

6. The growth in the strength, complexity, and importance of both party whip organizations in this century suggests a growing sense of party solidarity within the House. The whip organizations now involve 16 Republicans and 20 Democrats directly. These 36 men and women have made a commitment of time—which members of the House must necessarily hoard—to work for their respective parties within the House. Unless they felt that party work was worth doing, a sufficient number of such commitments, of a desirable calibre, might not be forthcoming.

7. The history of the party whip organizations suggests that the importance of the whip partly depends on the mode of leadership exercised by the Speaker or Minority Leader, and secondarily on the role of the Rules Committee Chairman. Strong, solitary leaders like Rayburn have relied less on the whip than leaders who seek and need the active help of others. Leaders with fewer resources, like McCormack and Halleck, necessarily rely more on others in the leadership circle—including the whip and his organization.

8. The contrast between the place of the Democratic whip organization and the Republican whip organization in 1962–1963 provides material for broader generalizations about the differences between the two parties in the House. The Democratic whip in these years was firmly lodged in a three-man leadership circle. His influence was great and his prospects for eventual advancement to Majority Leader were

good. The Republican whip, however, would never obtain another leadership post. In addition, he had to work not only with the Minority Leader but also subject to the decisions of the 35-man Republican Policy Committee, of which he was but one member.[60] The majority leadership appeared to be substantially more compact than the minority leadership.

9. At the same time several features of the two party whip organizations suggest that the customary characterization of the Democratic Party in the House as a loose coalition of disparate groups without much central allegiance and of the Republican Party in the House as a closely-knit body of men dedicated to common principles may be at least partially correct. The Democratic assistant whips are regarded primarily as informing agents rather than as pressuring agents, although individual assistant whips may on occasion choose to pressure their zone members. The Democratic whip's office keeps no systematic voting records with which to confront the less loyal members. The Republican assistant whips, however, are expected to work for a solid Republican vote in accord with the dictates of the Policy Committee. The Republican whip's office keeps voting records, even on teller votes, so that the whip may berate the goats and praise the sheep when the occasion demands. The method of selection of the assistant whips is also an important difference. The Democratic whip is presented with assistants he may not want. The Republican whip picks his own assistants.[61]

In short, the data suggest that a change is necessary in the typical description of the House which attributes, in the words of Professor Bone, "no consistently great influence in policy directing or in establishing party accountability for legislative program" to the party machinery.[62] As important pieces of party machinery the whip organizations possess such influence. How great and how consistent the influence, are still open questions. This article has attempted to provide some tentative answers to those questions.

NOTES

1. See Austin Ranney and Willmoore Kendall, *Democracy and the American Party System* (New York, 1956), p. 399; E. E. Schattschneider, *Party Government* (New York, 1942); and the Committee on Political Parties of the American Political Science Association, "Toward a More Responsible Two-Party System," *American Political Science Association Review,* 44 (Sept., 1950).

2. See David B. Truman, "The State Delegations and the Structure of Party Voting in the U.S. House of Representatives," *American Political Science Association Review,* 50 (Dec., 1956), 1023; Truman, *The Congressional Party* (New York, 1959), pp. vi–vii; Julius Turner, *Party and Constituency: Pressures on Congress* (Baltimore, 1951); and Avery Leiserson, *Parties and Politics* (New York, 1958), p. 379 (appendix).

3. Ralph Huitt, "Democratic Party Leadership in the Senate," *American Political Science Association Review,* 55 (1961), 334; see also Robert L. Peabody and Nelson W. Polsby, *New Perspectives on the House of Representatives* (Chicago, 1963), pp. 269–270.

4. See Huitt, *op. cit.;* Malcolm E. Jewell, "The Senate Republican Policy Committee and Foreign Policy," *Western Political Quarterly,* 12 (Dec.,

1959), 966–980; Hugh A. Bone, "An Introduction to the Senate Policy Committees," *American Political Science Association Review,* 50 (June, 1956), 339–359; George Galloway, "Leadership in the House of Representatives," *Western Political Quarterly,* 12 (1959), 417–441; and James A. Robinson, *The House Rules Committee* (Indianapolis, 1963). Paul Hasbrouck, *Party Government in the House of Representatives* (New York, 1927), is an older treatment of some parts of the House leadership.

5. These are "Whips' Effectiveness Tested on Close 1961 House Votes," *Congressional Quarterly,* Weekly Report, No. 24 (June 16, 1961), pp. 992–998; and Alfred Steinberg, "Shepherds of Capitol Hill," *Nation's Business* (Jan., 1952), pp. 31–33. The first article presents roll call data and infers "effectiveness" from them; but no direct link between the data and the whips is established. The second is a popular treatment of the role and importance of the whips.

   A short article for a small audience (University of Oklahoma alumni) but with some general interest is Carl Albert, "Oklahoma and the Democratic Whip," *Sooner Magazine* (July, 1955), pp. 18–19.

6. See Clem Miller, *Member of the House* (New York, 1962), pp. 52–54; DeAlva S. Alexander, *History and Procedure of the House of Representatives* (Boston, 1916), pp. 104–106; George Brown, *The Leadership of Congress* (Indianapolis, 1922), p. 222; Truman, *The Congressional Party, op. cit.,* pp. 227 ff.; Neil MacNeil, *Forge of Democracy* (New York, 1963), pp. 97–100; George Galloway, *History of the United States House of Representatives,* H. Doc. 246, 87th Cong., 1st sess. (1961), pp. 102–103; Floyd M. Riddick, *Congressional Procedure* (Boston, 1941), pp. 75–77; and Riddick, *The United States Congress: Organization and Procedure* (Manassas, Va., 1949), pp. 101–102.

7. Champ Clark, *My Quarter Century of American Politics* (New York, 1920), Vol. II, p. 337.

8. The name "whip" derives from the British fox-hunting term "whipper-in," used to describe the man responsible for keeping the hounds from leaving the pack. It was first applied to the British Parliament about 1770. For a description of the British whips see Roland Young, *The British Parliament* (London, 1962), pp. 75–77; also Eric Alexander, Viscount Chilston, *Chief Whip* (London, 1961).

   For a brief description of the whip in the United States Senate see a speech by J. Hamilton Lewis, long-time Democratic Senate whip, *Congressional Record,* Vol. 80, pt. 7, pp. 7044–7046 (1936).

9. See MacNeil, *op. cit.,* pp. 97–100; and Alexander, *op. cit.,* p. 104. See also David S. Barry, *Forty Years in Washington* (Boston, 1924), pp. 100 ff. for comments on one Republican whip in the late 19th Century, Omar Conger of Michigan.

10. Clark, *op. cit.,* p. 338, says he was acting as volunteer whip as late as 1909. Important Republicans who acted as volunteer whips in the late 19th Century were Thomas Reed of Maine and James Wilson of Iowa.

11. Alexander, *op. cit.,* note 6 above, p. 105, states that Watson was, in 1899 (his second term), the first whip chosen by party caucus; and he indicates that Tawney succeeded Watson. Alexander's assertion is repeated by MacNeil, p. 97; Galloway, *History,* p. 102; Steinberg, *op. cit.;* and in a speech by Representative Guy Hardy of Colorado in 1928, which is cited in Cannon's *Precedents,* Vol. VIII, p. 958 (1936).

   This view is mistaken. Tawney was the first whip and was succeeded by Watson in 1905; see the *New York Times,* Dec. 3, 1905, 3:2; the *Washington Post,* Dec. 3, 1905, 2:2 and Dec. 13, 1905, 4:6; Edward T. Taylor, *A History of the Committee on Appropriations, House of Representatives,* H. Doc. 299, 77th Cong., 1st sess. (1941), p. 51; and Charles W. Thompson, *Party Leaders of the Time* (New York, 1906), pp. 153, 195.

The exact date of Tawney's appointment as whip is as obscure as his method of appointment. Taylor, *loc. cit.,* gives the date as 1897 and says that Speaker Reed made the choice. Thompson, *op. cit.,* refers to Tawney as being whip in 1902, although he does not indicate how long he had then been so. Before 1920 the documentation for the identity of party whips was almost non-existent. I have therefore given footnote references identifying the whips before that date.

12. Kenneth W. Hechler, *Insurgency* (New York, 1940), p. 70.

13. See MacNeil and Alexander; also the *New York Times,* Jan. 20, 1928, and the *Washington Star,* March 14, 1809, 1:8; March 22, 1909, 1:5; and April 4, 1911, 4:2.

14. Cannon's *Precedents,* Vol. VIII, p. 961.

15. In 1919 the old-guard Republicans dominated the Party Conference, to the dismay of more progressive members. Fights over many issues, including the choice of the new whip, occurred in the Conference. See the *New York Times,* March 12, 1919, 1:4. Knutson, the winner, received 118 votes out of 182 cast.

16. The only reference to Burke as whip I could find was on the floor plan of the Capitol in the *Congressional Directory* for the 63d Congress. For Hamilton see the *Washington Star,* April 1, 1917, 1:2. Hamilton also returned a form to the office of the *Biographical Directory of Congress* in 1928 in which he indicated that he was the Republican whip in the 64th and 65th Congresses. Knutson listed his tenure as whip as the 66th and 67th Congresses, on a similar form. Vestal became whip in 1923, not in 1925 as the *Biographical Directory* states. The files of the *Biographical Directory* indicate that his service as whip began in 1923; so does his obituary in the *Anderson* (Ind.) *Daily Bulletin,* April 2, 1932.

17. See the *Washington Post,* Jan. 10, 1900, 4:5; and the *New York Times,* Jan. 10, 1900, 1:6. Sydney P. Epes of Virginia, who died two months later, was named assistant whip.

18. Lloyd's service as whip is mentioned in the following places: *Congressional Record,* Vol. 90, pt. 3, p. 3420 (1944); the *Hannibal* (Mo.) *Courier–Post,* April 4, 1944; and the *Canton* (Mo.) *Press–News,* April 4 (?), 1944. James E. Watson, in his memoirs, *As I Knew Them* (Indianapolis, 1936), p. 295, mentions Claude Swanson of Virginia as a Democratic whip. I have found no other substantiation for this, however. Lloyd was the designated Democratic whip during the entire time Watson was the Republican whip. I wish to thank Professor Clarence Berdahl for bringing Lloyd's service to my notice. See Berdahl's articles, "Some Notes on Party Membership in Congress," *APSA Review,* 43 (1949), 309–321, 492–508, 721–734, for a treatment of many important facets of party history.

19. The *Congressional Directory* floor plan of the Capitol for the 63d Congress shows Bell as whip. His obituary in the March 20, 1941, *Gainesville* (Ga.) *News* speaks of him as Democratic whip "for a term or two." Berdahl thinks that Bell was whip from 1909 until 1919; I have not been able to substantiate this. Bascom N. Timmons, in his *Garner of Texas* (New York, 1948), pp. 59–60, 61, 64, 74, indicates that John N. Garner was Democratic

whip, probably during the 1909–1913 period. I have been unable to find other evidence for this.

20. This expectation was not a guarantee, however. In 1962 all of the leaders advanced one place after the death of Speaker Rayburn. This provides some precedent but does not establish a pattern. For evidence that Albert's tenure as whip helped lead to his election as Majority Leader see Polsby, in Peabody and Polsby, *op. cit.*, pp. 246–247. It is customary, especially on the Democratic side, for the floor leader to become Speaker when that office falls vacant.

21. This statement is based on the floor plans of the Capitol in the *Congressional Directory* for each session. The record may be somewhat incomplete.

22. This information comes from a perusal of the Legislative Appropriations Acts in the *U. S. Statutes-at-Large*. The title "whip" was first used in the 1913 legislation.

23. When the Republicans captured the House in the 1952 elections John McCormack was slated to move from Majority Leader to minority whip. He asked Speaker Martin, Majority Leader Halleck, and Minority Leader Rayburn if he might keep one of his long-time employees as Administrative Assistant. He and the Republican whip, Les Arends, then agreed that they both would have Administrative Assistants.

24. The value of the party whip organizations was widely enough recognized in the House by the late 1950s for a portion of the Democratic membership to imitate the political parties and establish a third whip organization. In 1957 a loose alliance of liberal Democrats was formed in the House under the leadership of Representative Eugene McCarthy of Minnesota. This group immediately established a whip organization, which functioned at least sporadically. In 1959 both the Democratic Study Group and its whip organization were formally established. The Secretary of the DSG also serves as its whip.

25. See the speech by Majority Floor Leader John Q. Tilson of Connecticut, *Cong. Rec.,* Vol. 69, pt. 2, p. 1757 (1928).

26. Letter from Carl G. Bachmann to the author, August 15, 1963.

27. In 1949 Halleck expected Martin to appoint him Deputy Minority Leader and so did not desire to be whip. In 1955 Halleck saw no need to disturb the 11-year tenure of Arends as whip merely for the sake of a title.

28. Letter from Clarence Cannon to the author, September 23, 1963; Cannon's *Precedents,* Vol. VIII, pp. 961–962 (1936); and E. Pendleton Herring, "First Session of the Seventy-Third Congress," *American Political Science Association Review,* 28 (Feb., 1934), p. 69.

29. See the statement by John McCormack after Boland's death, *Congressional Record,* Vol. 88, pt. 3, p. 4318, 77th Cong., 2d sess. (1942). See also the *Washington Star,* August 18, 1935, D–2:6 and June 4, 1936, A–10:1; the *Washington Post,* August 25, 1935, III–3:2; and the *Scranton Times,* May 18, 1942.

30. The post of deputy whip as a formal leadership position was created in 1955 for Hale Boggs of Louisiana, the present whip. John Moss of California became deputy whip in 1962. Boland had a "principal assistant" or "chief assistant" whip, Thomas Ford of California. See the *Washington Star,* August 18, 1935, D–2:6, and *Congressional Record,* Vol. 88, pt. 3, p. 4320, 77th Cong., 2d sess. (1942).

31. Boland apparently appointed his own assistant whips. In 1939 he threatened to "fire" some of them for disloyalty to the President's program. *New York Times,* August 22, 1939, 20:3.

    The assistant whips may develop some independent weight in their state delegations. See the chapter by Alan Fiellin in Peabody and Polsby, *op. cit.,* p. 70.

32. In the Democratic Study Group the Secretary and whip since its founding has been Frank Thompson of New Jersey. He was elected initially and has continued to be re-elected every two years by the full membership of the DSG, which totaled 126 in 1963. He has appointed four regional whips, each of whom has either four or five regional subwhips reporting to him. The subwhips are responsible for calling from four to six other DSG members.

    The DSG whip organization takes no polls on legislation, since the group was formed on the basis of ideological congeniality. The organization distributes information on pending legislation and works for maximum attendance, particularly on teller votes on amendments in Committee of the Whole.

33. One primary fact determined the time span here studied—the availability of files.

34. This is not to suggest that Albert was not important as whip. Rayburn consulted him, but the whip organization as a whole was used less than in 1962–1963. It should be noted that when Albert became whip he replaced Percy Priest, who decided not to continue as whip in 1955 because he had become Chairman of the Committee on Interstate and Foreign Commerce. *Congressional Record,* Vol. 101, pt. 1, pp. 191–192 (1955).

35. An unusual instance of this occurred in the drive for adjournment in October, 1962, when the leadership was having difficulty in keeping a quorum in Washington. The whip's office called or sent telegrams to all missing Democrats from east of the Mississippi at their homes, asking them to return. A similar situation, even more acute, developed in 1963 after President Kennedy's assassination, as the House struggled until Christmas eve to pass a foreign aid appropriations bill acceptable to President Johnson.

36. For the 87th Congress *Congressional Quarterly* reports that Boggs had a 73 per cent and Moss a 91 per cent Kennedy Support Score.

37. See footnote 40, *infra,* for a listing of the votes chosen.

38. This evidence that assistant whips were more loyal (hence, more liberal) should be compared with Duncan MacRae's suggestion that elected party leaders tend to take middle-of-the-road positions on issues. MacRae, *Dimensions of Congressional Voting* (Berkeley and Los Angeles, 1958), ch. 4.

    The *Congressional Quarterly* study of the whips, *op. cit.,* p. 994, concludes that in terms of Democratic party support for the first half of the 1961 session: "The performance of the whips was matched roughly by that of the membership as whole . . ." David Truman, *The Congressional Party, op. cit.,* p. 227, attributes some of the influence of the principal whips in the House to "their individual positions in the voting structure of the party." Donald Matthews, *U. S. Senators and Their World* (Chapel Hill, 1960), suggests that the Senate whips tend to fall off in party-line voting.

39. The Republicans, starting with a base of greater party agreement on is-

sues, look on their assistant whips as definite agents of the leadership. The method of appointment for Republican assistant whips—by the chief whip himself—insures some accountability to the leadership. On the Democratic side Boggs obviously cannot assume that the assistant whip appointed by Howard Smith will be an avid Administration supporter.

Boggs summarized the job of assistant whip in a telegram to the *Shreveport* (La.) *Times* in the fall of 1963:

> The assistant whips keep members in their zones informed as to which bills will be scheduled for a vote and when. On a request from the House leadership, they ascertain how each member in their zone will vote on a specific measure, and report the results to the leadership. When important bills are being considered by the House, they try to make sure that the members from their zone are present for key votes. The assistant whips are responsible solely to their party colleagues in their zones. The executive branch has absolutely no voice in either selecting or removing assistant whips.

40. The specific issues in 1962 were: (1) final passage of the resolution disapproving the reorganization plan which would have created an Urban Affairs Department, (2) final passage of the 1962 Revenue Act, (3) final passage of an increase in the national debt limit, (4) recommittal motion of the feed-grains section of the farm bill, (5) recommittal motion substituting a one-year extension of reciprocal trade for the Trade Expansion Act, (6) recommittal motion on the accelerated public works bill, and (7) final passage of the bill authorizing the President to purchase U.N. bonds.

   The specific issues in 1963 were: (1) adoption of the resolution permanently enlarging the Rules Committee, (2) passage of an amendment to a supplemental appropriations bill adding $450 million to the accelerated public-works program, (3) recommittal motion deleting medical student loan provisions from the Health Professions Educational Assistance Act, (4) final passage of an increase in the national debt limit, (5) final passage of a bill authorizing a voluntary feed-grains acreage diversion program for 1964–1965, (6) final passage of Area Redevelopment Act amendments, (7) final passage of a second debt-limit extension, (8) recommittal motion on the tax bill making a tax cut dependent on reduced governmental spending, (9) final passage of a third debt-limit extension, and (10) final passage of the cotton bill.

   The recommittal motion on the 1963 tax bill did not fully meet the stated criteria, because part of the poll on the recommittal motion was taken through the Democratic members of the Committee on Ways and Means. The 15 zones used by these men when acting as the Democratic Committee on Committees were also employed in this poll and the results were channeled first to Chairman Mills and then to the whip's office. Aside from this significant deviation, however—a display of Mills's independent power—the whip's office performed its normal functions during this struggle. Since the bill was one of the most important to the Administration and the House leadership in 1963, an accurate picture of the whip system could hardly be given without including it here.

   A few examples in the text will come from whip operations on bills other than the 17 listed above.

41. The three lost were Urban Affairs and the farm bill in 1962 and the Area Redevelopment Act amendments in 1963. The phrase "close margin" means roll calls on which a change of 25 votes or less would

alter the result. Urban Affairs, the recommittal motion on the trade bill, and U.N. bonds were not "close" in 1962. Only the medical student loan provisions was not "close" in 1963. Nine of the 17 voting results could have been changed by a shift of 15 or fewer votes.

42. The Majority Manager of Telephones on the floor also instructs his operators to call each member's office when a vote is near but the operators do not specify what is at issue.

43. The *Congressional Quarterly* study of the first half of 1961, *op. cit.,* pp. 993–994, documents the high voting turnout in that session and suggests the whip organizations might be part of the cause.

44. The assistant whips had attendance records much like those of all Democrats on all roll calls, but on the 17 key votes they did somewhat better than the rank and file. In 1962 the assistant whips voted 83.4 per cent of the time on all roll calls and 84.7 per cent in 1963. But on the 17 key votes their voting attendance rose to 96 per cent.

45. The Democratic whip's office also relays to the leadership whatever information it receives about Republican voting probabilities. Such information may come from lobbyists, Executive officials, or personal contacts between Democratic and Republican members. The Republican and Democratic whips' offices do not, of course, trade information.

    Information on Republican voting tends to be quite unreliable when it reaches the Democratic whip's office. For example, during the debt-limit fight in May, 1963, it was supposed that at least eight to 10 Republicans would vote for the increase. Only one did. When the Administration lost the Area Redevelopment bill in June, 1963, the whip's office had received information that 21 Republicans would vote for the bill. Only 15 did. During the 1963 struggle over enlarging the Rules Committee six Republicans who finally voted with the Democratic leadership had been written off as lost to Halleck and Judge Smith.

46. There are several reasons for a member's making an inaccurate report of his position. He might want to avoid leadership pressure by not alerting anyone to his opposition. He might be annoyed at the inconvenience of repeatedly reporting his position. Finally, he might use the report of opposition as a bargaining device. For example, on the poll on the debt limit increase in May, 1963, a loyal Administration supporter from the midwest reported "doubtful" and, at the same time, indicated his eagerness for final Treasury confirmation that a new Internal Revenue Service installation would be located in his district.

47. Conceivably, some inferences might be drawn from a comparison of the winning percentage on roll calls used by *Congressional Quarterly* in computing its Presidential Support Index with the Administration's record of success on the key votes analyzed here. The question could be put whether the President won a greater percentage of the time when the Democratic whip organization was fully engaged in the battle. On the 17 key votes the President won 14 times—82 per cent support—as against an overall 85 per cent winning record (on 60 roll calls) in 1962. From this it might be argued that the whip organization made no material difference, since the winning percentages are about the same. But it might also be argued that since the roll calls used here represent the "toughest" of the more numerous roll calls chosen by *Congressional Quarterly* the winning percentage is higher than could be expected without concentrated whip activity.

48. Three of the 13 voted with the leadership even though they were not ulti-mately needed. The other 10 voted nay but remained on the floor after voting, ready to change their votes if necessary.

49. Seven of these 10, largely at the urging of Mills, voted aye even though not needed. Mills was anxious to have a respectably large margin of victory. He was trying to set a precedent for November, when another debt limit increase would be necessary.

50. Truman, "The State Delegations," *op. cit.,* p. 1045.

51. Turner, *op. cit.,* p. 23.

52. Truman, *The Congressional Party, op. cit.,* p. 245.

53. Truman's reference to "the ambiguity surrounding the term 'the leader-ship' " (*ibid.,* p. 282) is also to the point here. "The leadership" is a fairly precise term when used in connection with a specific piece of legis-lation. It always includes the Speaker, Majority Leader, whip, and Com-mittee Chairman. It may include the deputy whip, a Subcommittee Chair-man or a senior Committee member who is going to act as floor manager of the bill.

54. *Ibid.,* p. 285.

55. Raymond Bauer, Ithiel de Sola Pool, and Lewis A. Dexter, *American Busi-ness and Public Policy* (New York, 1963), p. 466.

56. Truman, *The Congressional Party, op. cit.,* p. 278.

57. See *ibid.,* ch. 8.

58. On implicit bargaining see Lewis A. Froman, Jr., *People and Politics* (Englewood Cliffs, N.J., 1962), pp. 55–56.

59. Again this coincides with the findings of Bauer, Pool, and Dexter, *op. cit.* The importance of information is highlighted by Charles Clapp, *The Con-gressman* (Washington, Brookings Institution, 1963). He reports, p. 302, that criticism of both party whip organizations by House members cen-ters "around the failure to perform the informing function." Lewis Anthony Dexter, in Peabody and Polsby, *op. cit.,* pp. 312 ff., discusses "the tyranny of information" in another context.

60. See the forthcoming book by Charles Jones on the House Republican Policy Committee.

61. The voting records of the 1963 Republican and Democratic assistant whips over the previous two years indicate that each party organization had a similar number of "mavericks." Five Democratic assistant whips had a mean Larger Federal Role Support Score 22.6 per cent lower than the mean Support Score of all 16 assistant whips who had been members of the 87th Congress. Five Republican regional and assistant whips had a mean Larger Federal Role Support Score 23 per cent higher than the mean Support Score of all 14 regional and assistant whips who had been members of the 87th Congress. The Support Scores for individual mem-bers come from *Congressional Quarterly Almanac* for 1962.

   Both the Republican and Democratic assistant whips had served, on the average, slightly more than nine years in the House by the end of 1963.

62. Hugh Bone, *American Politics and the Party System* (New York, 1955), p. 597.

15

THE FORMATION OF THE DEMOCRATIC STUDY GROUP

MARK F. FERBER

The Democratic party leadership cannot always lead the Democratic party in the House because the party itself is frequently divided. The situation of near paralysis that sometimes results is not equally beneficial to all congressmen, and thus, not tolerable to them all. Paralysis, or the inability to lead, generally favors those who least prefer changes in public policy. Thus, while conservatives can live with division and disunity, liberals find it more difficult to do so. From this dilemma arose the Democratic Study Group, a group of liberal, Democratic congressmen organized for the purpose of supplying a measure of coherence to the efforts of like-minded Democrats who could not always look to the Speaker or majority leader for vigorous leadership in policy areas where the party was deeply split. The study group has been influential in tiding the Democratic party in the House over an awkward period when the South, while declining numerically in the Democratic caucus, still holds many influential positions in the committee structure, owing to the seniority system, and maintains a substantial threat of coalescing with Republicans on measures sponsored by a Republican administration.

During the Kennedy and Johnson administrations, the study group was a useful device for strengthening the hand of House Democratic leaders in dealing with conservative Democratic chairmen, and more than once the study group was able to prevent the Speaker and southern conservatives from taking steps inimical to the interests of the liberal majority of House Democrats. Mark Ferber is Special Assistant to the President of the University of California. The following selection from his doctoral dissertation, published here for the first time, is based on extensive field work.

As the first session of the Eighty-sixth Congress (1959–1960) drew to a close, frustration within the liberal ranks in the House soared with the Washington summer temperature. While the traditionally conservative Senate appeared to be moving in a more liberal direction, it seemed that the liberals in

Printed by permission of the author.

the House were incapable of translating their increased strength into legislative results.

Many pieces of legislation considered vital to the liberal program had been sidetracked by one or another of the devices available to the conservative forces. Civil rights, one of the key items on the liberal agenda, was locked in the Rules Committee with little

chance of seeing daylight. The Depressed Area bill, which had been passed by the Senate and reported out by
the House Banking and Currency Committee early in the session, joined federal aid to education legislation and
the Civil Rights bill in the pigeonhole
that Rules Committee Chairman Howard Smith reserved for measures meeting with his disapproval. Twice, a
conservative president had exercised
the power of the veto to whittle down
the Housing bill to its bare essentials,
and the veto, or its threat, had been
effective in keeping a number of liberal
measures pared down to minimum
standards and expenditures. Finally,
the Landrum–Griffin bill had shown
that the conservative forces could not
only block liberal legislation but could
take the initiative and pass bills that
liberals viewed with distaste. Their
lack of communications, coordination,
and general ability in parliamentary
maneuver became increasingly apparent to the liberals as the session progressed, and it was against this background and state of mind that the
Democratic Study Group came into
existence.

The Early Efforts

Actually, the concept of a group of
liberal congressmen banding together
on a wide range of program goals was
not unique with the liberals in the
Eighty-sixth Congress. In general,
however, earlier efforts had tended
to be on an issue-by-issue, ad hoc
basis.[1] Gradually, from 1953 on, a
small group of liberals found themselves joining together with increased
frequency. Prominent among this
group were Congressmen Eugene Mc-
Carthy and John Blatnik (Minn.), Lee
Metcalf (Mont.), Frank Thompson
(N.J.), Stewart Udall (Ariz.), and Chet
Holifield and John Moss (Calif.).
While this pattern of interaction did

not bring about the formal trappings
that were to characterize the Democratic Study Group, it did point up
the advantages that joint action could
produce. Nothing like officers or a
staff developed, but Representative
McCarthy emerged as the generally
recognized leader of the group and
provided a good deal of informal leadership.

In 1957, following Eisenhower's landslide victory over Adlai Stevenson in
the face of Democratic majorities in
both houses of Congress, the group,
now frequently referred to as Mc-
Carthy's "Mavericks" or "Marauders,"
increased the frequency of its meetings. Operating on an informal basis,
they attempted to influence legislation
by increased communication on specific issues and with the creation of
an embryonic whip system for alerting
members to crucial votes on the floor.
On January 8, 1957, twenty-eight of the
liberals announced a broad, legislative
program that they hoped to promote
during the Eighty-fifth Congress.[2] On
the 30th of the same month, seventy-
nine members lent their names to this
"Democratic State of the Union Message" or "liberal manifesto" as it came
to be known. The even division of
forces in the House, however, precluded any major effort on the part
of the group, and little, other than the
germ of an idea about organization,
grew out of these efforts.

As the Eighty-fifth Congress drew to
a close, the nucleus of the McCarthy
group [3] sensed that Democratic chances
looked good in the upcoming 1958
elections. To help strengthen their
position in the House, they decided
to contact liberal candidates and offer
help in their respective elections.
Therefore, on August 25, 1958, twelve
Democratic members of the House
signed a joint letter to some eighty
new candidates offering "considerable

material available here in Washington that might be of assistance to you in your campaign."[4] These new candidates were urged to contact Representative Frank Thompson (N.J.), for help. In the landslide Democratic election of 1958, many of those helped by the McCarthy group were, in fact, elected and looked immediately to Thompson, Metcalf, and the others for directions when they arrived in Washington. Many of these new members were among the group that met to discuss plans to change the Rules Committee.[5]

While the actual impact of this "help" is difficult to measure, there can be no doubt about its effect upon the new members. From Woodrow Wilson on, political scientists have written about the quandry and confusion facing the new member of Congress.[6] In this respect, the Class of 1958 was certainly no different from its predecessors. Yet, with Thompson, Metcalf, Udall, and a host of experienced congressmen there to help, many of the problems traditionally facing new members were eased. Temporary office space was provided the newcomers until their own offices were assigned. Materials were made available dealing with the range of issues likely to come up in the forthcoming session of Congress. Socialization and a general "getting to know each other" took place far more rapidly as a result of the calculated efforts on the part of the old McCarthy group. Seminars, run for the administrative assistants to the new group of congressmen, dealt with such subjects as the prerogatives available to all members (reduced rate radio and TV facilities, district office space, and so forth), and other aspects involved in setting up a congressional office in Washington.

Thus, during the early days of the new Congress a pattern of contact was established that was to become formalized in September with the formation of the Democratic Study Group. Increasingly, as the session moved along its desultory path, the necessity for organization impressed itself upon an ever larger number of liberal members. In particular, a group of them, concentrated in the Committee on Education and Labor, met together to discuss common problems and the possibilities of a more formal organization.

The nature of this committee and the subject matter that came before it made it a natural point of interest to the liberal forces. Although Speaker Rayburn had refused to accede to their designs for altering the Rules Committee, he had strengthened the liberal side on the Education and Labor Committee. The opening of the Eighty-sixth Congress had found five Democratic vacancies available on the committee, and all of these had been filled by freshmen from the northern and western parts of the country who were committed to many of the liberal programs that were being fought through the committee.[7]

In addition, Lee Metcalf (Mont.), who was ultimately to become the first chairman of the Democratic Study Group, had previously served on the committee for some time and was one of the chief congressional proponents of federal aid to education. As a result of his abilities he had been tapped by the House leadership for service on the more powerful Ways and Means Committee, but he remained in constant contact with his former associates on Education and Labor. Also serving on the committee were Udall, Thompson, James Roosevelt (Calif.), and Edith Green (Ore.), all of whom were to figure prominently in the formation of the group.

As the session wore on, and particularly after passage of the Landrum–Griffin Act had demonstrated their weaknesses, the liberals on the Education and Labor Committee continued to hold informal discussions among themselves. In addition, many disgruntled freshmen were brought into the conversations along with such veterans as Holifield (Calif.), Sidney Yates (Ill.), and William Green (Pa.). Finally, although he did not join the group formally, Congressman Richard Bolling (Mo.), recognized as a protegé of Speaker Rayburn, was a frequent participant in these meetings. Bolling's close friendship with the Speaker made him an important addition to the group; furthermore, as a link between the liberal organization and the established leadership, Bolling played an essential role in seeing to it that the organization stayed within the accepted norms of the House of Representatives.

Against a background of growing frustration, two factors combined to give special impetus to the establishment of the Democratic Study Group and to the particular leadership structure that developed. First, the chaos characterizing the liberal forces during the Landrum–Griffin debate provided a catalyst for action. The abysmal state of organization, the total absence of communication, and the general ineptitude in debate that had led to passage of an antilabor bill provided an example that was obvious to everyone. The importance of the Landrum–Griffin Act in the genesis of the Democratic Study Group cannot be overemphasized.

A second factor of significance was the deep concern felt by many of the older members of the McCarthy group over the splintering up into small groups that was occurring within the liberal camp. Frustrated by the course of the session, some of the more extreme members from northern and western states had been meeting and taking action that could only undermine a united liberal effort in the House. Thus, in a futile attempt to retaliate against southern conservatives, this small band had tried to hold up peanut and cotton legislation without recognizing the consequences for nonsouthern peanut and cotton districts and with seeming disregard for the opprobrium that such action brought from the Speaker and other senior members.

Many of these members had also participated in a series of meetings under the general leadership of Congressman James Roosevelt (Calif.). Calling themselves the "Liberal Project" and moving far beyond the day-to-day concerns of legislation before the Eighty-sixth Congress, the group had met with outside experts for a series of conferences primarily concerned with broad issues in the field of foreign affairs and disarmament.[8] The emergence of Roosevelt as the leader of this small band posed a special problem to Metcalf, Thompson, and the other, older members of the McCarthy group. While the son of the former President had served since 1955 in the House, his reputation among his fellow members had been made far more on the basis of headlines and speaking than by dint of hard, legislative homework. It seemed apparent to the members who ultimately moved into the leadership positions of the Democratic Study Group that Roosevelt had consistently been playing to an audience outside the House of Representatives and outside his own congressional district. It was felt that he was using the House as a forum to reach a national audience, and in the day-to-day workings within committee and in strategy meetings, his penchant for grabbing headlines rather than doing hard work had made him less than popular with many of his colleagues. This behavior also led the more senior members to view him as "irresponsible." At the same time, the image of the Roosevelt name, coupled with his own dynamic personality, made him a threat to a well-organized "working" group of Democratic congressmen.

In order to forestall the organization of smaller groups and to contain extremist elements, as well as to improve communication and coordination, it was decided to form an organization of congressional liberals. In early September, Metcalf and Thompson, after talking with Bolling, went to see Speaker Rayburn to acquaint him with their plans. While the Speaker was far from excited about the proposal, he did recognize the legitimacy of their claims and gave them his limited blessing.

The Formation of the Group

Having assured the Speaker that their efforts in no way constituted a threat to his leadership and, thus, having neutralized what could have been a major hurdle to their plans, the founders of the Democratic Study Group set to work.

Capitalizing on the deep concern shared by all the liberal members over the fate of the pigeonholed Civil Rights bill, they sent the following letter to approximately eighty-five members from northern and western states: [9]

Dear Colleague:

You are invited to a meeting of northern and western Democrats to be held tomorrow morning—Saturday—at 10 A.M., in the Public Works Committee Room, 1304, New House Office Building.

Action on civil rights, one pressing matter still unresolved, will be discussed. Also, we would like to take this opportunity to consider what should be done to prepare the most effective operation next year on imperative issues of concern to an effective party program.

We are mindful of the shortness of this invitation, but feel it is the last opportunity to meet and plan together, in order to avoid some of the mistakes of this session and make an affirmative record in the next year.

If you cannot be present, we would appreciate your sending a staff member to represent you.

Sincerely,

John A. Blatnik	George Rhodes
Chet Bowles	Henry S. Reuss
Lee Metcalf	Frank Thompson, Jr.

Given the short notice and the fact that the meeting was on a Saturday morning, the planners were quite pleased and surprised with the turnout. More than forty members or their representatives were present. The idea of a formal organization apparently had appeal for many of the liberal group, and the ideas of the original planners met with considerable approval.

"It was like an old time revival meeting," said one of the staff people who participated, "as member after member got up to confess his own failure or frustration and to signify his own willingness to work with others for the common good."[10] This feeling of enthusiasm was to characterize the remaining meetings of the group during the closing days of the session. As attendance increased, the leaders of the emerging group continued to be pleased by the response that their plans seemed to evoke.

The first meeting, on Saturday, September 5, 1959, was presided over by Metcalf. Having elicited generalized support for the notion of a formal organization, it was necessary to set up precise outlines for the group. A twelve-man Select Planning Committee, under the Chairmanship of Congressman B. F. Sisk (Calif.), was established to prepare plans and report back at a meeting set up for Tuesday, September 8. In addition, the newly formed group decided to hold a caucus immediately preceding the opening of the second session of the Eighty-sixth Congress in January, 1960, in order to plan broad strategy for the session. Hope was also voiced about the possibility of undertaking some research on key liberal issues during the three months between adjournment and the opening of the second session.

On Monday, September 7, Sisk's Planning Committee met in his office and worked up the details of the organizational outlines that the group should take. In addition to a chairman, vice-chairman, and secretary, the Select Planning Committee recommended the creation of a thirty-three-man policy committee to serve as a kind of "oversized" executive committee. The Planning Committee also envisioned this policy committee as serving as a whip organization for the entire liberal group. Dividing the country outside of the South into six regions, Sisk's committee suggested representation of the policy committee in rough proportion to each region's Democratic strength in the House. While one commentator's observation that the large-sized committee "exemplifies the liberals' ineptitude for tight organization"[11] may have been correct, the positive benefit of attaching many members to positions of importance (with a consequent stake in the organization) seems to have been a factor which was given greater weight by the Planning Committee. As we shall see, the large policy committee idea met with resistance from the start, and subsequent organizational modifications did reduce it to the role of a whip organization.

The second meeting of what was to become the Democratic Study Group took place as planned on Tuesday, September 8. Again using the cement of civil rights to attract a good attendance, Metcalf's announcement of the meeting featured the fact that "Congressman Manny Celler will discuss strategy on the Civil Rights discharge petition." Metcalf then went on to note that "the Interim Planning Committee . . . will offer recommendations on other subjects of urgent interest to the group."[12]

At the Tuesday meeting, which was chaired by Congressman Sisk, so much time was consumed by the discussion of civil rights matters that the only proposal of the Select Planning Committee that could be acted upon was approval of the initial slate of officers. Hence, another meeting of the whole group was scheduled for the next day. To House Democrats who had not responded to previous invitations, the following notice went out:[13]

Dear Democratic Colleague:

This is to invite you to attend a meeting to be held tomorrow morning, Wednesday, September 9, at 10:00 A.M., in the House Judiciary Committee Room 346. This will be a follow-up of previous meetings of northern and western Democrats.

We hope that you will take the time to come and sit down with us to discuss our mutual problems and how we can attain the legislative aims of our Democratic Party.

Sincerely,

John A. Blatnik   Henry S. Reuss
Chet Bowles   George M. Rhodes
Lee Metcalf   Frank Thompson, Jr.
Bernie Sisk

More than fifty offices responded, and the turnout at the September 9 meeting was so encouraging to the founders of the group that they decided to move ahead with the election of officers.[14] With Sisk presiding, the group unanimously elected Metcalf as Chairman, Frank Thompson as Secretary, and James Roosevelt as Vice-chairman.

Roosevelt's inclusion had been made to ensure the broadest possible involvement among liberal ranks in the Congress. As leader of the so-called red-hots, it was important to the future operation of the Democratic Study Group that he be included in the leadership. At the same time, however, as vice-chairman, he was the natural choice to succeed Metcalf as chairman in the event that Metcalf vacated the post.[15] Given Roosevelt's reputation in the House, this distinct possibility did not augur well for the future of the group.

The solution to what could have been a serious organizational problem was solved by surrounding Roosevelt with additional vice-chairmen. Thus, once the initial selections had been made, a "discussion" of the proposed organizational pattern broke out. It was pointed out that the thirty-three-man policy committee conceived by the Sisk committee was too large and cumbersome to function as a genuine leadership element. On the other hand, the three men already selected were obviously too small a group to represent the different shades of opinion within the group.

A "compromise" between the original plan and the suggestions and criticisms voiced at the meeting was finally developed. Adopting the regional principle that had been the basis for appointment to the original policy committee, one vice-chairman was proposed from *each* of the regions. These vice-chairmen, together with the chairman and secretary, would form an Executive Committee to plan the work of the group and formulate an agenda for the coming session of Congress. This solution won the overwhelming support of those present at the meeting and the group proceeded to select John Blatnik (Minn.), Sidney Yates (Ill.), Abraham Multer (N.Y.), Frank Coffin (Maine), and William Green (Pa.), as vice-chairmen on a co-equal basis with Roosevelt.

With the election of twenty members to the Policy Committee, the group broke up for the session.[16] Highlighting their refusal to abide by the traditional folkways of the House which place a heavy premium on seniority, it is interesting to note that five of the twenty members of the Policy Committee were freshmen who had only been elected to Congress the preceding year.[17] It was understood that all of the elections would be "temporary," pending an early January caucus in which all organizational decisions would be reviewed and plans for the second session of the Congress developed. In the interim, the Executive Committee was to proceed with research and planning.

During the next few days, the Executive Committee selected a name for the group. After considerable discussion, the suggestion of Congressman Chet Holifield (Calif.), to adopt the neutral-sounding name, "Democratic Study Group," was accepted.

On September 12, 1959, Metcalf, as the temporary chairman of the DSG, addressed a letter to all northern and western Democratic members of the House.[18]

Appended to the letter was a return slip indicating the name of the congressman, his district address, office number in Washington, and suggesting that if he were interested in co-operating with the DSG, he should return the slip to Metcalf. The results of this mailing were more than satisfactory to the leadership of the new group, and these return slips became the basis for the membership list of the Democratic Study Group.

The Composition of the Group

In many respects, the members of the Democratic Study Group were remarkably similar to the average member of Congress. In other ways, however, certain distinctions characterized group members. Because some of these differences may help to account for the particular behavior or issue-orientation of the Democratic Study Group, it is important to note where the group differed from the Congress as a whole.

Although the study group claimed an initial membership of "around" 125, the actual membership list has been kept secret by all of those associated with the organization. From published material and interviews, however, it is possible to construct a list of ninety-four members of the original group.[19]

. . .

While the study group and its leadership subgroup contained a large number of members from safe districts, the percentage from fighting and marginal districts was much larger than among Democrats generally. In part, the study group can be seen as a reflection of the tension and frustration that these members experienced during the first session. In particular, it is important to note that twenty-two of the twenty-six Democratic Study Group members from marginal districts were freshmen. (See Table 1.) Most of these had been swept into office during the landslide election of 1958 and had campaigned on extremely liberal platforms. Their first year in office, however, had been a time of chaos and disorganization for the liberals and the study group offered a vehicle for trying to translate their campaign oratory into practical results.

It was this climate of opinion among many disorganized individuals that allowed the leadership group to structure an organization like the Democratic Study Group. The "leaders" themselves tended, like the Democratic party as a group, to come from safe districts. The feeling of frustration provided them with the raw material to build the type of organization that they had been talking about since the

Dear Fellow Democrat:

Democrats in the Congress are being criticized, unfairly at times, for failure to carry out to a greater extent the legislative program spelled out in the Democratic Platform. One reason for lack of success in some of our efforts has been a breakdown of communication among members who favor such a program.

To remedy this lack of communication, and thus to achieve a better record next year than this, a number of us felt that we should have an organization before which we could discuss legislation, both as introduced and as reported, and be able to present the problems of our Districts, States and Regions to others.

We have held several meetings and have organized the Democratic Study Group on a preliminary basis. More than 70 members have attended one or more of these meetings. We have established a tentative whip organization. We have elected a temporary steering committee, responsible to the will of a majority of the board group of participating Members of the House. Meetings during the past week will permit research and organizational details to go forward during the recess. The organization is subject to ratification and such modification as may be voted at a meeting of Democratic Members participating to be called early in January 1960.

Of course, we all realize that there will be basic conflicts between individual beliefs and among the interests of the Districts we represent. But these may be resolved in a freer discussion of each other's problems than we are able to get from floor debate. No individual participating will be asked to bind himself to a group decision.

We would welcome your participation. If you wish to join us, please fill out the form below and return it to me.

Sincerely,
Lee Metcalf
Temporary Chairman
Democratic Study Group

TABLE 1   Party Competition for House Seats, Eighty-sixth Congress

CATEGORY	HOUSE	GOP	DEMOCRATS	DSG	LEADERS
Safe	260 (59.6%)	44 (28.8%)	216 (76.4%)	55 (58.5%)	17 (63.0%)
Fighting	71 (16.3%)	48 (31.4%)	23 (8.1%)	13 (13.8%)	5 (18.5%)
Marginal	105 (24.1%)	61 (39.8%)	44 (15.5%)	26 (27.7%)	5 (18.5%)
Totals:	436 (100%)	153 (100%)	283 (100%)	94 (100%)	27 (100%)

Source: Congressional Quarterly, Weekly Report, Vol. XX, Special Supplement.

days of the old "McCarthy Marauders."

Two factors that may help to account for the development of the Democratic Study Group revolve around the age and seniority of its members. Since power and status in the House are, at least in part, a function of the member's length of service, it would not be surprising to find a large grouping of younger and less senior members in an organization which sought to alter the power structure in the House.

These generalizations are confirmed by the data presented in Table 2. In general, the members of the Democratic Study Group were younger and less senior than the House or either political party, and the group included a larger percentage of freshmen than the other categories.

Since a good deal of the power within the House devolves upon the highly structured committee system, the relative force of the Democratic Study Group on the different committees is of key importance in analyzing its strength and weakness.

In the 86th Congress, the members of the Democratic Study Group held the number of seats on the twenty standing committees as shown in Table 3.

In general, the membership of the Democratic Study Group was spread throughout the committees of the House. Power for the group was concentrated in Banking and Currency, Education and Labor, and Foreign Affairs, and the newly created Committee on Science and Astronautics. In all of these committees but the last, the study group also had the advantage of cooperative chairmen. In the three most prestigious committees, Appropriations, Ways and Means, and Rules, their numbers were restricted, but they had sufficient strength to be heard.

Religion and race

The religious divisions in the House provide us with interesting contrasts between the two political parties and between the Democratic Study Group and the rest of the Democratic party. The frequently heard expression that the Republican party is congenial to white Protestant Americans, while the Democrats tend to give greater representation to minority groups, is certainly borne out by our data. Additionally, the image of the South as essentially a Protestant center, regardless of party affiliation, emerges from our study. Of the 120 members from the southern area (eleven ex-confederate states plus Oklahoma and Kentucky), only 7, or 5.8 per cent, were Catholic, and no Jews sit in Congress from these states. (See Table 4.)

As Table 4 suggests, when compared to the House as a whole, or to the full membership of each of the political parties, the Democratic Study Group

TABLE 2 Age, Seniority, and Number of Freshmen, Eighty-sixth Congress

	HOUSE	REPUBLICANS	DEMOCRATS	DSG	LEADERS
Average Age	52.4	53.8	50.9	46.8	46.6
Seniority *	5.4	5.5	5.2	3.4	3.5
Freshmen	82 (18.8%)	19 (12.4%)	63 (22.2%)	34 (36.1%)	6 (22.2%)

* Measured in numbers of terms served in Congress.
Sources: Congressional Quarterly, *Weekly Report*, Vol. XX, No. 5 (February 2, 1960), for ages; *Congressional Directory*, Eighty-sixth Congress 1st session, for seniority and freshmen.

TABLE 3   Distribution of Seats on the Twenty Standing Committees, Eighty-sixth Congress

COMMITTEE	TOTAL	REPUBLICAN	DEMOCRATIC	DSG
Agriculture	34	12	22	3
Appropriations	50	20	30	8
Armed Services	37	14	23	6
Banking/Currency	30	11	19	13
District of Columbia	25	9	16	3
Education/Labor	30	10	20	12
Foreign Affairs	32	11	21	9
Government Operations	30	11	19	8
House Administration	25	9	16	6
Interior/Insular Affairs	30	12	18	7
Interstate/Foreign Commerce	33	12	21	4
Judiciary	32	11	21	6
Merchant Marine and Fisheries	31	11	20	8
Post Office and Civil Service	25	9	16	8
Public Works	34	12	22	4
Rules	12	4	8	1
Science and Astronautics	25	9	16	9
Un-American Activities	9	4	5	0
Veterans' Affairs	23	8	15	4
Ways/Means	24	9	15	6

tended to overrepresent both Catholic and Jewish members while underrepresenting Protestants. The "leadership" of the study group, however, tended to give less representation to Catholic members. This latter fact can be largely explained by the heavy concentration of Catholic members from a relatively small number of urban areas, many of them still boss controlled. For example, more than half of the seventy-six Catholic Democrats in the Eighty-sixth Congress came from New York City (eight), Chicago (seven), Philadelphia (four), Massachusetts (eight), Connecticut (five), and New Jersey (five). While the study group did not fight the large Democratic machines around the country, members from these areas

TABLE 4   Religious Affiliation of House Members, Eighty-sixth Congress

GROUP	PROTESTANT	ROMAN CATHOLIC	JEWISH	OTHER *	TOTAL
House	331 (75.9%)	91 (20.8%)	10 (2.3%)	4 (1.0%)	436
Republicans	137 (89.5%)	14 (9.2%)	1 (0.7%)	1 (0.7%)	153
Democrats	194 (68.6%)	77 (27.0%)	9 (3.2%)	3 (1.2%)	283
DSG	50 (53.3%)	36 (38.3%)	7 (7.2%)	1 (1.0%)	94
Leaders	21 (77.7%)	4 (14.8%)	2 (7.4%)	0 (0.0%)	27

* Includes 1 Sikh and 3 "not given."
Source: Congressional Quarterly, *Weekly Report*, Vol. XX.

were frequently not the most energetic congressmen in the Democratic camp. Thus, many were nominal members of the study group but did not participate in its inner workings.

While the religious distribution of these congressmen makes for interesting data, the significance of these data is more difficult to analyze. In particular, the relationship between religious affiliation and voting or issue-orientation is not an automatic one. It could certainly be argued, however, that the issues of federal aid to parochial schools and birth control may create a major problem for the Democratic Study Group because these issues may divide Catholic and non-Catholic liberals. At this point, it is sufficient to note, with regard to the religious factor, that the Democratic Study Group did give greater representation to both Catholic and Jewish members than either the House as a whole or either of the two political parties.

The factor of race presents an easier, if less meaningful, picture. Only four Negroes served in the Eighty-sixth Congress. All were Democrats and two (Nix, Pa., and Diggs, Mich.) were members of the Democratic Study Group. The two nonmembers (Dawson, Ill., and Powell, N.Y.), were both committee chairmen, and both had built unique careers in the House. Dawson was part of the House "establishment," while Powell had followed a highly erratic path. Both frequently voted with the liberals, but neither was prepared to become part of a group effort nor to accept the discipline that was involved by membership in the group.

The Recess

With the end of the first session, the research operation of the Democratic Study Group began to function. Eschewing the heavy barrage of press releases that had frequently tended to characterize liberal efforts in the past, the Executive Committee quietly set about producing factual material that could be of benefit to members both during the recess as they toured their home districts and as background material for the fight during the second session of the Congress. Some of the more experienced administrative assistants prepared a series of staff papers which allowed the members to talk knowledgeably in their home districts about some of the crucial problems facing the Congress. This staff work produced, for the first time, a set of research papers aimed directly at the liberal members of Congress and covering some of the issues in which they were interested.

As an example, following President Eisenhower's attack on the spending record of the first session of the Eighty-sixth Congress,[20] an eight-page, single-spaced pamphlet was mimeographed and sent to all of the members.[21] Utilizing speeches from the *Congressional Record*, statistical data, and other information, the paper refuted the President point by point and attempted to show how the programs envisioned by the liberals would have aided the economy in recovering from the recession of 1958.

Other publications distributed during the recess included *The Fight in 1959*, which consisted of speeches and appendix material from the *Congressional Record* covering the important issues that had been before the first session, and a summary of the activities of the so-called Republican–Southern Democratic Coalition.[22]

During the recess, meetings continued to be held in Washington among those members of the group who had returned from visits to their constituencies or had decided to remain in the Capitol. A rough plan of organization for the opening of the second session was worked out, and the increasing response from members who had not attended the September meetings indicated that the possibilities for an effective organization were increasing.

While, as we have noted, the new group consciously shied away from overexposure through the news media, word of the undertaking gradually began to spread. Recognizing that the newspapers could magnify their efforts into a "revolt" against the established House leadership, Metcalf and Thompson went out of their way to point up their basic accord with the Speaker and Majority Floor Leader. Nothing, they recognized, could sidetrack the development of the group faster than the express disapproval of the leadership, and they spared no effort to ensure that this did not take place.

The first press release of the group, sent out on December 21, 1959, gives a clear emphasis to the image the group was trying to create. Noting that "A number of newspapermen have asked about current and future activities of the Democratic Study Group," the release merely made available to the press a letter and memorandum that had been sent to members of the study group on December 18.[23] For our purposes, the memorandum is particularly interesting in terms of setting the "tone" that Metcalf and Thompson hoped to establish for the group. After noting that "we have been unable to communicate effectively, to study legislation from a broad policy viewpoint, or to work together to the degree necessary to implement a legislative program consistent with our Democratic Platform and vital to our Districts, States, regions, the Nation and the free world . . ." the memo specifically went on to point out that the members of the Democratic Study Group "have no conflicts with the Democratic leadership of the House, nor with the National Committee or Advisory Council. To the degree that our Democratic Study Group can be made an effective instrument, we will supplement and assist the leadership in furthering our party's program."[24] By maintaining a frank and candid relationship with the press corps and by holding down the more flamboyant liberal rhetoric, Metcalf and Thompson were able to build a favorable image in the press while keeping a lid on all talk of "revolt."

Actually, very little press coverage was given to the new group, and those stories that did appear were generally favorable. The first piece that attempted to analyze the Democratic Study Group appeared in the *Wall Street Journal*, on November 23, 1959. Written by Robert Novak, one of the more perceptive journalists covering Capitol Hill, the *Journal* article pointed out how the liberals, having been "frustrated over the course of this year's session . . . [were] changing tactics for the year ahead."[25] Novak noted the liberals' highly publicized and unsuccessful attempt to "clip the powers of the Rules Committee" in January 1959 and contrasted it with the Study Group's "reticence to discuss . . . plans . . . and scheming behind closed doors."[26]

As the opening of the second session of the Eighty-sixth Congress drew near, mention in the press of the new liberal organization in the House became more frequent. Generally, references to the study group appeared in articles dealing with the battle that was beginning to form over the civil rights issue, but a few articles, usually favorable, dealt with the events leading up to the group's formation and its goals for the coming session.[27]

The careful groundwork and moderate tone taken by Metcalf and Thompson produced the kind of coverage that they had hoped for. Most of the stories that mentioned the Democratic Study Group took pains to point out the absence of any "revolt" against the established Democratic leadership. Drew Pearson, for example, noted that the target of the Group was "not Mr. Sam whom they love, but Dixiecrats who vote with the Republicans."[28] The *St. Louis Post-Dispatch* headlined a story by one of its Washington correspondents, "Liberal Bloc Is Trying to Avoid Fight With House Leadership."[29]

This strategy with regard to the leadership was highly successful. Having been informed of their activities from the start, Rayburn adopted a somewhat paternalistic attitude toward the study group and on one occasion was quoted as referring to the group as "good boys" who "probably will be a help."[30] This view was also confided to Bolling, who continued to serve as an informal link between the Speaker and the study group. Rayburn's problems with the obstreperous Rules Committee and his belief that the Democratic Study Group was being led by "responsible" members undoubtedly helped to place the group in a favorable light. The continued attitude of "responsible" action and the growing effectiveness of the group in the second session of the Eighty-sixth Congress fostered Rayburn's positive view of them. When, in January 1961 the Speaker found himself engaged in a struggle with Chairman Smith over expanding the size of the Rules Committee, it was the Democratic Study Group that provided the bulk of the votes for the Speaker, and Bolling and Thompson were largely responsible for directing the attack on Rayburn's behalf.[31]

The Presession Caucus

As 1959 faded into history, the leadership of the Democratic Study Group began a round of meetings aimed at developing strategy for the 1960 session of the Eighty-sixth Congress. Of particular importance was the establishment of legislative priorities that could ensure the support of a maximum number of nonsouthern Democrats and the development of strategies for bringing these measures through the complicated legislative mill.

On January 5, the Executive and Policy committees met together for the express purpose of deciding those issues on which the group should focus during the forthcoming session. After a lengthy closed-door meeting, agreement was reached on the following seven substantive issues: civil rights, federal aid to education, depressed areas, increased minimum wages, housing and urban renewal, farm program, and broadened social security coverage to include medical care financed under the Social Security system. With the possible exception of the farm program, it was felt that these issues contained no serious, divisive elements for northern and western liberals and could thus ensure maximum cohesion of the group. Like other earlier decisions, however, final approval was left to the caucus of all members that had been scheduled for January 7.

The caucus itself indicated the success of the work that had been undertaken during the recess. While exact figures are unavailable, more than one hundred congressional offices were represented at the meeting. All told, thirty-four different states outside of the South were involved through one or more members. The cautious approach of the leadership and its efforts to hold the legislative goals to those issues which united liberals produced widespread consensus among the participants at the meeting. The temporary elections of Metcalf, Thompson, the six regional vice-chairmen, and the Policy Committee members were all ratified by the full membership of the group. In addition, widespread agreement was achieved for the legislative priorities that had been established at the earlier meeting of the Policy Committee.

The only major modification to the initial format concerned the actual operational organization of the group itself. After approving the issues on which to concentrate, considerable discussion was devoted to the most practical way to approach each substantive area. It soon became apparent that the large-sized Policy Committee would not be suited to this highly technical role. After a number of alternatives had been offered, it was decided to form task forces for each of the issues that the Democratic Study Group had decided to pursue in the second session. These specialized groups would be responsible for keeping members informed on the substance of the legislation and for developing specific parliamentary strategies in their respective areas. Metcalf was given responsibility for determining the special interests of the various members and assigning them to the task force where their talents could best be utilized.

The following congressmen were named to head task forces: Clem Miller, area redevelopment; James Roosevelt, civil rights; Frank Thompson, education; George McGovern, farm policy; Martha Griffiths, housing; James Quigley, minimum wage; and Thaddeus Machrowicz, social security. In addition, two more generalized task forces, foreign policy and economic policy, were created and chaired by Frank Coffin and Henry Reuss. With the establishment of these issue-oriented task forces, the Policy Committee's priority-setting function disappeared. The Policy Committee, however, was maintained in order to perform the vital role of a whip organization for alerting members to crucial floor activity.

To assess fully the impact of the Democratic Study Group, it is important to recognize some of the problems that those who formed the group were attempting to solve by its creation.

The Communications Problem

One of the major problems facing the liberals within the Eighty-sixth Congress was a breakdown in any kind of communication pattern between members representing districts across the country from the Northeast through the Midwest to the Pacific Coast. Little has been written about this problem, yet it is important to recognize that the average congressman is tied to an extraordinarily structured set of relationships which take up a good deal of his working time.[32] In addition to belonging to a party which places certain demands on his time, the average member is associated with a state delegation and, most importantly, is directly oriented toward his formal committee assignments. Demands not directly related to the work of Congress, but intimately involved with his own chances for reelection, take up a considerable portion of his working day. The running of an office, which is a uniquely personal aspect of congressional life, consumes vast amounts of time. Finally, in all but the safest of congressional districts, the care and feeding of the district and the problem of keeping in front of hometown media are of signal import. Furthermore, this role of "representative" forces the average congressman to spend a good deal of time dealing with administrative agencies and various offices of the federal government, seeing to it that son John gets the service discharge that his mother is requesting, checking into a pension problem for an elderly constituent, making certain that private bills flow through the normal channels of Congress, leading local businessmen through the myriad agencies that might be able to help in the packaging of some local product.

While the size of the House seems reasonably small, one is impressed with the general lack of familiarity among most of the junior members. True, they recognize their colleagues away from the Congress, and a general aura of comraderie exists when they meet, but, during the early years of his tenure, the typical congressman generally does not get to know very well those members beyond his state delegation, his committee, and those occupying offices near him. Only after time, as the congressman moves from committee to committee, as his stature rises within the House, and his abilities come to the fore, does he gain wide acquaintanceship on anything but a most casual basis with many of his fellow members.[33]

The meetings at cocktail parties or in the general social world of Washington are remarkably devoid of serious policy comment, and the result is a general breakdown among large groups of congressmen sharing similar policy goals. It was this breakdown that the Democratic Study Group sought to counter through regular communication, both written and face to face, between its members. Once the group was operating, a steady barrage of mimeographed material circulated among the members. This included highly technical communications dealing with the substance of issues and messages dealing with strategy for individual, legislative measures. There were also occasional meetings of the group to strengthen the "sense of belonging" that the leaders felt was so essential.

To this latter end, a series of programs was set up with various experts. These were aimed at discussing broad problems that did not have an immediate legislative aspect, but which could serve as a forum for introducing the various members of the DSG to each other on an informal basis and for heightening a spirit of group participation. In a period of only two months, the congressmen who participated had meetings with Louis Bean, the election analyst; James Warburg, speaking on foreign policy; Richard Scammon, another elections specialist; and Louis Harris, who had done a good deal of polling for Democratic organizations. None of the discussions was aimed at highlighting a particular legislative problem, but, in the view of most of the participants, these meetings tended to cement the group into a more cohesive whole.

An additional aspect of the communications problem was the relationship of the group to the "leadership" of the House. Communication between the average member and the leadership—the Speaker, the Majority Floor Leader, and a few key individuals—had been a problem for some time. Many members freely admitted that on a large number of issues, even where they were prepared to "go along" with the leadership, they really did not know the position the leadership was taking. Rayburn, in particular, tended to keep his thoughts to himself on all but the most critical pieces of legislation. Whether or not the Speaker had in mind conserving his immense prestige is unknown, but clearly in the absence of strong leadership, and with a hostile president in the White House, many of the junior members of the Eighty-sixth Congress were virtually rudderless in their search for direction. Thus, the leaders of the Democratic Study Group hoped to provide direction and to channel the efforts of these congressmen in a unified bloc. The experiences during the first session clearly indicated the necessity for doing so and greatly increased the willingness of many members to participate in the group.

The Problem of Research

While the creation of a communications network was admittedly an important problem, the information that went into that network was of equal or greater importance. Again, the leaders of the Democratic Study Group recognized this need and sought, by a careful division of labor, to utilize the available talents for optimum benefit to the group.

Like the problem of getting to know his colleagues, the problem of "getting to know" the substance of all but a narrow range of issues is an enormous one for the average congressman. Unless he has had a very specialized background, he is simply overwhelmed by the mass of legislation coming before him. This problem has been greatly complicated in recent decades by the immense complexity of the issues that are dealt with through the legislative process. No longer is it merely a question of Congress laying down broad rules for new programs; the need for increasingly detailed concern with the specifics of ongoing programs, an understanding of highly complicated amendments to existing frameworks, and knowledge for dealing with highly technical matters tend to characterize modern law making.

In all but those bills coming before his committee, the average congressman is at the mercy of "a few friends," outside interest groups, and, when the circumstances are right, the outputs of a friendly executive branch. In the case of liberal Democrats during the Eighty-sixth Congress, this latter, highly important factor was totally missing. In addition, special note should be taken of the fact that liberals were seeking to create new programs in the face of a bureaucracy that was opposed to many of their plans. The result was that once the member had settled into his office, many of the programs that had sounded wonderful back in the home district began to evaporate in the absence of the detailed information necessary to carry them through the legislative process. Complicated statistics, detailed legal passages, and the other technical aspects of bill drafting were beyond the resources available to the average congressman.

By pooling resources, the group was able to provide itself with a small staff. William Phillips, who was serving as administrative assistant to Congressman George Rhodes (Pa.), was selected for the job of staff director. With a master's degree in political science, and with several years of work "on the Hill," Phillips brought a wide perspective to the job. Operating out of Rhodes' office, he embarked on a research program aimed at achieving the goals of the group. He worked closely with the administrative assistants of several other members and developed, in the interim between the end of the first session and the beginning of the second, a series of fact sheets dealing with the critical issues coming before the Congress. These, as was noted, were made available to members in an effort to improve their ability to articulate before constituents in their respective districts. In addition, Phillips drew up a plan for research after the session began. The various issues were parceled out to administrative assistants and other interested helpers, and the inflow of information began. While a certain amount of "unnecessary" work was accomplished during this period, when the actual task forces were set up on specific issues, the papers developed during the interim often served as a basis for discussion.

An additional source of information, albeit a weak one, was the Legislative Reference Service in the Library of Congress. By channeling requests through the congressional offices themselves, the staff of the study group was able to get a good deal of supplemental information from the Reference Service. Unfortunately for most congressmen, the service has never been able to provide the kind of research facility that had been hoped for in the Reorganization Act of 1946. Hemmed in by a small budget, forced by the folkways of the Hill to devote a considerable amount of time to the requests of more-senior members, handicapped by the size of its staff, the service had done a remarkable job under the circumstances. However, as a major source of creative information for the Democratic Study Group, it was early discovered that the Legislative Reference Service would be inadequate.

One of the key tasks performed by Phillips and his small group was the collection of massive amounts of data from the various interest groups. Each congressman's desk is daily flooded by messages from a variety of special interests all seeking to plead their cause. Far from the traditional notions of "lobbying," much of this information is scholarly and is presented with graphs and accompanying charts, with myriad statistics, and with excellently worded briefs. The real problem, in the office of a single congressman, is separating these valuable data from the immense volume of messages that continually flow across his desk.

The group of administrative assistants was able to go through this material carefully and identify whatever would serve the cause of the Democratic Study Group. Again, in the face of an administration that was increasingly hostile to even providing a bare minimum of information, this source of data proved very helpful to the DSG.

Another major aspect of the research problem revolved around the highly complex rules of procedure that operate within the House. Quite apart from their excellent work relating to substantive issues that were to be debated, the staff of the Democratic Study Group produced a number of significant reports dealing directly with these procedures and the relationship between the established rules and specific legislative strategies of concern to the group. While these were particularly helpful to the younger members, their use was certainly not limited to this group. For reasons not yet researched, even some of the more-senior liberals seemed equally unfamiliar with the subtleties of the highly developed House rules. Here again, by doing a thorough research job and by utilizing the talents of the limited number of liberals who were at home with the complexities of parliamentary procedure, the staff of the group was able to develop detailed memoranda for the membership which were to be of major importance in the session to come. The group's ability to employ successfully such unusual procedures as "Calendar Wednesday," was, in large part, due to careful preparation by the staff and leadership. While the time demands of the typical liberal members precluded a thorough study of the rules, the study group was able to provide this information for its members.

"The Balance of Power"

Another positive virtue flowing from organization, as viewed by those in leadership positions within the group, was the increased bargaining position that a formal group would give to liberal demands upon the leadership of the Congress. As David Truman's careful analysis suggests, in the weak party system of Congress, one of the primary functions of the "leadership" is essentially that of negotiating between the various elements of the respective political parties.[34] While certain schisms have existed within Republican ranks, such division had tended to be a particular problem for the Democrats. Faced with a basic division along sectional lines, the leadership has traditionally been forced to rely on negotiation and bargaining to achieve any kind of cohesion. The conservatives, since they occupied many of the formal seats of power (committee chairmanships, ranking memberships, and so forth), seemed able to produce a more unified stance than the unorganized liberal groupings. Organized within their own informal, southern "caucus," they had tended to operate remarkably well as a group. The liberals, on the other hand, were often divided into numerous, small factions, frequently squabbling with one another. The result had been to weigh the balance, with regard to the House leadership, in favor of the conservatives.

By organizing around a set of positions that they could all agree on, the leadership of the Democratic Study Group felt that their ability to bargain with Rayburn and McCormack would be increased because pressure for a common set of priorities could be brought to bear on the Speaker. This is not to suggest that Rayburn was necessarily opposed to the aims of the Democratic Study Group, but, rather, that his own position was in large part determined by the various pressures mounting on both sides of the liberal-conservative scale. With a single set of legislative priorities, the leaders of the Democratic Study Group were able to maximize liberal effectiveness on each of the issues as they came up. Instead of 120 members with different priorities for the same ten pieces of legislation, the leaders of the group could now concentrate on one issue at a time and on building up the pressure of the entire membership. In addition, the psychological pressure on liberals to conform to agreements that had been made within the context of the group reduced the possibility of the conservatives being able to whittle away individual members who might otherwise have been concerned only with the various pieces of legislation that were under consideration.

Thus, as the opening of a new session appeared, a new element was injected into congressional politics. Having seen most of their cherished legislative hopes go down the drain in the first session, the liberals had erected an organization which, it was hoped, would be able to strengthen their position during the second session of the Eighty-sixth Congress.

NOTES

1. For a detailed account of the activities of such an ad hoc grouping in connection with the passage of the Employment Act of 1946, see Steven K. Bailey, *Congress Makes a Law* (New York: Columbia University Press, 1950).

2. For the text of the "manifesto," see *Congressional Record,* Vol. 103, pt. 1, pp. 1,324–1,325.

3. Without, however, McCarthy himself. He had announced for the Senate seat held by Republican Edward Thye and was engaged in what turned out to be a successful campaign.

4. Letter on the stationery of Congressman Lee Metcalf dated August 28, 1958, and signed by congressmen Thompson (N.J.), Metcalf (Mont.), Holifield (Calif.), Madden (Ind.), Moss (Calif.), Yates (Ill.), Blatnik (Minn.), Morgan (Pa.), Price (Ill.), Reuss (Wisc.), Udall (Ariz.), and Rhodes (Pa.).

5. Nothing came of these at this time. For an account, see *Congressional Quarterly Weekly Report,* XVII (January 9, 1959), p. 45.

6. Woodrow Wilson, *Congressional Government* (Paperback edition, New York: Meridan Books, 1956), pp. 59–62.

7. The five were John Brademas (Ind.), James O'Hara (Mich.), Roman Pucinski (Ill.), Robert Giamio (Conn.), and Dominick V. Daniels (N.J.).

8. Some of the papers discussed at these meetings were subsequently published, in 1962, to the great embarrassment of a number of liberal members and to the great glee of most Republicans. Denials of participation in the meetings were immediately forthcoming until only Roosevelt himself and Congressman Robert Kastenmeier (Wisc.), would admit to involvement in the "Project."

9. Letter dated September 4, 1959, in the files of the Democratic Study Group.

10. Interview with the author.

11. Robert Novak, "Congressional Liberals," *Wall Street Journal,* November 23, 1959, p. 1.

12. Letter dated September 5, 1959, in the files of the Democratic Study Group.

13. Letter dated September 8, 1959, in the files of the Democratic Study Group.

14. While the exact number of participants was kept confidential, several in attendance agreed that "more than fifty" offices were represented.

15. Which, in fact, occurred ten months later, when Metcalf ran successfully for the Senate.

16. Anderson (Mont.), Bowles (Conn.), Brademas (Ind.), Coad (Iowa), Denton (Ind.), Green (Ore.), Griffith (Mich.), Johnson (Colo.), Karth (Minn.), McGovern (S.D.), Clem Miller (Calif.), Moss (Calif.), Multer (N.Y.), Reuss (Wisc.), Rhodes (Pa.), Sisk (Calif.), Thompson (N.J.), Udall (Ariz.), Vanik (Ohio), and Yates (Ill.).

17. Bowles, Brademas, Johnson, Karth, and Miller.

18. Copy in the author's files.

19. For a list of the original members of the Democratic Study Group, see Mark F. Ferber "The Democratic Study Group" (unpublished Ph.D. Dissertation, U.C.L.A., 1964) Appendix I.

20. For the text of Eisenhower's speech, see *New York Times,* September 20, 1959, p. 1.

21. Democratic Study Group, "A Positive Democratic Answer to President Eisenhower's Attack on the Record of the First Session, 86th Congress," *Staff Memorandum* (Washington, D.C.: September, 1959, mimeographed).

22. Democratic Study Group, "The Republican-Southern Democratic Coalition, 1938–1959," *Staff Memorandum* (Washington, D.C.: December, 1959, mimeographed).

23. News release dated December 21, 1959, signed by Metcalf and Thompson.

24. *Ibid.*

25. Novak, *op. cit.*

26. *Ibid.*

27. See Robert C. Albright, "Political Survival Program Mapped by Democratic Liberals in House," *The Washington Post,* December 26, 1959, p. A 9; and "Liberal House Democrats Organize for Action," *Congressional Quarterly Weekly Reports,* Vol. XVIII, No. 1 (January 5, 1960), 12.

28. Drew Pearson, "Liberals to Battle House Coalition," *The Washington Post,* January 6, 1960, p. B 23.

29. See Thomas Ottenad's column, *St. Louis Post-Dispatch,* January 17, 1960, p. 1.

30. Rowland Evans, Jr., "Congress, Eyes on Politics," *New York Herald Tribune,* January 7, 1960, p. 1.

31. William R. MacKaye, *A New Coalition Takes Control: The House Rules Committee Fight of 1961* (Eagleton Institute Cases in Practical Politics; New York: McGraw-Hill Book Company, Inc., 1963).

32. For an excellent discussion of the various roles a legislator is expected to perform, see William C. Mitchell, "Occupational Role Strains: The American Public Official," in S. Sidney Ulmer (ed.), *Introductory Readings in Political Behavior* (Chicago: Rand McNally & Co., 1961), pp. 415–424.

33. See Charles Clapp, *The Congressman: His Job as He Sees It* (Washington, D.C.: The Brookings Institution, 1964), Chapter 1.

34. David Truman, *The Congressional Party, A Case Study* (New York: John Wiley & Sons, Inc., 1959), Chapter 6.